Mathematical Modeling and Intelligent Optimization in Green Manufacturing & Logistics

Mathematical Modeling and Intelligent Optimization in Green Manufacturing & Logistics

Editor

Yaping Ren

MDPI • Basel • Beijing • Wuhan • Barcelona • Belgrade • Manchester • Tokyo • Cluj • Tianjin

Editor
Yaping Ren
Jinan University (Zhuhai Campus)
China

Editorial Office
MDPI
St. Alban-Anlage 66
4052 Basel, Switzerland

This is a reprint of articles from the Special Issue published online in the open access journal *Mathematics* (ISSN 2227-7390) (available at: https://www.mdpi.com/si/mathematics/Model_Optim_Green_Manuf_Logist).

For citation purposes, cite each article independently as indicated on the article page online and as indicated below:

LastName, A.A.; LastName, B.B.; LastName, C.C. Article Title. *Journal Name* **Year**, *Volume Number*, Page Range.

ISBN 978-3-0365-7570-4 (Hbk)
ISBN 978-3-0365-7571-1 (PDF)

© 2023 by the authors. Articles in this book are Open Access and distributed under the Creative Commons Attribution (CC BY) license, which allows users to download, copy and build upon published articles, as long as the author and publisher are properly credited, which ensures maximum dissemination and a wider impact of our publications.

The book as a whole is distributed by MDPI under the terms and conditions of the Creative Commons license CC BY-NC-ND.

Contents

About the Editor . . . . **vii**

Yaping Ren, Xinyu Lu, Hongfei Guo, Zhaokang Xie, Haoyang Zhang and Chaoyong Zhang
A Review of Combinatorial Optimization Problems in Reverse Logistics and Remanufacturing for End-of-Life Products
Reprinted from: *Mathematics* **2023**, *11*, 298, doi:10.3390/math11020298 . . . . **1**

Ao Lv and Baofeng Sun
Multi-Objective Robust Optimization for the Sustainable Location-Inventory-Routing Problem of Auto Parts Supply Logistics
Reprinted from: *Mathematics* **2022**, *10*, 2942, doi:10.3390/math10162942 . . . . **25**

Xiaodong Li, Yang Xu, Kin Keung Lai, Hao Ji, Yaning Xu and Jia Li
A Multi-Period Vehicle Routing Problem for Emergency Perishable Materials under Uncertain Demand Based on an Improved Whale Optimization Algorithm
Reprinted from: *Mathematics* **2022**, *10*, 3124, doi:10.3390/ math10173124 . . . . **47**

Jianxun Li, Wenjie Cheng, Kin Keung Lai and Bhagwat Ram
Multi-AGV Flexible Manufacturing Cell Scheduling Considering Charging
Reprinted from: *Mathematics* **2022**, *10*, 3417, doi:10.3390/math10193417 . . . . **65**

Ming Wan, Ting Qu, Manna Huang, Xiaohua Qiu, George Q. Huang, Jinfu Zhu and Junrong Chen
Cloud-Edge-Terminal-Based Synchronized Decision-Making and Control System for Municipal Solid Waste Collection and Transportation
Reprinted from: *Mathematics* **2022**, *10*, 3558, doi:10.3390/math10193558 . . . . **81**

Leilei Meng, Biao Zhang, Yaping Ren, Hongyan Sang, Kaizhou Gao and Chaoyong Zhang
Mathematical Formulations for Asynchronous Parallel Disassembly Planning of End-of-Life Products
Reprinted from: *Mathematics* **2022**, *10*, 3854, doi:10.3390/math10203854 . . . . **101**

Chengshuai Li, Biao Zhang, Yuyan Han, Yuting Wang, Junqing Li and Kaizhou Gao
Energy-Efficient Hybrid Flowshop Scheduling with Consistent Sublots Using an Improved Cooperative Coevolutionary Algorithm
Reprinted from: *Mathematics* **2023**, *11*, 77, doi:10.3390/math11010077 . . . . **117**

Ying Tian, Zhanxu Gao, Lei Zhang, Yujing Chen and Taiyong Wang
A Multi-Objective Optimization Method for Flexible Job Shop Scheduling Considering Cutting-Tool Degradation with Energy-Saving Measures
Reprinted from: *Mathematics* **2023**, *11*, 324, doi:10.3390/math11020324 . . . . **145**

Jia Mao, Jinyuan Cheng, Xiangyu Li, Honggang Zhao and Ciyun Lin
Optimal Design of Reverse Logistics Recycling Network for Express Packaging Considering Carbon Emissions
Reprinted from: *Mathematics* **2023**, *11*, 812, doi:10.3390/math11040812 . . . . **177**

Bao Chao, Peng Liang, Chaoyong Zhang and Hongfei Guo
Multi-Objective Optimization for Mixed-Model Two-Sided Disassembly Line Balancing Problem Considering Partial Destructive Mode
Reprinted from: *Mathematics* **2023**, *11*, 1299, doi:10.3390/math11061299 . . . . **209**

About the Editor

Yaping Ren

Yaping Ren, Ph.D., is Associate Professor in the Department of Industrial Engineering of the College of Intelligent Science and Engineering in Jinan University. In September 2019, he received his Ph.D. degree from the School of Mechanical Science and Engineering, Huazhong University of Science and Technology. From September 2017 to August 2019, he conducted joint doctoral training at Purdue University. He is mainly engaged in intelligent optimization and scheduling research for manufacturing/transportation logistics. So far, he has presided over two national research projects, five provincial and ministerial research projects, and one project funded by the Fundamental Research Funds for the Central Universities. Thirty-six SCI/EI high-level academic papers of his have been published and accepted, among which twenty-two SCI papers and four EI papers have been published and accepted with him as the first author/corresponding author, including *IEEE Transactions on Systems, Man, and Cybernetics: Systems*; *IEEE Transactions on Industrial Informatics*; *IEEE Transactions on Intelligent Transportation Systems*; *Robotics and Computer-Integrated Manufacturing*; *Journal of Cleaner Production*; *Expert Systems with Applications*; and other top journals in Zone 1 of the Chinese Academy of Science Journal Partition, as well as several authoritative Chinese journals such as *Journal of Mechanical Engineering* and *Computer Integrated Manufacturing Systems*. More than thirty national invention patents have been applied, twelve of which have been authorized. He has won three provincial and ministerial awards and is the youth editorial board member of journals such as *Journal of Applied Basic and Engineering Science and Mechanical and Electrical Engineering Technology*.

Review

A Review of Combinatorial Optimization Problems in Reverse Logistics and Remanufacturing for End-of-Life Products

Yaping Ren [1,2,3], Xinyu Lu [4], Hongfei Guo [1,2,3,*], Zhaokang Xie [4], Haoyang Zhang [4] and Chaoyong Zhang [5]

1. School of Intelligent Systems Science and Engineering, Jinan University, Zhuhai 519070, China
2. Institute of Physical Internet, Jinan University, Zhuhai 519070, China
3. CBA and BF+B International Joint Research Center for Smart Logistics, Jinan University, Zhuhai 519070, China
4. School of Management, Jinan University, Guangzhou 510632, China
5. State Key Lab of Digital Manufacturing Equipment and Technology, Huazhong University of Science and Technology, Wuhan 430074, China
* Correspondence: ghf-2005@163.com

Abstract: During the end-of-life (EOL) product recovery process, there are a series of combinatorial optimization problems (COPs) that should be efficiently solved. These COPs generally result from reverse logistics (RL) and remanufacturing, such as facility location and vehicle routing in RL, and scheduling, planning, and line balancing in remanufacturing. Each of the COPs in RL and remanufacturing has been reviewed; however, no review comprehensively discusses and summarizes the COPs in both. To fill the gap, a comprehensive review of the COPs in both RL and remanufacturing is given in this paper, in which typical COPs arising at the end of the product life cycle are discussed and analyzed for the first time. To better summarize these COPs, 160 papers published since 1992 are selected and categorized into three modules: facility location and vehicle routing in RL, scheduling in remanufacturing, and disassembly in remanufacturing. Finally, the existing research gaps are identified and some possible directions are described.

Keywords: reverse logistics; remanufacturing; EOL product; combinational optimization

MSC: 90-10

1. Introduction

Reverse logistics (RL) and remanufacturing are the two main processes for end-of-life (EOL) products' recovery, aiming to maximize resource utilization by means of collecting, disassembling, refurbishing, and reassembling to grant the EOL products the same quality and functionality as new products. In order to improve the efficiency of product recovery, it is vital to solve the combinatorial optimization problems (COPs) involved effectively; therefore, scholars have conducted much research on them.

The concept of RL was put forward by Stock [1] in 1992, whose essence was to transfer EOL products from the consumer to the producer for processing. The COPs in RL include facility location and the vehicle-routing problem (VRP). The facility location is to build an appropriate network structure to determine the location of various facilities, such as collection centers, remanufacturing centers, distribution centers, etc. The VRP is to formulate a specific transportation plan to transport EOL products to the above facilities, including the driving path, number of vehicles, types of vehicles, etc. There are some reviews about the facility location and VRP in RL [2–5].

However, only the transportation process of RL cannot truly realize the reuse of resources; remanufacturing is the key to achieve sustainable development [6]. Remanufacturing is a process to recover EOL products to the same state as new products through inspection, disassembly, cleaning, maintenance, replacement, reassembly, etc. [7]. The COPs involved include disassembly sequence planning (DSP), disassembly-line-balancing problem (DLBP), disassembly scheduling, production scheduling, reassembly, etc. There are also some reviews about each of the COPs in remanufacturing [8–11].

Relevant reviews have been provided for each COP involved in RL and remanufacturing as shown in Table 1. However, it lacks a literature to review all COPs from the perspective of the recovery process for EOL products recovery, which is important to draw a framework of COPs for product recovery. In this paper, the COPs involved in RL and remanufacturing are divided into three categories, namely, facility location and VRP in RL, scheduling in remanufacturing, and disassembly in remanufacturing. These COPs are analyzed from two perspectives: a mathematical model and intelligent optimization methods, to fill the blanks of current research.

The rest of this article is organized as follows: Sections 2–4 summarize the mathematical model of facility location and VRP in RL, scheduling in remanufacturing, and disassembly in remanufacturing, respectively. Section 5 analyzes and discusses the literature from the perspective of optimization methodology and problem uncertainty. Section 6 summarizes the full text and proposes the future research directions.

Table 1. Previous reviews about RL and remanufacturing.

Article	Area	Perspectives
[2]	Facility location in RL	A comprehensive review of remanufacturing RL and closed-loop supply chain network design.
[3]	Facility location in RL	A review of various quantitative models that have been proposed to solve RL network design.
[4]	VRP in RL	Extensively analyzed the existing literature of the VRP in RL to identify the current trends, research gaps, and the limitations in the adaptability to real world.
[5]	VRP in RL	Reviewed the major contribution about waste collection in VRP.
[8]	DLBP in remanufacturing	Reviewed recent models to summarize the input data, parameters, decision variables, constraints, and objectives of the DLBP.
[9]	DSP in remanufacturing	Reviewed the existing DSP methods from the perspectives of disassembly mode, disassembly modelling, and planning method.
[10]	Scheduling in remanufacturing	Classified the scheduling literature in remanufacturing into single and multiple products, disassembly, and integrated scheduling, and further subdivided through part capacity, commonality, and deterministic/stochastic parameters.

2. Facility Location and VRP in RL

Before remanufacturing EOL products, collecting them from users is the first step, which is essentially a process of RL. To perform this efficiently, it is necessary to properly plan the location of various facilities and products' flow routes. Specifically, companies need to choose how to collect EOL products from users and transport them to collection centers, where to inspect EOL products, where to remanufacture EOL products to make them available for resale, and how to sell remanufactured products to potential users [12]. That is to solve the problem of facility location and the VRP in RL.

2.1. Facility Location in RL

Generally, the facility location determines the location of the collection center, remanufacturing center, distributing center, and so on to minimize the logistics costs. Scholars have designed different network structures based on these facilities, which can be summarized as three types. This section will analyze the three kinds of network structures from the perspective of mathematical models, including: general network structure, closed-loop network structure, and hybrid network structure.

2.1.1. General Network Structure

The general network structure consists of four parts: consumers, collection centers, remanufacturing centers, and secondary markets, as shown in Figure 1. The collection center collects EOL products from consumers, inspects and disassembles the products, and then, according to the value of the components, chooses to discard or remanufacture; finally, the remanufactured finished products flow back to the market for sale. It is worth noting that in this network structure, remanufactured products are usually different from new products and mainly flow to the second-hand market.

Figure 1. General network structure.

It can be seen from Table 2 that most researchers choose the single-objective mixed-integer linear programming (MILP) model when establishing the mathematical model of the general network structure. Two papers established the mixed-integer nonlinear programming model (MILNP) [13,14], and they were single-objective optimization to maximize the total profit or minimize the total cost [14–20]. However, while minimizing the total cost, Roghanian and Pazhoheshfar [21] considered the uncertainty of capacity, demand, and product quantity in RL parameters, so they proposed a probabilistic mixed-integer linear programming model (P-MILP) and converted it into an equivalent deterministic model when solving. Tari and Alumur [22] considered the fairness between different companies and the problem of providing a stable product flow for each company while minimizing the total cost, thus establishing multi-objective mixed-integer linear programming (M-MILP).

In addition to minimizing the total cost and maximizing the total profit, the main purpose of establishing the mathematical model is to find out the location, capacity, and quantity of the core facilities, such as the collection center and the remanufacturing center that need to be opened in the RL network. Sasikumar et al. [13] provided decisions related to the number and location of facilities to be opened and the allocation of corresponding product flows through the establishment of MILP. Roghanian and Pazhoheshfar [21] proposed a multi-product, multi-stage RL network problem. It was not only necessary to determine the subset of disassembly centers and machining centers to be opened, but also necessary to determine the transportation strategy to meet the needs of manufacturing centers and recycling centers, with the minimum fixed opening cost and total transportation cost. Alshamsi and Diabat [16] also introduced important transportation considerations by providing options for using internal fleets and outsourcing options. Liao [14] introduced a modular remanufacturing process and emission reduction; two papers [14,16] also considered the carbon footprint while determining the location of factories (inspection/remanufacturing), the transportation of cores/remanufactured products between factories, and the route of vehicles between factories.

Table 2. Mathematical model of general network structure.

NO	Years	Type	Num. of Objectives	Products	Solution
[13]	2010	MINLP	One (maximize profit)	Tire retreading	Lingo 8.0
[15]	2012	MILP	One (maximize profit)	Washing machines and tumble dryers	CPLEX
[21]	2014	P-MILP	One (minimize the total cost)	Hypothetical problem	Genetic algorithm
[22]	2014	M-MILP	Three (minimize total cost, ensure equity among different firms, and provide stable product flow to each company within the planning scope)	Electrical waste and electronic equipment	CPLEX
[16]	2015	MILP	One (maximize profit)	Washing machines and tumble dryers	CPLEX
[17]	2016	MILP	One (maximize profit)	Vehicles	CPLEX
[18]	2017	MILP	One (maximize profit)		Genetic algorithm
[14]	2018	MINLP	One (maximize profit)	Waste recycling	Hybrid genetic algorithm
[19]	2019	MILP	One (minimize the total cost)	Lithium-ion batteries	Three-phase heuristic
[20]	2020	MILP	One (maximize profit)	Numerical research	CPLEX

2.1.2. Closed-Loop Network Structure

To protect the environment, many countries expand producer responsibility through legislation. Driven by economic benefits, many manufacturers began to integrate RL [23], thus evolving a closed-loop network structure (CLNS), as shown in Figure 2. The CLNS integrates forward logistics and reverse logistics, producing huge economic and environmental benefits, and is the most widely studied network structure by scholars. In the CLNS, manufacturers obtain raw materials from suppliers, and the products manufactured are sold to customers through distributors. The products used by customers are collected by the collection center and selectively sent to the remanufacturing center. After remanufacturing, they return to forward logistics. In the CLNS, the terminals of forward logistics and reverse logistics are the same customer group.

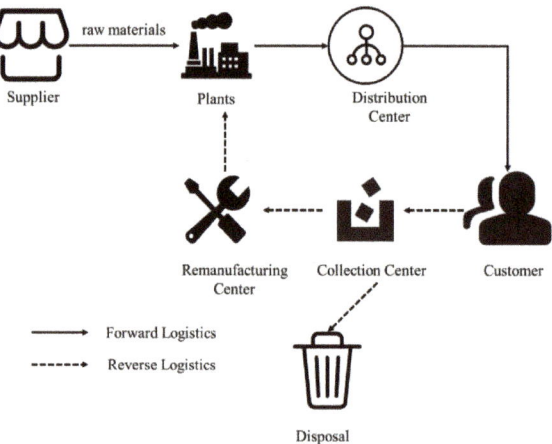

Figure 2. Closed-loop network structure.

Tables 3 and 4 are, respectively, the previous mathematical model research on CLNS and the corresponding abbreviations of terms. In paper [24], the environmental problems are integrated into an integer CLNS model, and a genetic algorithm based on the spanning tree structure is proposed to solve the NP-hard problem. Pishvaee et al. [25] also established a multi-objective fuzzy mathematical model to design the environmental protection supply chain. They used life cycle assessment to quantify the environmental impact of the network. Zohal and Soleimani [26] also regard the model as a green CLNS according to the CO2 emissions of the gold industry. As shown in Table 3, most scholars are studying how to use metaheuristics and heuristic algorithms to solve the model. Devika et al. [27] proposed six different mixed metaheuristics to solve the sustainable CLNS problem they developed. In paper [28], a CLNS decision model under uncertainty was proposed, and the imperialist competitive algorithm, particle swarm optimization, and genetic algorithm were used to solve the large-scale NP-hard model developed by them. In another study, Fard et al. [29] considered the three-level decision model to express their forward/reverse supply chain network design problem, and adopted a variety of metaheuristic algorithms, including tabu search, variable neighborhood search, particle swarm optimization, water wave optimization, and Keshtel algorithm. The results show that the metaheuristic algorithm is an effective method to solve the model in practice.

Table 3. Mathematical model of CLNS.

NO	Years	Type	Objectives	Network Stages	Solution	Outputs
[24]	2010	MILP	MC, MEI	SC, PC, DC, CZ, RYC	E	FL, PA, I, PT, TM, CR
[30]	2011	MILP	MC, MEI, MS	SC, PC, DC, CZ, CC, RDC, RCC, RMC, RYC, DIC	OM	SO, FL, A, PA, PT, TA, NP
[31]	2012	SMIP	MC	SC, PC, DC, CZ, CC, RDC, RCC, RMC, RYC, DIC	OM	SO, FL, A, PA, PT, TA, NP
[25]	2012	MILP	MC	PC, DC, RCC	OM	FL, FC, A, PA
[27]	2014	FMIP	MC, MEI	PC, CZ, CC, RCC (Steel), RCC(Plastic), DIC	IFS	FL, TA, PA, NP
[32]	2015	SMIP	MC	CZ, CZ, CC, RDC, RCC, DIC	E	FL, TA, QND
[26]	2016	MINLP	MC	SC, PC, CZ, W, DC, RMC, RCC	E, OM	FC, TA, UP, I, NP
[28]	2017	MILP	MC	SC, PC, DC, CZ, D, RMC, RDC, DIC	GA	FL, PA, TA
[29]	2018	MILP	MC, MEI	CC, DC, CZ, SC, RYC	OM	FL, A, NP, CS, TA
[33]	2019	MINLP	MC, MEI, MS	SC, PC, DC, CZ, CC, RDC, RCC, RMC, RYC, DIC	OM	SO, FL, A, PA, PT, TA, NP, DC

Table 4. Abbreviations comparison table.

Item	Content	Notation
Objectives	Min cost/max profit	MC
	Min environment impacts	MEI
	Max social benefits	MS
Network Stages	Supply centers	SC
	Production centers	PC
	Distribution centers	DC
	Warehouses	W
	Customer zones (retail outlets)	CZ
	Collection/inspection centers	CC
	Dismantlers	D
	Redistribution centers	RDC
	Recovering centers	RCC
	Remanufacturing centers	RMC
	Recycling centers	RYC
	Disposal/incineration centers	DIC
Solution Method	Exact	E
	Genetic-algorithm-based	GA
	Other metaheuristics	OM
	Interactive fuzzy solution approach	IFS
Outputs	Suppliers/orders	SO
	Facilities location	FL
	Facility capacity	FC
	Allocation	A
	Discount	DC
	Production amount	PA
	Utilization of production centers	UP
	Production technology	PT
	Transportation amount	TA
	Transportation mode	TM
	Number of vehicles	NV
	Inventory	I
	Number of used products which are processed	NP
	Carbon credits sold/purchased	CS
	Quantity of non-satisfied demand	QND

2.1.3. Hybrid Network Structure

Some scholars have put forward the concept of hybrid facilities, that is, the merger of a manufacturing center and remanufacturing center, and the merger of a distribution center and collection center, as shown in Figure 3, thus representing integrated forward and reverse logistics [34]. Due to the existence of mixed facilities, RL can use the nodes of forward logistics to optimize its design, thereby effectively reducing or eliminating the cost of building new RL networks. Therefore, in recent years, it has also become a research hotspot of scholars.

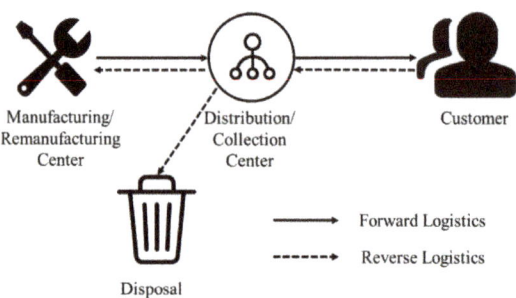

Figure 3. Hybrid network structure.

In this growing research field, the number of literature sources is growing rapidly. Fleischmann et al.'s pioneering work in hybrid network structure modeling studied the impact of product recycling on the design of a logistics network [35]. The study argued that the impact of product recycling depended heavily on the environment. In some cases, it may be feasible to integrate this activity into the existing logistics structure, while in other cases, it may be necessary to redesign the logistics network in an overall manner. Since this study, Salma et al. [36] incorporated capacity constraints, demand uncertainty, and returns into the multi-product planning based on this model. Later, they integrated strategic and tactical decisions by considering two inter-related time scales: at the strategic level, they gave a discretization of the time range, which must meet the needs and reporting values; at the tactical level, more detailed planning was allowed to achieve this goal [37]. Cardoso et al. [38] analyzed the integration of RL activities under demand uncertainty, took the maximum expected net present value as the objective function, and made decision variables for facility size and location, process installation, forward and reverse logistics, and inventory level. Later, the author expanded this work to solve the uncertainty and characterize the elastic closed-loop network structure [39].

Subsequently, environmental and social sustainability issues began to be considered. Paksoy et al. [40] analyzed the supply plan and considered the emission cost (total cost minimization) and the profit maximization of the recycled products in the economic objective function. Mota et al. [41] considered the sustainability of the economy, environment, and society. They proposed a mathematical model with the minimization of the total cost of the network structure as the economic objective function; the minimization of the life cycle assessment index ReCipe as the environmental objective function; and the location of the network structure activities in underdeveloped areas as the social objective function. Gao et al. [42], based on the existing forward logistics network, proposed a double-objective stochastic integer programming model aiming at economic and environmental benefits, which aimed to support production, remanufacturing, and waste activities by addressing the uncertainty factors of new product demand and the return volume of old products in the customer area.

2.2. VRP in RL

After locating critical facilities, the next question is how to reversely transport EOL products, that is, the vehicle-routing problem in RL. The VRP in RL refers to how to arrange vehicle types, quantities, capacities, routes, etc., to collect waste products from customers, to achieve the goal of the minimum cost or the shortest route. Collection is the starting point of EOL product recovery, so scholars have carried out much research to improve the efficiency of this link.

The VRP in RL can be described as: a certain number of customers must use a certain number of fleets with limited capacity, which are usually assumed to be the same. The vehicles are stationed in a central parking lot and return after collecting waste products from customers according to the route requirements. Cao et al. [10] used RL to reuse the Internet of Things through identifying the resources required for road infrastructure, and modeled RL to transfer the Internet of Things from a tailings dam to a processing plant, and then to a road construction site. For minimizing the total cost, Richnák and Gubová [44] established a heterogeneous-fleet electric-vehicle path-recovery time window model considering vehicle load constraints. The type of vehicle limited the weight of recyclable waste and the time limit allowed by the customer. Chen et al. [45] proposed a nonlinear programming model including the number of second-hand products and reprocessed products. For both types of requirements, analysis and insight were provided in the form of a complete strategy consisting of different scenarios that allow optimal decisions to be made under a variety of conditions. Through sensitivity analysis, numerical examples supplemented the understanding of the model. Santana et al. [46] considered the risks in the e-waste recycling process and modeled the reverse logistics process of electrical and electronic equipment as a MILP with biological objectives under uncertainty. The cooperative alliance strategy was employed by Mishra et al. [47] to actualize the constrained capabilities of VRP in RL. The cooperative mechanism made it possible to prevent inefficient resource distribution, cut back on circular logistics, and minimize long-distance travel. In order to minimize recovery tasks, Chen et al. [48] used an improved ant colony algorithm to handle vehicle design and route optimization problems. Foroutan et al. [49] established a mixed-integer nonlinear programming model for multi-mode green vehicle routing and scheduling with the objective of minimizing operating costs and environmental costs and considering return, lead time, and delay costs. A mathematical model for the recovery of EOL cars was developed by Chaabane et al. [50] by combining the traditional VRP with the receiving and delivery problem as well as the restrictions of various vehicle kinds and time periods.

The multi-vehicle routing optimization problem with time limitations has also been the subject of interest for scholars' in-depth research. In order to meet the needs of minimizing transportation and procurement costs, the research in the literature [51] included choosing suppliers and setting up homogeneous fleets to buy various products from chosen suppliers. It also defined new branching rules, introduced new inequality families, and established the competitiveness of the new branching price-reduction method. To optimize the multi-depot production material-allocation system and research the routing problem of delivery vehicles, Xu et al. [52] took into account a variety of factors, including multiple warehouses, multiple vehicle types, multiple commodities, mismatches between customer supply and demand, and arbitrary segmentation of delivery and delivery demands. Fan et al. [53] designed a genetic variable neighborhood algorithm for multi-vehicle routing optimization problem with fuzzy set requirements by improving the adaptive search strategy. A multi-mode electric vehicle routing optimization model was developed by Guo et al. [54] taking into account the differentiating service costs under the consideration of vehicle diversity, charging strategy, person vehicle matching, and service time difference.

With the improvement in logistics network and the development of e-commerce, in order to improve customer satisfaction, logistics service providers need to handle a large number of delivery orders and return orders at the same time. In this case, the joint optimization of simultaneous pickup and delivery VRP (VRPSPD) can significantly improve the utilization rate of vehicles [55].

Studies have shown that solving the problem of collecting refurbished goods in forward and reverse logistics can improve the utilization rate of refurbished products, shorten the return time, and improve customer satisfaction [55]. Dethloff [56] studied VRPSPD in order to avoid redundant handling work, considering that customers have both picking and delivery needs. They developed an insertion-based heuristics method, which can be used to construct initial feasible solutions, which can be improved by subsequent application of the local search process. A specific case of VRPSPD that allows for the decomposition of the picking and delivery needs was developed by Masson et al. [57]. This method can be used in real-world transportation systems with many of pickup trucks but few deliveries. Nagy et al. [58] proposed a VRP with separable delivery and picking, and studied the cost reduction caused by demand segmentation of simultaneous delivery and pickup. In order to optimize vehicle scheduling to satisfy freight requests, Ghilas et al. [59] created a VRPSPD with scheduling lines and took synchronization and time window limitations into account in the solution algorithm. Gschwind et al. [60] evaluated the performance of branch cut and price algorithms in VRPSPD to solve the shortest path issue under time windows and resource limitation. Goeke [61] investigated the VRPSPD of electric cars, in which the route design of electric vehicles attempted to optimize the pick-up and delivery services in metropolitan areas with a lower environmental impact. Wolfinger [62] proposed a mixed-integer programming model to develop a single warehouse VRPPD with split load, and tested the algorithm performance through extensive computing experiments through large-scale neighborhood search. Haddad et al. [63] developed a multi-warehouse VRPPD to design a sustainable picking and distribution route between multiple warehouses. The efficiency of transportation can be increased at the same time, within the limitations of vehicle capacity and time window.

3. Scheduling in Remanufacturing

The remanufacturing system is generally composed of three subsystems: disassembly, reprocessing and reassembly, as shown in Figure 4. Previous research usually took the scheduling of reprocessing and reassembly as the production scheduling in remanufacturing. Disassembly scheduling can be defined as the problem of determining which products or subassemblies, how many, and when to disassemble EOL products to satisfy the demand of their parts or components. This paper reviews scheduling in remanufacturing into disassembly scheduling, production scheduling, and integrated scheduling

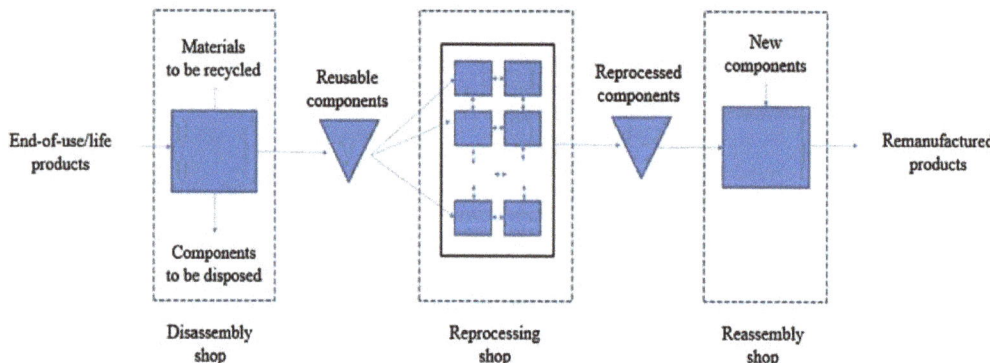

Figure 4. Composition of a typical remanufacturing system.

3.1. Disassembly Scheduling in Remanufacturing

In the last few years, there has been a growing interest in the disassembly-scheduling problem. Since Gupta and Taleb [64] described the basic form of the disassembly-scheduling problem, a number of research articles have been released. We review literature sources on approaches employed to model capacitated or incapacitated problems.

The majority of the early research took into account the scheduling issue of incapable disassembly. Firstly, Gupta and Taleb [64] proposed a reverse material requirement planning algorithm (RMRP) without an explicit objective function. Later, Taleb et al. [65] proposed a different RMRP algorithm to reduce the number of products that needed to be disassembled by taking into account the commonality of parts in this fundamental instances. In order to reduce the total cost of setup, disassembly operations, and inventory holding, Kim et al. [66] applied a heuristics algorithm and a linear programming (LP) relaxation technique to the basic problem put forth by Taleb et al. [65]. In order to reduce the total cost of product purchase, installation, disassembly operation and inventory holding, Lee et al. [67] adopted a two-stage heuristic algorithm to solve the problem based on the research of Gupta and Taleb [64]. Lee and Xirouchakis [68] proposed and solved three integer programming models for three problem cases, i.e., a single product type without parts commonality and single and multiple product types with parts commonality, they used CPLEX to solve the problem. Inderfurth and Langella [69] adopted a heuristic algorithm to reduce the estimated cost of disassembly operation, purchase and disposal, taking into account such factors as multiple product types, commonality of components, two-stage structure and uncertainty of production rate. Later, Kongar and Gupta [70] further improved their earlier work by incorporating uncertainty into the consideration of the problem and expressing the uncertainty of the problem through fuzzy goal programming [71]. Barba-Gutierrez and Adenso-Diaz [72] extended their earlier work by integrating uncertainty requirements. Barba-Gutierrez, Adenso-Diaz et al. [73], proposed an algorithm: F-RMRP (RMRP based on fuzzy logic) to solve the problem. Kim and Lee [74] considered a multi-period version problem and proposed a heuristic algorithm using priority rules to solve it. Recently, Kim et al. [75] proposed a two-stage heuristic algorithm based on their earlier model of Kim and Lee [74]. Most recent studies considered the capability of the disassembly-scheduling problem. Lee et al. [76] proposed an integer programming model whose objective function was to minimize the sum of disassembly operation, product purchase, and inventory carrying costs. Later, Kim et al. [77] proposed an optimization algorithm with the minimum number of disassembled products as the objective function. Later, Kim et al. [78], based on the research of Kim et al. [77], considered the more complex actual situation, added the minimum installation, disassembly operation and inventory carrying cost into the objective function, and proposed a Lagrange heuristic algorithm to solve the problem. In addition, Prakash et al. [79] proposed a disassembly-scheduling problem model for parts commonality and proposed a constrained simulated annealing algorithm to solve it. Liu and Zhang [80] built a non-convex mixed-integer model based on the research of Prakash et al. [79]. Aiming at the optimal collection price, appropriate disassembly time and quantity of recycled products, Liu and Zhang proposed a particle swarm optimization algorithm based on dynamic programming to solve the problem. Ullerich and Buscher [81] established an integer linear programming model considering complete disassembly scheduling by considering the capacity constraints of each time period. Later, Ji et al. [82] added the consideration of start-up and setup costs on the basis of Ullerich and Buscher [81], and proposed a Lagrange relaxation heuristic algorithm to solve the problem. Godichaud et al. [83] built an MILP model considering the penalty cost of sales loss and disassembly capacity overload, and proposed a genetic algorithm to solve it. Hrouga et al. [84] adopted a hybrid genetic algorithm and fix-and-optimization heuristic algorithm to solve the disassembly batch scale problem of multi-type products with sales loss and capacity constraints. Based on the original study by Hrouga et al. [85], the problems of disassembly batch size under sales loss, multiple product types, and two-tier and capacity constraints were considered by Hrouga et al. [84], and the objective function was to minimize the sum of installation, inventory, sales losses and overload costs. An efficient optimization method based on a genetic algorithm and fix-and-optimization heuristic was proposed. Kim and Xirouchakis [86] considered the problem of multi-cycle, multi-product type, two-level product structure and random demand, aiming to minimize the sum of expectation setting, inventory holding and penalty costs of unmet requests, and proposed a Lagrange relaxation heuristic algorithm for solving the problem. Inderfurth and Langella [69] proposed a disassembly-scheduling problem of random output considering the impact of yield uncertainty on the stochastic scale model and binomial model, and proposed a two-root three-leaf mathematical model to describe the problem. Liu and Zhang [80] constructed a mixed-integer nonlinear programming considering the capable disassembly-scheduling problem of stochastic yield and demand, and proposed an algorithm based on external approximation to solve it. Tian and Zhang [87] considered the problems of capable disassembly scheduling and pricing, and established a non-convex mixed-integer model with the objective of determining the appropriate collection price of recycled products and the appropriate disassembly time and quantity, which was solved by the algorithm combining particle swarm optimization and dynamic programming. Zhou, He et al. [88] considered the capability disassembly-scheduling problem with the uncertainty of demand and disassembly operation time, constructed a new stochastic programming model, and proposed a hybrid genetic algorithm to solve it. Yuan, Yang et al. [89] proposed a capable fuzzy disassembly-scheduling model with cycle time and environmental cost as parameters, proposed a mixed-integer mathematical programming model with the goal of minimizing cycle time and environmental cost, and proposed a metaheuristic algorithm based on the fruit fly optimization algorithm to solve the problem. Slama, Ben-Ammar et al. [90] constructed a new mixed-integer programming model with the goal of maximizing disassembly process gain by considering external procurement, defects and late-order items, setup time, and capable dynamic batch problems. Slama et al. [91] considered the random multi-period disassembly batch problem and proposed a special optimization method according to specific different scenarios. (i) A two-stage mixed-integer linear programming model was proposed to solve all possible scenarios of small cases. (ii) The sample average approximation method based on Monte Carlo simulation was proposed for all possible scenarios of medium-scale examples. (iii) For all possible scenarios of large-scale instances, an optimization algorithm based on Monte Carlo simulation and genetic algorithm was proposed.

3.2. Production Scheduling in Remanufacturing

Process planning and production scheduling for remanufacturing are more challenging than traditional manufacturing because there are many uncertain factors in the remanufacturing system, for example, there are uncertainties in the processing route and time of processing different kinds of materials in the remanufacturing process. These uncertainties will lead to the failure of the usual process planning and scheduling methods. Therefore, many researchers have conducted a great amount of meaningful exploration on the uncertainty of remanufacturing production.

Wen H et al. [92] took the minimum remanufacturing time as the objective function, established a production-scheduling comprehensive optimization model with double random variable constraints, and proposed a hybrid algorithm of stochastic simulation technology, a neural network, and a genetic algorithm to solve the problem. He P [93] proposed a quality evaluation standard for the remanufacturing production-scheduling problem under the two uncertain conditions of randomness and fuzziness of job scheduling. Then, based on this, he built a remanufacturing production-scheduling model under uncertain conditions, and adopted the hybrid algorithm of the BP neural network and genetic algorithm to solve the problem. Peng S et al. [94] took the high value-added cylinder block of the engine as the research object, took the minimum manufacturing span as the objective function, considered the uncertainty of processing time and path, and proposed a new rule-based dynamic window algorithm to solve the problem. Zhang [95] considered the remanufacturing production scheduling problem under random and fuzzy conditions, built a quality evaluation method for remanufacturing recovered resources, and based on this, established a remanufacturing production scheduling model under uncertain conditions, and proposed a hybrid algorithm combining a double-fuzzy algorithm, BP neural network, and genetic algorithm to solve the problem. Shi J et al. [96] proposed a new double-fuzzy remanufacturing scheduling model, which considered many double uncertainties in remanufacturing and used double fuzzy variables to describe these uncertainties. Extended discrete particle swarm optimization algorithm was used to solve the problem.

3.3. Integrated Scheduling in Remanufacturing

Kim et al. [97] encouraged the integration of all remanufacturing operations (disassembly, remanufacturing/repair, and reassembly) into remanufacturing scheduling decisions. The past research on the scheduling problem of integrated remanufacturing system can be divided into flow shop type and job shop type. The flow-shop-type reprocessing shop is oriented to small-batch, multiple varieties of personalized remanufacturing products; the job-shop-type reprocessing shop is oriented to small-batch, multiple varieties of a single type of remanufacturing product type.

For the remanufacturing system with a flow-shop-type reprocessing shop, Stanfield, King et al. [98], aiming to minimize in-process operations and maximizing system utilization, proposed a stochastic scheduling heuristic algorithm to solve the problem. In addition, Kim et al. [99], aiming to minimize the total flow time of a remanufacturing system with parallel flow-shop reprocessing lines, proposed three heuristic algorithms for solving the problem, namely, the heuristic algorithm based on priority rules, the heuristic algorithm based on Nawaz–Enscore–Ham and the iterative greedy algorithm. Later, Kim et al. [75], based on the research by Kim et al. [99], proposed an algorithm based on priority rules to minimize the total delay. Qu et al. [100] proposed a new FPA algorithm based on the hormone regulation mechanism to solve the waiting-free flow-shop scheduling problem, and introduced hormone-regulatory factors to enhance the global search capability of the algorithm. Wang et al. [101] studied the scheduling problem of a remanufacturing system with a parallel disassembly workstation, parallel flow-shop-reprocessing line, and parallel reassembly workstation, and adopted the improved multi-objective invasive weed optimization algorithm to solve it. Wang, Tian et al. [102] considered the scheduling problem with parallel disassembly workstations, multiple parallel flow-shop-reprocessing lines, and parallel reassembly workstations. Aiming to minimize the total energy consumption, they proposed an improved genetic algorithm to solve the problem.

For the remanufacturing system with a shop–shop reprocessing shop, Guide Jr [103] proposed a drum-slow Okinawa scheduling method for a military warehouse. Subsequently, Daniel and Guide Jr [104] reported the performance of various scheduling rules and order release strategies based on the drum-cached Okinawa scheduling method. In addition, Souza et al. [105] proposed a two-stage solution, aiming to meet the profit maximization of customer service level, built a queuing network model, and solved using priority rules. See Guide Jr et al. [106] and Li et al. [107] for other models and solving algorithms. Kang and Hong [108] studied the disassembly and reassembly optimization problem; established an integer programming model; and solved the problem with the minimum disassembly cost, inventory cost, and manufacturing cost of new parts as targets. Lin D et al. [109] took the optimal factory selection and optimal remanufacturing job scheduling as objectives under resource constraints, and used linear physical programming and the multi-level-coded genetic algorithm to solve the problem. Giglio et al. [110] considered an integrated-batch-size and energy-saving job-shop scheduling problem, constructed a mixed-integer programming model, and proposed a relaxation-fixed heuristic algorithm to solve it. Yu and Lee [111] considered the scheduling problem of a remanufacturing system with parallel disassembly workstations, shop-like reprocessing workstations, and parallel reassembly workstations, constructed an integer programming model, and proposed two solving algorithms: a decomposition algorithm and integration algorithm.

Li et al. [112] proposed a hybrid metaheuristic algorithm embedded with a colored, timed Petri net scheduling strategy to solve the problem of the optimal recovery route and recovery operation sequence for searching the worn core on the workstation, aiming to minimize the total production cost. Fu, Zhou et al. [113] adopted a multi-objective discrete Drosophila optimization algorithm to solve the stochastic multi-objective disassembly reprocessing–reassembly integrated scheduling problem in order to minimize the expected production cycle and total delay. Zhang, Zheng et al. [114] considered the integrated process planning and scheduling problem of a remanufacturing system containing a parallel disassembly workstation, a flexible job-shop-type reprocessing shop, and a parallel reassembly workstation, and proposed an improved artificial swarm algorithm to solve it.

4. Disassembly in Remanufacturing

Disassembly refers to obtaining valuable components from EOL products with various resource constraints. Disassembly in remanufacturing mainly includes two COPs: disassembly sequence planning (DSP) and disassembly line balancing problem(DLBP). DSP means obtaining the required components in an optimal sequence. DLBP means assigning disassembly operations to different workstations on a disassembly line to achieve one or multi-objectives.

4.1. Disassembly Sequence Planning

The most common objective of DSP is to improve the disassembly efficiency and reduce the cost. Disassembly sequence planning can be divided into three steps as shown in Figure 5: First, choosing a suitable disassembly mode which could be complete/partial disassembly or sequential/parallel disassembly. Second, building a model about the disassembly relationship of parts or components of EOL products. Third, choosing an optimization method to solve the DSP problem. There has been a great amount of research on DSP, and various methods have been developed. The most commonly used methods are heuristic algorithms. Additionally, the most prominent advantage of the heuristic algorithms is that they can obtain high-quality solutions in an acceptable time for large-scale problems [115]. For example, Tseng et al. [116] developed a new block-based genetic algorithm (GA) with the penalty function matrix in the crossover and mutation mechanism for disassembly sequence planning. Similarly, ElSayed et al. [117] and Li et al. [118] used a GA to address DSP on different occasions. It is obvious that a GA is easy to use and effective. However, more and more studies have investigated other heuristic algorithms. Zhong et al. [119] solve the DSP including fasteners using Dijkstra's algorithm and particle swarm optimization (PSO), which is another metaheuristic algorithm. Guo et al. [120] proposed a lexicographic multi-objective scatter search method to overcome the complexity explosion caused by a large-scale DSP considering a multi-objective resource-constrained operation. Liu et al. [121] built the disassembly model by using the modified feasible-solution-generation method, and a robotic DSP was solved by using an enhanced discrete bee colony algorithm. Additionally, Tao et al. [122] proposed an improved Tabu search heuristic algorithm with an exponentially decreasing diversity management strategy; a partial and parallel DSP problem was solved to show the proposed algorithm was feasible and efficient. Guo et al. [123] and Ren et al. [124–127] investigated various types of DSP problems by using different heuristic algorithms. In summary, a heuristic algorithm is one of the most effective methods to solve DSP.

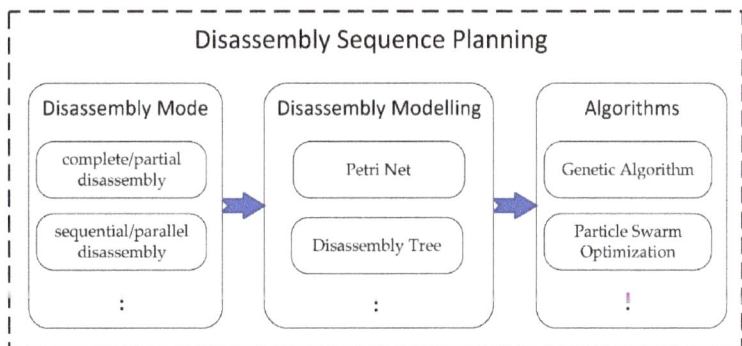

Figure 5. The three steps in DSP.

There are few studies which have investigated the exact mathematical methods. The exact mathematical methods can quickly obtain high-quality solutions for small-scale problems without traversing the entire solution space [115]. However, exact mathematical methods are more restrictive than other techniques. If the problem is large-scale, that is, with many variables and constraints, it is difficult to obtain a solution in an acceptable time. However, still some valuable papers are proposed because exact mathematical methods still have the advantage of quickly producing solutions when solving small-scale problems. For example, Zhu et al. [128] introduced a disassembly information model with dynamic capabilities to handle state-dependent information and presented a linear-programming-based optimization model to obtain the optimal disassembly sequence. Costa et al. [129] developed a recursive branch-and-bound algorithm to obtain the optimal disassembly sequence. They also proposed a best-first search algorithm to accelerate the optimization process. Some literature sources [130–132] also investigated the exact mathematical methods, but the solutions were not good enough when encountering large-scale DSP.

4.2. Disassembly-Line-Balancing Problem

The DLBP was first proposed by Güngör and Gupta [133] and more and more studies have investigated this problem. As Figure 6 shows, the main difference between DSP and the DLBP is the disassembly operation assigned to the workstation, which makes the DLBP more complex than DSP. Hence, there are some unique variables in the DLBP, such as objectives which could minimize the number of workstations or idle time [134].

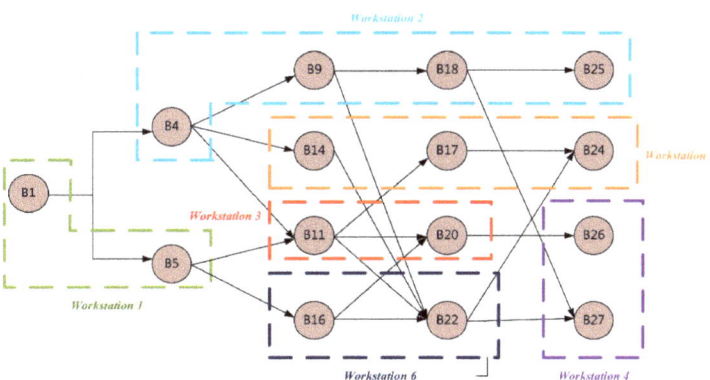

Figure 6. An example of the DLBP.

Like DSP, many studies have also applied a metaheuristic algorithm to solve the DLBP. For example, Yin et al. [135] considered a partial DLBP with multi-robot workstations; they established an exact mixed-integer programming model and proposed a multi-objective hybrid driving algorithm to effectively address the above problem. Li et al. [136] introduced the profit-oriented U-shaped partial DLBP for the first time. They established an integer linear programming model for solving the small-scale problem. Additionally, a novel discrete cuckoo search algorithm was implemented and improved to solve the considered DLBP. Wang et al. [137] proposed a discrete multi-objective artificial bee colony algorithm to address the partial DLBP considering both economic benefits and environmental impacts. Ren et al. [138–141] also investigated the problem of disassembly line balancing and applied different heuristic methods to meet different objectives.

The exact mathematical methods can produce higher-quality solutions when solving the small-scale DLBP, so there are some papers which have investigated them. Yılmaz et al. [142] focused on a multi-objective DLBP considering the tactical-level strategies and operational-level scenarios. They also developed the improved augmented ϵ-constrained method to obtain the Pareto solutions for small-scale problems. Edis et al. [143] studied a DLBP with balancing issues, the hazardousness of parts, and other factors. They developed a generic MILP model for the above problem and their proposed method proved effective after a series of tests. There are literature sources [144–146] which have also studied the exact mathematical methods to solve the DLBP, but still could avoid the problem of not being able to produce better solutions when encountering large-scale problems.

In conclusion, the DLBP has been well-researched and developed over decades. The exact mathematical methods and heuristics algorithm have shown their effectiveness at different scales of problems.

4.3. Integrated Disassembly and Reassembly

Reassembly is the operation following disassembly. Reassembly refers to the assembly of reused parts, remanufactured parts, and original manufacturing parts through specific processes to produce reusable products. However, because it is not the same as normal assembly, reassembly will encounter different problems. For example, uncertainty in reassembly can lead to a huge increase in the complexity of the problem. The quantity or quality of the remanufactured parts is uncertain, which leads to a decline in production efficiency, to unstable product quality, and to many other problems [147].

A few literature sources investigated the optimization of only reassembly but without considering disassembly. For example, Su et al. [148] proposed an optimal selective-assembly method for remanufacturing based on an ant colony algorithm in order to gain optimal reassembly combinations and reduce the influence of the uncertainty factors on the quality. Additionally, Liu et al. [149] proposed a simulated annealing genetic algorithm to solve the assembly deviation degree on-line optimization model.

As mentioned above, optimization that only considers reassembly is incomplete. Therefore, it is necessary to consider the complexities of reassembly when solving any disassembly problem, that is, the integrated problem of disassembly and reassembly. For example, Behdad and Thuston [150] proposed graph-based integer linear programming combined with multi-attribute utility analysis to obtain the optimal sequence of disassembly operations which considers the costs and uncertainties of both disassembly and reassembly. Su et al. [151] developed a multi-objective optimization method based on the TS-NSGAII hybrid algorithm which provided a new direction for the optimization of the remanufacturing system. Li et al. [152] established an optimization decision-making model for the reassembly process, and proposed a decision-making method based on the improved T-S FNN which focused on minimizing the remanufacturing time and costs. Oh and Behad [153] proposed a network flow graph and integer linear programming to produce solutions of the type and number of parts that should be reassembled and procured. Some literature sources focused on the whole remanufacturing system; Lahmar et al. [154] studied the remanufacturing production planning problem to minimize economic costs and carbon emissions. They developed a non-dominated sorting genetic algorithm (NSGA-II)-based approach to overcome the complexity of the whole remanufacturing system. Polotski et al. [155] investigated a hybrid manufacturing–remanufacturing system considering the optimization of manufacturing, remanufacturing, and maintenance policies. The stochastic dynamic programming approach was used to address this problem. In summary, it is a trend to study the optimization of the whole remanufacturing system in order to fully optimize all aspects of the system.

5. Analysis and Discussion

This section will discuss and analyze the above-mentioned literature sources from two aspects: optimization methodology and problem uncertainty.

5.1. Optimization Methodology

The problems described in Section 2 to Section 4 are essentially COPs. For COPs, the most important step is how to solve them after establishing the relevant mathematical model, and the solution methods are mainly divided into exact and heuristic or metaheuristic algorithms. The exact algorithm includes the branch and bound method, the dynamic programming method, the cutting-plane method, etc. However, due to the complexity of practical problems and the NP-hard attribute of most COPs, it is difficult for the exact algorithm to obtain a satisfactory solution for large-scale problems in a reasonable time. Therefore, most of the current research focuses on the development of heuristic or metaheuristic algorithms. This section will analyze the solution methods of the COPs mentioned in the above sections.

Tables 5–7 summarize exact algorithms, heuristic or metaheuristic algorithm, and some other algorithms, respectively. From the results of horizontal comparison, the number and types of heuristic or metaheuristic algorithm are far greater than those of the exact algorithm. This shows that in the field of RL and remanufacturing, using heuristic or metaheuristic algorithms to solve problems is the mainstream method of current research. Moreover, some classical algorithms have many applications in different problems, such as genetic algorithms [156], particle swarm optimization [157], ant colony algorithms [158], simulated annealing [159], and Tabu search [160].

Table 5. Exact algorithms.

Area	Methods	Reference
Facility location and VRP in RL	Lingo	[13,25,31,40]
	CPLEX	[15–17,20,22,30,37–39,42]
	Branch and bound	[36,51,57,60,63]
Scheduling in remanufacturing	CPLEX	[77]
	Dynamic programming	[87]
Disassembly in remanufacturing	CPLEX	[143]
	Improved augmented Epsilon constraint	[145]

Table 6. Heuristic or metaheuristic algorithms.

Area	Methods	Reference
Facility location and VRP in RL	Genetic algorithm	[14,18,21,23,24,43,49]
	Three-phase heuristic approach	[19]
	Three different hybridization methods	[27]
	Hybrid genetic algorithm and particle swarm optimization	[32]
	Ant colony algorithm	[26,48]
	Imperialist competitive algorithm	[28]
	Tri-level metaheuristics	[29]
	Hybrid Keshtel and genetic algorithm	[33]
	Parallel differential evolutionary algorithm	[55]
	Simulated annealing	[49]
	Two-phased heuristic	[50]
	Insertion-based heuristics	[56]
	Tabu search	[58,61]

Table 6. *Cont.*

Area	Methods	Reference
Scheduling in remanufacturing	Neighborhood search	[59,62,63]
	Genetic algorithm	[83,102,109]
	Two-phased heuristic	[67,75,82,105]
	One-to-many heuristic	[69]
	One-to-one heuristic	
	Greedy algorithm	[74]
	Simulated annealing	[79,111]
	Particle swarm optimization	[80,87,96]
	Fruit fly optimization	[89,113]
	Hybrid genetic algorithm	[84,85,88,90–93,95]
	CDS	[98]
	Nawaz–Enscore–Ham-based	[75,99]
	Priority-rule-based heuristic	[75]
	Integrated gradients	[75]
	Flower pollination algorithm	[100]
	Multi-objective invasive weed optimization	[101]
	Hybrid metaheuristic using simulated annealing and tabu search	[107]
	Hybrid metaheuristic using SA and MST rule	[112]
	Artificial bee colony algorithm	[114]
Disassembly in remanufacturing	Genetic algorithm	[116–118,124,125]
	Particle swarm optimization	[119]
	Scatter search algorithm	[120]
	Discrete bees algorithm	[121,126,127,137]
	Tabu search	[122,151]
	Variable neighborhood search	[127,138]
	Greedy search algorithm	[129]
	Two-phase algorithm	[131]
	Hybrid driving algorithm based on a three-layer encoding method	[135]
	Discrete cuckoo search	[136]
	2-optimal algorithm	[139]
	Gravitational search algorithm	[140]
	Fast-ranking heuristic approach	[141]
	Non-dominated sorting genetic algorithm-II	[142,151,154]
	Two-stage parameter-adjusting heuristic	[144]
	Branch and fathoming algorithm	[146]
	Ant colony algorithm	[148]
	Simulated annealing genetic algorithm	[149]

Table 7. Other algorithms.

Area	Methods	Reference
Facility location and VRP in RL	Integrating the sample average approximation scheme with an importance sampling strategy	[34]
	ReCiPe life cycle assessment methodology	[41]
	Fermatean fuzzy CRITIC-EDAS approach	[47]
Scheduling in remanufacturing	Reverse material requirement planning algorithm	[64,65,72]
	Fuzzy goal programming technique	[70]
	Outer approximation-based solution algorithm	[80]
	Dynamic window approach	[94]
	Drum–buffer–rope-based scheduling approach	[103,104]
Disassembly in remanufacturing	Choquet integral	[123]
	Immersive computing technology	[132]
	Multi-attribute utility analysis	[150]
	Takagi–Sugeno fuzzy neural network	[152]

Deep reinforcement learning (DRL) solving COPs in the process of EOL product recovery has attracted extensive attention in recent years. Bengio et al. [161] proposed three types of paradigms for the application of machine learning to COPs. Lei et al. [162] proposed an end-to-end DRL framework to solve the TSP and the CVRP. Yang et al. [163] proposed the framework of robotic disassembly sequence planning using DRL to solve the robotic disassembly sequence planning problem. In general, compared with heuristic or metaheuristic algorithms, DRL is seldom used to solve COPs in the process of EOL product recovery at present. However, DRL has been proved to be superior to metaheuristic algorithms in solving certain problems. Therefore, future research can focus more on DRL.

5.2. Problem Uncertainty

Due to the complexity of the reality and the instability of the state of EOL products, the recovery process will face a series of uncertainties. At present, most of the studies only have considered the deterministic conditions, but the uncertain studies are more practical.

In the stage of facility location and the VRP in RL, it is easy to face uncertainty of quantity, facility capacity, demand, etc. Therefore, Roghanian and Pazhoheshfar [21] considered the uncertainty degree of the demands, capacities, and quantity of EOL products, and proposed a P-MILP model to decide which subsets of processing and disassembly centers will be opened. Lee et al. [34] established a two-stage stochastic programming model which assumed the demand of forward items and the supply of returned products on customers to be stochastic parameters with known distribution. To solve the OOPRLP selection problem with unknown attributes and decision-maker weights, Arunodaya et al. [47] developed a hybrid methodology that combined CRITIC and EDAS methods with Fermatean fuzzy sets (FFSs). In addition, there is also other research on uncertainty in the collection stage of EOL products [36,38,39].

In the area of scheduling in remanufacturing, it often faces the uncertainty of the quality of old products, the demand for new products, and the supply of raw materials. Many scholars have studied the uncertainty in this field [95–97,113]. Kongar et al. [70] established a multi-criteria optimization model of a disassembly-to-order (DTO) system under uncertainty and adopted the fuzzy goal programming technique to solve the problem. Because real-world data on the demand for used components is frequently ambiguous, vague, or imprecise, Barba-Gutiérrez et al. [72] used a fuzzy logic approach to develop the reverse MRP algorithm, incorporating subjectivity and imprecision into the model formulation and solution process. Other similar studies such as Liu and Zhang [80] studied the capacitated disassembly-scheduling problem under stochastic yield and demand. Wen et al. [92] optimized the integration of remanufacturing production planning and a scheduling system under uncertainty. He [93] developed a useful optimization method for the production scheduling in remanufacturing under uncertain conditions. Peng et al. [94] studied a Petri-net-based scheduling scheme and energy model for the remanufacturing of a cylinder block under uncertainty.

In the field of disassembly in remanufacturing, there are many failure features, such as wear, fracture, deformation, and corrosion, which may influence the disassembly time and cost. Behdad et al. [132] used immersive computing technology as a tool to explore an alternative disassembly sequence scheme in an intuitive manner, taking into account uncertain conditions such as time, cost, and the probability of causing damage. Liu et al. [144] researched the DLBP with partial uncertain knowledge, that is, the task-processing time mean and covariance matrix. A new distributionally robust formulation with a joint chance constraint was proposed. Behdad and Thurston [150] considered the costs and uncertainties associated with disassembly and reassembly. To find the best set of tradeoffs, graph-based integer linear programming was combined with multi-attribute utility analysis.

6. Conclusions

The COPs in RL and remanufacturing have important academic value and practical value. In this paper, we divided the COPs into three categories, including facility location and the VRP in RL, scheduling in remanufacturing, and disassembly in remanufacturing; each of them contained several subcategories. At present, the research on these COPs mainly focuses on mathematical models and optimization methodology, which are also the two perspectives of this paper to review the current literature.

At the mathematical model level, through the analysis of this paper, the following suggestions are proposed for future research. Firstly, concerning the facility location and VRP in RL, researchers can pay more attention to the hybrid network structure, as described in Section 2, which can reduce the cost of logistics facilities and improve logistics efficiency. In addition to the uncertainty of the quantity and quality of EOL products, the demand for remanufactured products is also uncertain. Therefore, how to study the hybrid network structure under uncertain conditions may be the direction that researchers should work hard towards. Secondly, in the area of scheduling in remanufacturing, scholars can consider more practical factors, such as multi-objective, limited buffer, uncertainty of task arrival time, etc. Moreover, the combination of the disassembly process and the scheduling process is also a direction that can be considered. Thirdly, for disassembly in remanufacturing, researchers can conduct more study on two-sided or U-shaped disassembly lines. Due to the danger of disassembly operations, human–robotic cooperation is also a field of concern. Similarly, due to the poor quality of EOL products, how to carry out disassembly sequence planning in the case of disassembly failure will be a reality that has to be considered.

At the optimization methodology level, DRL can solve the COPs end-to-end, thus avoiding the complex design of traditional optimization algorithms and its characteristics of low efficiency and high complexity. Therefore, researchers can consider developing relevant DRL algorithms.

Author Contributions: Conceptualization, Y.R.; project administration, H.G.; writing—original draft preparation X.L., Z.X. and H.Z.; writing—review and editing, X.L.; supervision, C.Z. All authors have read and agreed to the published version of the manuscript.

Funding: The research is financially supported by the National Natural Science Foundation of China (No. 52205526, No. 52205538), the Basic and Applied Basic Research Project of Guangzhou Basic Research Program (202201010284), the National Foreign Expert Project of Ministry of Science and Technology of China (G2021199026L), the Guangdong Province Graduate Education Innovation Project (82620516), the National Key Research and Development Program of China (2021YFB3301701), the Guangzhou Leading Innovation Team Program (201909010006), the Guangdong Province "Quality Engineering" Construction Project (210308), the Research Project of Characteristic Innovation of University Teachers (2021DZXX01), and Zhuhai Science and Technology Planning Project in the Field of Social Development (2220004000302).

Data Availability Statement: Not applicable.

Conflicts of Interest: The authors declare no conflict of interest.

References

1. Stock, J.R. *Reverse Logistics: White Paper*; Council of Logistics Management: Lombard, IL, USA, 1992.
2. Zhang, X.; Zou, B.; Feng, Z.; Wang, Y.; Yan, W. A Review on Remanufacturing Reverse Logistics Network Design and Model Optimization. *Processes* **2021**, *10*, 84. [CrossRef]
3. Chanintrakul, P.; Coronado Mondragon, A.E.; Lalwani, C.; Wong, C.Y. Reverse logistics network design: A state-of-the-art literature review. *Int. J. Bus. Perform. Supply Chain Model.* **2009**, *1*, 61–81. [CrossRef]
4. Waidyathilaka, E.; Tharaka, V.K.; Wickramarachchi, A.P.R. Trends in Green Vehicle Routing in Reverse Logistics. In Proceedings of the International Conference on Industrial Engineering and Operations Management (IEOM), Bangkok, Thailand, 5–7 March 2019.
5. Han, H.; Ponce Cueto, E. Waste collection vehicle routing problem: Literature review. *PROMET Traffic Transp.* **2015**, *27*, 345–358. [CrossRef]
6. Majumder, P.; Groenevelt, H. Competition in remanufacturing. *Prod. Oper. Manag.* **2001**, *10*, 125–141. [CrossRef]
7. Nasr, N.; Thurston, M. Remanufacturing: A key enabler to sustainable product systems. *Rochester Instit. Technol.* **2006**, *23*, 14–17.
8. Laili, Y.; Li, Y.; Fang, Y.; Pham, D.T.; Zhang, L. Model review and algorithm comparison on multi-objective disassembly line balancing. *J. Manuf. Syst.* **2020**, *56*, 484–500. [CrossRef]
9. Zhou, Z.; Liu, J.; Pham, D.T.; Xu, W.; Ramirez, F.J.; Ji, C.; Liu, Q. Disassembly sequence planning: Recent developments and future trends. *Proc. Instit. Mech. Eng. Part B J. Eng. Manuf.* **2019**, *233*, 1450–1471. [CrossRef]
10. Morgan, S.D.; Gagnon, R.J. A systematic literature review of remanufacturing scheduling. *Int. J. Prod. Res.* **2013**, *51*, 4853–4879. [CrossRef]
11. Wang, Y.; Mendis, G.P.; Peng, S.; Sutherland, J.W. Component-oriented reassembly in remanufacturing systems: Managing uncertainty and satisfying customer needs. *J. Manuf. Sci. Eng.* **2019**, *141*, 021005. [CrossRef]
12. Fleischmann, M.; Bloemhof-Ruwaard, J.M.; Beullens, P.; Dekker, R. Reverse logistics network design. In *Reverse Logistics*; Springer: Berlin/Heidelberg, Germany, 2004; pp. 65–94.
13. Sasikumar, P.; Kannan, G.; Haq, A.N. A multi-echelon reverse logistics network design for product recovery—A case of truck tire remanufacturing. *Int. J. Adv. Manuf. Technol.* **2010**, *49*, 1223–1234. [CrossRef]
14. Liao, T.Y. Reverse logistics network design for product recovery and remanufacturing. *Appl. Math. Model.* **2018**, *60*, 145–163. [CrossRef]

15. Alumur, S.A.; Nickel, S.; Saldanha-da-Gama, F.; Verter, V. Multi-period reverse logistics network design. *Eur. J. Oper. Res.* **2012**, *220*, 67–78. [CrossRef]
16. Alshamsi, A.; Diabat, A. A reverse logistics network design. *J. Manuf. Syst.* **2015**, *37*, 589–598. [CrossRef]
17. Demirel, E.; Demirel, N.; Gökçen, H. A mixed integer linear programming model to optimize reverse logistics activities of end-of-life vehicles in Turkey. *J. Clean. Prod.* **2016**, *112*, 2101–2113. [CrossRef]
18. Alshamsi, A.; Diabat, A. A Genetic Algorithm for Reverse Logistics network design: A case study from the GCC. *J. Clean. Prod.* **2017**, *151*, 652–669. [CrossRef]
19. Reddy, K.N.; Kumar, A.; Ballantyne, E.E.F. A three-phase heuristic approach for reverse logistics network design incorporating carbon footprint. *Int. J. Prod. Res.* **2019**, *57*, 6090–6114. [CrossRef]
20. Reddy, K.N.; Kumar, A.; Sarkis, J.; Tiwari, M.K. Effect of carbon tax on reverse logistics network design. *Comput. Ind. Eng.* **2020**, *139*, 106184. [CrossRef]
21. Roghanian, E.; Pazhoheshfar, P. An optimization model for reverse logistics network under stochastic environment by using genetic algorithm. *J. Manuf. Syst.* **2014**, *33*, 348–356. [CrossRef]
22. Tari, I.; Alumur, S.A. Collection center location with equity considerations in reverse logistics networks. *INFOR Inf. Syst. Oper. Res.* **2014**, *52*, 157–173. [CrossRef]
23. Zarei, M.; Mansour, S.; Husseinzadeh Kashan, A.; Karimi, B. Designing a reverse logistics network for end-of-life vehicles recovery. *Math. Probl. Eng.* **2010**, *2010*, 649028. [CrossRef]
24. Wang, H.F.; Hsu, H.W. A closed-loop logistic model with a spanning-tree based genetic algorithm. *Comput. Oper. Res.* **2010**, *37*, 376–389. [CrossRef]
25. Pishvaee, M.S.; Torabi, S.A.; Razmi, J. Credibility-based fuzzy mathematical programming model for green logistics design under uncertainty. *Comput. Ind. Eng.* **2012**, *62*, 624–632. [CrossRef]
26. Zohal, M.; Soleimani, H. Developing an ant colony approach for green closed-loop supply chain network design: A case study in gold industry. *J. Clean. Prod.* **2016**, *133*, 314–337. [CrossRef]
27. Devika, K.; Jafarian, A.; Nourbakhsh, V. Designing a sustainable closed-loop supply chain network based on triple bottom line approach: A comparison of metaheuristics hybridization techniques. *Eur. J. Oper. Res.* **2014**, *235*, 594–615. [CrossRef]
28. Fard, A.M.F.; Gholian-Jouybari, F.; Paydar, M.M.; Hajiaghaei-Keshteli, M. A bi-objective stochastic closed-loop supply chain network design problem considering downside risk. *Ind. Eng. Manag. Syst.* **2017**, *16*, 342–362.
29. Fard, A.M.F.; Hajaghaei-Keshteli, M. A tri-level location-allocation model for forward/reverse supply chain. *Appl. Soft Comput.* **2018**, *62*, 328–346. [CrossRef]
30. Pishvaee, M.S.; Rabbani, M.; Torabi, S.A. A robust optimization approach to closed-loop supply chain network design under uncertainty. *Appl. Math. Model.* **2011**, *35*, 637–649. [CrossRef]
31. Chaabane, A.; Ramudhin, A.; Paquet, M. Design of sustainable supply chains under the emission trading scheme. *Int. J. Prod. Econ.* **2012**, *135*, 37–49. [CrossRef]
32. Soleimani, H.; Kannan, G. A hybrid particle swarm optimization and genetic algorithm for closed-loop supply chain network design in large-scale networks. *Appl. Math. Model.* **2015**, *39*, 3990–4012. [CrossRef]
33. Hajiaghaei-Keshteli, M.; Fathollahi Fard, A.M. Sustainable closed-loop supply chain network design with discount supposition. *Neural Comput. Appl.* **2019**, *31*, 5343–5377. [CrossRef]
34. Lee, D.H.; Dong, M.; Bian, W. The design of sustainable logistics network under uncertainty. *Int. J. Prod. Econ.* **2010**, *128*, 159–166. [CrossRef]
35. Fleischmann, M.; Beullens, P.; Bloemhof-Ruwaard, J.M.; Van Wassenhove, L.N. The impact of product recovery on logistics network design. *Prod. Oper. Manag.* **2001**, *10*, 156–173. [CrossRef]
36. Salema, M.I.G.; Barbosa-Povoa, A.P.; Novais, A.Q. An optimization model for the design of a capacitated multi-product reverse logistics network with uncertainty. *Eur. J. Oper. Res.* **2007**, *179*, 1063–1077. [CrossRef]
37. Salema, M.I.G.; Barbosa-Povoa, A.P.; Novais, A.Q. Simultaneous design and planning of supply chains with reverse flows: A generic modelling framework. *Eur. J. Oper. Res.* **2010**, *203*, 336–349. [CrossRef]
38. Cardoso, S.R.; Barbosa-Póvoa, A.P.F.D.; Relvas, S. Design and planning of supply chains with integration of reverse logistics activities under demand uncertainty. *Eur. J. Oper. Res.* **2013**, *226*, 436–451. [CrossRef]
39. Cardoso, S.R.; Barbosa-Póvoa, A.P.; Relvas, S.; Novais, A.Q. Resilience metrics in the assessment of complex supply-chains performance operating under demand uncertainty. *Omega* **2015**, *56*, 53–73. [CrossRef]
40. Paksoy, T.; Bektaş, T.; Özceylan, E. Operational and environmental performance measures in a multi-product closed-loop supply chain. *Transp. Res. Part E Logist. Transp. Rev.* **2011**, *47*, 532–546. [CrossRef]
41. Mota, B.; Gomes, M.I.; Carvalho, A.; Barbosa-Povoa, A.P. Towards supply chain sustainability: Economic, environmental and social design and planning. *J. Clean. Prod.* **2015**, *105*, 14–27. [CrossRef]
42. Gao, X. A novel reverse logistics network design considering multi-level investments for facility reconstruction with environmental considerations. *Sustainability* **2019**, *11*, 2710. [CrossRef]
43. Cao, S.; Liao, W.; Huang, Y. Heterogeneous fleet recyclables collection routing optimization in a two-echelon collaborative reverse logistics network from circular economic and environmental perspective. *Sci. Total Environ.* **2021**, *758*, 144062. [CrossRef]
44. Richnák, P.; Gubová, K. Green and reverse logistics in conditions of sustainable development in enterprises in Slovakia. *Sustainability* **2021**, *13*, 581. [CrossRef]

45. Chen, Z.-S.; Zhang, X.; Govindan, K.; Wang, X.-J.; Chim, K.-S. Third-party reverse logistics provider selection: A computational semantic analysis-based multi-perspective multi-attribute decision-making approach. *Expert Syst. Appl.* **2021**, *166*, 114051. [CrossRef]
46. Santana, J.C.C.; Guerhardt, F.; Franzini, C.E.; Ho, L.L.; Ribeiro, S.E.R., Jr.; Cânovas, G.; Yamamura, C.L.K.; Vanalle, R.M.; Berssaneti, F.T. Refurbishing and recycling of cell phones as a sustainable process of reverse logistics: A case study in Brazil. *J. Clean. Prod.* **2021**, *283*, 124585. [CrossRef]
47. Mishra, A.R.; Rani, P.; Pandey, K. Fermatean fuzzy CRITIC-EDAS approach for the selection of sustainable third-party reverse logistics providers using improved generalized score function. *J. Ambient Intell. Hum. Comput.* **2022**, *13*, 295–311. [CrossRef]
48. Chen, C.-M.; Xie, W.-C.; Li, L.-L.; Fan, S.-S.; Jiang, W.-B. The Research on Logistics Vehicle Path Optimization of Improved Ant Colony Algorithm. *Adv. Sci. Lett.* **2012**, *11*, 493–497. [CrossRef]
49. Foroutan, R.A.; Rezaeian, J.; Mahdavi, I. Green vehicle routing and scheduling problem with heterogeneous fleet including reverse logistics in the form of collecting returned goods. *Appl. Soft Comput.* **2020**, *94*, 106462. [CrossRef]
50. Chaabane, A.; Montecinos, J.; Ouhimmou, M.; Khabou, A. Vehicle routing problem for reverse logistics of End-of-Life Vehicles (ELVs). *Waste Manag.* **2021**, *120*, 209–220. [CrossRef]
51. Desrosiers, J.; Lübbecke, M.E. Branch-price-and-cut algorithms. In *Encyclopedia of Operations Research and Management Science*; John Wiley & Sons: Chichester, UK, 2011; pp. 109–131.
52. Xu, D.; Li, K.; Zheng, P.; Tian, Q. Multi-parking, multi-vehicle, multi-category supply and demand unmatched and arbitrarily splittable delivery vehicle routing problem optimization. *J. Manag.* **2020**, *17*, 1086–1095.
53. Fan, H.; Liu, H.; Liu, P.; Ren, X. Optimization of the simultaneous distribution and collection path of irregular vehicles with fuzzy collection demand. *Control Theory Appl.* **2020**, *1*, 14.
54. Guo, F.; Yang, J.; Yang, C. Research on path optimization and charging strategy of multi-model electric vehicles considering differentiated service time. *Chin. Manag. Sci.* **2019**, *27*, 118–128.
55. Zhang, M.; Pratap, S.; Zhao, Z.; Prajapati, D.; Huang, G.Q. Forward and reverse logistics vehicle routing problems with time horizons in B2C e-commerce logistics. *Int. J. Prod. Res.* **2021**, *59*, 6291–6310. [CrossRef]
56. Dethloff, J. Vehicle routing and reverse logistics: The vehicle routing problem with simultaneous delivery and pick-up. *OR-Spektrum* **2001**, *23*, 79–96. [CrossRef]
57. Masson, R.; Ropke, S.; Lehuédé, F.; Péton, O. A branch-and-cut-and-price approach for the pickup and delivery problem with shuttle routes. *Eur. J. Oper. Res.* **2014**, *236*, 849–862. [CrossRef]
58. Nagy, G.; Wassan, N.A.; Speranza, M.G.; Archetti, C. The vehicle routing problem with divisible deliveries and pickups. *Transp. Sci.* **2015**, *49*, 271–294. [CrossRef]
59. Ghilas, V.; Demir, E.; Van Woensel, T. An adaptive large neighborhood search heuristic for the pickup and delivery problem with time windows and scheduled lines. *Comput. Oper. Res.* **2016**, *72*, 12–30. [CrossRef]
60. Gschwind, T.; Irnich, S.; Rothenbächer, A.K.; Tilk, C. Bidirectional labeling in column-generation algorithms for pickup-and-delivery problems. *Eur. J. Oper. Res.* **2018**, *266*, 521–530. [CrossRef]
61. Goeke, D. Granular tabu search for the pickup and delivery problem with time windows and electric vehicles. *Eur. J. Oper. Res.* **2019**, *278*, 821–836. [CrossRef]
62. Wolfinger, D. A large neighborhood search for the pickup and delivery problem with time windows, split loads and transshipments. *Comput. Oper. Res.* **2021**, *126*, 105110. [CrossRef]
63. Haddad, M.N.; Martinelli, R.; Vidal, T.; Ochi, L.S.; Martins, S.; Jamilson, M.; Souza, J.F.M.; Hartl, R. Large neighborhood-based metaheuristic and branch-and-price for the pickup and delivery problem with split loads. *Eur. J. Oper. Res.* **2018**, *270*, 1014–1027. [CrossRef]
64. Gupta, S.M.; Taleb, K.N. Scheduling disassembly. *Int. J. Prod. Res.* **1994**, *32*, 1857–1866. [CrossRef]
65. Taleb, K.N.; Gupta, S.M.; Brennan, L. Disassembly of complex product structures with parts and materials commonality. *Prod. Plan. Control* **1997**, *8*, 255–269. [CrossRef]
66. Kim, H.J.; Lee, D.H.; Xirouchakis, P.; Züst, R. Disassembly scheduling with multiple product types. *CIRP Ann.* **2003**, *52*, 403–406. [CrossRef]
67. Lee, D.H.; Kim, H.J.; Choi, G.; Xirouchakis, P. Disassembly scheduling: Integer programming models. *Proc. Instit. Mech. Eng. Part B J. Eng. Manuf.* **2004**, *218*, 1357–1372. [CrossRef]
68. Lee, D.H.; Xirouchakis, P. A two-stage heuristic for disassembly scheduling with assembly product structure. *J. Oper. Res. Soc.* **2004**, *55*, 287–297. [CrossRef]
69. Inderfurth, K.; Langella, I.M. Heuristics for solving disassemble-to-order problems with stochastic yields. *Or Spectr.* **2006**, *28*, 73–99. [CrossRef]
70. Kongar, E.; Gupta, S.M. Disassembly to order system under uncertainty. *Omega* **2006**, *34*, 550–561. [CrossRef]
71. Kongar, E.; Gupta, S.M. A multi-criteria decision making approach for disassembly-to-order systems. *J. Electron. Manuf.* **2002**, *11*, 171–183. [CrossRef]
72. Barba-Gutiérrez, Y.; Adenso-Díaz, B. Reverse MRP under uncertain and imprecise demand. *Int. J. Adv. Manuf. Technol.* **2009**, *40*, 413–424. [CrossRef]
73. Barba-Gutiérrez, Y.; Adenso-Diaz, B.; Gupta, S.M. Lot sizing in reverse MRP for scheduling disassembly. *Int. J. Prod. Econ.* **2008**, *111*, 741–751. [CrossRef]

74. Kim, D.H.; Lee, D.H. A heuristic for multi-period disassembly leveling and scheduling. In Proceedings of the 2011 IEEE/SICE International Symposium on System Integration (SII), Kyoto, Japan, 20–22 December 2011; pp. 762–767.
75. Kim, D.H.; Doh, H.H.; Lee, D.H. Multi-period disassembly levelling and lot-sizing for multiple product types with parts commonality. *Proc. Instit. Mech. Eng. Part B J. Eng. Manuf.* **2018**, *232*, 867–878. [CrossRef]
76. Lee, D.H.; Xirouchakis, P.; Zust, R. Disassembly scheduling with capacity constraints. *CIRP Ann.* **2002**, *51*, 387–390. [CrossRef]
77. Kim, J.-G.; Jeon, H.-B.; Kim, H.-J.; Lee, D.-H.; Xirouchakis, P. Capacitated disassembly scheduling: Minimizing the number of products disassembled. In Proceedings of the International Conference on Computational Science and Its Applications, Singapore, 9–12 May 2005; pp. 538–547.
78. Kim, H.J.; Lee, D.H.; Xirouchakis, P. A Lagrangean heuristic algorithm for disassembly scheduling with capacity constraints. *J. Oper. Res. Soc.* **2006**, *57*, 1231–1240. [CrossRef]
79. Prakash, P.K.S.; Ceglarek, D.; Tiwari, M.K. Constraint-based simulated annealing (CBSA) approach to solve the disassembly scheduling problem. *Int. J. Adv. Manuf. Technol.* **2012**, *60*, 1125–1137. [CrossRef]
80. Liu, K.; Zhang, Z.H. Capacitated disassembly scheduling under stochastic yield and demand. *Eur. J. Oper. Res.* **2018**, *269*, 244–257. [CrossRef]
81. Ullerich, C.; Buscher, U. Flexible disassembly planning considering product conditions. *Int. J. Prod. Res.* **2013**, *51*, 6209–6228. [CrossRef]
82. Ji, X.; Zhang, Z.; Huang, S.; Li, L. Capacitated disassembly scheduling with parts commonality and start-up cost and its industrial application. *Int. J. Prod. Res.* **2016**, *54*, 1225–1243. [CrossRef]
83. Godichaud, M.; Amodeo, L.; Hrouga, M. Metaheuristic based optimization for capacitated disassembly lot sizing problem with lost sales. In Proceedings of the 2015 international conference on industrial engineering and systems management (IESM), Seville, Spain, 21–23 October 2015; pp. 1329–1335.
84. Hrouga, M.; Godichaud, M.; Amodeo, L. Efficient metaheuristic for multi-product disassembly lot sizing problem with lost sales. In Proceedings of the 2016 IEEE International Conference on Industrial Engineering and Engineering Management (IEEM), Bali, Indonesia, 4–7 December 2016; pp. 740–744.
85. Hrouga, M.; Godichaud, M.; Amodeo, L. Heuristics for multi-product capacitated disassembly lot sizing with lost sales. *IFAC-PapersOnLine* **2016**, *49*, 628–633. [CrossRef]
86. Kim, H.J.; Xirouchakis, P. Capacitated disassembly scheduling with random demand. *Int. J. Prod. Res.* **2010**, *48*, 7177–7194. [CrossRef]
87. Tian, X.; Zhang, Z.H. Capacitated disassembly scheduling and pricing of returned products with price-dependent yield. *Omega* **2019**, *84*, 160–174. [CrossRef]
88. Zhou, F.; He, Y.; Ma, P.; Lim, M.K.; Pratap, S. Capacitated disassembly scheduling with random demand and operation time. *J. Oper. Res. Soc.* **2022**, *73*, 1362–1378. [CrossRef]
89. Yuan, G.; Yang, Y.; Tian, G.; Fathollahi-Fard, A.M. Capacitated multi-objective disassembly scheduling with fuzzy processing time via a fruit fly optimization algorithm. *Environ. Sci. Pollut. Res.* **2022**; ahead-of-print.
90. Slama, I.; Ben-Ammar, O.; Dolgui, A.; Masmoudi, F. New mixed integer approach to solve a multi-level capacitated disassembly lot-sizing problem with defective items and backlogging. *J. Manuf. Syst.* **2020**, *56*, 50–57. [CrossRef]
91. Slama, I.; Ben-Ammar, O.; Dolgui, A.; Masmoudi, F. Genetic algorithm and Monte Carlo simulation for a stochastic capacitated disassembly lot-sizing problem under random lead times. *Comput. Ind. Eng.* **2021**, *159*, 107468. [CrossRef]
92. Wen, H.; Hou, S.; Liu, Z.; Yongjiang, L. An optimization algorithm for integrated remanufacturing production planning and scheduling system. *Chaos Solitons Fractals* **2017**, *105*, 69–76. [CrossRef]
93. He, P. Optimization and simulation of remanufacturing production scheduling under uncertainties. *Int. J. Simul. Model.* **2018**, *17*, 734–743. [CrossRef]
94. Peng, S.; Li, T.; Zhao, J.; Guo, Y.; Lv, S.; Tan, G.Z.; Zhang, H. Petri net-based scheduling strategy and energy modeling for the cylinder block remanufacturing under uncertainty. *Robot. Comput. Int. Manuf.* **2019**, *58*, 208–219. [CrossRef]
95. Zhang, H.P. Optimization of remanufacturing production scheduling considering uncertain factors. *Int. J. Simul. Model.* **2019**, *18*, 344–354. [CrossRef]
96. Shi, J.; Zhang, W.; Zhang, S.; Chen, J. A new bifuzzy optimization method for remanufacturing scheduling using extended discrete particle swarm optimization algorithm. *Comput. Ind. Eng.* **2021**, *156*, 107219. [CrossRef]
97. Kim, H.J.; Lee, D.H.; Xirouchakis, P. Disassembly scheduling: Literature review and future research directions. *Int. J. Prod. Res.* **2007**, *45*, 4465–4484. [CrossRef]
98. Stanfield, P.M.; King, R.E.; Hodgson, T.J. Determining sequence and ready times in a remanufacturing system. *IIE Trans.* **2006**, *38*, 565–575. [CrossRef]
99. Kim, M.G.; Yu, J.M.; Lee, D.H. Scheduling algorithms for remanufacturing systems with parallel flow-shop-type reprocessing lines. *Int. J. Prod. Res.* **2015**, *53*, 1819–1831. [CrossRef]
100. Qu, C.; Fu, Y.; Yi, Z.; Tan, J. Solutions to no-wait flow shop scheduling problem using the flower pollination algorithm based on the hormone modulation mechanism. *Complexity* **2018**, *2018*, 1973604. [CrossRef]
101. Wang, W.; Tian, G.; Yuan, G.; Pham, D.T. Energy-time tradeoffs for remanufacturing system scheduling using an invasive weed optimization algorithm. *J. Intell. Manuf.* **2021**, 1–19. [CrossRef]

102. Wang, W.; Tian, G.; Zhang, H.; Xu, K.; Miao, Z. Modeling and scheduling for remanufacturing systems with disassembly, reprocessing, and reassembly considering total energy consumption. *Environ. Sci. Pollut. Res.* **2021**, *ahead-of-print*.
103. Guide, V.D.R., Jr. Scheduling using drum-buffer-rope in a remanufacturing environment. *Int. J. Prod. Res.* **1996**, *34*, 1081–1091. [CrossRef]
104. Guide, V.D.R., Jr. Scheduling with priority dispatching rules and drum-buffer-rope in a recoverable manufacturing system. *Int. J. Prod. Econ.* **1997**, *53*, 101–116.
105. Souza, G.C.; Ketzenberg, M.E.; Guide, V.D.R., Jr. Capacitated remanufacturing with service level constraints. *Prod. Oper. Manag.* **2002**, *11*, 231–248. [CrossRef]
106. Guide, V.D.R., Jr.; Souza, G.C.; Van Der Laan, E. Performance of static priority rules for shared facilities in a remanufacturing shop with disassembly and reassembly. *Eur. J. Oper. Res.* **2005**, *164*, 341–353. [CrossRef]
107. Li, L.; Li, C.; Tang, Y. A color petri net based scheduling model for remanufacturing system with stochastic process routing. In Proceedings of the 2014 IEEE International Conference on Automation Science and Engineering (CASE), New Taipei, Taiwan, 18–22 August 2014; pp. 474–479.
108. Kang, C.; Hong, Y.S. Dynamic disassembly planning for remanufacturing of multiple types of products. *Int. J. Prod. Res.* **2010**, *50*, 6236–6248. [CrossRef]
109. Lin, D.; Teo, C.C.; Lee, C.K.M. Heuristics for integrated job assignment and scheduling in the multi-plant remanufacturing system. *Int. J. Prod. Res.* **2015**, *53*, 2674–2689. [CrossRef]
110. Giglio, D.; Paolucci, M.; Roshani, A. Integrated lot sizing and energy-efficient job shop scheduling problem in manufacturing/remanufacturing systems. *J. Clean. Prod.* **2017**, *148*, 624–641. [CrossRef]
111. Yu, J.M.; Lee, D.H. Scheduling algorithms for job-shop-type remanufacturing systems with component matching requirement. *Comput. Ind. Eng.* **2018**, *120*, 266–278. [CrossRef]
112. Li, L.; Li, C.; Li, L.; Tang, Y. An integrated approach for remanufacturing job shop scheduling with routing alternatives. *Math. Biosci. Eng.* **2019**, *16*, 2063–2085. [CrossRef]
113. Fu, Y.; Zhou, M.C.; Guo, X.; Qi, L. Stochastic multi-objective integrated disassembly-reprocessing-reassembly scheduling via fruit fly optimization algorithm. *J. Clean. Prod.* **2021**, *278*, 123364. [CrossRef]
114. Zhang, W.; Zheng, Y.; Ahmad, R. The integrated process planning and scheduling of flexible job-shop-type remanufacturing systems using improved artificial bee colony algorithm. *J. Intell. Manuf.* **2022**, 1–26. [CrossRef]
115. Guo, X.; Zhou, M.C.; Abusorrah, A.; Alsokhiry, F.; Sedraoui, K. Disassembly sequence planning: A survey. *IEEE/CAA J. Autom. Sin.* **2020**, *8*, 1308–1324. [CrossRef]
116. Tseng, H.-E.; Chang, C.-C.; Lee, S.-C.; Huang, Y.-M. A block-based genetic algorithm for disassembly sequence planning. *Expert Syst. Appl.* **2018**, *96*, 492–505. [CrossRef]
117. ElSayed, A.; Kongar, E.; Gupta, S.M.; Sobh, T. A robotic-driven disassembly sequence generator for end-of-life electronic products. *J. Intell. Robot. Syst.* **2012**, *68*, 43–52. [CrossRef]
118. Li, H.J.; Jiang, J.; Wang, Y.F. Disassembly sequence planning based on extended interference matrix and genetic algorithm. *Comput. Eng. Des.* **2013**, *34*, 1064–1068.
119. Zhong, L.; Youchao, S.; Okafor, E.G.; Haiqiao, W. Disassembly sequence planning for maintenance based on metaheuristic method. *Aircr. Eng. Aerosp. Technol.* **2011**, *83*, 138–145. [CrossRef]
120. Guo, X.; Zhou, M.; Liu, S.; Qi, L. Lexicographic multiobjective scatter search for the optimization of sequence-dependent selective disassembly subject to multiresource constraints. *IEEE Trans. Cybern.* **2019**, *50*, 3307–3317. [CrossRef]
121. Liu, J.; Zhou, Z.; Pham, D.T.; Xu, W.; Ji, C.; Liu, Q. Robotic disassembly sequence planning using enhanced discrete bees algorithm in remanufacturing. *Int. J. Prod. Res.* **2018**, *56*, 3134–3151. [CrossRef]
122. Tao, F.; Bi, L.; Zuo, Y.; Nee, A.Y.C. Partial/parallel disassembly sequence planning for complex products. *J. Manuf. Sci. Eng.* **2018**, *140*, 011016. [CrossRef]
123. Guo, H.; Chen, Z.; Ren, Y.; Qu, T.; Li, J. Research on disassembly sequence and disassembly length integrated decision of End-of-life products based on parts recovery comprehensive evaluation. *J. Mech. Eng.* **2022**, *58*, 258–268.
124. Ren, Y.; Zhang, C.; Zhao, F.; Xiao, H.; Tian, G. An asynchronous parallel disassembly planning based on genetic algorithm. *Eur. J. Oper. Res.* **2018**, *269*, 647–660. [CrossRef]
125. Ren, Y.; Meng, L.; Zhang, C.; Zhao, F.; Saif, U.; Huang, A.; Mendis, G.P.; Sutherland, J.W. An efficient metaheuristics for a sequence-dependent disassembly planning. *J. Clean. Prod.* **2020**, *245*, 118644. [CrossRef]
126. Ren, Y.; Tian, G.; Zhao, F.; Yu, D.; Zhang, C. Selective cooperative disassembly planning based on multi-objective discrete artificial bee colony algorithm. *Eng. Appl. Artif. Intell.* **2017**, *64*, 415–431. [CrossRef]
127. Lu, Q.; Ren, Y.; Jin, H.; Meng, L.; Li, L.; Zhang, C.; Sutherland, J.W. A hybrid metaheuristic algorithm for a profit-oriented and energy-efficient disassembly sequencing problem. *Robot. Comput. Integr. Manuf.* **2020**, *61*, 101828. [CrossRef]
128. Zhu, B.; Sarigecili, M.I.; Roy, U. Disassembly information model incorporating dynamic capabilities for disassembly sequence generation. *Robot. Comput. Integr. Manuf.* **2013**, *29*, 396–409. [CrossRef]
129. Costa, C.M.; Veiga, G.; Sousa, A.; Rocha, L.; Oliveira, E.; Cardoso, H.L.; Thomas, U. Automatic generation of disassembly sequences and exploded views from solidworks symbolic geometric relationships. In Proceedings of the 2018 IEEE International Conference on Autonomous Robot Systems and Competitions (ICARSC), Torres Vedras, Portugal, 25–27 April 2018; pp. 211–218.

130. Lambert, A.J.D.; Gupta, S.M. Methods for optimum and near optimum disassembly sequencing. *Int. J. Prod. Res.* **2008**, *46*, 2845–2865. [CrossRef]
131. Ma, Y.S.; Jun, H.B.; Kim, H.W.; Lee, D.-H. Disassembly process planning algorithms for end-of-life product recovery and environmentally conscious disposal. *Int. J. Prod. Res.* **2011**, *49*, 7007–7027. [CrossRef]
132. Behdad, S.; Berg, L.P.; Thurston, D.; Vance, J.M. Leveraging virtual reality experiences with mixed-integer nonlinear programming visualization of disassembly sequence planning under uncertainty. *J. Mech. Des.* **2014**, *136*, 041005. [CrossRef]
133. Gungor, A.; Gupta, S.M. Disassembly line balancing. In Proceedings of the 1999 Annual Meeting of the Northeast Decision Sciences Institute, Newport, RI, USA, 24–26 March 1999.
134. Özceylan, E.; Kalayci, C.B.; Güngör, A.; Gupta, S.M. Disassembly line balancing problem: A review of the state of the art and future directions. *Int. J. Prod. Res.* **2019**, *57*, 4805–4827. [CrossRef]
135. Yin, T.; Zhang, Z.; Zhang, Y.; Wu, T.; Liang, W. Mixed-integer programming model and hybrid driving algorithm for multi-product partial disassembly line balancing problem with multi-robot workstations. *Robot. Comput. Integr. Manuf.* **2022**, *73*, 102251. [CrossRef]
136. Li, Z.; Janardhanan, M.N. Modelling and solving profit-oriented U-shaped partial disassembly line balancing problem. *Expert Syst. Appl.* **2021**, *183*, 115431. [CrossRef]
137. Wang, K.; Li, X.; Gao, L.; Li, P.; Sutherland, J.W. A discrete artificial bee colony algorithm for multiobjective disassembly line balancing of end-of-life products. *IEEE Trans. Cybern.* **2021**, *52*, 7415–7426. [CrossRef] [PubMed]
138. Ren, Y.; Zhang, C.; Zhao, F.; Triebe, M.J.; Meng, L. An MCDM-based multiobjective general variable neighborhood search approach for disassembly line balancing problem. *IEEE Trans. Syst. Man Cybern. Syst.* **2018**, *50*, 3770–3783. [CrossRef]
139. Ren, Y.; Zhang, C.; Zhao, F.; Tian, G.; Lin, W.; Meng, L.; Li, H. Disassembly line balancing problem using interdependent weights-based multi-criteria decision making and 2-Optimal algorithm. *J. Clean. Prod.* **2018**, *174*, 1475–1486. [CrossRef]
140. Ren, Y.; Yu, D.; Zhang, C.; Tian, G.; Meng, L.; Zhou, X. An improved gravitational search algorithm for profit-oriented partial disassembly line balancing problem. *Int. J. Prod. Res.* **2017**, *55*, 7302–7316. [CrossRef]
141. Ren, Y.; Meng, L.; Zhang, C.; Lu, Q.; Tian, G. Multi-criterion decision making for disassembly line balancing problem. *Procedia CIRP* **2019**, *80*, 542–547. [CrossRef]
142. Yılmaz, Ö.F.; Yazıcı, B. Tactical level strategies for multi-objective disassembly line balancing problem with multi-manned stations: An optimization model and solution approaches. *Ann. Oper. Res.* **2021**, *319*, 1793–1843. [CrossRef]
143. Edis, E.B.; Ilgin, M.A.; Edis, R.S. Disassembly line balancing with sequencing decisions: A mixed integer linear programming model and extensions. *J. Clean. Prod.* **2019**, *238*, 117826. [CrossRef]
144. Liu, M.; Liu, X.; Chu, F.; Zheng, F.; Chu, C. Robust disassembly line balancing with ambiguous task processing times. *Int. J. Prod. Res.* **2020**, *58*, 5806–5835. [CrossRef]
145. Budak, A. Sustainable reverse logistics optimization with triple bottom line approach: An integration of disassembly line balancing. *J. Clean. Prod.* **2020**, *270*, 122475. [CrossRef]
146. Han, H.J.; Yu, J.M.; Lee, D.H. Mathematical model and solution algorithms for selective disassembly sequencing with multiple target components and sequence-dependent setups. *Int. J. Prod. Res.* **2013**, *51*, 4997–5010. [CrossRef]
147. Liu, C.; Zhu, Q.; Wei, F.; Rao, W.; Liu, J.; Hu, J.; Cai, W. A review on remanufacturing assembly management and technology. *Int. J. Adv. Manuf. Technol.* **2019**, *105*, 4797–4808. [CrossRef]
148. Su, B.; Huang, X.M.; Ren, Y.H.; Wang, F.; Xiao, H.; Zheng, B. Research on selective assembly method optimization for construction machinery remanufacturing based on ant colony algorithm. *J. Mech. Eng.* **2017**, *53*, 60–68. [CrossRef]
149. Liu, W.; Sun, Z.; Ge, M.; Wang, C.; Wang, Q. Remanufacturing Quality Optimization Method of Complex Mechanical Products Based on Assembly Deviation Degree. *China Mech. Eng.* **2014**, *25*, 1473.
150. Behdad, S.; Thurston, D. Disassembly and reassembly sequence planning tradeoffs under uncertainty for product maintenance. *J. Mech. Des.* **2012**, *134*, 041011. [CrossRef]
151. Su, C.; Shi, Y.; Dou, J. Multi-objective optimization of buffer allocation for remanufacturing system based on TS-NSGAII hybrid algorithm. *J. Clean. Prod.* **2017**, *166*, 756–770. [CrossRef]
152. Li, C.; Feng, Y.; Du, Y. Decision-making method for used components remanufacturing process plan based on modified FNN. *Comput. Integr. Manuf. Syst.* **2016**, *22*, 728–737.
153. Oh, Y.; Behdad, S. Simultaneous reassembly and procurement planning in assemble-to-order remanufacturing systems. *Int. J. Prod. Econ.* **2017**, *184*, 168–178. [CrossRef]
154. Lahmar, H.; Dahane, M.; Mouss, N.K.; Haoues, M. Production planning optimisation in a sustainable hybrid manufacturing remanufacturing production system. *Procedia Comput. Sci.* **2022**, *200*, 1244–1253. [CrossRef]
155. Polotski, V.; Kenne, J.P.; Gharbi, A. Joint production and maintenance optimization in flexible hybrid Manufacturing–Remanufacturing systems under age-dependent deterioration. *Int. J. Prod. Econ.* **2019**, *216*, 239–254. [CrossRef]
156. Holland, J.H. Genetic algorithms. *Sci. Am.* **1992**, *267*, 66–73. [CrossRef]
157. Kennedy, J.; Eberhart, R. Particle swarm optimization. In Proceedings of the ICNN'95-International Conference on Neural Networks, Perth, WA, Australia, 27 November–1 December 1995; Volume 4, pp. 1942–1948.
158. Dorigo, M.; Birattari, M.; Stutzle, T. Ant colony optimization. *IEEE Comput. Intell. Mag.* **2006**, *1*, 28–39. [CrossRef]
159. Kirkpatrick, S.; Gelatt, C.D., Jr.; Vecchi, M.P. Optimization by simulated annealing. *Science* **1983**, *220*, 671–680. [CrossRef]
160. Glover, F.; Laguna, M. Tabu search. In *Handbook of Combinatorial Optimization*; Springer: Boston, MA, USA, 1998; pp. 2093–2229.

161. Bengio, Y.; Lodi, A.; Prouvost, A. Machine learning for combinatorial optimization: A methodological tour d'horizon. *Eur. J. Oper. Res.* **2021**, *290*, 405–421. [CrossRef]
162. Lei, K.; Guo, P.; Wang, Y.; Wu, X.; Zhao, X. Solve routing problems with a residual edge-graph attention neural network. *Neurocomputing* **2022**, *508*, 79–98. [CrossRef]
163. Yang, C.; Xu, W.; Liu, J.; Yao, B.; Hu, Y. Robotic Disassembly Sequence Planning Considering Robotic Movement State Based on Deep Reinforcement Learning. In Proceedings of the 2022 IEEE 25th International Conference on Computer Supported Cooperative Work in Design (CSCWD), Hangzhou, China, 4–6 May 2022; pp. 183–189.

Disclaimer/Publisher's Note: The statements, opinions and data contained in all publications are solely those of the individual author(s) and contributor(s) and not of MDPI and/or the editor(s). MDPI and/or the editor(s) disclaim responsibility for any injury to people or property resulting from any ideas, methods, instructions or products referred to in the content.

Article

Multi-Objective Robust Optimization for the Sustainable Location-Inventory-Routing Problem of Auto Parts Supply Logistics

Ao Lv and Baofeng Sun *

College of Transportation, Jilin University, Changchun 130022, China
* Correspondence: sunbf@jlu.edu.cn

Abstract: A great loss of transportation capacity has been caused in auto parts supply logistics due to the independent transportation from auto parts suppliers (APSs) to the automobile production line (APL). It is believed that establishing distribution centers (DCs) for centralized collection and unified distribution is one effective way to address this problem. This paper proposes a unified framework simultaneously considering the location-inventory-routing problem (LIRP) in auto parts supply logistics. Integrating the idea of sustainable development, a multi-objective MIP model is developed to determine the location and inventory capacity of DCs and routing decisions to minimize the total system cost and carbon emissions while concerning multi-period production demand. In addition, a robust optimization model is developed further in the context of uncertain demand. Numerical experiments and sensitivity analyses are conducted to verify the effectiveness of our proposed deterministic and robust models. The results show that synergistically optimizing the location and capacity of DCs and routing decisions are beneficial in reducing total system cost and carbon emissions. The analysis can provide guidelines to decision-makers for the effective management of auto parts supply logistics.

Keywords: auto parts supply chain; sustainable logistics; robust optimization; location-inventory-routing optimization; multi-period demand

MSC: 90B05; 90B06; 90B10

1. Introduction

With the increase and diversification of end-customer demands in the commercial vehicle market, the automobile logistics service size and system complexity will unavoidably continue growing. As a core concept of the automobile supply chain, auto parts supply logistics has caught the abundant attention of academic and auto manufacturers [1]. The existing literature has indicated that if the auto parts are delivered separately by the auto part suppliers (APSs), several problems will be caused such as the great loss of transportation capacity and higher transport cost [2]. Hence, to address the practical issues of the auto parts supply logistics, our research aims to establish distribution centers (DCs) integrated with the routing problem [3] for centralized pickup and unified delivery. In order to better respond to the idea of emission reduction [4], it is critical to determine the location-inventory-routing problem from a sustainable perspective while reducing the total transport cost.

Our problem is a typical location-inventory-routing problem (LIRP) involving strategic, tactical, and operational decisions. Specifically, the strategic decisions are to determine the number and location of DCs, which undertake the tasks of the centralized pick-up of auto parts from APSs, storage, and their unified delivery to the automobile production line (APL). Unreasonable locations of the DCs are likely to fail in meeting production demands and reduce the operating efficiency of the auto parts supply logistics. The tactical decisions

are to determine the inventory capacity of the opened DCs. Subject to the construction budget, it is not ideal to establish DCs with a large inventory capacity. On the other hand, when the inventory capacity is insufficient, there is a risk of a shortage of auto parts in DCs. In that case, the required auto parts of the APL cannot be satisfied by DCs, requiring APSs to deliver auto parts directly to the APL, which will significantly increase the transport cost. Moreover, operational decisions refer to the assignment between DCs and APSs [5] routing decisions for centralized pickup and unified delivery. The location selection of DCs, inventory capacity, and routing decisions are interrelated. With respect to the periodicity and time-sensitive characteristics of auto parts, this paper considers multi-period production demand to describe the LIRP of auto parts supply logistics.

Another essential factor that has to be considered is the uncertain demand. In automobile production activities, the production demand in the APL depends on the market orders, which are impacted deeply by indeterministic factors. In order to make up for the production uncertainty, it is essential to expand the inventory capacity of DCs or to order more auto parts in advance. However, these solutions have the potential to increase the delivery cost significantly. At the same time, it is difficult to obtain an exact probability distribution of uncertain demand. Therefore, a robust optimization method is needed to deal with the uncertainty of production demand.

Overall, this paper proposes a unified framework to describe the multi-objective LIRP while considering the multi-period uncertain demand of auto parts supply logistics. The main contributions of this paper are as follows:

(1) Concerning the multi-period deterministic demand, this paper first proposes a multi-objective mixed-integer programming model (MIP) to investigate the LIRP in auto parts supply logistics from a sustainable perspective. Specifically, this model determines the location and capacity of DCs and routing decisions to minimize the total system cost and carbon emissions.

(2) Further, a robust optimization model is developed to capture the multi-period uncertain production demand in the APL. To the authors' knowledge, this is the first time the LIRP in auto parts supply logistics is simultaneously optimized while considering multi-period uncertain demand.

(3) Numerical experiments are conducted to demonstrate the usefulness of the proposed models. The sensitivity analysis results show that the location, inventory capacity, and delivery routing decisions are highly affected by various cost parameters.

The remainder of this paper is structured as follows. Section 2 briefly reviews the relevant literature, and the LIRP and the MIP model are formulated in Section 3. Numerical experiments, results analysis, and managerial insights are presented in Section 4. Finally, Section 5 summarizes the conclusions and future direction of this research.

2. Literature Review

As a typical topic, numerous studies focus on the LIRP in various fields. To comprehensively review the problem in auto parts supply logistics, we summarize the literature review from three aspects: the LIRP in the auto parts supply network, the environmentally sustainable LIRP, and the LIRP with uncertain factors.

2.1. LIRP in Auto Parts Supply Logistics

The complexities of the LIRP in auto parts supply logistics are closely related to location, inventory, and routing decisions. The location models have been widely investigated to determine the site of DCs. Ref. [6] developed a location model for an auto parts warehouse to minimize construction and transport costs. An improved particle swarm optimization algorithm was proposed and benchmark experiments were conducted to prove the effectiveness of the location model. In addition, the inventory capacity is another essential component in the LIRP, which is tightly associated with supply efficiency and inventory cost. In addition, route planning at the regional level has significant implications for regional transportation planning [7]. Compared to the zero inventory strategy that several automobile companies adopt, Ref. [8] proposed a new logistics strategy integrating progress-lane and vehicle routing problems. A mixed-integer model was established to minimize the total cost of inbound logistics, which is demonstrated to be more effective and economical than the zero inventory strategy. Further, Ref. [9] developed an adaptive Visual Basic Application (VBA) program to largely enhance the utilization rate of DCs and reduce the inventory cost. A multi-level location-inventory model was proposed by [10] and solved with the Lagrangian relaxation method. Concerning the auto parts demand, Ref. [11] provided the second weighted moving average method to forecast the future demand in advance, which is beneficial in reducing the inventory cost.

As auto parts transportation is the main component of the total system cost and the primary source of carbon emission [12,13], it is of great significance to optimize the routing problem in the auto parts supply logistics. Previous research has mainly concentrated on the location-inventory and routing problems separately. Therefore, it is essential to investigate the LIRP in auto parts supply logistics comprehensively.

2.2. Environmentally Sustainable LIRP

Traditional supply chain optimization problems mainly focus on minimizing the economic costs, which ignores the goal of reducing carbon emissions. With the popularity of the low-carbon concept, recent literature [14] has paid more attention to the LIRP from a sustainable view in various fields. For instance, to address the fresh food delivery problem, Ref. [15] proposed a model to discuss the vehicle routing problem with time windows (VRPTW) while decreasing carbon emissions. To deal with urban waste, Ref. [16] developed a multi-warehouse location-routing model and proposed a hybrid genetic algorithm and a simulated annealing algorithm. Numerical experiments demonstrated that the method and algorithm are effective in determining the location of parking lots and the vehicles routing to collect garbage. A two-layer planning model based on a carbon emission trading policy was developed in [17] to optimize the location problem of cold chain logistics. Similarly, Ref. [18] proposed an LIRP model that considers the carbon trading mechanism in the cold chain logistics network. Through simulation results, it was demonstrated that the improved NSGA-II can effectively reduce the carbon emissions of enterprises. Combining pollution-related routing, Ref. [19] developed a mathematical model to discuss the inventory-routing problem and proposed a hybrid adaptive particle swarm optimization algorithm. Considering the green location inventory problem, Ref. [20] developed a two-stage stochastic mathematical model and proposed a hierarchical heuristic algorithm. This study further proved the impact of the carbon trading scheme on strategic decision-making. To achieve a sustainable supply chain, Ref. [21] proposed a two-stage approach and built a multi-objective mixed-integer model. Based on the environmental consideration, the location-path-inventory system in a three-level supply chain network was studied, and Ref. [22] formulated a bi-objective mixed-integer programming model for the above system and developed a multi-objective particle swarm optimization algorithm.

Only a few studies discussed energy saving and emission reduction in auto parts supply logistics. To minimize the transport cost and carbon emissions, Ref. [23] established a routing planning model and verified the effectiveness through a real case. Based on emission reduction and resource sharing, a decision-making optimization model of the auto parts supply chain was established by [24] to minimize the total system cost and carbon emission. Variational inequality was utilized to analyze the optimal conditions.

In order to simultaneously minimize economic cost and carbon emissions, this study described a multi-objective model for the LIRP in the auto parts supply network.

2.3. LIRP with Uncertain Factors

Another key challenge for the LIRP is the demand uncertainty [25]. Reviewing the literature in the LIRP, researchers have made various assumptions when describing the demand. For instance, assuming that the demand is satisfied by a normal distribution, Ref. [26] formulated a dual-objective stochastic model to minimize the total cost and maximize the service time while considering various multi-period products, and a heuristic algorithm was adopted to obtain the Pareto set. Concerning the uncertain topology of the hub location, Ref. [27] proposed an interactive method to delineate the design problem of the dangerous goods transportation network. Two heuristics based on the lower bound and rolling horizon were proposed to solve the model in a large-scale case.

In the presence of demand uncertainty, robust optimization and stochastic optimization are two main streams. Ref. [28] formulated a stochastic programming mixed-integer model to determine the location and inventory strategy at the same time. Considering carbon emissions and energy consumption, Ref. [29] applied stochastic programming to the LIRP and proposed a sustainable closed-loop model to achieve economic, environmental, and social trade-offs. Robust optimization concentrates on min-max risk control. With respect to the uncertain demand in the medical supplier network, a robust LIRP model was proposed by [30] to reduce the total system cost effectively. Integrating with big data technology, Ref. [31] developed a multi-center location-routing optimization model of medical logistics considering several uncertain factors.

To give a clear representation of the innovation of this paper, we summarize the related literature review in Table 1. Up until now, there has been a lack of studies on a robust LIRP in auto parts supply logistics from a sustainable perspective while considering the multi-type, multi-period characteristic. To address the existing issues, this paper investigates the deterministic LIRP first and proposes a robust model combined with the multi-period uncertain demand to optimize the total transport cost and carbon emissions.

Table 1. List of referenced articles.

Article	Problem	Multi-Objective	Sustainable	Uncertainty	Optimization Method	Multi-Period
Ghasemi et al., 2022 [32]	LIRP			✓	Two-stage	
Yang et al., 2021 [33]	LIRP		✓		Integrated	
Biuki et al., 2020 [21]	LIRP	✓	✓	✓	Two-stage	✓
Chao et al., 2019 [34]	LIRP				Two-stage	✓
Li et al., 2022 [18]	LIRP	✓	✓		Integrated	
Ji et al., 2022 [22]	LIRP	✓	✓		Integrated	
Shang et al., 2022 [30]	LIRP			✓	Integrated	✓
Aydemir-Karadag, 2022 [35]	LIRP	✓	✓		Two-stage	✓
Liu et al., 2021 [36]	LIRP	✓	✓		Integrated	
Yavari et al., 2020 [37]	LIRP			✓	Integrated	✓
Song Wu, 2022 [38]	LIRP	✓			Integrated	✓
This Paper	LIRP	✓	✓	✓	Integrated	✓

3. Problem Description and Model Formulation

Motivated by a real-world problem, we aim to present a novel multi-objective optimization model for the LIRP in the auto parts supply network. First, problem formulation and modeling assumptions are described. Then, we develop an integrated deterministic MIP model. Finally, integrating multi-period uncertain demand, a robust optimization model is further developed, and the complex modeling process in this paper is delineated in Figure 1.

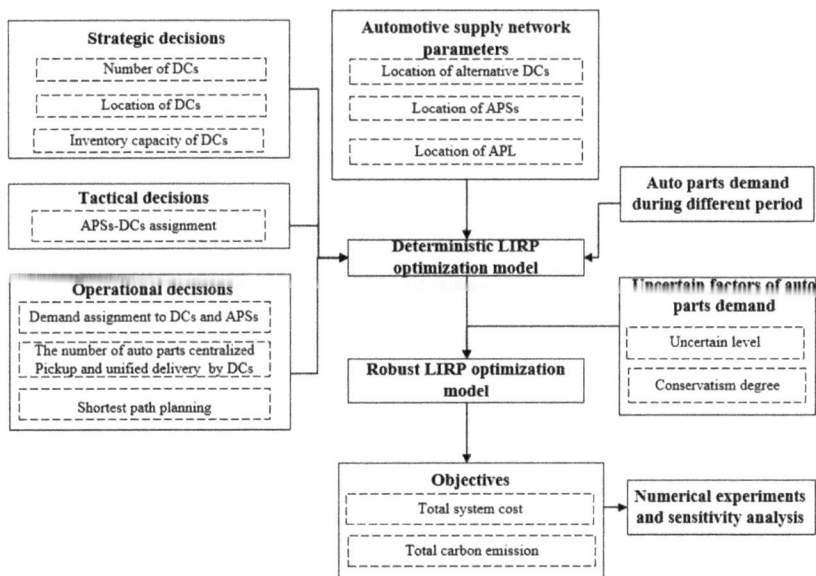

Figure 1. The research framework for auto parts supply logistics.

3.1. Problem Description

This paper considers an auto parts supply network, as shown in Figure 1. The strategical decisions in this paper are to determine the location and inventory capacity of DCs. Let $J = \{1, 2, \ldots \bar{J}\}$ represent the alternative points set of DCs, which is indexed by j. Denote y_j as a binary variable to describe if the alternative point j is selected as DCs. That is, if $y_j = 1$, the DC is opened. In addition, it is essential to determine a reasonable inventory level for the opened DCs. Let $L = \{1, 2, \ldots \bar{L}\}$ represent the inventory levels set. Denote $y_{jl} = 1$ to describe the opened DC, where j is equipped with the inventory level l. In addition, we have to decide the assignment between DCs and APSs, and we assume each APS has to be assigned with one DC. Suppose the set for APSs is $I = \{1, 2, \ldots \bar{I}\}$, which is indexed by i. If the APS i is assigned to DC j, we define $x_{ij} = 1$, otherwise $x_{ij} = 0$. To investigate the multi-periods production demand of the APL, the time is discretized into several equal periods $T = \{1, 2, \ldots, \bar{T}\}$, which is indexed by t. Once the APS i is assigned to DC j initially, the assignment will not change. As a side note, the auto parts demand in the APL is satisfied by DCs and APSs. We assume the auto parts demand of APS i is D_i^t. One part of the demand of the APS i is accommodated by the responding DC j, and another part of the demand is provided by APS i directly. Afterward, there is a need to pick-up auto parts centrally to the DCs so that the demand in the last period can be satisfied. Namely, the DCs will dispatch vehicles to the corresponding assigned APS i to pick-up auto parts according to the order quantity.

This will involve a vehicle routing problem to seek the shortest path. Three kinds of routes are included in Figure 2. The red lines are the direct delivery routing from APSs to the APL, and the black lines are the unified delivery routing from APSs to the APL. In addition, the blue lines are the centralized pickup routing from DCs to APSs and end at the same DCs. Specifically, in order to reduce the system operating cost and carbon emissions, this paper solves a joint decision-making LIRP in auto parts supply logistics.

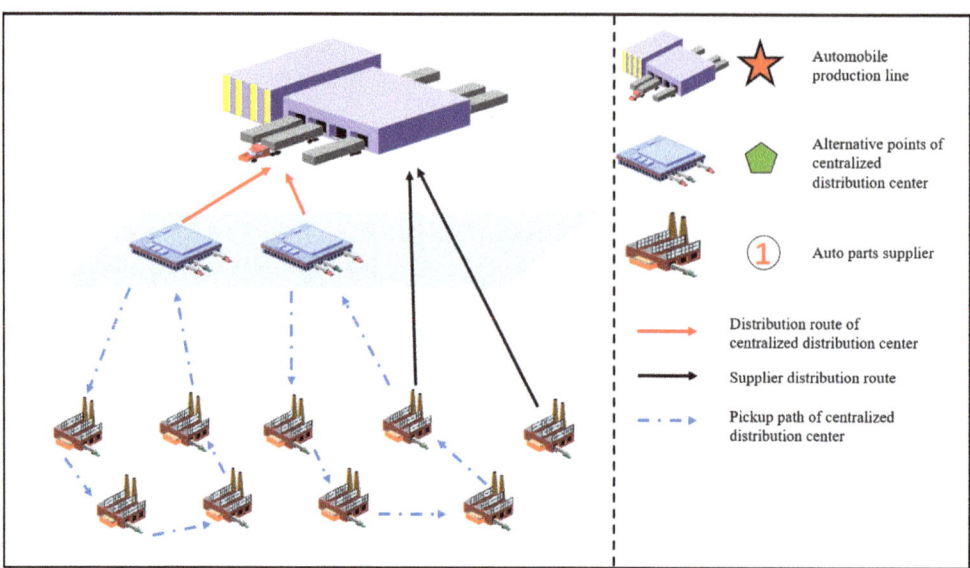

Figure 2. LIRP in the auto parts supply network.

3.2. Problem Assumption and Notations

To formulate the complex auto part supply network into a mathematical model, the following assumptions are proposed in this paper.

(1) We assume the APSs have the ability to provide sufficient auto parts and the shortage is out of our investigation scope.
(2) The production demand for the APL can be obtained from historical data and must be satisfied.
(3) It is essential to translate the auto parts into the standard unit so that the various auto parts can be classified as a unified specification.
(4) We suppose that each APSs only provide one kind of auto part.
(5) The carbon emission factor considered in this paper is the carbon emission from vehicles during transportation, and the calculation method refers to the literature [39].
(6) We assume sufficient vehicles to serve the pickup and delivery, and there is no difference in vehicle performance.

Specifications on variables and parameters used in the LIRP are shown in Table 2.

Table 2. Variables and parameters used in the LIRP.

Notations	Detailed Definition
Set	
I	The set for APSs, indexed by i
T	The set for time periods, indexed by t
J	The candidate point set for DCs, indexed by j
L	The set for capacity level, indexed by l
K	The set for APL, indexed by k

Table 2. Cont.

Notations	Detailed Definition
Parameters	Detailed definition
D_i^t	The auto parts demand from APS i during period t
UH	Unit inventory holding cost for auto parts
FW_l	Fixed cost for establishing one DC with inventory level l
FN	Unit transport cost from DCs to the APL
FZ	Unit transport cost from APSs to the APL directly
FG	Unit transport cost for picking up auto parts from DCs to corresponding APSs
WC_l	The inventory capacity corresponding to the inventory level l of the DC
VC	Vehicle capacity for picking up auto parts
M_0	A large positive number
CE	The factor for carbon emission
d_{ik}	Distance between APS and the APL
d_{jk}	Distance between DC and the APL
$d_{ii'}$	Distance between two APSs
d_{ji}	Distance between DC and the APS
Auxiliary variables	
SY_{ji}^t	The remaining quantity of auto part from APS i at DC j during period t
LC_{ji}^t	The quantity loaded in the vehicle that picks up auto parts from DC j after it finishes loading at APS i during the period t
or_{ji}^t	A positive integer, the quantity ordered from APS i for DC j during period t
q_{ji}^t	A binary, if there is a need for DC j to order auto parts from APS i during period t
Decision variables	
x_{ij}	A binary, equal to 1 if the APS i is assigned to DC j, 0 otherwise
y_j	A binary, equal to 1 if the candidate point j is selected as the DC, 0 otherwise
y_{jl}	A binary, equal to 1 if the capacity of DC j is level l, 0 otherwise
de_{ji}^t	A positive integer, the number of auto parts delivered from APS i to APL during period t when APS i is assigned to DC j
gy_{ji}^t	A positive integer, the number of auto parts of APS i delivered from DC j to APL during period t
$ro_{ii'}^t$	A binary, equal to 1 if the pickup routs from i to i' during period t, 0 otherwise
ro_{ji}^t	A binary, equal to 1 if the pickup routs from DC j to APS i during period t, 0 otherwise
ro_{ij}^t	A binary, equal to 1 if the pickup routs from APS i to DC j during period t, 0 otherwise

3.3. Deterministic Model

Here, we first formulate a deterministic model to describe the LIRP integrating with the prior known multi-period demand of the APL. Our objective is to find the most efficient x_{ij}, y_j, and y_{jl} and other routing decision variables under proper constraints. As a result, the proposed sustainable LIRP in auto parts supply logistics is formulated as follows:

Objective function:

$$\sum_{j \in J} \sum_{l \in L} FW_l \cdot y_{jl} + \sum_{j \in J} \sum_{i \in I} \sum_{t \in T} UH \cdot \sum_{t=1}^{T} SY_{ji}^t + \sum_{j \in J} \sum_{i \in I} \sum_{t \in T} FZ(de_{ji}^t/VC) \cdot d_{ik}$$
$$+ \sum_{j \in J} \sum_{t \in T} FN \left(\sum_{i \in I} gy_{ji}^t / VC \right) \cdot d_{jk} + \sum_{t \in T} \sum_{j \in J} \sum_{i \in I} FG \cdot ro_{ii'}^t \cdot d_{ii'} \quad (1)$$
$$+ \sum_{t \in T} \sum_{j \in J} \sum_{i \in I} FG \cdot ro_{ji}^t \cdot d_{ji} + \sum_{t \in T} \sum_{j \in J} \sum_{i \in I} FG \cdot ro_{ij}^t \cdot d_{ij}$$

$$\sum_{j\in J}\sum_{i\in I}\sum_{t\in T}CE\left(de_{ji}^{t}/VC\right)\cdot d_{ik}+\sum_{j\in J}\sum_{t\in T}CE\left(\sum_{i\in I}gy_{ji}^{t}/VC\right)\cdot d_{jk}$$
$$+\sum_{t\in T}\sum_{j\in J}\sum_{i\in I}CE\cdot ro_{ii'}^{t}\cdot d_{ii'}+\sum_{t\in T}\sum_{j\in J}\sum_{i\in I}CE\cdot ro_{ji}^{t}\cdot d_{ji} \qquad (2)$$
$$+\sum_{t\in T}\sum_{j\in J}\sum_{i\in I}CE\cdot ro_{ij}^{t}\cdot d_{ij}$$

Objective function (1) minimizes the total system cost, where the first term is the construction cost for DCs, the second term is the inventory holding cost, the third term is the total transport cost from APSs to the APL, the fourth term is the total transport cost from DCs to the APL, and the last term is the total transport cost for centralized pickup from DCs to APSs.

In additn, objective function (2) is the definition of carbon emissions released by transport vehicles, including the carbon emission released by transport vehicles that route from APSs to the APL, from DCs to the APL, and from DCs to APSs.

Constraints:

$$\sum_{j\in J}x_{ij}=1\forall i\in I \qquad (3)$$

Constraint (3) limits that each APS can only be assigned to one DC.

$$x_{ij}\leq y_{j}\forall i\in I,\forall j\in J \qquad (4)$$

Constraint (4) ensures that the APSs can only be assigned to the opened DC.

$$\sum_{l\in L}y_{jl}=y_{j},\forall j\in J \qquad (5)$$

Constraint (5) determines the capacity level of the opened DC.

$$\sum_{j\in J}gy_{ji}^{t}+\sum_{j\in J}de_{ji}^{t}=D^{t}\times CP_{i},\forall i\in I,\forall t\in T \qquad (6)$$

Constraint (6) represents that all the demands of the APL are satisfied by APS and corresponding DC. We denote gy_{ji}^{t} to indicate the number of auto parts of APS i delivered from DC j to the APL during period t, and de_{ji}^{t} is the quantity of auto parts delivered from APS i to the APL during period t when APS i is assigned to DC j.

$$gy_{ji}^{t}\leq M_{0}\cdot x_{ij}, \quad \forall j\in J, t\in T, i\in I \qquad (7)$$

$$de_{ji}^{t}\leq M_{0}\cdot x_{ij}, \quad \forall j\in J, t\in T, i\in I \qquad (8)$$

Constraints (7) and (8) ensure that auto parts supplies from DCs and APSs need to satisfy the assignment relationship between DCs and APSs.

$$SY_{ji}^{t}=SY_{ji}^{t-1}+or_{ji}^{t-1}-gy_{ji}^{t-1}, \quad \forall i\in I,\forall j\in J,\forall t\in T \qquad (9)$$

Constraint (9) indicates the inventory quantity conservation of auto parts from APS i stored in the corresponding assigned DC j. That is, the inventory quantity of auto parts from APS i during period t at DC j equals the inventory quantity during period $t-1$, plus the order quantity from APS i to DC j, minus the quantity delivered to the APL from DC j.

$$gy_{ji}^{t}\leq SY_{ji}^{t}, \quad \forall i\in I,\forall j\in J,\forall t\in T \qquad (10)$$

Constraint (10) ensures that the quantity of auto parts of APS i delivered from DC j to the APL during period t does not exceed the inventory quantity at DC j during period t.

$$\sum_{i\in I}SY_{ji}^{t}\leq \sum_{l\in L}WC_{l}\cdot y_{jl}, \quad \forall j\in J,\forall t\in T \qquad (11)$$

Constraint (11) guarantees that the total inventory quantity of all auto parts in the DC j at each period is less than the inventory capacity of DC j.

$$SY_{ji}^t \leq x_{ij} \cdot M_0, \quad \forall i \in I, \forall j \in J, \forall t \in T \tag{12}$$

Constraint (12) indicates that only if the APS i is assigned to the DC j, the DC j will store the auto parts of the APS i.

$$or_{ji}^t \leq M_0 \cdot x_{ij}, \quad \forall j \in J, t \in T, i \in I \tag{13}$$

Constraint (13) points out that only if the APS i is assigned to the DC j, the DC j will order auto parts from the APS i.

$$or_{ji}^t \leq M_0 \cdot q_{ji}^t, \quad \forall j \in J, t \in T, i \in I \tag{14}$$

$$q_{ji}^t \leq or_{ji}^t \quad \forall j \in J, t \in T, i \in I \tag{15}$$

Constraints (14) and (15) ensure that when the DC j has a clear ordering demand for the auto parts of APS i, the DC j will dispatch vehicles to APS i to pick-up the auto parts.

$$\sum_{i' \in I} ro_{ji'}^t = \sum_{i \in I} ro_{ij}^t, \quad \forall t \in T \ \forall j \in J \tag{16}$$

$$ro_{ji'}^t \leq q_{ji'}^t \quad \forall i' \in I \ \forall t \in T \ \forall j \in J \tag{17}$$

$$ro_{ij}^t \leq q_{ji}^t \quad \forall i \in I \ \forall t \in T \ \forall j \in J \tag{18}$$

Constraint (16) indicates that the vehicles dispatched by DC j will depart from DC j and finally arrive at DC j. Constraints (17) and (18) ensure that the first and final APSs picked up by the vehicles have a clear order need.

$$\sum_{i' \in N_j^t, i \neq i'} ro_{ii'}^t + ro_{ji'}^t = q_{ji'}^t \quad \forall i' \in N_j^t, \forall t \in T, \forall j \in J \tag{19}$$

$$\sum_{i' \in N_j^t, i \neq i'} ro_{ii'}^t + ro_{ij}^t = q_{ji}^t \quad \forall i \in N_j^t, \forall t \in T, \forall j \in J \tag{20}$$

Constraints (19) and (20) describe the path planning for the vehicles to pick-up auto parts. N_j^t is the set for APSs that are assigned to the same DC j and has order needs during period t.

$$LC_{ji}^t \leq q_{ji}^t \cdot M_0 \quad \forall i \in I, \forall t \in T, \forall j \in J \tag{21}$$

$$LC_{ji}^t \geq q_{ji}^t \quad \forall i \in I, \forall t \in T, \forall j \in J \tag{22}$$

Constraints (21) and (22) ensure that the auto parts of APS i loaded in the vehicles only occur at the APS, which has a clear order need.

$$LC_{ji}^t + (1 - ro_{ji}^t) \cdot M_0 \geq or_{ji}^t \forall i \in I, \forall t \in T, \forall j \in J \tag{23}$$

$$LC_{ji'}^t + (1 - ro_{ii'}^t) \cdot M_0 \geq LC_{ji}^t + or_{ji'}^t \quad \forall i, i' \in I \ (i \neq i'), \forall t \in T, \forall j \in J \tag{24}$$

Constraints (23) and (24) calculate the number of auto parts loaded in the vehicle after it finishes loading at APS i during the period t.

$$LC_{ji}^t \leq VC + (1 - ro_{ij}^t) \cdot M_0 \quad \forall i \in I, \forall t \in T, \forall j \in J \tag{25}$$

$$LC_{ji}^t \leq VC, \quad \forall i \in I, \forall t \in T, \forall j \in J \tag{26}$$

Constraints (25) and (26) require that the quantity of auto parts loaded in the vehicle is no more than the vehicle capacity.

$$or_{ji}^t \leq LC_{ji}^t \quad \forall i \in I, \forall t \in T, \forall j \in J. \tag{27}$$

Constraint (27) requires that the quantity loaded in the vehicle after it finishes loading at APS i is greater than the order quantity needed.

$$x_{ij}, y_j, y_{jl}, ro_{ii'}^t, ro_{ji}^t, ro_{ij}^t \in \{0,1\} \forall i \in I, \forall t \in T, \forall j \in J \tag{28}$$

$$de_{ji}^t, gy_{ji}^t \geq 0 \forall i \in I, \forall t \in T, \forall j \in J \tag{29}$$

Constraints (28) and (29) are the definitional domain of the decision variables.

Based on the above analysis, the comprehensive LIRP is formulated as the following MIP model.

Deterministic model:
$$\text{min Objective (1) (2)}$$
$$\text{s.t. Constraints (3) } - \text{ (29)}$$

3.4. Robust Model

In daily production activities, automobile production depends on the market demand, which is easily influenced by the preference of consumers and unexpected events. Various uncertain factors may lead to a sharp increase in auto parts demand. To avoid facing a shortage of auto parts, we try to develop a robust model to formulate the uncertain demand. To address the uncertain issue, this paper adopts the robust optimization method of [40] and proposes a robust LIRP optimization model that is able to describe the degree of conservation and uncertainty level.

We assume that the production demand for the APL during each period is unknown and belongs to the symmetric range $[D^t - \hat{D}^t, D^t + \hat{D}^t]$, where D^t is the nominal values and $\hat{D}^t$ is the maximum deviation value. For the sake of clarifying the uncertain $\hat{D}^t$, we introduce the concept of uncertainty level $\beta \in [0,1]$ to represent the proportion of deviation. Therefore, the automobile production demand for the APL falls in the range of $[D^t - \beta \cdot \hat{D}^t, D^t + \beta \cdot \hat{D}^t]$. Subsequently, we let ρ describe the number of periods at which the production demand is uncertain, and the value of ρ falls in the range of $\rho \in [0, \overline{T}]$, in which $\overline{T}$ is the total number of planning periods. Specifically, if $\rho = 0$, there is no uncertainty protection, and the model is deterministic. On the other hand, if $\rho = T$, there exists uncertain demand during each period, indicating that the production scheme of the APL is fairly conservative. Then, we employ a set $U = \{(t|\hat{D}^t > 0)\}$ to describe the period set at which the production demand is uncertain. Based on the above analysis, a robust model is developed. Compared to the deterministic model, the difference is that constraint (6) is substituted by robustness constraints, which are formulated in (30) and (31).

Robust model:
$$\text{min (1), (2)}$$

Subject to: (3)–(5), (7)–(29)

$$\sigma^t = \begin{cases} 1 & t \in \left\{u^t \middle| max_{\{u^t|u^t \in U, |u^t|=\rho\}} \{\Sigma_{t \in u^t} \hat{D}^t\}\right\} \\ 0 & \text{others} \end{cases} \tag{30}$$

$$\sum_{j \in J} gy_{ji}^t + \sum_{j \in J} de_{ji}^t = D_i^t + CP_i \cdot \sigma^t \cdot \beta \cdot \hat{D}^t, \quad \forall i \in I, \forall t \in T \tag{31}$$

In constraint (30), a compensation coefficient is introduced and represented as σ^t, which describes the protection function against the worst case. Equation (31) describes the demand satisfaction constraints under uncertain scenarios.

3.5. Solution Approach

Regarding the multi-objective deterministic or robust model, the main challenge is deciding how to manage the trade-offs. We adopt the linear programming solver Gurobi to obtain the optimal solution. Gurobi allows the multi-objectives function to be treated hierarchically. In the hierarchical approach, the priority is set for each objective. Concerning the realistic problem, this paper first sets the same priority for the two objectives in the following sensitivity analysis. Afterward, this paper generates a series of coupled priorities to obtain the Pareto solution. The priority determination method is subjective to a certain extent. The data envelopment analysis (DEA) method in [41] will be discussed in a future study.

4. Numerical Experiments

To illustrate the practical application of the proposed models, we conduct numerical experiments based on actual data provided by an automobile manufacturer located in Changchun, China. The following experiments are run by Gurobi 9.5.1 software on a personal computer equipped with an AMD Ryzen 7,5700 G with Radeon Graphics 3.80 GHz and 32.0 GB RAM, using the Microsoft Windows 10 operating system.

The auto parts supply network consists of 30 APSs, 12 DCs, and 1 APL. Figure 3 graphically describes the location distribution of APSs, DCs, and the APL. In addition, the units of travel cost, carbon emissions, and distance are measured with RMB (yuan), kilogram (KG), and kilometers (KM), respectively. Next, we analyze in detail the sensitivity of the deterministic model, the advantages of the robust optimization model, and the usefulness of our proposed models.

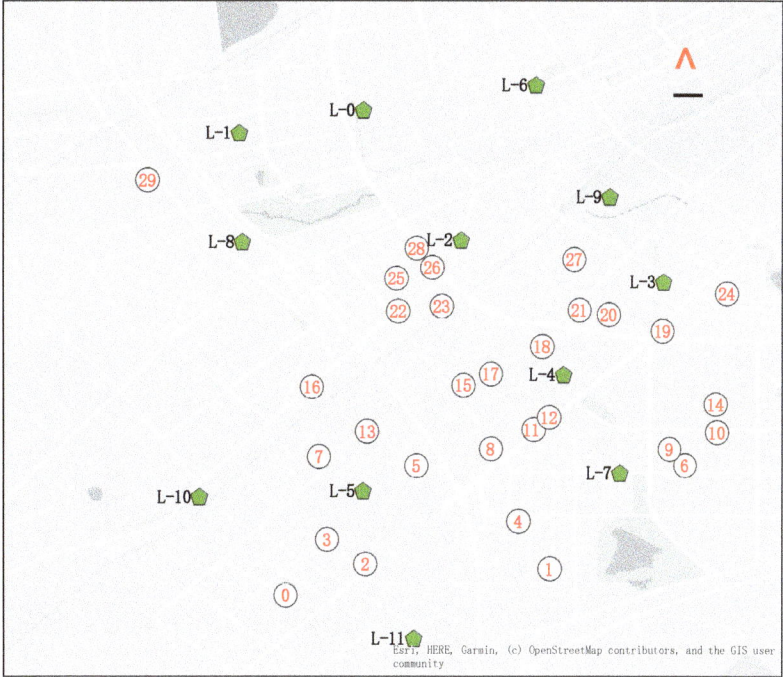

Figure 3. Description of the study area.

We obtain experimental data from surveying and collecting the material and data in Changchun. Through a series of data processing and simplification processes, the parameters involved in these experiments are listed in Table 3. The automobile demand of the APL is derived from the actual statistical data. According to the corresponding relationship between the automobile and the auto parts, we multiply the coefficients to acquire the auto parts demand of each APS. In this paper, we consider four production periods of the automobile APL, and the vehicle capacity is set as 1500. In addition, the inventory capacity can be chosen from the set (8000, 9000, 10,000, and 11,000). Suppose the unit transport cost from DCs to the APL and from APSs to the APL are the same and set as 20. However, the unit transport cost for picking up auto parts from DCs to the corresponding APSs is less and assumed as 14. Define the unit inventory holding cost for auto parts as 0.1. Finally, the factor of carbon emission is defined as 0.3.

Table 3. Key input parameters.

T	VC	WC_l	UH	FN/FZ	FG	CE
4	1500	(8000, 9000, 10,000, 11,000)	0.1	20	14	0.3

4.1. Sensitivity Analysis of Deterministic Model

This section conducts sensitivity experiments to investigate the impact of essential parameters on the LIRP under deterministic demand. Namely, we discuss how the unit inventory holding cost (UH), unit transport cost from DCs to the APL (FN), unit transport cost from APSs to the APL directly (FZ), and unit transport cost for picking up auto parts from DCs to corresponding APSs (FG) influence the total system cost and the carbon emission. The results are shown in Figures 4 and 5, respectively.

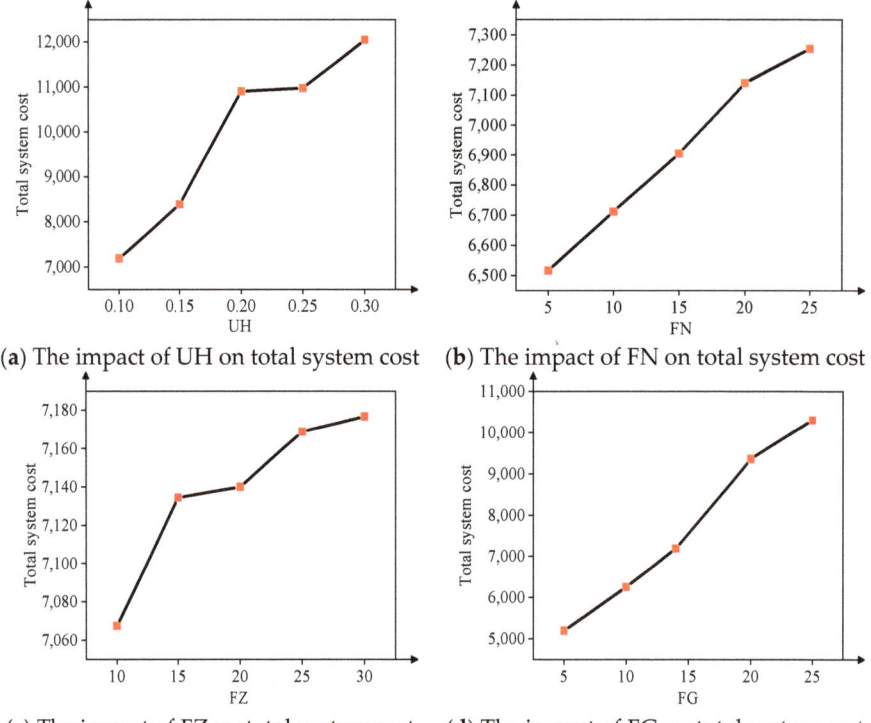

(**a**) The impact of UH on total system cost (**b**) The impact of FN on total system cost

(**c**) The impact of FZ on total system cost (**d**) The impact of FG on total system cost

Figure 4. The impact of various parameters on the total system cost.

As can be seen from Figure 4, there is an evident increase in the total system cost with the growth of UH, FN, FZ, and FG, which is in accordance with the realistic situation. For example, Figure 4a describes the relationship between total system cost and the unit inventory holding cost (UH). When the UH changes from 10 to 15, the total system cost increases sharply. As UH continues to increase, the growth rate will slow down. Hence, we can draw the conclusion that the total system cost is more sensitive to the UH when it is lower than 15.

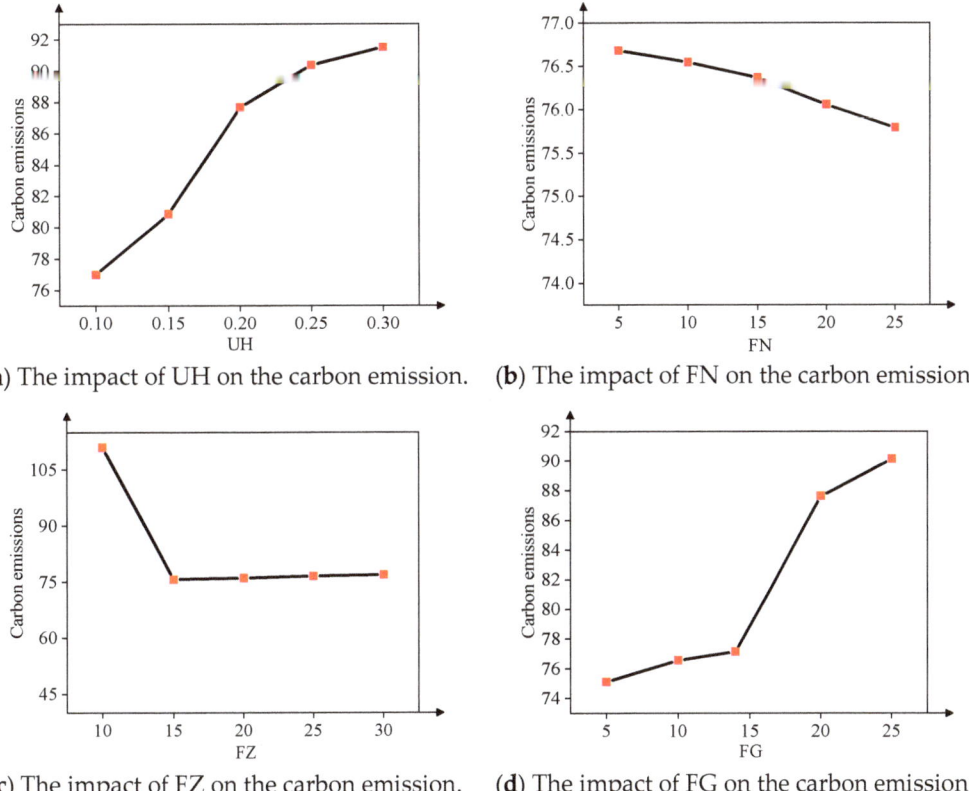

(a) The impact of UH on the carbon emission.

(b) The impact of FN on the carbon emission.

(c) The impact of FZ on the carbon emission.

(d) The impact of FG on the carbon emission.

Figure 5. The impact of various parameters on the carbon emission.

Further, we analyze how these parameters influence the carbon emissions in Figure 5. Figure 5b,c show that the carbon emission slightly decreases with the growth of the FN and FZ. On the contrary, Figure 5a,d indicate that carbon emission rises significantly with the increase in UH and FG.

According to Figures 4 and 5, it can be observed that both objectives are closely associated with the UH and FG. The main reason is that the variations in UH and FG greatly influence the delivery routing of auto parts. We propose the indicator Supplier Delivery Amount (SDA) to represent the number of auto parts delivered from APSs to the APL directly. Analogously, Distribution Center Delivery Amount (DCDA) is proposed to describe the number of auto parts supplied from DCs to the APL. In addition, Supplier Delivery Amount Percentage (SDAP) is proposed to capture the proportion of SDA in the total number of auto parts transported.

Therefore, we summarize these indicators under different values of UH and FG in Table 4. It is easy to observe that the SDAP increases from 0% to 14.89% with the growth of UH, which means that if the unit inventory cost is high, more auto parts will be delivered from APSs to the APL directly. Therefore, there is a need for more vehicles to undertake auto parts transport activities. Consequently, the total system cost and the carbon emission will arise. Compared to the UH, FG has a similar effect on the system performance of the auto parts supply logistics network. A larger value for FG indicates that the centralized pickup cost from DCs to corresponding APSs is high, resulting in more auto parts being delivered from APSs to DCs directly, and the SDAP increases from 0% to 21.88%.

Table 4. Statistical data for the delivery routing of auto parts under various UH and FG.

SA	UH					FG				
	0.1	0.15	0.2	0.25	0.3	5	10	14	20	25
SDA	0	874	886	2566	3561	0	0	0	4377	5233
DCDA	23,912	23,038	23,026	21,379	20,351	23,912	23,912	23,912	19,535	18,679
SDAP	0.00%	3.66%	3.71%	10.59%	14.89%	0.00%	0.00%	0.00%	18.30%	21.88%

To graphically depict the delivery routing decisions under different values of UH, we portray the delivery routing distribution during periods $t = 2$ and $t = 3$ in Figure 6, respectively. Figure 6a,b describe the routing decisions under the circumstance of UH = 0.1, and Figure 6c,d assume UH = 1.5.

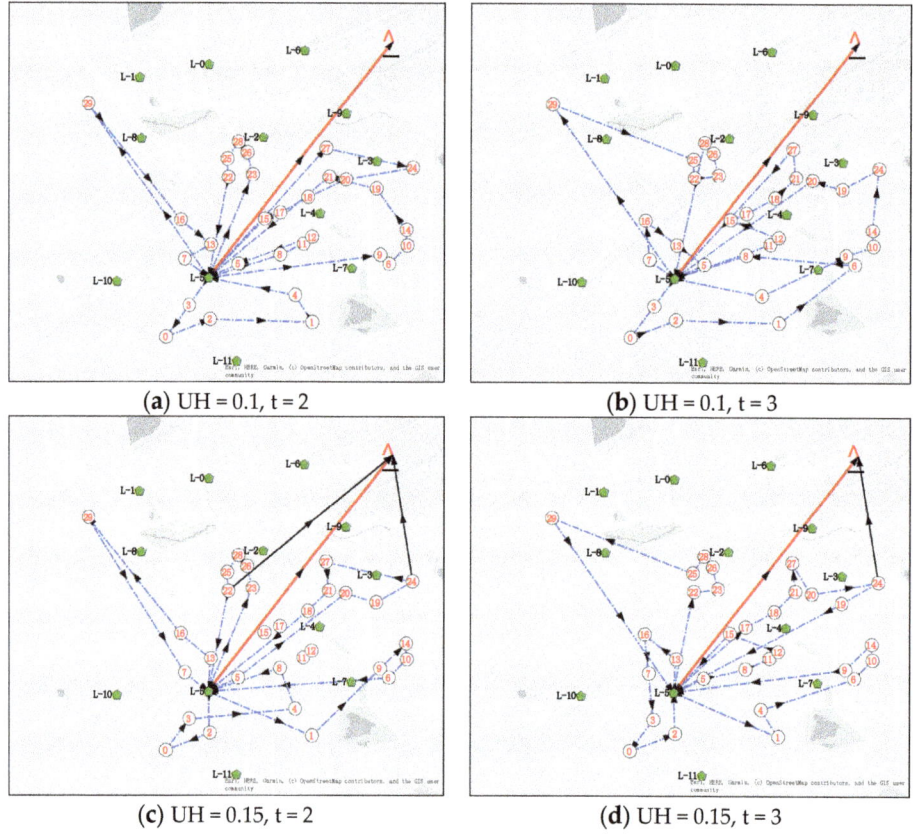

Figure 6. The impact of UH on the routing decisions.

As can be seen in Figure 6, candidate L_5 is chosen as DCs and the delivery routing decisions are described. The blue dotted line is the delivery routing from DCs to the corresponding APSs to pick up auto parts, and each circle represents an assigned vehicle. In addition, the solid black lines depict the routing from APSs to the APL, while the solid red line describes the delivery routing from DCs to the APL. Through the comparison between Figure 6a,c, it is clear that there are two extra direct delivery routes from APSs to the APL, and the result again verifies the idea that a higher UH will increase the number of auto parts delivered directly from APSs to the APL. We can obtain the same conclusion by comparing Figure 6b,d. The impact of FG on the delivery decisions is similar to UH, and it is not described in this article, to avoid repetition.

However, compared to UH and FG, FZ has a distinct influence on auto parts delivery routing decisions. In the following, we analyze the delivery routing of auto parts under various FZ in Table 4. Higher FZ indicates that the unit transport cost from APSs to the APL is high. With the FZ upward, more auto parts are assigned to DCs to reduce the transport cost by centralized pickup. Table 5 shows that as the FZ increases from 10 to 15, the SDAP will decrease from 37.09% to 1.09%.

Table 5. Statistical data on the delivery routing of auto parts under various FZ.

SA	FZ				
	10	15	20	25	30
SDA	8772	260	0	0	0
DCDA	15,140	23,652	23,912	23,912	23,912
SDAP	37.09%	1.09%	0.00%	0.00%	0.00%

Similar to Figure 6, to graphically depict the delivery routing decisions under different values of FZ, we portray the routing distribution during periods t = 2 and t = 3 in Figure 7. Figure 7a,b delineate the routing decisions under the condition of FZ = 10, and Figure 7c,d suppose FZ = 15.

Analogous to Figure 6, candidate point L_5 is selected as DCs. Figure 6a,b show that there are a total of five routes from APSs to the APL during periods t = 2 and t = 3 when FZ = 10. However, when FZ = 15 in Figure 6c,d, the total number of routes from APSs to the APL is reduced to one. This is in accordance with Table 6 that higher FZ leads to more auto parts being delivered through DCs, which perform centralized pickup and unified delivery.

Table 6. Variations in LIRP decisions under different uncertainty levels ($\rho = 1$).

Uncertainty Level	DC	WC	SDA	DCDA	SDAP
30%	L_5	9000	2313	24,161	8.74%
60%	L_5	9000	4827	24,209	16.62%
90%	L_5	10,000	7410	24,188	23.45%

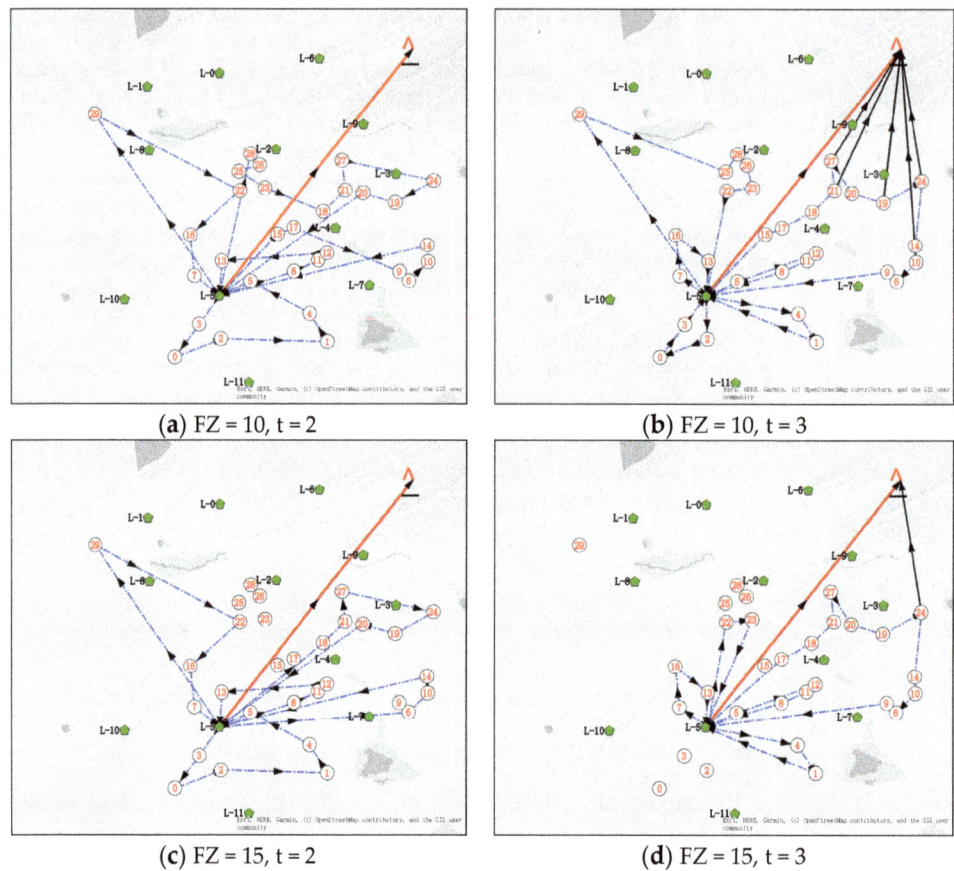

Figure 7. The impact of FZ on the routing decisions.

The above parameters influence the system performance by affecting the location of DCs, inventory capacity, and delivery routing decisions. Overall, we can conclude that the total system cost and carbon emission are sensitive to the above four parameters.

Concerning the relationship between the total system cost and carbon emission, the Pareto-set output from the deterministic model under different weights is depicted in Figure 8, where one point in the figure represents a particular LIRP solution. The Pareto set has a total system cost ranging from 7062 RMB to 7166 RMB and the carbon emission ranges from 74 kg to 77 kg. It can also be seen in Figure 8 that carbon emission and total system cost have the same tendency, which proves the essence of considering the sustainable LIRP in auto parts supply logistics.

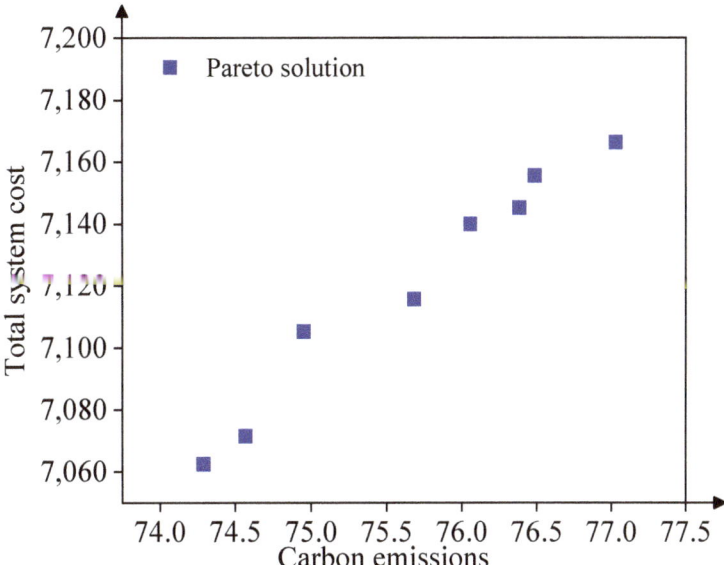

Figure 8. Pareto set of LIRP.

4.2. Sensitivity Analysis of Robust Model

The above parameters sensitivity analysis in the deterministic model are suitable for the robust model. Except for these analyses, this section further discusses how the uncertainty level and the degree of conservatism influence the LIRP. Here, we first define that the deviation value $\hat{D}^t$ equals the nominal values D^t. According to the same input parameters as the deterministic model, it is assumed that the uncertain demand is likely to occur at any period, and, as introduced in 3.4, we use $\beta \in [0,1]$ to represent the uncertainty level. This paper adopts ρ to describe the degree of conservatism.

First, we discuss the effect of uncertainty level on the system performance in Figure 9. Three kinds of degrees of conservatism are considered. Figure 9a delineates the variation in total system cost with increased uncertainty level, and Figure 9b shows the variation in carbon emissions. It can be seen from Figure 8 that with the increase in the uncertainty level, the total system cost and carbon emissions increase significantly under different degrees of conservatism.

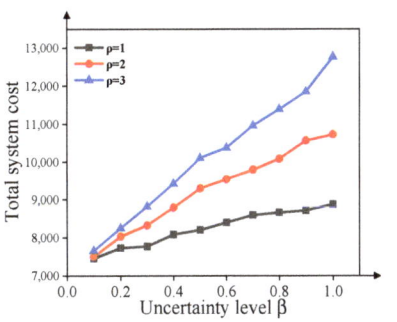

(**a**) Effect of uncertainty level on the total system cost

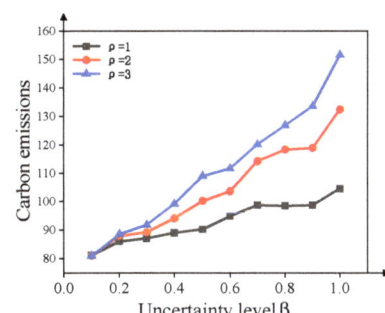

(**b**) Effect of uncertainty level on the carbon emission

Figure 9. Effect of uncertainty level on the system performance.

To further depict the impact of uncertainty level on the location of DCs, inventory capacity, and delivery routing decisions, we take the degree of conservatism $\rho = 1$ as an example and analyze how the decision variables change when the uncertainty level ranges from 30% to 90%. The results are shown in Table 6, where the value of DC is the selected candidate point for DCs and WC is the inventory capacity for DCs.

As shown in Table 6, although the location of DC does not change, the inventory capacity of DC increases from 9000 to 10,000 when the uncertainty level grows. Another interesting finding is that the proportion of auto parts delivered from APSs to the APL directly increases from 8.74% to 23.45%. The reason may be that when the uncertainty level grows, the production demand in the APL for the worst case is extremely high, which is likely to exceed the inventory capacity of DCs. Therefore, the auto parts in APSs close to the APL will be transported directly without needing transfers in DCs. The detailed delivery routing decisions are graphically shown in Figure 10. It is clear to see that more solid black lines are depicted with the increase in the uncertainty level, verifying that more auto parts close to the APL are delivered directly.

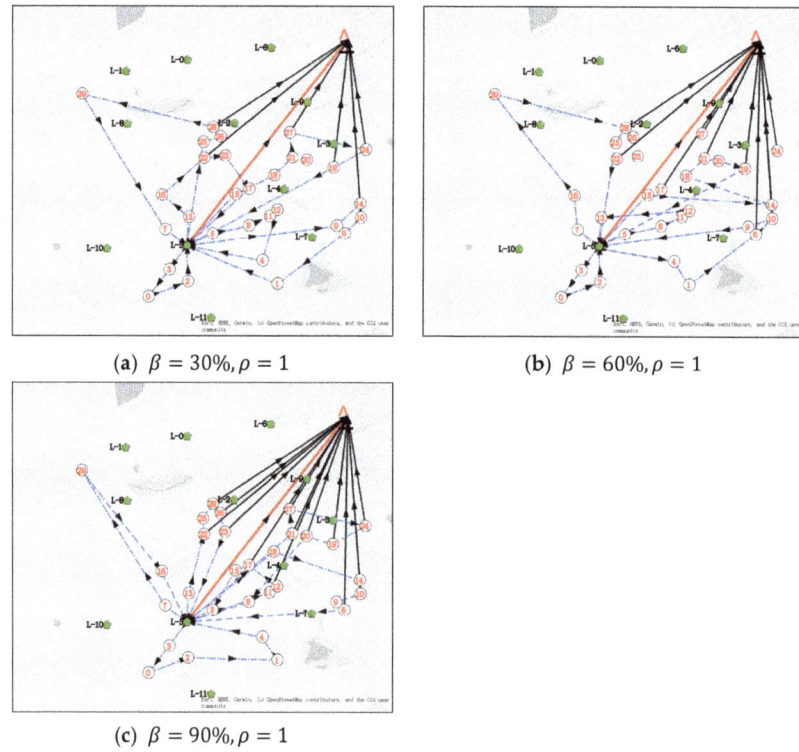

(a) $\beta = 30\%, \rho = 1$

(b) $\beta = 60\%, \rho = 1$

(c) $\beta = 90\%, \rho = 1$

Figure 10. The impact of uncertainty level on the delivery routing decisions.

Subsequently, the effects of the degree of conservatism on the location, inventory, and delivery routing decisions are summarized in Table 7. We take the uncertainty level $\beta = 100\%$ as an example and analyze how the decision variables change when the degree of conservatism changes from 1 to 3. Similar to the uncertainty level, the inventory capacity increases from 10,000 to 11,000 with the growth of the degree of conservatism, and the proportion of auto parts delivered from APSs to the APL directly increases from 29.48% to 55.10%. This is because more production demand is needed under a more conservative environment. Limited to the inventory capacity, more auto parts close to the APL will be delivered directly, and the detailed delivery routing distribution is similar to Figure 9, which we do not display again.

Table 7. Variations in LIRP decisions under different conservatism degrees ($\beta = 100\%$).

Degree of Protection	DC	WC	SDA	DCDA	SDAP
1	L_5	10,000	9566	22,886	29.48%
2	L_5	10,000	18,439	22,126	45.46%
3	L_5	11,000	26,353	21,471	55.10%

4.3. Model Comparisons

At present, the auto parts are delivered directly from APSs to the APL, resulting in a large waste in vehicle capacity and a high transport cost. This paper proposes a robust LIRP in auto parts supply logistics to address the real problem of establishing DCs to minimize the total system cost. We define the two scenarios as "Without DCs" and "With DCs". In the following, we conduct comparative analyses on the utilization rate of vehicle capacity, total system cost, and carbon emission. The results are summarized in Table 8.

Table 8. Comparative analyses between without and with DCs.

Scenarios	The Utilization Rate of Vehicle Capacity	Carbon Emission	Total System Cost
Without DCs	17.71%	221.1108	14,740.72
With DCs	96.29%	76.05862	7139.92

Obviously, the total system cost and carbon emissions will decrease when establishing DCs using the proposed LIRP model, and the utilization rate of vehicle capacity will be dramatically improved. Consequently, we can draw the conclusion that the proposed LIRP model is largely effective in the auto parts supply logistics network.

Moreover, to demonstrate the significance of considering uncertain demand, we compared the system performance between the scenarios "Without DCs" and "With DCs" under uncertain demand. Assuming the degree of conservatism $\rho = 3$, we further discuss the variation in total system cost and carbon emission while the uncertainty level changes from 0.1 to 1. As shown in Figure 11, the total system cost and the carbon emission obtained by our robust LIRP model are significantly lower than the scenario "without DCs".

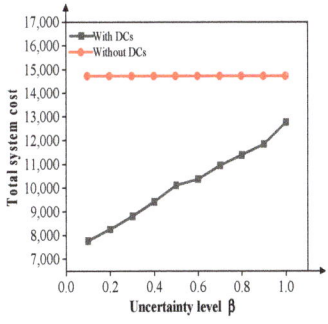
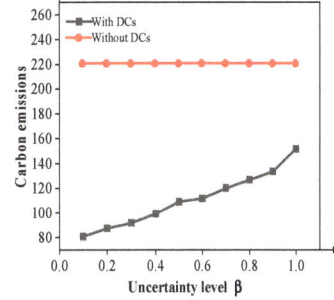

(a) Comparison in total system cost (b) Comparison in Carbon emissions

Figure 11. Comparative analyses between without and with DCs considering uncertain demand.

5. Discussion

In this paper, a multi-objective MIP model is proposed to deal with the LIRP of the automotive parts supply chain with deterministic and uncertain demands. The objective of the model is to minimize the cost and carbon emissions in the whole system.

Based on the above numerical analysis, we can have the following practical implications and insights on the LIRP system design problem. First, the model proposed in this paper provides an integrated optimization scheme for automotive parts supply chain optimization and gives a basis for micro-analysis of operation strategies. Compared with the two-stage model [35], the integrated optimization model we choose can more adequately consider the relationship between the three-level decisions. Second, compared to the LIRP model of [42], we fully consider the idea of sustainability, which largely reduces carbon emissions released from transport vehicles, and the results reveal that the total system cost optimization direction is consistent with sustainable optimization. Finally, considering the uncertainty in production demand, the robust optimization approach adopted in this paper significantly outperforms the emergency order direct delivery by APSs in terms of both total system cost reduction and carbon emission reduction.

The environment is becoming an increasingly important criterion in planning automotive parts supply networks. The model presented in this paper has the potential to assist decision-makers and managers solve the LIRP in the supply network configuration. It also provides constructive suggestions for auto parts supply chain planners to select the reasonable DC location and determine the cost-optimal routing decisions for centralized collection and unified distribution. The results demonstrate that the method proposed in this paper would contribute to significant savings in total system cost and reduce the environmental impact.

Although this study proves that the LIRP model we proposed is effective in auto parts supply logistics, there is still a few limitations that we would like to emphasize for future research. First, for the sake of simplification, only one APL is considered. It is more realistic to investigate multiple APLs, which will increase the complexity of this problem. Secondly, as the number of periods and APSs increases, the size of the problem could become very large, making it difficult to address by the solver. Therefore, it is necessary to explore an efficient algorithm. With various metaheuristics available and many possibilities for customization, future work might explore the best options for realistic networks.

6. Conclusions

This paper proposes a unified framework simultaneously considering the location-inventory-routing problem in auto parts supply logistics, which are rarely considered from a sustainable perspective. Within this framework, a novel multi-objective MIP model is proposed to estimate the system performance. Specifically, this model determines the location and capacity of DCs and routing decisions to minimize the total system cost and carbon emissions while considering multi-period production demand. Concerning uncertain factors in production activities, a robust optimization method is developed further in the context of uncertain demand in the APL. A numerical example is investigated to illustrate the effectiveness of the proposed framework in the LIRP. Sensitivity analyses of essential parameters yield several managerial insights. The results show that the location, inventory capacity, and delivery routing decisions are highly affected by various cost parameters. Finally, we observe that the utilization of vehicle capacity will be dramatically improved by our LIRP model, indicating that studying the LIRP of auto parts supply logistics is extremely meaningful.

The current research can be extended in various directions to optimize the automotive parts supply network LIRP. First, it is idealistic to assume the auto parts are classified as a unified specification in the context of actual situations. It is of great significance to discuss the diverse specifications of auto parts. Secondly, it seems that uncertain incidents can occur in random stages. Hence, it is not enough to consider the uncertain demand in the APL, but the uncertain circumstance during the supply and transportation should also be taken into account. Finally, the urban road network structure deeply affects transportation routing decisions, which will be included in our future study.

Author Contributions: Conceptualization, B.S.; methodology, A.L.; software, A.L.; validation, B.S.; formal analysis, A.L.; investigation, A.L.; resources, A.L.; data curation, A.L.; writing—original draft preparation, A.L.; writing—review and editing, A.L.; visualization, A.L.; supervision, A.L.; project administration, A.L.; funding acquisition, B.S. All authors have read and agreed to the published version of the manuscript.

Funding: This research was funded by the National Natural Science Foundation of China (grant number 61873109); the Natural Science Foundation of Jilin Province (grant number 20210101055JC); the FAW Technology Innovation Project (grant number KF2020-70006).

Institutional Review Board Statement: Not applicable.

Informed Consent Statement: Not applicable.

Data Availability Statement: Not applicable.

Acknowledgments: The authors appreciate the support from Jilin University.

Conflicts of Interest: The authors declare no conflict of interest.

References

1. Ranjbaran, F.; Kashan, A.H.; Kazemi, A. Mathematical formulation and heuristic algorithms for optimisation of auto-part milk-run logistics network considering forward and reverse flow of pallets. *Int. J. Prod. Res.* **2020**, *58*, 1741–1775. [CrossRef]
2. La Rosa, L.M.V.-D.; Villarreal-Villarreal, L.A.; Alarcón-Martínez, G. Quality and innovation as drivers for manufacturing competitiveness of automotive parts suppliers. *TQM J.* **2019**, *33*, 966–986. [CrossRef]
3. Wang, Y.; Chen, F. Packed parts delivery problem of automotive inbound logistics with a supplier park. *Comput. Oper. Res.* **2019**, *101*, 116–129. [CrossRef]
4. Yu, W.; Wang, T.; Xiao, Y.; Chen, J.; Yan, X. A Carbon Emission Measurement Method for Individual Travel Based on Transportation Big Data: The Case of Nanjing Metro. *Int. J. Environ. Res. Public Health* **2020**, *17*, 5957. [CrossRef]
5. Wu, W.; Zhou, W.; Lin, Y.; Xie, Y.; Jin, W. A hybrid metaheuristic algorithm for location inventory routing problem with time windows and fuel consumption. *Expert Syst. Appl.* **2021**, *166*, 114034. [CrossRef]
6. Yaobao, Z.; Ping, H.; Shu, Y. An Improved Particle Swarm Optimization for the Automobile Spare Part Warehouse Location Problem. *Math. Probl. Eng.* **2013**, *2013*, 726194. [CrossRef]
7. Russo, F.; Rindone, C. Regional Transport Plans: From Direction Role Denied to Common Rules Identified. *Sustainability* **2021**, *13*, 9052. [CrossRef]
8. Mao, Z.; Huang, D.; Fang, K.; Wang, C.; Lu, D. Milk-run routing problem with progress-lane in the collection of automobile parts. *Ann. Oper. Res.* **2020**, *291*, 657–684. [CrossRef]
9. Khongkaew, P. Random Location under Fixed Zone Storage Strategy A Case Study of Automobile and Electronic Parts Manufacturing Factory. In Proceedings of the International Conference on Industrial Engineering and Operations Management, Bangkok, Thailand, 5–7 March 2019.
10. Diabat, A.; Richard, J.-P.; Codrington, C.W. A Lagrangian relaxation approach to simultaneous strategic and tactical planning in supply chain design. *Ann. Oper. Res.* **2013**, *203*, 55–80. [CrossRef]
11. Zeng, R. Research on the Demand Prediction of Parts Inventory for Auto Customer Service. *J. Phys. Conf. Ser.* **2020**, *1654*, 012115. [CrossRef]
12. Li, J.; Wang, F.; He, Y. Electric Vehicle Routing Problem with Battery Swapping Considering Energy Consumption and Carbon Emissions. *Sustainability* **2020**, *12*, 10537. [CrossRef]
13. Zou, Y.; Wu, H.; Yin, Y.; Dhamotharan, L.; Chen, D.; Tiwari, A.K. An improved transformer model with multi-head attention and attention to attention for low-carbon multi-depot vehicle routing problem. *Ann. Oper. Res.* **2022**, 1–20. [CrossRef]
14. Qiu, Y.; Qiao, J.; Pardalos, P.M. A branch-and-price algorithm for production routing problems with carbon cap-and-trade. *Omega* **2017**, *68*, 49–61. [CrossRef]
15. Chen, J.; Dan, B.; Shi, J. A variable neighborhood search approach for the multi-compartment vehicle routing problem with time windows considering carbon emission. *J. Clean. Prod.* **2020**, *277*, 123932. [CrossRef]
16. Yu, V.F.; Aloina, G.; Susanto, H.; Effendi, M.K.; Lin, S.-W. Regional Location Routing Problem for Waste Collection Using Hybrid Genetic Algorithm-Simulated Annealing. *Mathematics* **2022**, *10*, 2131. [CrossRef]
17. Zhang, S.; Chen, N.; She, N.; Li, K. Location optimization of a competitive distribution center for urban cold chain logistics in terms of low-carbon emissions. *Comput. Ind. Eng.* **2021**, *154*, 107120. [CrossRef]
18. Li, K.; Li, D.; Wu, D. Carbon Transaction-Based Location-Routing- Inventory Optimization for Cold Chain Logistics. *Alex. Eng. J.* **2022**, *61*, 7979–7986. [CrossRef]

19. Kumar, R.S.; Kondapaneni, K.; Dixit, V.; Goswami, A.; Thakur, L.; Tiwari, M. Multi-objective modeling of production and pollution routing problem with time window: A self-learning particle swarm optimization approach. *Comput. Ind. Eng.* **2016**, *99*, 29–40. [CrossRef]
20. Wang, M.; Wu, J.; Kafa, N.; Klibi, W. Carbon emission-compliance green location-inventory problem with demand and carbon price uncertainties. *Transp. Res. Part E Logist. Transp. Rev.* **2020**, *142*, 102038. [CrossRef]
21. Biuki, M.; Kazemi, A.; Alinezhad, A. An integrated location-routing-inventory model for sustainable design of a perishable products supply chain network. *J. Clean. Prod.* **2020**, *260*, 120842. [CrossRef]
22. Ji, S.; Tang, J.; Sun, M.; Luo, R. Multi-objective optimization for a combined location-routing-inventory system considering carbon-capped differences. *J. Ind. Manag. Optim.* **2022**, *18*, 1949. [CrossRef]
23. Quan, C.; He, Q.; Ye, X.; Cheng, X. Optimization of the Milk-run route for inbound logistics of auto parts under low-carbon economy. *J. Algorithms Comput. Technol.* **2021**, *15*, 17483026211065387. [CrossRef]
24. Liu, Z.; Hu, B.; Huang, B.; Lang, L.; Guo, H.; Zhao, Y. Decision Optimization of Low-Carbon Dual-Channel Supply Chain of Auto Parts Based on Smart City Architecture. *Complexity* **2020**, *2020*, 2145951. [CrossRef]
25. Govindan, K.; Mina, H.; Esmaeili, A.; Gholami-Zanjani, S.M. An Integrated Hybrid Approach for Circular supplier selection and Closed loop Supply Chain Network Design under Uncertainty. *J. Clean. Prod.* **2019**, *242*, 118317. [CrossRef]
26. Nekooghadirli, N.; Tavakkoli-Moghaddam, R.; Ghezavati, V.; Javanmard, S. Solving a new bi-objective location-routing-inventory problem in a distribution network by meta-heuristics. *Comput. Ind. Eng.* **2014**, *76*, 204–221. [CrossRef]
27. Zahiri, B.; Suresh, N.C. Hub network design for hazardous-materials transportation under uncertainty. *Transp. Res. Part E: Logist. Transp. Rev.* **2021**, *152*, 102424. [CrossRef]
28. Zahiri, B.; Suresh, N.C.; de Jong, J. Resilient hazardous-materials network design under uncertainty and perishability. *Comput. Ind. Eng.* **2020**, *143*, 106401. [CrossRef]
29. Zhalechian, M.; Tavakkoli-Moghaddam, R.; Zahiri, B.; Mohammadi, M. Sustainable design of a closed-loop location-routing-inventory supply chain network under mixed uncertainty. *Transp. Res. Part E Logist. Transp. Rev.* **2016**, *89*, 182–214. [CrossRef]
30. Shang, X.; Zhang, G.; Jia, B.; Almanaseer, M. The healthcare supply location-inventory-routing problem: A robust approach. *Transp. Res. Part E Logist. Transp. Rev.* **2022**, *158*, 102588. [CrossRef]
31. Yuan, Z.; Gao, J. Dynamic Uncertainty Study of Multi-Center Location and Route Optimization for Medicine Logistics Company. *Mathematics* **2022**, *10*, 953. [CrossRef]
32. Ghasemi, P.; Goodarzian, F.; Muñuzuri, J.; Abraham, A. A cooperative game theory approach for location-routing-inventory decisions in humanitarian relief chain incorporating stochastic planning. *Appl. Math. Model.* **2022**, *104*, 750–781. [CrossRef]
33. Yang, Y.; Zhang, J.; Sun, W.; Pu, Y. Research on NSGA-III in Location-routing-inventory problem of pharmaceutical logistics intermodal network. *J. Intell. Fuzzy Syst.* **2021**, *41*, 699–713. [CrossRef]
34. Chao, C.; Zhihui, T.; Baozhen, Y. Optimization of two-stage location–routing–inventory problem with time-windows in food distribution network. *Ann. Oper. Res.* **2019**, *273*, 111–134. [CrossRef]
35. Aydemir-Karadag, A. Bi-Objective Adaptive Large Neighborhood Search Algorithm for the Healthcare Waste Periodic Location Inventory Routing Problem. *Arab. J. Sci. Eng.* **2022**, *47*, 3861–3876. [CrossRef]
36. Liu, A.; Zhu, Q.; Xu, L.; Lu, Q.; Fan, Y. Sustainable supply chain management for perishable products in emerging markets: An integrated location-inventory-routing model. *Transp. Res. Part E Logist. Transp. Rev.* **2021**, *150*, 102319. [CrossRef]
37. Yavari, M.; Enjavi, H.; Geraeli, M. Demand management to cope with routes disruptions in location-inventory-routing problem for perishable products. *Res. Transp. Bus. Manag.* **2020**, *37*, 100552. [CrossRef]
38. Song, L.; Wu, Z. An integrated approach for optimizing location-inventory and location-inventory-routing problem for perishable products. *Int. J. Transp. Sci. Technol.* **2022**. [CrossRef]
39. Qin, G.; Tao, F.; Li, L. A Vehicle Routing Optimization Problem for Cold Chain Logistics Considering Customer Satisfaction and Carbon Emissions. *Int. J. Environ. Res. Public Health* **2019**, *16*, 576. [CrossRef]
40. Bertsimas, D.; Sim, M. The Price of Robustness. *Oper. Res.* **2004**, *52*, 35–53. [CrossRef]
41. Musolino, G.; Rindone, C.; Vitetta, A. Evaluation in Transport Planning: A Comparison between Data Envelopment Analysis and Multi Criteria Decision Making Methods. In Proceedings of the 31st Annual European Simulation and Modelling Conference, Lisbon, Portugal, 25–27 October 2017; pp. 233–237.
42. Saragih, N.; Bahagia, S.; Suprayogi, S.; Syabri, I. Location-inventory-routing model with considering urban road networks. *J. Ind. Eng. Manag.* **2021**, *14*, 830–849. [CrossRef]

Article

A Multi-Period Vehicle Routing Problem for Emergency Perishable Materials under Uncertain Demand Based on an Improved Whale Optimization Algorithm

Xiaodong Li [1,†], Yang Xu [1,*,†], Kin Keung Lai [2,†], Hao Ji [1], Yaning Xu [1] and Jia Li [3]

1. College of Economics and Management, Yi'an Technological University, Yi'an 710021, China
2. Department of Industrial and Manufacturing Systems Engineering, Hong Kong University, Hong Kong 999077, China
3. Institute of Service Assurance Centre, Air Force Medical University, Xi'an 710000, China
* Correspondence: xuyang@chd.edu.cn
† General Research Project on Major Theoretical and Practical Issues in Philosophy and Social Sciences of Shaanxi Province, 2022ND0185.

Abstract: The distribution of emergency perishable materials after a disaster, such as an earthquake, is an essential part of emergency resource dispatching. However, the traditional single-period distribution model can hardly solve this problem because of incomplete demand information for emergency perishable materials in affected sites. Therefore, for such problems we firstly construct a multi-period vehicle path distribution optimization model with the dual objectives of minimizing the cost penalty of distribution delay and the total corruption during delivery, and minimizing the total amount of demand that is not met, by applying the interval boundary and most likely value weighting method to make uncertain demand clear. Then, we formulate the differential evolutionary whale optimization algorithm (DE-WOA) combing the differential evolutionary algorithm with the whale algorithm to solve the constructed model, which is an up-and-coming algorithm for solving this type of problem. Finally, to validate the feasibility and practicality of the proposed model and the novel algorithm, a comparison between the proposed model and the standard whale optimization algorithm is performed on a numerical instance. The result indicates the proposed model converges faster and the overall optimization effect is improved by 23%, which further verifies that the improved whale optimization algorithm has better performance.

Keywords: emergency material distribution; multi-period; uncertain demand; perishable materials; whale optimization algorithm; differential evolution algorithm

MSC: 90B06

1. Introduction

Large-scale sudden natural or man-made disasters occur frequently around the world every year, posing serious threats and impacts on society, human production, and life [1]. How to respond quickly effectively to these unpredictable emergencies has attracted much attention from governments and management at all levels, and has also placed high requirements on them from all aspects [2].

A scientific distribution and reasonable delivery of emergency relief materials, a key aspect of emergency relief work, can reduce the damage to property and casualties caused by disasters, improve the efficiency of rescue work and release the psychological pressure on the victims [3–5]. Due to the suddenness of disasters and the urgency of rescues, the demand for perishable emergency supplies for affected locations is often vague [6]. In addition, the longer the transport time, the more serious the spoilage phenomenon. Currently, this problem can be solved by a single-period delivery model. However, in this case, plenty of restrictions influence the solution's precision. For example, the actual demand for one disaster site is much greater than the maximum loading capacity of a vehicle, and the number of vehicles is limited. Thus, the single-period delivery cannot satisfactorily solve this problem. To more efficiently solve this problem, we consider a multi-period distribution model. Given the situation of sufficient supplies in the distribution center, one can use it to make decisions on the distribution vehicle's path and the distribution quantity in each period to minimize the cost penalty of distribution delay and total corruption during delivery, and minimize the total amount of demand that is not met, which is worthy of studying to improve relief work's efficiency and reduce losses in disaster areas.

The remainder of this paper is organized as follows. Section 2 performs literature reviews relevant to this study. Section 3 constructs the optimization model with the bi-objective and multi-period vehicle path distribution, and proposes the improved differential whale optimization algorithm, which is a novel algorithm for solving the vehicle path problem with multi-objective optimization. Section 4 presents a practical example to verify the validity of the proposed model and algorithm. A comparison of the solution results of the algorithm before and after the improvement reveals that the improved differential evolutionary whale optimization algorithm optimizes better regarding the two objectives of minimizing the distribution delay penalty and corruption cost, and minimizing the unsatisfied degree of demand. Finally, conclusions and possible future research are given in Section 5.

2. Literature Review

The vehicle routing problem (VRP), as a classical problem in the field of operations research and combinatorial optimization, has been widely studied and played a significant role in transportation, logistics production and emergency rescue since its introduction in 1959 by Dantzig and Ramser [7]. A large number of experts and scholars have conducted in-depth research and analysis on it so far. Many variants of the VRP problem have been derived, and related theories and models have become relatively mature, among which, the multi-period vehicle path problem (PVRP) is one. Traditional vehicle paths and their derivatives are mostly deterministic vehicle path optimization problems, where the relevant variables are known in advance. However, in practice, uncertain information abounds whether in production transport or emergency relief, including demands, road conditions, casualties and so on. It can be divided into fuzzy information, random information and dynamic information concerning the properties of uncertain information. Therefore, the analysis and research of uncertain vehicle path optimization problems have become the focuses of experts and scholars. With the increasing development of intelligent optimization algorithms in recent years, a good research foundation has been laid for solving such problems.

The problem of optimizing the routes of emergency material distribution vehicles is a typical VRP problem in which the distribution center provides materials to some demand points with different quantities of materials, and vehicles are assigned to appropriate routes which form closed loops such that departure and final return are both the distribution center, so that the demand points' needs are met. Such goals of minimum transport costs, shortest driving distance and time spent under certain constraints should also be accounted for. Given the condition of the demand of distribution being known, the shortest driving distance is used as a goal to indicate the shortest resource allocation time, and a suitable distribution path is selected for a vehicle to satisfy the distribution demand of each affected location. Zhou et al. constructed a heterogeneous vehicle path optimization model for the vehicle path problem in which the pre-emergency transporters' vehicles are insufficient; the maximum system satisfaction and the minimum total time and the total cost were considered as the goals [8]. Li Zhuo et al., focusing on different interests of demand points and transporters, developed a multi-objective hybrid vehicle path optimization model with a soft time window, and a non-dominated sorting ant colony algorithm was proposed to solve this model. An arithmetic case analysis indicated the effectiveness of the modified algorithm [9].

For the multi-site, open-emergency material distribution vehicle path problem considering secondary disasters, with the objective of shortest transportation time, Tan Jie et al. established two types of mathematical planning models that, under the one-sided fuzzy soft time window and fuzzy demand constraints, consider the risk of random failure at supply points, and designed an improved variable neighborhood search algorithm to solve the problem [10].

To solve the site-path problem of post-disaster emergency relief, different objectives and models were developed by scholars. With the objectives of maximizing rescue efficiency and minimizing the total cost, Cao Yinyu et al. developed a multi-stage site-path optimization model under the constraint of demand uncertainty and proposed an improved fast non-dominated genetic algorithm [11]. To maximize the matching degree of emergency demand at each dispatch point in the current stage, minimize the variance of the average matching degree of emergency demand at the previous k stages of dispatch and minimize the total travel time of the dispatch path, Liu Yang et al. constructed a multi-stage distribution and dispatching model for emergency relief supplies based on the historical travel time functions of road sections to portray the dynamics of the traffic on a road network [12]. In addition, an integrated optimization algorithm and coding adjustment strategy were made for the solution of multi-stage distribution and dispatching of disaster relief supplies. With the objective of minimizing the maximum distribution time, Zhou Yufeng et al. formulated an emergency facility siting-allocation model applicable to the initial post-earthquake relief phase by considering the phase characteristics, facility disruption scenarios, multi-species uncertain demand, facility capacity limitations, etc. The defuzzification of uncertain demand was processed through the expectation value formula of interval boundary, and on this basis, the result could be obtained by the proposed hybrid integer coding genetic algorithm [13].

The period vehicle routing problem (PVRP) was firstly proposed by Bekrami and Bodin in 1974 [14], arguing that different customers have different access frequencies for the recycling of industrial waste in New York City. Christofides et al. (1984) initially constructed a mathematical model of PVRP [15]. After nearly forty-five years of development, PVRP has been further extended in practical applications, such as the period vehicle routing problem with time window (PVRPTW), multidepot and periodic vehicle routing problems (MAPVRP) and the dynamic multi-period vehicle routing problem (DPVRPD) [16–19], and other existing studies mostly used heuristic algorithms to solve the extended PVRP model.

Wang et al. (2019) put forward a multi-stage model for distributing emergency supplies to multiple affected locations with the objectives of minimizing losses caused by shortages, total fixed costs of transportation and distribution costs. They designed and constructed a nonlinear utility function to reflect the negative utility caused by a lack of funding, and experiment results proved the feasibility of this model [20]. With the objectives of minimizing total delay time and total system loss for distribution of emergency supplies, Wang Yanyan et al. developed a dynamic distribution optimization decision model that uses fuzzy information conditions with multiple demand points, multiple distribution centers, multiple supplies, multiple periods and multiple objectives. After analyzing the clarification methods of the interval objective function, interval fuzzy constraints and triangular fuzzy constraints, they designed a two-dimensional Euclidean distance-based objective empowerment fuzzy algorithm to solve the model [21]. With the dual objectives of minimizing the risk of sending unsatisfying amounts of resources and minimizing the risk of resources not reaching disaster areas, Zhou et al. considered of the inherent nature of the multi-period dynamic emergency resource scheduling (ERS) problem to establish a multi-objective optimization model for the multi-period dynamic emergency resource scheduling (ERS) problem, and a decomposition-based multi-objective evolutionary algorithm (MOEA/D) was made to achieve great performance [22].

The vehicle routing problem for perishable goods (VRPFPG) is one of the vehicle routing problems (VRP) [23]. Large quantities of perishable goods around the world are transported from suppliers to consignees on a daily basis. Perishable goods, such as food and pharmaceuticals, require special handling during transportation due to their limited lifespans, and they must be transported as fast as possible before they deteriorate. Besides transport time constraints, the high frequency of transport can generate high transportation costs, which makes the optimization of perishable materials particularly vital. With the multiple objectives of minimizing operational costs, spoilage costs and carbon emissions, and maximizing customer satisfaction, Zulvia et al. paid attention to time windows, different travel times during peak and off-peak hours and working hours to develop a green VRP model and design a multi-objective gradient evolution (MOGE) algorithm whose results showed great performance [24].

To solve the perishable with uncertain demand material distribution vehicle path problem, researchers constructed various models with different objectives. With minimum total cost, maximum product freshness and minimum carbon emission as objectives, Qian Zhang et al. established a multi-objective optimization model for distribution path planning, and designed the main objective method and fruit fly algorithm based on robust optimization to deal with the uncertainty problem [25]. With the objective of minimizing the operating cost and emission cost, Babagolzadeh et al. constructed a two-stage stochastic planning model to determine the optimal replenishment strategy and transportation plan in the presence of carbon tax controls and uncertain demand, and an improved result was obtained by the proposed mathematical algorithm with respect to iterative local search (ILS) algorithm and mixed integer programming [26]. With the objectives of minimizing costs, minimizing environmental impacts and maximizing customer service levels, Talouki et al. formulated a dynamic green vehicle path model for perishable material under green transportation conditions in view of time window implementation, and then designed an algorithm based on a new augmented-constrained heuristic for solutions [27]. With the goal of profit maximization, Wu et al. developed a variable fractional inequality distribution path optimization model considering the uncertainty of perishable food demand for high speed rail and designed an augmented Lagrangian with the Euler algorithm based on the pairwise algorithm [28].

For the problem of uncertainty in demand and return of perishable goods with different periods, with the objective of minimizing the total cost of the system, Guo Jiangyan et al. constructed a multi-period closed-loop logistics network for perishable goods and figured out a mixed-integer linear programming (MILP) model solving by a proposed genetic algorithm [29].

For the problems of high-frequency distribution, uncertain demand and return of fresh goods due to perishability, with the objective of minimizing the total cost of the system, Yang et al. constructed the corresponding fuzzy mixed-integer linear programming (FMILP) model for the system and designed genetic algorithm (GA) and particle swarm optimization (PSO) algorithms to solve it [30].

The vehicle path problem is considered as an NP-hard problem, so it may be time-consuming and ineffective to use ordinary mathematical methods, such as exact algorithms, to deal with it. Most scholars nowadays use intelligent optimization algorithms for solving such problems. The whale optimization algorithm (WOA) is a biomimetic metaheuristic algorithm developed by Mirjalili et al. in 2016 to simulate the feeding mode of whales [31]. In recent years, it has been successfully applied to some large-scale optimization problems with the advantages of few artificial parameters and simple operation, such as resource scheduling problems [32], workflow planning for construction sites, site selection and path planning [33] and neural network training [34]. However, because the traditional WOA has the disadvantages of slow late convergence and easily falling into a local optima, some scholars have combined other algorithms with it to improve its performance in operation speed. Rohit Salgotra et al. addressed the problems of poor search performance and easily falling into a local optimum of the WOA algorithm. Three different improved versions, including WOA-adversarial-based learning, exponentially reduced parameters and worst-particle elimination and reinitialization methods, have been proposed to improve its exploratory capabilities. These properties have been exploited to improve the exploration capabilities of WOA by maintaining the diversity among search agents [35]. Shang Mang et al. proposed a WOA-based vehicle path optimization method for the distribution logistics of the VRP problem; modified the WOA algorithm using random inertia weights and a non-uniform variation strategy; and verified the effectiveness of the improved algorithm by testing functions. The verification results showed that the improved whale optimization algorithm can efficiently optimize the distribution path for vehicles and reduce the distribution cost of logistics [36].

As a novel algorithm, the WOA algorithm has attracted extensive attention from scholars in various fields since a basis has been built for the research, development and improvement of the algorithm, and application studies have been conducted regarding engineering, scheduling, optimization and site selection. Additionally, there is a richness in algorithm improvement. However, there are fewer applications in vehicle path research, so further development and utilization are needed.

A great deal of research has been carried out in the existing literature on the optimization of vehicle paths for the distribution of emergency and perishable materials. In addition to large demands for emergency supplies, such as communication equipment, quilts and tents, in the early stage of post-disaster relief, there also would be large demands for life-saving and living emergency supplies, such as medicines and foodstuffs. As for the perishable characteristics of these emergency supplies, along with the likelihood of severe damage to some roads, there is often uncertainty about the needs of the affected sites, making it difficult for these emergency perishable supplies to be delivered quickly and meet demand requirements at once. Therefore, in order to improve the optimization efficiency, this paper combines the differential evolutionary algorithm with the whale optimization algorithm to solve the vehicle path problem for the distribution of emergency perishable materials with dual objectives, which is rarely studied at present. Finally, further verification of the effectiveness of the improved whale optimization algorithm at solving the realistic vehicle path problem through examples shows convincing performance.

3. Multi-Period Optimization Model and DE-WOA Algorithm

The distribution vehicle path problem for emergency perishable materials has special characteristics compared to the same problem for general emergency materials, which negatively affect the solving process. The standard whale optimization algorithm greatly improves the operation efficiency of the algorithm because of the relatively simpler process and searching mechanism. Thus, it is suitable for solving the problem of emergency perishable material distribution optimization. This sub-section, while taking the uncertain demand situation into account, analyses the situation of adequate supplies in distribution centers and constructs a multi-period vehicle path distribution optimization model with the dual objectives of minimizing the cost penalty of distribution delay and total corruption during delivery, and minimizing the total amount of demand that is not met. The improved differential evolutionary whale algorithm is designed to solve the model by combining the features of the differential evolutionary algorithm with the standard whale optimization algorithm with strong global search capability.

3.1. Description of the Problem

Given a simple discrete undirected road traffic network $G = (V, E)$, where $V = (v_0, v_1, v_2, \ldots, v_n)$ is the set of nodes and v_0 denotes the distribution center for emergency perishable relief supplies, $v_1, v_2, \ldots, v_n$ denotes the affected point and $E = \{e(v_i, v_j) | v_i, v_j \in V\}$ is the set of edges. Assume that the supplies are sufficient. The demand for emergency perishable supplies at the affected point v_i is represented by interval boundary $\tilde{D}_i (i = 1, 2, \ldots, n)$. The distribution center v_0 possesses a sufficient emergency perishable supply, and the total quantity is S. The spoilage rate of emergency perishable supplies during the distribution process will linearly change along with the distribution time, and it is θt_j. The demand for emergency perishables at each site can be hardly met at once due to uncertain information on demand and limited vehicle capacity.

v_0: The distribution center now has k vehicles available with a maximum capacity of R for each; d_{ij} represents the distance between any two points; v_{ij}, depending on the road conditions, represents the actual speed of the vehicle on edge (i, j) during transportation, and $\bar{v}_{ij}$ represents the average speed of the vehicle so that the actual time for the vehicle to reach the disaster site j is $t_j = d_{ij}/v_{ij}$ and the ideal time is $\bar{t}_j = d_{ij}/\bar{v}_{ij}$. c_j is defined as the delay penalty, relying on the demand and the degree of damage at the disaster site. The distribution service will deliver emergency perishable materials to each disaster site and back to the distribution center until all the needs of the disaster sites are met. The most probable value weighting method is used to identify the uncertain demand, and the distribution route and the amount of each demand point in each period are decided with the dual objectives of minimizing the cost penalty of distribution delay and the total corruption during delivery, and minimizing the total amount of demand that is not met.

The model was constructed based on the following assumptions.

(1) The demand points' locations and total amounts are known.
(2) A tour of one vehicle is a closed loop such that its departure and final return are both the distribution center.
(3) The condition of the roads and the extent of damage to the affected sites are known for each period, so vehicles' ideal and actual speeds can be calculated.

3.2. Model Building and Notation Definition

The symbols and parameters used in this model are defined in Table 1. Decision variables are identified in Table 2.

Table 1. The symbols and parameters used in the model.

P	Collection of distribution periods
Z	The set of all nodes
R	The maximum load capacity per vehicle
$\tilde{D}_{ip}$	Disaster site i demand for emergency perishable goods for period p
S	Total amount of material in distribution center
t_0	The ideal arrival time of vehicles
t_j	The actual time of arrival of the vehicle
c	Cost of delay penalties per unit of vehicle delivery time
k	The number of vehicles that can be arranged
δ	The minimum permissible rate of spoilage of material during vehicle transport
ω	Vehicle utilization

Table 2. Decision variables.

x_{ijk}^p	1, if vehicle transports material from point i to point j in period p 0, otherwise
y_{ik}^p	1, if the task at point i is performed by vehicle k 0, otherwise
d_{ipk}	Volume of emergency perishable materials provided by vehicle k to disaster site i in period p

Taking into account all the objectives and constraints, the model is developed.

$$\min \sum_{i \in Z} \sum_{p \in P} (t_j - t_0) c_{1j} x_{ijk}^p + c_{2j} d_{ipk} \theta t_j, \text{ while } t_j \leq t_0, t_j - t_0 = 0 \quad (1)$$

$$\min \left\{ \sum_{p \in P} 1 - d_{ipk}(1 - \tilde{\theta} t_j) / \tilde{D}_{ip}, i \in Z, k \in K \right\} \quad (2)$$

$$s.t. \sum_{i \in Z} d_{ipk} y_{ik}^p \leq R, \ k \in K, \ p \in P; \tag{3}$$

$$\sum_{i \in Z} \sum_{k \in K} d_{ipk} \leq S, \ p \in P; \tag{4}$$

$$0 \leq \sum_{k \in K} d_{ipk} \theta t_j \leq \widetilde{D}_{ip}, \ i \in Z, \ p \in P; \tag{5}$$

$$\sum_{i \in S} \sum_{j \in S} x_{ijk}^p \leq |S| - 1, \ k \in K, \ p \in P; \tag{6}$$

$$\sum_{j \in Z} x_{nik}^p = \sum_{j \in Z} x_{ink}^p \leq 1, \ i \in Z, \ k \in K, p \in P; \tag{7}$$

$$\sum_{j \in Z, i \neq j} x_{ijk}^p \leq 1, \ i \in Z, \ k \in K, p \in P; \tag{8}$$

$$x_{ijk}^p \leq y_{ik}^p; \tag{9}$$

$$0 \leq \frac{d_{ipk} \theta t_j}{d_{ipk}} \leq \delta; \tag{10}$$

$$\frac{d_{ipk}}{R_k} \geq \omega; \tag{11}$$

$$x_{ijk}^p = 0 \text{ or } 1, \ y_{ik}^p = 0 \text{ or } 1, \ (i,j) \in Z, \ p \in P; \tag{12}$$

$$d_{ipk} \geq 0; \tag{13}$$

Equations (1) and (2), respectively, represent the dual objectives that minimize the cost penalty of distribution delay and the total corruption during delivery and minimize the total amount of demand that is not met. Equation (3) guarantees the load amount of each vehicle does not exceed the maximum capacity per vehicle. Equation (4) ensures that the total amount of distribution in each period is less than the available amount in the distribution center. Equation (5) is aimed at restricting the amount of emergency perishable supplies delivered to the disaster site in each period that does not exceed its ideal demand. Equation (6) indicates that the sub-loop in the distribution process is broken. Equation (7) guarantees each vehicle starts and ends transportation at the distribution center. Equation (8) presents a vehicle does not pass through the same path twice or more in any period. Equation (9) ensures that the vehicle serves a disaster site before passing through. Equation (10) indicates the degree of spoilage of emergency perishable materials during distribution should be less than a given rate. Equation (11) represents that each vehicle's utilization rate for each period should be more than a given rate. Equation (12) is related to the integer variable constraint. Equation(13) represents the non-negative constraint.

Where $\widetilde{D}_{ip} = \widetilde{D}_{ip} + |\widetilde{D}_{i(p-1)} - \sum d_{ik(p-1)}|$ when $p \geq 2$.

3.3. Clarity of Ambiguous Needs

In this paper, uncertain demand is expressed as interval boundary:

$$\widetilde{D}_{ip} = [q_{1i}, q_{2i}, q_{3i}], \ q_{1i} \leq q_{2i} \leq q_{3i} \tag{14}$$

The affiliation function is:

$$\mu_{\widetilde{D}_i}(x) = \begin{cases} 0 & x \leq q_{1i}, x \geq q_{3i} \\ (x - q_{1i})/(q_{2i} - q_{1i}) & q_{1i} < x < q_{2i} \\ (q_{3i} - x)/(q_{3i} - q_{2i}) & q_{2i} < x < q_{3i} \end{cases} \tag{15}$$

where q_1i, q_2i and q_3i represent the left boundary, the point with affiliation 1 (most likely value) and the right boundary of the interval boundary, respectively. The interval boundary is constant with the weights given by experts or decision-makers. $\tilde{D}_{ip} = [q_{1i}, q_{2i}, q_{3i}]$ is expressed by the Equation (16)

$$\tilde{D}_{ip} = w_1 q_{1i} + w_2 q_{2i} + w_3 q_{3i}. \tag{16}$$

w_1 is the weight of the lower boundary, w_2 is the weight of the most probable value and w_3 is the weight of the upper boundary.

Such methods that determine weights by experience and knowledge of experts or decision makers are relatively subjective. The results thus are influenced by strong human elements. Some more objective methods to identify fuzzy weights were developed, such as the same weight method and hierarchical analysis. The most common is the most likely method. The most likely value of the interval boundary is given the highest weight, as it is most accurate. The value of boundary is less accurate; thus, they are assigned smaller weights.

To indicate differences between the three estimates $q_{1,q}$ and q_3, the weights of them are consequently determined by $w_1 = w_3 = 1/6$ and $w_2 = 4/6$. Therefore, Equation (15) can be converted into Equation (16).

$$\tilde{D}_{ip} = \frac{q_{1i} + 4q_{2i} + q_{3i}}{6} \tag{17}$$

After replacing Equation (5) with Equation (17), the updated constraint is shown as Equation (18):

$$0 \leq \sum_{k \in K} d_{ipk} \leq \frac{1}{6} q_{1i} + \frac{4}{6} q_{2i} + \frac{1}{6} q_{3i}, \ i \in Z, \ p \in P \tag{18}$$

$$\min \left\{ \sum_{p \in P} 1 - d_{ikp}(1 - \tilde{\theta} t_j) / \frac{1}{6} q_{1i} + \frac{4}{6} q_{2i} + \frac{1}{6} q_{3i}, \ i \in Z, \ k \in K \right\} \tag{19}$$

3.4. Handling of Dual Targets

The ϵ conventional method aims to convert a muti-objective problem into a single-objective optimization problem by linear weighting. However, because of the non-uniformity of the objective magnitude, the solution of the original problem and that of the converted problem are not in simple one-to-one correspondence. The weights of each objective may largely affect the accuracy of solutions. This paper takes advantage of the idea of the constraint method (Haimes et al. 1971), combining it with an improved differential evolutionary whale algorithm.

In this case, two single-objective optimization problems are solved by converting one of the dual objectives into the other's constraints based on the importance of the objectives in each period in turn and solving them separately to obtain the Pareto solution set of the model.

1. Construct a single objective optimization problem with objective A and objective B, respectively, and find the value domain (upper and lower bounds) of the two objective functions.

Objective A.

$$\min \sum_{j \in Z} \sum_{p \in P} (t_j - t_0) c_{1j} x_{ijk}^p + c_{2j} d_{ipk} \theta t_j, \ while \ t_j \leq t_0, \ t_j - t_0 = 0 \tag{20}$$

s.t. $constraint(1) - constraint(13)$

Objective B.

$$\min \left\{ \sum_{p \in P} 1 - d_{ipk}(1 - \tilde{\theta} t_j) / \tilde{D}_{ip}, \ i \in Z, \ k \in K \right\} \tag{21}$$

s.t. $constraint(1) - constraint(13)$

2. Step 1 finds the minimum value of objective A as m, and then adds $Z_A \leq a$ as a constraint to get the result of objective B. Construct a single-objective optimization problem for objective B. If the problem has a feasible solution, find the optimal solution for objective B as Z_B^*, and go to Step 3; if there is no feasible solution, go to Step 4.

3. Then, add $Z_B \leq Z_B^*$ as a constraint to objective A to construct a single objective optimization problem for objective A. Similarly, if there is a feasible solution to the problem, the optimal solution to objective A is found at Z_A^*, at which point the solution obtained in the above step is counted in the Pareto solution set; if there is no feasible solution, then go to step 4.

4. Make $a = a + \epsilon$. ϵ is a fixed step; go to step 2 to continue solving.

5. Stop when a is greater than the maximum value of target A.

3.5. The Basic Process of DE-WOA

The improved differential evolutionary whale algorithm is computed as Figure 1.

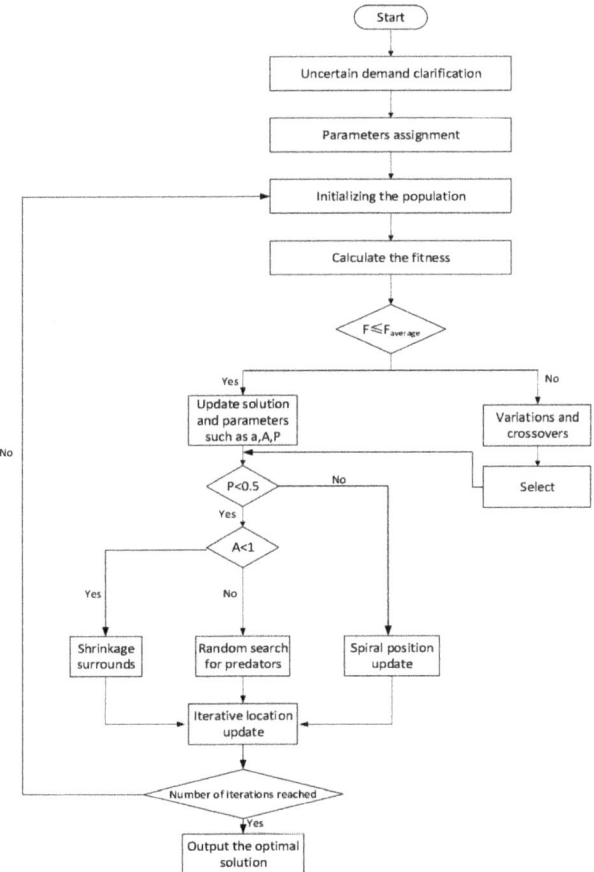

Figure 1. Flowchart of the DE-WOA algorithm.

Step 1: Uncertain demand clarification. The demand parameters in the model are the interval boundary. The most probable weight method is used to convert the interval boundary into definite values and replace them in the model.

Step 2: Initialize parameters. Assign values to parameters, such as population size pop, the maximum number of iterations M, the logarithmic spiral shape constant b, the scaling factor F and the crossover probability CR.

Step 3: Calculate the individual fitness function at F' and the population average fitness function at $F'_{average}$. Based on the obtained fitness function values, record the location of the global optimal solution in the initial population x_{best}, where the global optimal value is F'_{best}.

Step 4: When $F' \leq F'_{average}$, iteratively update the solution and calculate the values of parameters such as a, A, p, C and l; otherwise adapt it for global exploitation using $X_i(t+1) = X_{best}(t) - A * D, A = 2a * r - a, C = 2 * r$ to expand the population diversity.

Step 5: When $P < 0.5$ and $|A| < 1$, the whale position is updated using $D = |C * X_{best}(t) - x_i(t)|$; when $P \geq 0.5$ and $|A| < 1$, the whale position is updated using $D' = |X_{best}(t) - x_i(t)|$; when $P < 0.5$ and $|A| \geq 1$, the whale position is updated using $D = |C * X_{rand}(t) - x_i(t)|$.

Step 6: Update the global optimal solution x_{best} and the global optimal value F'_{best}.

Step 7: Stop the iteration if the algorithm stopping condition is met; otherwise, repeat step 4–step 7.

4. Analysis of Numerical Examples and Computational Results

In this section, we report the results of numerical experiments that were applied to verify the feasibility and effectiveness of the constructed model and proposed algorithm. All experiments were tested on a PC equipped with an Intel(R) Core(TM) i7-9750H CPU @ 2.60 GHz 2.59 and 8 GB of RAM. The model programming was solved by Python 3.8.1.

4.1. Parameter Setting

There are one distribution center and ten disaster locations labeled in order from 0 to 10. Related information, including coordinate values, is shown in Table 3. The network topology between the distribution center and the affected points is shown in Figure 2.

Table 3. Coordinates of the distribution center and locations of affected points.

	No.	X	Y
Distribution Center	0	30	70
Affected sites	1	35	55
	2	38	73
	3	25	70
	4	30	55
	5	32	85
	6	38	62
	7	43	79
	8	40	60
	9	38	85
	10	24	65

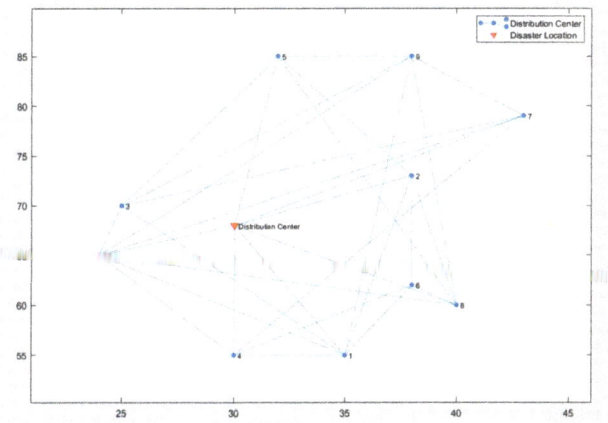

Figure 2. Network topology in the affected area.

Due to the lack of information on data from the affected areas, the demand for emergency perishable goods and the speed of vehicle movements at each affected location need to be estimated based on published information, such as local casualties and the probability of secondary disasters. The specific demand parameters q_1 (pessimistic value), q_2 (most likely value) and q_3 (optimistic value) are shown in Table 4.

Table 4. Demand parameters.

Point of Need	0	1	2	3	4	5	6	7	8	9	10
q_1	0	103	52	78	210	53	41	43	80	65	52
q_2	0	125	70	86	226	70	50	56	91	74	61
q_3	0	140	82	100	242	81	56	64	100	81	70
Demand	0	123.833	69	87	226	69	49.5	55.163	90.667	73.667	61

The distribution center has three small trucks of the same type. In order to obtain a more accurate distribution time, the actual distance between any two points is measured according to the latitude and longitude of the map, and the maximum speed of the vehicles traveling on each road is estimated according to the road damage. The transport network parameters (a, b) and vehicle parameters are shown in Tables 5 and 6.

Table 5. Transport network parameters.

	1	2	3	4	5	6	7	8	9	10
0	(30,30)	(22.4,38)	(-,-)	(6.5,45)	(18.6,60)	(-,-)	(-,-)	(32.5,35)	(15.2,41)	(7.7,46)
1	0,0	(40.6,37)	(31.5,40)	(-,-)	(15.7,42)	(20.4,33)	(-,-)	(43.7,37)	(22.1,41)	(-,-)
2	(40.6,37)	0,0	(51.2,40)	(36.2,38)	(25.6,42)	(-,-)	(17.5,39)	(-,-)	(-,-)	(27.1,45)
3	(-,-)	(51.2,40)	0,0	(-,-)	(-,-)	(34.6,47)	(15.3,39)	(-,-)	(22.2,30)	(-,-)
4	(6.5,45)	(36.2,38)	(-,-)	0,0	(-,-)	(17.8,33)	(-,-)	(33.6,42)	(-,-)	(29.5,40)
5	(18.6,60)	(25.6,42)	(-,-)	(-,-)	0,0	(-,-)	(29.3,36)	(19.3,42)	(-,-)	(-,-)
6	(-,-)	(-,-)	(34.6,47)	(17.8,33)	(-,-)	0,0	(-,-)	(-,-)	(42.1,36)	(14.2,45)
7	(-,-)	(17.5,39)	(15.3,39)	(-,-)	(29.3,36)	(-,-)	0,0	(-,-)	(23.4,35)	(-,-)
8	(32.5,35)	(-,-)	(-,-)	(33.6,42)	(19.3,42)	(-,-)	(-,-)	0,0	(-,-)	(47.1,60)
9	(15.2,41)	(-,-)	(-,-)	(-,-)	(-,-)	(42.1,36)	(23.4,35)	(-,-)	0,0	(38.9,39)
10	(7.7,46)	(27.1,45)	(29.5,40)	(29.5,40)	(-,-)	(14.2,45)	(-,-)	(47.1,60)	(38.9,39)	0,0

Table 6. Vehicle parameters.

Vehicle Type	Quantity (Volume)	Max. Loading Capacity (kg)	Average Travel Speed (km/h)
Small trucks	3	500	60

In Table 5, a denotes the distance between two points (km), b denotes the actual speed of the vehicle traveling between this path v_k (km/h) and "-" denotes that this section is impassable, resulting in the delivery time parameters shown in Table 7.

Table 7. Distribution time parameters.

	0	1	2	3	4	5	6	7	8	9	10
0	0	0.5	0.22	-	0.04	0	-	-	0.39	0.12	0.02
1	0.5	0	0.42	0.26	-	0.11	0.28	-	0.45	0.17	-
2	0.22	0.42	0	0.43	0.35	0.18	-	0.16	-	-	0.15
3	-	0.26	0.43	0	-	-	0.16	0.14	-	0.37	-
4	0.04	-	0.35	-	0	-	0.24	-	0.24	-	0.25
5	0	0.11	0.18	-	-	0	-	0.33	0.14	-	-
6	-	0.28	-	0.16	0.24	-	0	-	-	0.47	0.08
7	-	-	0.16	0.14	-	0.33	-	0	-	0.28	-
8	0.39	0.45	-	-	0.24	0.14	-	-	0	-	0
9	0.12	0.17	-	0.37	-	-	0.47	0.28	-	0	0.35
10	0.22	-	0.15	-	0.25	-	0.08	-	0	0.35	0

4.2. Results

After several trials, the parameters of the improved whale algorithm (DE-WOA) based on the difference algorithm were set as shown in Table 8.

Table 8. DE-WOA parameter settings.

Parameter	Description	Value
pop_num	Initial population size	80
Max_iteration	Maximum number of iterations	300
R	Maximum vehicle loading capacity	500 kg
θ	Corruption rate	0.02 kg/h
σ	Minimum permissible rate of spoilage of materials during vehicle transport	0.90
k	Number of vehicles	3
β	Minimum allowable loading rate during vehicle transport	0.5

After five trials, a Pareto frontier solution set for the problem was obtained and is shown in Figure 3. The horizontal coordinates and vertical coordinates, respectively, represent the value of objective A (the distribution delay penalty and corruption cost) and the value of objective B (total amount of demand that is not met). Each point represents a distribution solution that satisfies the Pareto optimum. The decision maker can choose a relative compromise by weighing the relationship between multiple objectives according to the situation in practice.

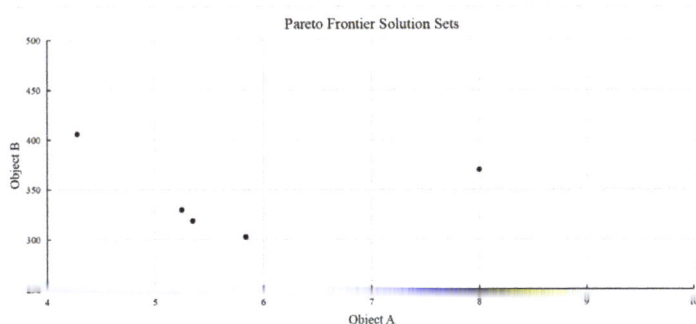

Figure 3. Pareto frontier solution set.

The relationship between the transport volume and the optimal solution at each affected point is obtained, and the optimal path is output as shown in Tables 9 and 10.

Table 9. Relationship between transport volumes at affected sites and optimal path.

First Period	Affected Sites	Transport Volume	Second Period	Affected Sites	Transport Volume
	0	0		0	0
	5	69	Vehicle 1	2	73.2
Vehicle 1	1	123.83		0	0
	8	90.67		10	63.66
	0	0		8	86
	2	69	Vehicle 2	5	74.37
	7	55.17		7	50
Vehicle 2	3	87		3	92.8
	6	49.5		9	74.33
	9	73.67		0	0
	0	0		4	232.83
Vehicle 3	10	61	Vehicle 3	6	53.5
	4	226		1	156
	0	0		0	0

Table 10. Distribution vehicle paths and objective function values.

Periodicity	Vehicles	Transport Routes	Objective A	Objective B
1	1	0-5-1-8-0	318.760	5.358
	2	0-2-7-3-6-9-0		
	3	0-10-4-0		
2	1	0-2-0	490.679	7.790
	2	0-10-8-5-7-3-9-0		
	3	0-4-6-1-0		

4.3. Algorithm Comparison

Two algorithms, the standard whale algorithm (WOA) and the improved differential evolutionary whale algorithm (DE-WOA), were used to solve the algorithms, resulting in the set of Pareto front solutions under both algorithms shown in Figure 4. It can be seen from Figure 4 that the Pareto ranks of the solutions of the improved differential evolutionary whale algorithm are lower than the Pareto ranks of the solutions of the standard whale algorithm, thereby indicating that the improved differential evolutionary whale algorithm can effectively improve the local search capability and increase the diversity of solutions in the population.

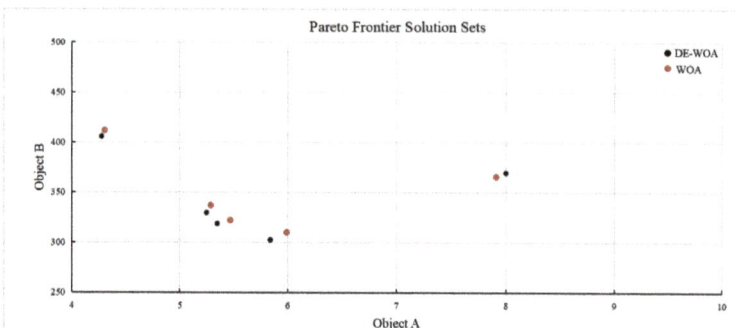

Figure 4. Set of Pareto front solutions under both algorithms.

After 100 runs of both algorithms, the optimal objective values were obtained as shown in Table 8, and the convergence of the algorithms under the two objectives was obtained as shown in Figures 5 and 6.

1. Comparison of target results.

Algorithms	Minimal Distribution Delay Penalty and Corruption Costs	Minimize Total Amount of Demands That Are Not Met
WOA	332.120	6.015
DE-WOA	318.760	5.358

2. Analysis of convergence effects.

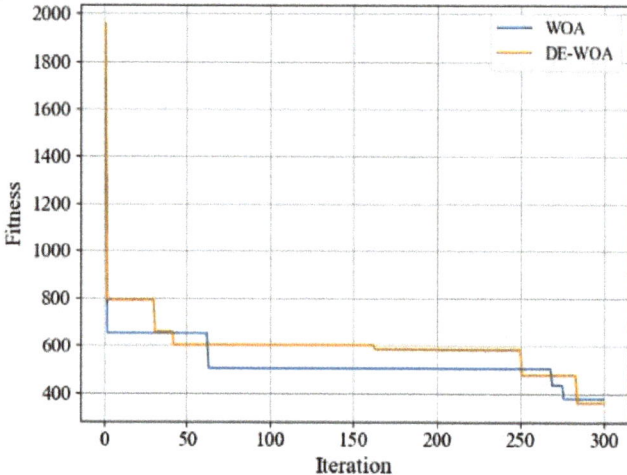

Figure 5. Convergence diagram of distribution delay penalty and corruption costs.

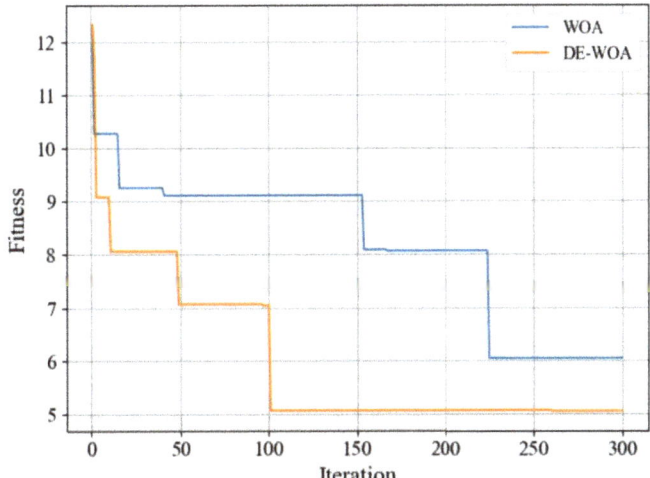

Figure 6. Convergence diagram of total amount of demand that is not met.

By comparison, it can be seen that the improved differential evolutionary whale algorithm outperformed the standard whale algorithm in terms of solution results and converged faster when solving. This shows that the improved differential evolutionary whale algorithm outperforms the standard whale algorithm in solving the dual objective model of this paper, thereby also verifying the validity of the model and algorithm.

5. Discussion and Conclusions

For the optimization problem of the multi-cycle distribution of emergency perishable materials under a uncertain demand, this paper draws the following conclusions.

(1) In this paper, we studied the multi-cycle distribution problem for emergency perishable materials under the situation of sufficient materials in distribution centers after disasters, and considered characteristics such as the degree of road destruction in real situations. We established a dual-objective PVRP distribution optimization model minimizing the cost penalty of distribution delay and the total corruption during delivery, and minimizing the total amount of demand that is not met. Additionally, the uncertain demand in the model is processed using the interval number and the most probable weight method, and the dual objective is processed with the idea of a constraint method. It was verified by an example that the solution is more accurate and faster after the model is processed.

(2) Combined with the real application conditions and scenarios, the whale optimization algorithm was chosen due to the characteristics of the model for optimization. To solve the shortcomings of small population diversity and falling into a local optimum of the standard whale optimization algorithm, the idea of combination with the differential evolution algorithm was proposed. It was improved by adding the characteristics of easy operation and strong global search ability of the differential evolution algorithm. Finally, the analysis of the numerical calculation results of the earthquake in Jiuzhaigou County, Sichuan, showed that the improved differential evolutionary whale algorithm can find a better distribution solution than the standard whale optimization algorithm with less distribution time and the less material corruption. Additionally, it improves the demand satisfaction, and converges faster, which further verifies the feasibility and applicability of the algorithm in practical applications.

The main purpose of this paper was to provide a set of scientific distribution scheme for emergency rescue, through the reasonable distribution of emergency perishable materials and reasonable arrangement of vehicles, so as to effectively reduce the damage caused by an earthquake, reduce casualties, improve the rescue work efficiency, etc. The research model and algorithm proposed in this paper can be applied not only to the disaster scenario, but also to the logistics distribution in urban and rural areas in practical daily life, which can effectively improve the operation efficiency among supply chains.

The model we proposed in this paper also has a few shortcomings. This case operates under the assumption that the distribution center has sufficient supplies and only distributes a single variety of perishable materials, though in practice the distribution center is often short of supplies and the demand for emergency perishable materials at the disaster site is often multi-species. In future work, we will take this shortcoming into account and consider how to combine and distribute multiple species of emergency perishable materials and improve the model to take more factors into account and build a more realistic emergency material distribution model. At the same time, as the complexity of the model increases, more efficient algorithms should be designed to correspondingly solve the model.

Author Contributions: Conceptualization, X.L.; Data curation, X.L.; Formal analysis, X.L.; Funding acquisition, Y.X. (Yang Xu); Investigation, X.L.; Methodology, X.L.; Project administration, Y.X. (Yang Xu), K.K.L., H.J. and Y.X. (Yaning Xu); Resources, Y.X. (Yang Xu) and K.K.L.; Software, X.L. and H.J.; Supervision, Y.X. (Yang Xu), K.K.L., H.J. and Y.X. (Yaning Xu); Validation, Y.X. (Yang Xu) and K.K.L.; Visualization, K.K.L. and Jia Li; Writing—original draft, X.L.; Writing—review & editing, X.L. and Y.X. (Yang Xu). All authors have read and agreed to the published version of the manuscript.

Funding: This research was funded by General Research Project on Major Theoretical and Practical Issues in Philosophy and Social Sciences of Shaanxi Province of funder grant number 2022ND0185. The APC was funded by Yang Xu.

Data Availability Statement: Not applicable

Conflicts of Interest: The authors declare no conflict of interest

Abbreviations

VRP	Vehicle Routing Problem
PVRP	Period Vehicle Routing Problem
PVRPTW	Period Vehicle Routing Problem with Time Window
MAPVRP	Multidepot and Periodic Vehicle Routing Problems
DPVRPD	The Dynamic Multi-period Vehicle Routing Problem
ERS	Emergency Resource Scheduling
MOAE/D	Multi-objective Evolutionary Algorithm
VRPFPG	The vehicle routing problem for perishable goods
MOGE	Multi-objective Gradient Evolution Algorithm
MILP	Mixed-integer Linear Programming
GA	Genetic Algorithm
PSO	Particle Swarm Optimization
WOA	Whale Optimization Algorithm
DE	Differential Evolutionary Algorithm
DE-WOA	Differential Evolutionary-Whale Optimization Algorithm

References

1. Chang, M.; Tseng, Y.; Chen, J. A scenario planning approach for the flood emergency logistics preparation problem under uncertainty. *Transp. Res. Part E Logist. Transp. Rev.* **2007**, *43*, 737–754. [CrossRef]
2. Liu, X.; Zhao, M. Reprint of: Regional risk assess-ment for urban major hazards based on GIS geoprocess-ing to improve public safety. *Saf. Sci.* **2017**, *97*, 112–119.
3. Mackenzie, C.; Zobel, C. Allocating resources to enhance resilience, with application to Superstorm Sandy and anelectric utility. *Risk Anal.* **2016**, *36*, 847–862. [CrossRef]
4. Wu, B.; Yan, X.; Wang, Y.; Zhang, D.; Guedes, S. Three-stage decision-making model under restricted conditions for emergency response to ships not under control. *Risk Anal.* **2017**, *37*, 2455–2474. [CrossRef]

5. Feng, C.; Xiang, Y.; Xue, K.; Feng, R. Multi-objective optimization model of the emergency logistics distribution with multicycle and multi-item. *Chin. J. Manag. Sci.* **2017**, *25*, 124–132.
6. Wang, H.J.; Wang, Q.; Ma, S.H. Decision-Making for Emergency Materials Dynamic Dispatching Based on Fuzzy Demand and Supply. *Chin. J. Manag. Sci.* **2014**, *22*, 55–64.
7. Dantzig, G.; Ramser, J. The Truck Dispatching Problem. *Manag. Sci.* **1959**, *6*, 80–91. [CrossRef]
8. Zhou, H.B. Modeling and Optimization of Heterogeneous Vehicle Routing Problem in Emergency Resource Distribution after Disaster. *J. Phys. Conf. Ser.* **2019**, *1302*, 042002. [CrossRef]
9. Li, Z.; Li, Y.Z.; Li, W.X. Muti-objective optimization model and solution algorithm for emergency material transportation path. *J. Comput. Appl.* **2019**, *39*, 2765–2771.
10. Tan, J; Li, W.L.; L, K.K. The Open Vehicle Routing Problem of Emergency Logistics Considering Secondary Disasters. *Syst. Eng.* **2021**, *39*, 61–71.
11. Gao, X.Y.; Ni, J. Multi-stage bi-objective emergency location-routing optimization with fuzzy requirement. *Appl. Res. Comput.* **2022**, *39*, 391–397.
12. Liu, Y.; Zhang, G.F.; Su, Z.P.; Jiang, J.G. Modeling and solving multi-phase allocation and scheduling of emergency relief supplies. *Control. Decis.* **2019**, *34*, 2015–2022.
13. Zhou, Y.F.; Chen, N.; Li, Z.; Gong, Y. Optimization Design of Emergency Logistics Network Considering Facility Disruption Scenarios during the Early Stage of Post-Earthquake Relief. *Oprations Res. Manag. Sci.* **2020**, *29*, 107–112.
14. Beltrami, E.; Bodin, L. Networks and vehicle routing for municipal waste collection. *Networks* **1974**, *4*, 65–94. [CrossRef]
15. Christofides, N.; Beasley, J.E. The period routing problem. *Networks* **1984**, *14*, 237–256. [CrossRef]
16. Cai, W.J.; Wang, C.Y.; Yu, B. Improved Ant Colony Algorithm for Period Vehicle Routing Problem. *Oprations Res. Manag. Sci.* **2014**, *23*, 70–77.
17. Michallet, J.; Prins, C.; Amodeo, L.; Yalaoui, F.; Vitry, G. Multi-start iterated local search for the periodic vehicle routing problem with time windows and time spread constraints on services. *Comput. Oper. Res.* **2014**, *41*, 196–207. [CrossRef]
18. Vidal, T.; Crainic, T.G.; Gendreau, M.; Lahrichi, N.; Rei, W. A Hybrid Genetic Algorithm for Multidepot and Periodic Vehicle Routing Problems. *Oper. Res.* **2012**, *60*, 611–624. [CrossRef]
19. Wen, M.; Cordeau, J.F.; Laporte, G.; Larsen, J. The dynamic multi-period vehicle routing problem. *Comput. Oper. Res.* **2010**, *37*, 1615–1623. [CrossRef]
20. Wang, Y.Y.; Bier Vicki, M.; Sun, B.Q. Measuring and Achieving Equity in Multiperiod Emergency Material Allocation. *Risk Anal. Off. Publ. Soc. Risk Anal.* **2019**, *39*, 2408–2426. [CrossRef]
21. Zhou, Y.W.; Liu, J.; Zhang, Y.T.; Gan, X.H. A Multi-objective Evolutionary Algorithm for Multi-Period Dynamic Emergency Resource Scheduling Problems. *Transp. Res. Part E* **2016**, *99*, 77–95. [CrossRef]
22. Wang, Y.Y.; Sun, B.Q. Muti-period Optimization Model of Multi-type Emergency Materials Allocation Based on Fuzzy Information. *Chin. J. Manag. Sci.* **2020**, *28*, 40–51.
23. Adenso-Diaz, B.; Gonzalez, M.; Garcia, E. A hierarchical approach to managing dairy routing. *Interfaces* **1998**, *28*, 21–31. [CrossRef]
24. Zulvia, F.E.; Kuo, R.J.; Nugroho, D.Y. A many-objective gradient evolution algorithm for solving a green vehicle routing problem with time windows and time dependency for perishable products. *J. Clean. Prod.* **2020**, *242*, 118428. [CrossRef]
25. Zhang, Q.; Xiong, Y.; He, M.K.; Zhang, H. Multi-objective Model of Distribution Route Problem for Fresh Electricity Commerce under Uncertain Demand. *J. Syst. Simul.* **2019**, *31*, 1582–1590.
26. Babagolzadeh, M.; Shrestha, A.; Abbasi, B.; Zhang, Y.; Woodhead, A.; Zhang, A. Sustainable cold supply chain management under demand uncertainty and carbon tax regulation. *Transp. Res. Part D* **2020**, *80*, 102245. [CrossRef]
27. Talouki, R.Z.; Javadian, N.; Movahedi, M.M. Optimization and incorporating of green traffic for dynamic vehicle routing problem with perishable products. *Environ. Sci. Pollut. Res. Int.* **2021**, *28*, 36415–36433. [CrossRef]
28. Wu, X.; Nie, L.; Xu, M.; Yan, F. A perishable food supply chain problem considering demand uncertainty and time deadline constraints: Modeling and application to a high-speed railway catering service. *Transp. Res. Part E* **2018**, *111*, 186–209. [CrossRef]
29. Guo, J.Q.; Yang, X.H. Robust optimization model of multi-period closed-loop logistics network for perishable products. *Appl. Res. Comput.* **2020**, *37*, 774–778+783.
30. Yang, X.H.; Guo, J.Q. Multi-period multi-decision closed-loop logistics network for fresh products with fuzzy variables. *J. Comput. Appl.* **2019**, *39*, 2168–2174.
31. Mirjalili, S.; Lewis, A.The whale optimization algorithm. *Adv. Eng. Softw.* **2016**, *95*, 51–67. [CrossRef]
32. Sha, J.X. Application of ameliorative whale optimization algorithm to optimal allocation of multi-objective water resources. *Water Resour. Hydropower Eng.* **2018**, *49*, 18–26.
33. Prakash, D.B.; Lakshminarayana, C. Optimal sitting of capacitors in radial distribution network using whale optimization algorithm. *Alex. Eng. J.* **2017**, *56*, 499–509. [CrossRef]
34. Aljarah, I.; Faris, H.; Mirjalili, S. Optimizing connection weights in neural networks using the whale optimization algorithm. *Soft Comput.* **2018**, *22*, 1–15. [CrossRef]
35. Salgotra, R.; Singh, U.; Saha, S. On some improved versions of whale optimization algorithm. *Arab. J. Sci. Eng.* **2019**, *44*, 9653–9691. [CrossRef]
36. Shang, M.; Wan, Z.P.; Cao, J.W.; Kang, J.Y. Logistics path optimization based on improved whale optimization algorithm. *Math. Pract. Theory* **2019**, *49*, 210–218.

Article

Multi-AGV Flexible Manufacturing Cell Scheduling Considering Charging

Jianxun Li [1], Wenjie Cheng [1], Kin Keung Lai [2,*] and Bhagwat Ram [3]

[1] School of Economics and Management, Xi'an University of Technology, Xi'an 710048, China
[2] International Business School, Shaanxi Normal University, Xi'an 710048, China
[3] Centre for Digital Transformation, Indian Institute of Management Ahmedabad, Vastrapur 380015, India
* Correspondence: mskklai@outlook.com

Abstract: Because of their flexibility, controllability and convenience, Automated Guided Vehicles (AGV) have gradually gained popularity in intelligent manufacturing because to their adaptability, controllability, and simplicity. We examine the relationship between AGV scheduling tasks, charging thresholds, and power consumption, in order to address the issue of how AGV charging affects the scheduling of flexible manufacturing units with multiple AGVs. Aiming to promote AGVs load balance and reduce AGV charging times while meeting customer demands, we establish a scheduling model with the objective of minimizing the maximum completion time based on process sequence limitations, processing time restrictions, and workpiece transportation constraints. In accordance with the model's characteristics, we code the machine, workpiece, and AGV independently, solve the model using a genetic algorithm, adjust the crossover mutation operator, and incorporate an elite retention strategy to the population initialization process to improve genetic diversity. Calculation examples are used to examine the marginal utility of the number of AGVs and electricity and validate the efficiency and viability of the scheduling model. The results show that the AVGs are effectively scheduled to complete transportation tasks and reduce the charging wait time. The multi-AGV flexible manufacturing cell scheduling can also help decision makers to seek AGVs load balance by simulation, reduce the charging times, and decrease the final completion time of manufacturing unit. In addition, AGV utilization can be maximized when the fleet size of AGV is 20%-40% of the number of workpieces.

Keywords: AGV scheduling; flexible manufacturing cell; AGV charging; genetic algorithm

MSC: 68T20

1. Introduction

An AGV is a transport vehicle that can navigate autonomously and carry out spontaneous or controlled transportation along a prescribed route [1]. It assists intelligent factories to realize workpiece production tasks under the condition of unmanned driving. In order to efficiently use AGVs to participate in intelligent operations, it is necessary to integrate information such as processes, equipment, and workpieces into workshop scheduling. This kind of scheduling is actually the Flexible Job-Shop Scheduling Problem (FJSP) that has evolved from the traditional Job-Shop Scheduling (JSP). There is an exceptionally rich domain of research that covers many aspects of AGV scheduling and proposes numerous approaches. The majority of interest in AGV scheduling stems from its potential impact in practice by increasing efficiency and lowering costs. However, due to its complexity and numerous features, it remains a challenging problem [2]. The literature review and discussion in this paper are limited to the number of available AGVs, the power threshold, and the charging time in AGV and machine task scheduling issues with single or multiple objectives AGVs. The scheduling optimization problem of AGVs is the primary focus of

Citation: Li, J.; Cheng, W.; Lai, K.K.; Ram, B. Multi-AGV Flexible Manufacturing Cell Scheduling Considering Charging. *Mathematics* **2022**, *10*, 3417. https://doi.org/10.3390/math10193417

Academic Editor: Yaping Ren

Received: 22 August 2022
Accepted: 17 September 2022
Published: 20 September 2022

Publisher's Note: MDPI stays neutral with regard to jurisdictional claims in published maps and institutional affiliations.

Copyright: © 2022 by the authors. Licensee MDPI, Basel, Switzerland. This article is an open access article distributed under the terms and conditions of the Creative Commons Attribution (CC BY) license (https://creativecommons.org/licenses/by/4.0/).

related research. Fu et al. [3] elaborated the analysis process, scheduling rules and optimization methods for the AGV scheduling optimization problem. Bilge and Ulusoy [4] proposed a pseudo-polynomial-time algorithm to obtain optimal machine and vehicle schedules. Abdelmaguid et al. [5] studied a hybrid genetic algorithm approach to schedule the machines and used a heuristic technique to obtain a vehicle assignment. The authors addressed the operations scheduling and provided the vehicle assigning heuristic with a starting time for each operation, as well as its predecessor operation in the job sequence. Zhang et al. [6] proposed a mixed integer linear programming model for the joint production and transportation scheduling in flexible manufacturing system (FMS) without considering the transportation tasks associated with each job from the lower and upper area to the machine. Fontes and Homayouni [7] established a new mixed integer linear programming model to solve the joint production transportation scheduling problem, which integrated the machine scheduling problem and the AGV scheduling problem, and used two sets of chain decision strategies (machine and AGV). Using the hybrid taboo bat algorithm, Yonglai et al. [8] carried out in-depth analysis on AGV material distribution scheduling and provided an effective solution for workshop material distribution scheduling by multiple AGVs under certain constraints. In addition, Liu et al. [9] also adopted the improved pollen algorithm to study the co-integration AGV manufacturing unit scheduling problem. Regarding the average delay in flexible manufacturing units with AGVs, Heger [10,11] studied the dynamic priority assignment rules of AGVs using sorting and routing rules. Xu and Guo [12] discussed the multi-objective and multi-dimensional green scheduling method of FMS with AGV by means of the evolutionary algorithm of segmented coding, and Zhang et al. [13] studied the AGV allocation problem for mixed-flow assembly lines considering the load capacity of AGVs. Umar et al. [14] considered the path conflict problem of AGV during transportation, and solved the problem with an improved genetic algorithm, but the algorithm has a long running time and low efficiency. Mousavi et al. [15] compared the genetic algorithm with the particle swarm algorithm that combined the multi-objective AGV scheduling in order to solve the proposed model in the flexible manufacturing system, which was different from the conventional intelligent algorithm Nouri et al. [16] proposed; a hybrid meta-heuristic algorithm based on the clustering multi-agent model, which simultaneously scheduled the machines and AGVs, treated AGVs as special machines for coding. Zhang et al. [17] proposed a two-stage solution approach and a particle sworn optimization method to solve an energy-efficient path planning model of a single-load AGV. The authors analyzed the AGV energy consumption characteristics by motion state and vehicle structure, where it was found that energy consumption was an independent optimization objective in AGV path planning.

The above research has effectively advanced the exploration of AGVs' participation in intelligent job scheduling. However, there are relatively few studies on the AGV charging problem in the workshop scheduling problem in the existing literature, and only a few experts and scholars have discussed the related issues. A typical example was given by Dehnavi et al. [18], who studied the optimization problem of AGV charging station location in manufacturing units through GAMES simulation. Zhengfeng and Yangyang [19] studied the job-shop workshop scheduling problem under the consideration of multiple charging AGVs. Wang et al. [20] studied an AGV scheduling method that integrated AGV energy consumption and workshop complexity. However, this type of research adopted the AGV to perform a task and then returned immediately, and did not perform the task continuously. This was not in line with the reality that the AGV could continue to perform transportation multiple times after being charged that directly affected the determination of the number and scale of AGVs in the workshop, their work efficiency, and its evaluation. Fazlollahtabar and Saidi-Mehrabad [21] examined literature related to different methodologies to optimize AGV systems for the problems of scheduling and routing at manufacturing, distribution, trans-shipment, and transportation systems. The authors categorized the methodologies into simulation studies, metaheuristic techniques, artificial intelligent, exact, and heuristics mathematical methods. Further, De Ryck et al. [22] overviewed a number of AGV-related control algorithms and techniques that were employed in not only the early stages of AGVs, but also the algorithms and techniques used in the most recent AGV-systems, as well as the algorithms and techniques with high potential.

Extant literature shows that experts and scholars have fully realized the significant role played by intelligent robots in the manufacturing industry, and have carried out research on the scheduling problem of flexible manufacturing cells with AGVs. The model realizes the solution to the problem and optimizes the scheduling optimization objective. However, the charging ability and continuous working ability of AGVs are rarely addressed in the model in literature. In particular, most of the existing literature assumes that the charging process is completed immediately and there is no waiting. Moreover, the selection of AGVs to transport workpieces is based purely on the customer's demand for completion time without regard to AGV priority, resulting in load imbalance in AGVs. Therefore, the calculation result is quite different from the actual scheduling AGV result, and sometimes a part of the workpieces cannot be completed according to customer demands. The load imbalance even caused some AGVs not to undertake any transportation tasks, but some AGVs are always in the working state. Then, the core question of research is: how to schedule AGVs to balance the distribution of transportation tasks and minimize the maximum completion time, while meeting customer demands, and considering the charging process and waiting time of AGVs?

Aiming to seek the marginal utility and load balance of AGV with charging, this paper studies the allocation and handling process scheduling problems of AGVs on the basis of FJSP. The AGV comprehensively considers factors such as workpiece scheduling, transportation task scheduling, scheduling priority, and charging constraints, to build models, and we solve these through genetic algorithms and complete use of AGV capabilities to obtain optimal production efficiency. To achieve this objective, we describe the problem and its formulation in Section 2. Further, algorithm development and solutions are given in Section 3. Section 4 presents numerical experiments followed by conclusion and future remarks in Section 5.

2. Mathematical Modelling

2.1. Problem Description

Given the number of machines, workpieces, and customer demands, the multi-AGV flexible manufacturing cell scheduling model explores the optimal distribution of multiple AGVs with charging, so as to complete all the processing tasks and minimize the final completion time of the manufacturing unit. In the model, AGVs must transport workpiece to machine according to the corresponding handling procedure. The total time consumption includes not only AGV transportation time and machine processing time, but also AGV charging time and waiting time. The problem of charging multiple AGVs in FJSP can be described as: there are n workpieces to be machined in a machining cell, expressed as $J = \{J_1, J_2, J_3, \ldots, J_n\}$, each workpiece $J_i(J_i \in J)$ has $p(p \geq 1)$ different machining operations. Each operation O_{ij} can be machined by an optional set of machines, the processing time of it is different for different operations $O_i(O_i \in O)$ of each workpiece. The processing time of the same process varies with the change of the machine, and the processing sequence of the workpiece has been specified in the process route file in advance. Workpiece J_i contains $p+1$ handling procedures T_{ij}, and the distance between each processing machine is measured by the AGV travel time. In the course of processing, k AGV handling robots $R = \{R_1, R_2, \ldots, R_k\}$ take out the workpiece blanks from the loading station and transport the workpiece J to m different machines $M = \{M_1, M_2, \ldots, M_m\}$ for processing until the last process of the workpiece is completed, and the AGV transports the processed workpiece to the unloading station. The AGV charging method is to stay and charge at the charging station. The charging time cannot be ignored; it affects the final scheduling decision. Therefore, the charging time is taken into account in the AGV's handling time. The issues that need to be considered are the selection of the processing machine where the process is located, the sequence of each process in the machine, and the

AGV allocation problem that considers charging. In order to build a multi-AGV flexible manufacturing cell scheduling model with charging, this paper introduces the symbol definitions in Table 1, and assumes the following conditions:

(1) The machine follows the principle of first-come, first-served. Each machine can process only one workpiece at a time, and each AGV can transport only workpiece for one operation at a time; (2) Each machine and workpiece have the same priority except for user requirements, and the processing and AGV transport process are uninterrupted; (3) There is a workpiece buffer area next to each machine. Ignoring the workpiece congestion, the buffer capacity is unlimited; (4) Ignore the time the AGV takes to load and unload workpieces in the warehouse or machine buffer; (5) Initially, the AGV position and the initial workpiece position are located in the loading station, and the workpieces that have completed all processes are placed in the unloading station; (6) If two adjacent processes of the same workpiece are in the same machine, the AGV handling resources will not be occupied; (7) The AGV handling speed remains unchanged during transportation, is not affected by the load, and does not consider path conflicts; (8) The difference between power consumption of the AGV with or without a load is not considered, the unit power consumption is fixed; and (9) After the AGV completes the handling of a process, if the power is less than the threshold, it returns to the charging pile for charging. When the power is greater than the threshold and meets the AGV to perform the handling task, it waits for the next handling task. The following table provides symbols that satisfy assumptions and model requirements.

Table 1. Symbol definitions.

Symbol	Description
$M_l, l \in \{1,2,\ldots,m\}$	Indicates the l-th processing machine, and the total number of processing machines is m.
$R_r, r \in \{1,2,\ldots,k\}$	Indicates the r-th AGV, the total number of AGV is k.
$J_i, C_i, i \in \{1,2,\ldots,n\}$	Indicates the i-th workpiece and the time of completion, and the total number of workpiece is n.
$O_{ij}, j \in \{1,2,\ldots,p\}$	Indicates the j-th processing operation of the i-th workpiece, and the maximum number of operations of the workpiece is p.
T_{ij}	Indicates the j-th delivery operation by AGV of the i-th workpiece, and the maximum transportation process of the workpiece is $p+1$.
t_{ijs}, t_{ije}	Machining process O_{ij} start time and end time.
τ_{je}	Latest finish time of the j-th processing operation required by customer.
T_{l-ij}	The processing time of the process O_{ij} in the processing machine M_l.
$R_{r-able}, R_{r-actual}$	Available time and actual power of the r-th AGV.
$T_{r-pos-M_{ij}}$	The time from the current position of the r-th AGV to the machine $M_{ij}(M_{ij} \in M_l)$ where O_{ij} is located.
$T_{r-pos-O_{ij}-\Delta}$	The time from the current position of the r-th AGV to loading station Δ where workpiece for O_{ij} is located.
$T_{r-O_{ij}-\Delta}$	The wait time of the r-th AGV at loading station Δ for O_{ij}.
$R_{r-total}$	The actual total travel time of the AGV to complete the transportation task (load + no load).
$R_{r-ijs}, R_{r-ije}, R_{r-ij}$	AGV start time, completion time, and time consumption of the transportation process T_{ij}.
U_{max}, U_{rt}	Maximum load of AGV, and the load of the r-th AGV at time t.
$\{U_{r1}, U_{r2}, \ldots, U_{rh}\}$ $\{U_{rt1}, U_{rt2}, \ldots, U_{rth}\}$	The transportation load sequences completed by the r-th AGV, and the completion time sequences of the corresponding transportation load.
$E_{rt}, E_{consumption}$	The battery power of the r-th AGV at time t, AGV energy consumption per unit time.
E_{max}, E_{min}	Battery maximum power, the minimum power that AGV can continue to work.

There are multiple AGVs in the manufacturing unit, and they stop working when the power stored in their batteries is exhausted, they are then required to be charged again. Therefore, it is necessary to define the available time parameters of the AGVs to ensure that when the AGVs are dispatched for handling, the AGVs are in the available state, not the charging state. The driving path of the AGV can be divided into three sections: the no-load time to the task location; the waiting time when waiting for the task profile to complete the previous process; and the time for the loaded profile to go to the destination machine. The waiting time is sometimes 0. Because the calculation of AGV power consumption is based on the driving power consumption, it is necessary to define the three states of AGV driving. The sum of the above three parts is the total time R_{r-ij} required to complete the task. In the case when waiting time is 0, there is $R_{r-ij} = R_{r-total}$.

Due to the flexibility of selecting machines for processing in FJSP, the decision variable $P_{ij}^{M_l}$ needs to be set. It means assigning machine M_l to complete the machining work of O_{ij}. Similarly, the handling task needs to assign one AGV from multiple AGVs to perform the task, so it is also necessary to define decision variables to specify the AGV to perform the work. The specific decision variable symbols and meanings are as follows:

$$\partial_{ij-i'j'}^{M} = \begin{cases} 1, O_{ij} \text{ is machined on the same machine before } O_{i'j'} \\ 0, else \end{cases}$$

$$\partial_{ij-i'j'}^{R} = \begin{cases} 1, T_{ij} \text{ is being transported by the same AGV before } T_{i'j'} \\ 0, else \end{cases}$$

$$P_{ij}^{M_l} = \begin{cases} 1, \text{Operation } O_{ij} \text{ is processed on machine } M_l \\ 0, else \end{cases}$$

$$P_{ij}^{R_r} = \begin{cases} 1, \text{Conveying process } T_{ij} \text{ is transported by AGV}(R_r) \\ 0, else \end{cases}$$

2.2. Model Formulations

The multi-AGV flexible manufacturing cell scheduling considering charging problem is actually a typical Flexible Job-shop Scheduling Problem. Because of the continuity of the system, it is not suitable to be solved by Mixed Integer Linear Programming or Multi-stage Stochastic Programming. Considering the complexity of Deep Q-learning in the calculation of partial derivatives, we employed Multivariate Nonlinear Programming, so as to comprehensively describe system constraints and process status. The scheduling objective is to minimize the maximum time cost of production. The completion time of the last process of the workpiece is t_{ipe}, then the objective function that can be expressed as:

$$f = \min_{1 \leq i \leq n}(\max(C_i)) \tag{1}$$

The flexible manufacturing cell scheduling constraints considering multi-AGV charging are:

$$C_i \geq t_{ips} + T_{l-ij} + T_{r-l-u}, R_{r-i(j+1)s} \geq t_{ijs} + T_{l-ij}, t_{i(j+1)s} \geq R_{r-ijs} + R_{r-ij} \tag{2}$$

$$\partial_{ij-i'j'}^{M_l} + \partial_{i'j'-ij}^{M_l} = 1, \sum_{M_l \in (M_1, M_2, \cdots, M_m)} P_{ij}^{M_l} = 1 \tag{3}$$

$$t_{ijs} + T_{l-ij} \leq t_{i'j's} + (1 - \partial_{ij-i'j'}^{M_l}) \times Q, P_{ij}^{M_l} \times P_{i'j'}^{M_l} \times (t_{i'j's} + T_{l-i'j'}) \leq t_{ijs} + \partial_{ij-i'j'}^{M_l} \times Q \tag{4}$$

$$\partial_{ij-i'j'}^{R_r} + \partial_{i'j'-ij}^{R_r} = 1 \tag{5}$$

$$R_{r-ijs} + R_{r-ij} \leq R_{r-i'j's} + (1 - \partial_{ij-i'j'}^{R_r}) \times Q, P_{ij}^{R_r} \times P_{i'j'}^{R_r} \times (R_{r-i'j's} + R_{r-i'j'}) \leq t_{ijs} + \partial_{ij-i'j'}^{R_r} \times Q \tag{6}$$

$$\sum_{R_r \in (R_1, R_2, \cdots, R_k)} P_{ij}^{R_r} = 1 \tag{7}$$

$$R_{r-ijs} = \max \left\{ R_{r-able} + T_{r-pos-M_{i(j-1)}}, t_{i(j-1)e} \right\} \tag{8}$$

$$R_{r-ije} = R_{r-ijs} + R_{r-ij} \tag{9}$$

$$R_{r-ij} = T_{agv} \times (R_{r-able} + T_{r-pos-M_{i(j-1)}} - t_{i(j-1)e}) + T_{r-O_{ij}-\Delta} + T_{r-M_{i(j-1)}-M_{ij}}$$

$$T_{agv} = \begin{cases} -1, R_{r-able} + T_{r-pos-M_{i(j-1)}} < t_{i(j-1)e} \\ 0, \text{else} \end{cases} \tag{10}$$

$$R_{r-total} = T_{r-pos-O_{ij}-\Delta} + T_{r-O_{ij}-\Delta} + T_{r-\Delta-M_{ij}} \tag{11}$$

$$R_{r-actual} = E_{\max} - (R_{r-total} \times E_{average}), R_{r-ct} = (E_{\max} - R_{r-actual})/E_v \tag{12}$$

$$\Theta_r = \Theta \times \frac{1}{\sum_{U_{rth} \leq t} U_{rh} + 1} \times \frac{E_{rt}}{E_{\max} - E_{\min}} \tag{13}$$

$$\Omega_r = \Omega \times T_{r-O_{ij}-\Delta} \times \tau_{je} \times \frac{E_{\max} - E_{\min}}{E_{rt}} \tag{14}$$

$$\forall t_{ije} \leq \tau_{je}, \forall t_{ijs} \leq R_{r-ije}, \forall U_{rt} \leq U_{\max} \tag{15}$$

$$\forall E_{rt} \leq E_{\max}, \forall E_{rt} \geq E_{\min} \tag{16}$$

$$[(\forall R_{r-ijs}(r \in R_r)) \cap (\neg \exists R_{r'-ijs}(r' \in R_r))] \cap [\neg \exists r \neq r'(T_{r-O_{ij}-\Delta} = T_{r'-O_{ij}-\Delta})] \tag{17}$$

$$i \in \{1, 2, \ldots, n\}, j \in \{1, 2, \ldots, p\}, r \in \{1, 2, \ldots, k\} \tag{18}$$

In the above inequalities and equations, constraint (2) represents the process sequence constraint of the same workpiece, which means that the maximum completion time of the workpiece is jointly constrained by the start processing time of the last process, the processing time, and the AGV handling time, and the AGV start handling time must be greater than the completion time of the previous process. Equation (3) represents the constraints of processing machine resources, requiring that one machine can process only one workpiece at a time, and the workpiece can be allocated to only one machine for processing. Here, Q is a positive integer that represents the elasticity of the system. Equation (4) indicates that the two machining processes on the same machine satisfy the sequence relationship. Equations (5)–(12) represent the AGV resource constraints, where Equation (5) indicates that an AGV can handle only one workpiece at a time, and Equation (6) indicates that the two handling processes completed by the same AGV satisfy the sequence relationship. Equation (7) means that a workpiece can be transported by only one AGV at a time. Equation (8) indicates that the start time of the AGV is constrained by the available time of the AGV, the time from the AGV to the processing equipment of the previous process, and the completion time of the previous process of the workpiece. Formula (9) indicates that the completion time of the AGV handling task is constrained by the time when the AGV starts to transport and the time from the current position to the processing machine. Equation (10) indicates that the actual transportation time is constrained by the available time of the AGV, the current position of the AGV, the start position of the transportation, and the completion time of the previous process. Equation (11) represents the constraint on the total transportation time of the AGV. Equation (12) represents the constraint on the actual power of the AGV and the charging time of the AGV. Equation (13) represents the priority of selecting the AGV, which is composed of two parts, one is the load size of the completed task, and the other is the current power situation. To achieve load balancing, the AGV with sufficient power and small historical load is preferentially selected to undertake transportation task. Θ is a constant for equivalent conversion. Equation (14) represents the priority of the AGV loading workpiece for O_{ij}. The AGV with earlier completion time and arrival time, and smaller power, has a higher priority for loading workpiece and a lower wait time. Here, Ω is a constant for equivalent conversion. Equation (15) indicates the time constraint and load constraint of any processing operation required by the customer. Equation (16) indicates the power constraint on which the AGV can continue to work. Equation (17) indicates the constraint to avoid deadlocks. The AGV must exclusively serve the operation O_{ij} in order. At the same time, only one AGV can serve one operation, and only one AGV can pick up workpiece for an operation from loading station. Equation (18) are the space sizes of all entities in the system.

3. Solution Algorithms

The scheduling problem of flexible manufacturing units with AGVs considering charging can be divided into three sub-problems, namely, assigning processes to machines, sequencing processes assigned to each machine, and AGV allocation for transportation tasks. Ant Colony Algorithm, Gray Wolf Algorithm, and Deep Learning Network, is applied to obtain optimal strategy, but all of these received local solutions. However, Genetic Algorithm is more inclined to global search, which can quickly retrieve all feasible solutions and prevent the convergence of local optimal solutions too fast. Thus, aiming at the above three problems, this paper introduces the elite retention strategy and uses the genetic algorithm to solve it. First, all feasible solutions are divided into three segments of chromosomes: process, machine, and the AGV, then the population is obtained after initialization, and then decoding is performed after performing crossover and mutation. Finally, the fitness value is calculated to complete the selection until it reaches the threshold of the number of iterations. The core algorithm part is as follows.

3.1. Coding and Initialization

3.1.1. Encoding Operation

The genetic algorithm involves three segments of chromosome coding: process coding, machine coding, and AGV coding. The process code describes the sequence of the production process, and its gene length is $L_1 = \sum_{i=1}^{n} (P_i + 1)$. The machine code indicates the processing machine where the process of each workpiece is located, and the length of the gene string is $L_2 = \sum_{i=1}^{n} P_i$. The AGV code corresponds to the task code, and the length of the gene string is the length of the AGV task code string. For example, in the code shown in Figure 1, process codes are sorted from left to right, the first number 3 represents the first process of workpiece No. 3, and the fourth number 2 represents the workpiece No. 2. The fifth number 3 of the machine code indicates that the second process of the workpiece No. 2 is processed by machine No. 3, and the tenth number 4 indicates that the unloading task is virtualized by the virtual equipment, that is, the unloading station. The fourth number of the AGV code is 1. The fourth task representing the process code, that is, the second process of workpiece No. 2, is transported by the AGV numbered 1. If the handling process is assigned to the corresponding AGV code, a sequence with process handling will be generated: $(O_{31}, M_3, T_{1-03}), (O_{11}, M_1, T_{2-01}), (O_{21}, M_2, T_{2-02})$, The corresponding handling time series is [1, 1, 3].

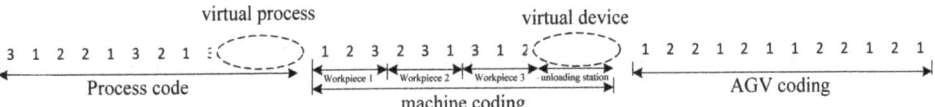

Figure 1. Individual coding gene string.

3.1.2. Initialization Operation

During initialization, depending upon the requirement of minimizing the maximum completion time, the machine with the shortest processing time is selected with a probability of 0.2, and the AGV code is initialized according to the principle of uniform distribution to balance the usage efficiency of the AGV and avoid idleness. After obtaining the fitness according to the objective function, the roulette method is used to select individuals from the population of size N. The probability that individual i can be retained for the next generation is related to the fitness value f_i, and the probability is $p_i = f_i / \sum_{i=1}^{N} f_i$. In addition, considering that after a series of genetic manipulations in the parent generation, individuals with high fitness have a certain probability of being eliminated, which may lead to a decrease in the average fitness of the group. To this end, we use an elite retention strategy to ensure the top 10% of the parent population do not participate in crossover and mutation. When there are multiple optimal solutions at the same time, the overall handling time of the AGV is used as the second evaluation criterion to calculate the total running time $\sum_{i=1}^{k} R_{r-total}$ of the AGV. The individuals are sorted in sequence according to formula: $F = F + 0.0001 \times \sum_{i=1}^{k} R_{r-total}$, and the individual with the smallest AGV total running time is taken as the optimal solution. After participating in the crossover mutation, a new species population of size P excepting the elite is generated, and then 10% of the worst solutions are replaced with the optimal solution stored by the parent population to maintain the next generation of the parent population and ensure excellent genetic continuity and diversity.

3.2. Crossover and Mutation Operations

3.2.1. Crossover Operation

The interleaving operation of the process code uses the POX method. Select all processes for a certain workpiece from the parent P1, keep the positions of all processes of the workpiece unchanged on the chromosome, and keep them separate from the child individual C1. Randomly generate the parent P2, and encode the parent individual P2. (Except for the process selected in the previous step). Fill in the blank positions of C1 in turn. Similarly, the corresponding parts of P1 and P2 are combined in order to obtain the offspring individual C2. As shown in Figure 2a, all processes of workpiece 3 in the parent P1 are randomly selected and inherited to the offspring C1, and are kept in the position in the gene string remains unchanged. Then, all the processes of the parent P2, except for workpiece 3, are sequentially filled in the remaining gene string vacancies of the offspring C1 to form a complete offspring C1. Similarly, the remaining parts of P1 and P2 can be merged. The offspring C2 is obtained. The crossover selection of machine gene strings is operated using the Multi-point Preservative Crossover (MPX) method, which is used for machine crossover for chromosome process assignment, and the process order is reserved for the offspring, as shown in Figure 2b. For the parent gene string P1 And P2, the randomly generated 0_1 sequence, exchange the genes located at positions 2, 5, 6, 8, and 12, of the chromosome, and cross to generate offspring C1 and C2, that is, 1 corresponds to the same position of the parent P1 and P2 and the rest of the positions remain unchanged. The crossover of the AGV gene string is consistent with the MPX crossover method of the machine gene string. As shown in Figure 2c, the genes at positions 3, 6, 8, 10, and 12 are exchanged.

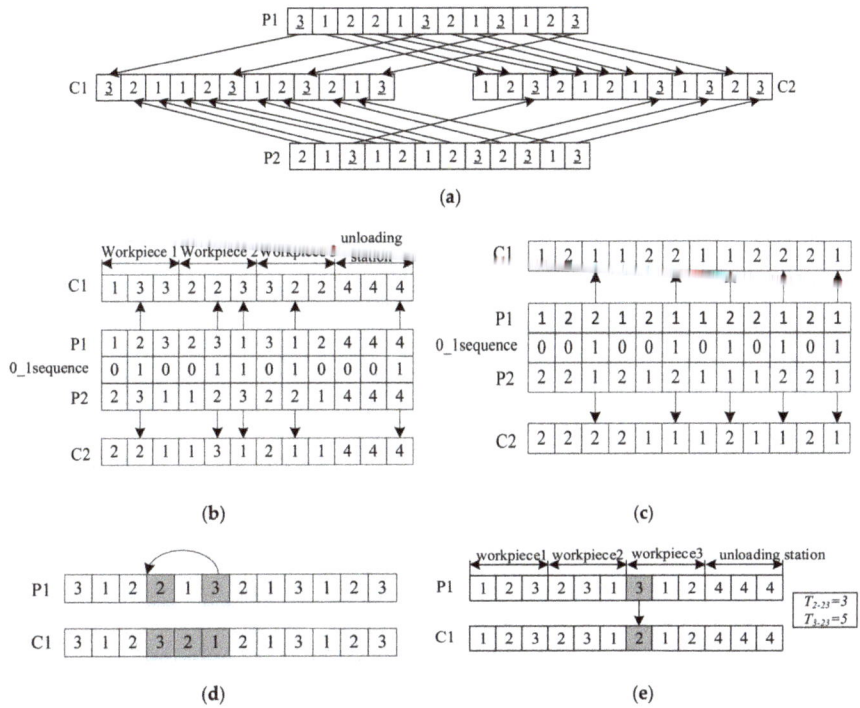

Figure 2. Chromosome crossover operation and mutation operation. (**a**) POX crossover operation of process code; (**b**) MPX interleaving operation of machine code; (**c**) MPX crossover operation of AGV code; (**d**) Mutation operation of process code; (**e**) Mutation operation of machine code.

3.2.2. Mutation Operation

For process code, the extended insertion mutation method is adopted, that is, a gene at a given position is randomly selected in the chromosome encoded by the process, and it is randomly inserted into another position in the chromosome under the constraint that the sequence of processes of the same workpiece is fixed. The sequence of the gene after the insertion is set back one space. As shown in Figure 2d, insert the second process of workpiece No. 3 at chromosome position 6 of parent P1 into the second process of workpiece No. 2 at chromosome position 4, the second process of workpiece 2 originally at position 4. The process needs to be moved one bit backwards. As shown in Figure 2e, the mutation operation of the machine code randomly selects one of the two machine codes, and selects the machine with the shortest processing time in the machine group. The gene at position 7 is replaced, that is, the processing machine of the first process of workpiece 3 is replaced, and the original processing machine No. 3 and processing time 5 are mutated into processing machine No. 2 and processing time 3. The AGV coding mutation operation is the same as the machine coding. For example, the AGV No. 1 at position 6 in the parent P1 chromosome is randomly selected according to the probability, and replaced by AGV No. 2, and the feasible solution progeny C1 for handling the AGV is obtained.

3.3. Fit Function and Decoding

The fitness function solved by the genetic algorithm for scheduling of multi-AGV flexible manufacturing units considering charging is $f = \max_{1 \leq i \leq n}(C_i)$, the maximum completion time. The smaller the f is, the better is the individual. The decoding operation of chromosomes is actually the process of converting chromosomes into feasible solutions for scheduling, which can obtain the process profile, the machine used in the process and its processing time, the AGV trolley transported, and its handling time, etc.

Step 1: Select a process chromosome from the process and machine code in turn to judge the task type, convert it into the corresponding process O_{ij}; the machine M_l corresponding to the process; the corresponding processing time T_{l-ij} and the completion time $t_{i(j-1)e}$ of the previous process $O_{i(j-1)}$ in the machine.

Step 2: Obtain the transportation task sequence T_{ij}, and the transportation start point (L or machine), end point (U or machine) and transportation time.

Step 3: Read the AGV chromosome code in sequence, obtain the AGV status information, and assign the handling tasks to the corresponding AGVs in sequence.

Step 4: Calculate the time $T_{r-pos-M_{i(j-1)}}$ from the AGV to the starting point of the handling task and the time R_{r-ijs} when the transportation starts, update time R_{r-ij} it takes for the AGV to handle the j process of Profile i, and calculate the total transportation time $R_{r-total}$, current actual power $R_{r-actual}$, and available time R_{r-able} for the AGV to perform each handling task.

Step 5: Based on the AGV status information, see whether the actual power of the AGV is less than the threshold; if it is less than the threshold, it will be charged at the loading station L, and calculate the charging time R_{r-ct}, and then update the available time R_{r-able} of the AGV.

4. Analysis of Examples

In order to verify the performance of the model and the algorithm, genetic algorithm and MATLAB programming are used to solve the FJSP 10×8 problem, FJSP 15×8 problem and FJSP 25 × 8 problem. We conduct hyper-parameter fine-tuning by GeatPy. Based on Values Exchanged Recombination and Mutation for Binary Chromosomes, the automated machine learning method is applied to obtain the optimal crossover and mutation operation probabilities. With the constructed field vector, objective vector, and fitness vector, we use the Elite Copy Selection method for fitness selection, and use the constraint violation value matrix to store the degree of individual violation constraints. After 1628 times evolution by Evolution Tracker, we acquire the parameters, as shown in Table 2. In addition, to reduce the problem scale, the maximum battery power is set to 100, the power threshold to 10, the number of charging piles to 1, the power consumption per unit time to 2, and the AGV charging rate to 6.

Table 2. The parameters of the algorithm model.

Parameters	Values
maximum battery power	100
power threshold	10
power consumption	2
AGV charging rate	6
population size	100
iteration threshold	10,000
mutation probability	0.208
crossover probability	0.846

4.1. Analysis of Results

According to the conversion time of 1:5, that is, one unit of time represents 5 min, we input the resource list and routing list according to the customer order. The final completion time of the manufacturing unit is optimally 227.5 min, which is about 3.79 h. The specific experimental results are shown in Figure 3. The black line in the figure is the driving path of AGV No. 1, and the red line is the driving path of AGV No. 2. The maximum completion time of the 10 × 8 scale case is a minimum of 45.5. The final completion time is measured by AGV removing all the workpieces. The production planning department can determine an appropriate time for different batches of production orders and draw actual schedules according to the scheduling plan. In the 10 × 8 calculation example, the two AGVs did not reach the power threshold, so the charging state wherein the AGV cannot be used does not appear in the Gantt chart. However, after the AGV completes the previous task and the handling time is greater than 90 units of time, it will fall below the power threshold and shall need to stop work for charging. In the case of 15 × 8 scale, the two AGVs reached the power threshold once and in the case of 20 × 8 scale, the two AGVs reached the power threshold twice. In both cases, the charging wait time is 0 and all transportation tasks are completed. However, in the 25 × 8 scale case, the charging wait time is 6 with all tasks completed. AGV1 reached the power threshold three times, and AGV2 reached the power threshold twice in this case. It means that the AGVs need to be recharged five times in total, which takes 438.06 units of time. Here, the current powers of AGVs when they go to charge are 11.25, 12.08, 12.67, 12.90, and 13.04, respectively. Although the current powers of the AGVs are higher than the minimum power E_{min}, they have to be charged because they cannot complete a single transportation task. Obviously, the larger the number of transportation tasks for workpieces, the more AGV charging times, and the longer the waiting time. From the perspective of AGV load, AGV1 and AGV2 each completed 17 transportation tasks in the case 10 × 8 scale, that is, the load balance ratio reaches the optimal state of value of 0. The load balance ratio is defined as $(\Psi_{max} - \Psi_{min})/\Psi_{avg}$. Here, Ψ_{max}, Ψ_{min} and Ψ_{avg} are the maximum, minimum, and average number of tasks completed by AGVs. As for the cases of 15 × 8 scale, 20 × 8 scale, and 25 × 8 scale, the load balance ratios are all less than 0.100, which are 0.074, 0.057, and 0.071, respectively. This shows that our model can effectively avoid AGV resource waste while meeting customer demands.

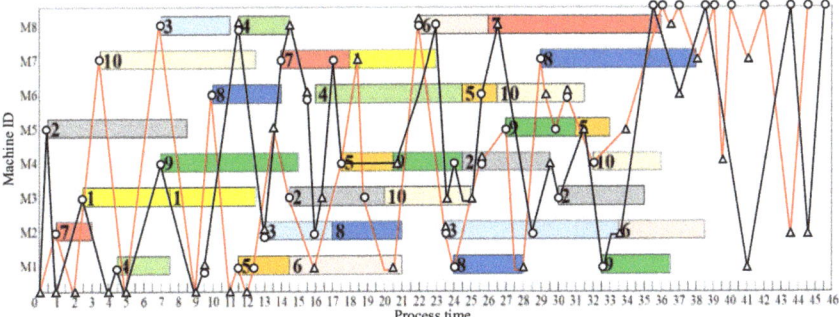

Figure 3. FJSP Gantt chart with 2 AGVs.

In general, the final completion time of manufacturing unit increases with the size of the problem. As shown in Table 3, when the number of AGVs is sufficient, the completion time grows in proportion to the problem scale. On average, for every 10 additional customer demands, the completion time increases by no more than 40 according to calculation examples. In contrast, if the number of AGVs is too small, the completion time will increase extremely with problem scale, and even some demands cannot be accomplished on time, as shown in the data marked with "*" in Table 3. Only if the AGVs exceeds 4 can all the problems of different scales from 20 × 8 to 100 × 8 be solved. Obviously, increasing the number of AGVs will improve the ability to solve problems. As the amount of AGVs increases exponentially, the completion time first decreases rapidly and then becomes stable. For example, in the case of 80 × 8 scale problem, when the number of AGVs is doubled from 1 to 32 successively, the completion time is improved by 128.57, 85.46, 50.07, 24.45, and 21.49, respectively. This shows that blindly increasing AGVs cannot significantly improve the scheduling effect, but will cause part of the AGVs to be idle. It can be found that when the number of AGVs exceeds 1/5 of the scale of workpieces, the improvement space of completion time is very small. In this case, each additional AGV reduces the completion time by a maximum of 3.17 unites. In order to obtain a more reasonable AGV fleet size, the marginal utility of the AGV is discussed in Section 4.2.

Table 3. Final completion time under different scales of problem and number of AGVs.

Number of AGVs	Scale of FJSP Problem									
	10 × 8	20 × 8	30 × 8	40 × 8	50 × 8	60 × 8	70 × 8	80 × 8	90 × 8	100 × 8
1	66.47	148.50	215.09 *	282.54 *	367.97 *	436.58 *	487.95 *	580.10 *	778.69 *	990.64 *
2	45.50	102.60	148.75	199.63	238.43 *	287.11 *	342.72 *	451.53 *	581.27 *	751.48 *
4	40.50	83.75	126.28	178.41	212.57	268.36	314.48	366.07	427.50 *	627.31 *
8	35.50	78.15	113.60	151.66	184.41	235.08	264.19	316.00	372.09	554.80
16	34.00	70.30	105.35	142.17	175.85	215.50	251.34	291.55	341.18	460.75
32	34.00	70.30	105.35	142.17	175.85	215.50	251.34	270.06	312.30	448.95

"*" means some demands cannot be accomplished on time.

4.2. AGV Marginal Utility

The number of AGVs is closely related to transportation allocation, and it also has a greater impact on optimization goals. Usually, the AGV is subject to transportation constraints and a dedicated AGV is equipped for various workpieces, but it may increase the cost of the enterprise. In order to deeply study the marginal utility of AGVs, this paper selects 10 × 8 examples, takes different numbers of AGVs, and calculates the data 10 times. The results are shown in Table 4. When its number is about 20% of the number of workpieces, the optimization effect is prominent and appears as an inflection point. On the contrary, the optimization effect gradually decreases. The reason for the inflection point is that when the AGV input is less than 20% of the number of workpieces, the turnover between the AGV and workpiece is complicated, and the AGV needs more. It takes at least 15 units of time to charge during the next shutdown. It can be seen that AGV transportation and charging greatly affects production efficiency. When the number of AGVs is greater than 80% of the number of workpieces, although a better solution is achieved, the optimal performance remains unchanged and the economic cost increases. Enterprises can assign AGVs according to the economic situation of the workshop and planning of the completion time. As shown in Tables 3 and 4, when the number of AGVs is greater than 2/5 of the number of workpieces, the marginal utility by increasing the AGV is less than 2.5. It means that when the AGV is 40% of the workpieces, the optimal schedule is almost reached and it is uneconomical to increase the number of AGVs again. Thus, according to the results of different scales and considering the fixed cost of AGVs, it is recommended that the number of AGVs should account for 20–40% of the scale of the workpieces, and the marginal utility is the most reasonable.

Table 4. AGV marginal utility.

Number of AGVs	1	2	3	4	5	6	7	8	9	10
AGV/workpiece (percentage)	10%	20%	30%	40%	50%	60%	70%	80%	90%	100%
Final completion time	66.47	45.50	43.00	40.50	38.50	37.00	36.00	35.50	34.00	34.00
Marginal utility	—	20.97	2.50	2.50	2.00	1.50	1.00	0.50	0.50	0

4.3. AGV Load and Charging

In order to verify the optimization of our model on the charging process and load balance, we conducted experiments in the case of 100 × 8 scale. The rapid increase in the scale of the problem makes it difficult to complete all transportation tasks when AGVs are insufficient. As shown in Table 5, while the number of AGVs is 1 and 2, respectively, 4 customer demands and 3 customer demands are uncompleted on time. Until the AGV exceeds 4, all the workpiece transportation tasks can be effectively completed. Thereafter, as the number of AGVs increases, the total charging times decreases almost exponentially and the waiting time drops sharply. When all transportation tasks are completed, the average wait time remains between 4 and 6. This indicates that the AVGs are effectively scheduled to accomplish all tasks, while maximizing the reduction of charging times and charging wait time. Especially when the AGVs exceeds 8, the charging times tend to be flat, and the utility brought by increasing AGV is not obvious. From the perspective of the AGV load, the load balance ratio is always less than 0.25, which means that the difference between the maximum and minimum load is less than 1/4 of the average load. This indicates that the loads of different AGVs are similar and tend to be balanced. In addition, the load balance ratio shows a bell-shaped trend of increasing first and then decreasing. The inflection point occurs when AGVs is 8, where the minimum load of AGVs changes by 20.7% and the maximum load of AGVs changes by only 17.3%. It means that when the charging times of AGVs do not decrease dramatically, the loads of AGVs will gradually become balanced based on scheduling priority. Furthermore, the rational load balance of AGVs is achieved when the charging times remains stable (the number of AGVs is greater than 12). That is, when considering charging, multi-AGV flexible manufacturing cell scheduling can assist decision makers to select a reasonable number of AGVs through simulation to meet the needs of all customers, reduce the charging times, and promote load balance.

Table 5. AGV load and charging.

Number of AGVs	1	2	4	6	8	10	12	14	16	18
Total waiting time for charging	421.28	109.46	57.88	38.61	21.05	15.20	11.92	8.90	0	0
Total charging times of AGVs	45	23	14	8	6	3	2	2	2	0
Maximum load of AGVs	362	186	132	98	81	69	55	48	43	39
Minimum load of AGVs	362	176	114	82	65	57	47	42	38	35
Average load of AGVs	362	181	121	91	72	60	52	45	40	36
Load balance ratio	0.000	0.055	0.149	0.177	0.221	0.199	0.155	0.133	0.124	0.110
Uncompleted demands on time	4	3	1	0	0	0	0	0	0	0

5. Conclusions

AGVs are powered by batteries, they move along the planned path, and have automatic guidance equipment such as magnetic strips, rails, or lasers, which can assist the workshop to complete a series of transportation tasks, providing a strong support for intelligent manufacturing enterprises to reduce the time consumption of the production process. Considering the influence of the available number of AGVs, the power threshold, and the charging time in the workshop scheduling, we adopted minimization of the maximum completion time as the optimization objective, and have constructed a multi-AGV flexible manufacturing unit scheduling model considering charging. The genetic algorithm was used to solve the problem, and the optimized process arrangement, the AGV driving path, and the scheduling plan after the AGV reached the power threshold were obtained, which further confirmed the impact of AGV transportation and charging on production efficiency. Compared with the models given in the literature [18,19], our model more comprehensively considers the charging time and charging waiting. The AGV scheduling priority is also designed to drive AGV load balance. The AGV with earlier completion time, arrival time, and smaller power, has a higher priority for loading workpiece and a lower wait time. To achieve load balancing, the AGV with sufficient power and a small historical load is preferentially selected to undertake the transportation task. After analyzing the marginal utility of the AGV under different problem scales, the results shows that the AGVs are effectively scheduled to complete transportation tasks, while reducing the charging times and charging wait time. It is clear that AGV utilization can be maximized when the number of AGV scales is 20–40% of the number of workpieces. Furthermore, the scheduling model of multi-AGV flexible manufacturing cell when considering charging can help decision makers minimize the maximum completion time by simulation, and seek load balance, while meeting customer demands. The limitations of the model research in this paper are as follows: (1) considering the complexity of research caused by diverse workpiece weights, we ignored the time-consuming differences generated by AGV loads in order to simplify model building; and (2) the objective function focuses on the final completion time cost of manufacturing unit without considering the fixed cost of the AGV. Therefore, future research can try to establish a multi-objective nonlinear programming model including time cost and fixed cost, and discuss the influence of different loads on AGV power consumption.

Author Contributions: Conceptualization, J.L. and W.C.; methodology, W.C.; software, W.C.; validation, J.L. and W.C.; formal analysis, J.L. and W.C.; investigation, W.C.; resources, W.C.; data curation, W.C.; writing—original draft preparation, W.C.; writing—review and editing, J.L., K.K.L. and B.R.; visualization, W.C.; supervision, K.K.L. and B.R. All authors have read and agreed to the published version of the manuscript.

Funding: This research received no external funding.

Data Availability Statement: The program code and data that support the plots discussed within this paper are available from the corresponding author upon request.

Conflicts of Interest: The authors declare no conflict of interest.

References

1. Lacomme, P.; Larabi, M.; Tchernev, N. Job-shop based framework for simultaneous scheduling of machines and automated guided vehicles. *Int. J. Prod. Econ.* **2013**, *143*, 24–34. [CrossRef]
2. Wu, N.; Zhou, M. Modeling and deadlock control of automated guided vehicle systems. *IEEE/ASME Trans. Mechatron.* **2004**, *9*, 50–57.
3. Fu, J.; Zhang, H.; Zhang, J.; Jiang, L. Review on AGV Scheduling Optimization. *J. Syst. Simul.* **2020**, *32*, 1664.
4. Bilge, Ü.; Ulusoy, G. A time window approach to simultaneous scheduling of machines and material handling system in an FMS. *Oper. Res.* **1995**, *43*, 1058–1070. [CrossRef]
5. Abdelmaguid, T.F.; Nassef, A.O.; Kamal, B.A.; Hassan, M.F. A hybrid GA/heuristic approach to the simultaneous scheduling of machines and automated guided vehicles. *Int. J. Prod. Res.* **2004**, *42*, 267–281. [CrossRef]
6. Zhang, Q.; Manier, H.; Manier, M.A. A genetic algorithm with tabu search procedure for flexible job shop scheduling with transportation constraints and bounded processing times. *Comput. Oper. Res.* **2012**, *39*, 1713–1723. [CrossRef]
7. Fontes, D.; Homayouni, S.M. Joint production and transportation scheduling in flexible manufacturing systems. *J. Glob. Optim.* **2019**, *74*, 879–908. [CrossRef]
8. Yonglai, W.; Wei, L.; Yanyan, L. Research on AGV Material Delivery Scheduling Problem Based on Hybrid Tabu Bat Algorithm. *Modul. Mach. Tool Autom. Manuf. Tech.* **2018**, *1*, 145–149.
9. Liu, E.H.; Yao, X.F.; Tao, T.; Jin, H. Improved flower pollination algorithm for job shop scheduling problems integrated with AGVs. *Comput. Integr. Manuf. Syst.* **2019**, *25*, 2219–2236.
10. Heger, J.; Voss, T. Reducing mean tardiness in a flexible job shop containing AGVs with optimized combinations of sequencing and routing rules. *Procedia CIRP* **2019**, *81*, 1136–1141. [CrossRef]
11. Heger, J.; Voß, T. Dynamic priority based dispatching of AGVs in flexible job shops. *Procedia CIRP* **2019**, *79*, 445–449. [CrossRef]
12. Xu, W.; Guo, S. A multi-objective and multi-dimensional optimization scheduling method using a hybrid evolutionary algorithms with a sectional encoding mode. *Sustainability* **2019**, *11*, 1329. [CrossRef]
13. Zhang, L.; Hu, Y.; Guan, Y. Research on hybrid-load AGV dispatching problem for mixed-model automobile assembly line. *Procedia CIRP* **2019**, *81*, 1059–1064. [CrossRef]
14. Umar, U.A.; Ariffin, M.K.A.; Ismail, N.; Tang, S.H. Hybrid multiobjective genetic algorithms for integrated dynamic scheduling and routing of jobs and automated-guided vehicle (AGV) in flexible manufacturing systems (FMS) environment. *Int. J. Adv. Manuf. Technol.* **2015**, *81*, 2123–2141. [CrossRef]
15. Mousavi, M.; Yap, H.J.; Musa, S.N.; Tahriri, F.; Md Dawal, S.Z. Multi-objective AGV scheduling in an FMS using a hybrid of genetic algorithm and particle swarm optimization. *PLoS ONE* **2017**, *12*, e0169817. [CrossRef] [PubMed]
16. Nouri, H.E.; Driss, O.B.; Ghédira, K. Simultaneous scheduling of machines and transport robots in flexible job shop environment using hybrid metaheuristics based on clustered holonic multiagent model. *Comput. Ind. Eng.* **2016**, *102*, 488–501. [CrossRef]
17. Zhang, Z.; Wu, L.; Zhang, W.; Peng, T.; Zheng, J. Energy-efficient path planning for a single-load automated guided vehicle in a manufacturing workshop. *Comput. Ind. Eng.* **2021**, *158*, 107397. [CrossRef]
18. Dehnavi, A.S.; Sabaghian, A.; Fazli, M. A Job shop scheduling and location of battery charging storage for the automated guided vehicles (AGVs). *J. Optim. Ind. Eng.* **2019**, *12*, 121–129.
19. Zhengfeng, L.; Yangyang, L. Research on job shop scheduling with multiple AGVs considering charging. *Comput. Integr. Manuf. Syst.* **2021**, *27*, 2872–2879.

20. Wang, F.; Zhang, Y.; Su, Z. A novel scheduling method for automated guided vehicles in workshop environments. *Int. J. Adv. Robot. Syst.* **2019**, *16*, 1729881419844152. [CrossRef]
21. Fazlollahtabar, H.; Saidi-Mehrabad, M. Methodologies to optimize automated guided vehicle scheduling and routing problems: A review study. *J. Intell. Robot. Syst.* **2015**, *77*, 525–545. [CrossRef]
22. De Ryck, M.; Versteyhe, M.; Debrouwere, F. Automated guided vehicle systems, state-of-the-art control algorithms and techniques. *J. Manuf. Syst.* **2020**, *54*, 152–173. [CrossRef]

Article

Cloud-Edge-Terminal-Based Synchronized Decision-Making and Control System for Municipal Solid Waste Collection and Transportation

Ming Wan [1,2,3], Ting Qu [1,3,4,*], Manna Huang [1,2,3], Xiaohua Qiu [1,2,3], George Q. Huang [1,3,5], Jinfu Zhu [6] and Junrong Chen [7]

1. GBA and B&R International Joint Research Center for Smart Logistics, Jinan University, Zhuhai 519070, China
2. School of Management, Jinan University, No.601 Huangpu Avenue West, Guangzhou 510632, China
3. Institute of Physical Internet, Jinan University (Zhuhai Campus), No.206 Qianshan Road, Zhuhai 519070, China
4. School of Intelligent Systems Science and Engineering, Jinan University (Zhuhai Campus), No.206 Qianshan Road, Zhuhai 519070, China
5. Department Industrial and Manufacturing Systems Engineering, The University of Hong Kong, Pokfulam Road, Hong Kong, China
6. Gongbei Street Office, 123 Gangchang Road, Xiangzhou District, Zhuhai 519020, China
7. Zhuhai Top Cloud Tech Co., Ltd., No.2021, Qianshan Mingzhu South Road, Xiangzhou District, Zhuhai 519070, China
* Correspondence: quting@jnu.edu.cn

Abstract: Due to dynamics caused by factors such as random collection and transportation requirements, vehicle failures, and traffic jams, it is difficult to implement regular waste collection and transportation schemes effectively. A challenge for the stable operation of the municipal solid waste collection and transportation (MSWCT) system is how to obtain the whole process data in real time, dynamically judge the process control requirements, and effectively promote the synchronization operation between multiple systems. Based on this situation, this study proposes a cloud-edge-terminal-based synchronization decision-making and control system for MSWCT. First, smart terminals and edge computing devices are deployed at key nodes of MSWCT for real-time collection and edge computing analysis of the whole process data. Second, we propose a collaborative analysis and distributed decision-making method based on the cloud-edge-terminal multi-level computing architecture. Finally, a "three-level and two-stage" synchronization decision-making mechanism for the MSWCT system is established, which enables the synchronization operation between various subsystems. With a real-world application case, the efficiency and effectiveness of the proposed decision-making and control system are evaluated based on real data of changes in fleet capacity and transportation costs.

Keywords: municipal solid waste; waste classification; waste logistics; waste collection and transportation; IoT; cloud-edge collaboration; synchronization

MSC: 00A06

1. Introduction

Waste classification is an efficient way for municipal solid waste management under the circular economy. It aims to maximize the value of recycling waste and achieve zero waste [1]. The municipal solid waste collection and transportation (MSWCT) system is the basis for ensuring waste classification [2]. The operation process of the system includes four parts: the classification and storage of waste at collection points, the classification and collection of collection vehicles, the compression and storage of transfer stations, and the classification and transportation of transit trucks. Additionally, the operational cost of the MSWCT system accounts for 60–80% of the total waste management cost [3,4]. As the MSWCT system operation process involves multiple units and decision-making subjects, there are management challenges.

Due to random waste generation, the uncertain system resources, and the complex driving paths, the operation process of the MSWCT system is subject to temporarily increased collection and transportation orders, vehicle failures, traffic jams, and other dynamic disturbances. It may affect the MSWCT scheme and progress of the system [5]. In addition, due to the lack of synchronization within and between units of the MSWCT system [6], the dynamic disturbances of some units may cause a bullwhip effect. It may result in poor operation of the overall system. This may cause the entire system to not run smoothly, causing problems such as overflowing trash bins, full loading of transfer stations, and odors in trash bins. Therefore, how to realize the synchronized decision making and control of the system in a dynamic environment is the key to the management and control of the MSWCT system [6,7].

For the above issues, relevant government departments and participating companies have introduced the latest technologies of Internet of Things (IoT), aiming to obtain real-time system data through the ubiquitous perception capabilities of IoT, and enable the visualization of the operation process [8–12]. The development and wide application of IoT technologies has improved the real-time data acquisition capability of the collection and transportation process, and has enabled the system to capture dynamic disturbances timely. However, the IoT information management system of local subsystems is still unable to meet the requirements of real-time synchronized decision making and control of the MSWCT system. There are three major challenges: (1) how to obtain the global system disturbance information in real time; (2) how to dynamically judge process control requirements after the occurrence of system dynamics; and (3) how to realize the synchronized operation among subsystems after clarifying the process dynamic control requirements, and achieve the global optimization.

In order to address the above challenges, this paper proposes a cloud-edge-terminal-based synchronized decision-making and control system (CET-SDCS) for MSWCT. First, through the deployment of a large number of terminal collection devices and an appropriate amount of edge computing devices, the accurate collection and efficient transmission of real-time data in the whole process of the system is realized. Secondly, after the system detects the occurrence of dynamics, the system will use the cloud-edge collaborative analysis and processing to achieve accurate judgment of the dynamic level. Finally, through the analysis of the multi-stage synchronized mechanism, the high real-time performance of the MSWCT system is realized as high-precision, high-cooperative synchronized decision-making and control.

The novelty and contribution of this paper is mainly to use the cloud-edge-terminal architecture to build a set of synchronized decision-making systems for MSWCT management, in order to realize distributed synchronized decision-making between multiple regions and multiple subjects. It is an innovative application of the synchronization mechanism and method in the MSWCT system, which significantly improves system operation efficiency and reduces system operation cost. Case examples for the management of municipal solid waste are provided.

The remainder of this paper is organized as follows: Section 2 briefly reviews relevant literature on three types of research: IoT-enabled intelligent waste logistics management, the concept of cloud-edge collaboration and its applications, and synchronized optimization of complex systems in dynamic environments; Section 3 provides the problem description; Section 4 introduces the CET-SDCS framework, device deployment, and operation mechanism; Section 5 provides a case study on how CET-SDCS improves the efficiency of the real-world municipal solid waste collection and transportation operation and recovery of usable value; and Section 6 summarizes the findings of this paper and future research directions.

2. Literature Review

We summarize related research from three aspects: Internet of Things (IoT)-enabled waste logistics management, the cloud-edge collaboration concept and its application, and synchronized optimization of complex systems in dynamic environments.

2.1. Smart Waste Logistics Management Enabled by IoT

The whole life cycle management of municipal solid waste has received considerable attention from scholars in recent years [13–16]. Due to the low efficiency of traditional waste collection and transportation, more and more cities are choosing to use IoT to drive the comprehensive, coordinated, and sustainable development of sanitation [17]. At present, the application of the IoT in urban domestic waste treatment, mainly based on more mature technology such as RFID electronic tags, GPS, etc., through the combination of a variety of technologies, so that enterprises can effectively improve the efficiency of waste collection [18]. As described by [19], modern tracking devices, such as volume sensors, can be used to obtain real-time information to minimize the distance covered and the number of vehicles required for collection by optimizing the route plan. Ref. [20] proposed a novel model, structure, and smart sensing algorithm for a real-time solid waste monitoring system, and this information can be used to optimize collection routes and reduce collection costs and carbon emissions, thus contributing to environmental sustainability. Ref. [21] optimized waste collection routes by locating and tracking bins to reduce costs and increase recycling rates. Ref. [22] presented a smart waste collection path problem that attempted to use real-time data on the bins to optimize the collection routes with three different business management approaches to process the information transmitted by the sensors. Ref. [23] proposed that IoT can also be used for intelligent coordination of waste trucks to improve the management efficiency of waste disposal companies and to reduce harmful emissions from waste trucks.

2.2. Cloud-Edge Collaboration Concept and Its Application

The concept of cloud computing was first introduced by Armbrust M in 2005, who defined cloud computing as both the applications delivered as services over the Internet and the hardware and systems software in the data centers that provide those services [24]. Its advantages include reduced computational costs, software costs, and improved computational performance, while the availability of virtually unlimited storage and low-cost processing power enables a new model of computing.

Edge computing can be traced back to the content delivery network proposed by Akamai in 1998, and the concept of edge computing was formally introduced in 2013 [25], and has been developed rapidly since then. Edge computing is a new computing mode, which is an open platform that integrates core capabilities of the network, computing, storage, and application close to objects or data sources to provide services closest to objects or data sources [26,27]. Edge computing is essentially an extension of the definition of cloud computing. Unlike cloud computing, edge computing is located at the edge of the network, near IoT devices [28]. They complement each other. Edge computing needs the support of a cloud computing center with powerful computing capacity and mass storage, while cloud computing center also needs edge devices to deal with mass data and private data to relieve the pressure of network broadband and the cloud data center. In the era of Internet of everything, there are many cases of cloud computing and edge computing combined together [29].

2.3. Synchronized Optimization of Complex Systems under Dynamics

Synchronization has received increasing attention in recent years as an important production control mechanism in Industry 4.0. Ref. [30] defined the concept of synchronization decision making as "a dynamic collaborative decision making approach in which the system autonomously mobilizes the most appropriate capacity or resources within and outside the system to best respond to dynamic disturbances throughout the life cycle of the production system". Ref. [31] proposed an IoT-based production logistics linkage system that responds to the dynamics of the manufacturing system execution process, thus reducing the delivery time. Ubiquitous technology is employed to synchronize production and logistics at the operational level to create a close decision–execution loop [32]. Ref. [33] presented a new view of coordinated decision making in integrated supply chain scheduling, i.e., coordinated lot delivery and order acceptance, and developed coordinated order acceptance and supply chain scheduling for lot direct delivery using three PL suppliers, and proposed two mixed integer plans. Ref. [34] proposed a multi-level cloud computing digital twin system for real-time monitoring, decision making, and control of production logistics linkage systems. In an IoT-driven production logistics linkage (PLS) system with complete real-time information, the negative impact of dynamics on the overall operational state of its system is evaluated to deal with dynamics in the most efficient and cost-effective way. Ref. [35] discussed the problem of route determination of collection vehicles at the transfer station, as well as their synchronization. The results show that the approach combining the collection phase with the transport phase can achieve a consistent reduction in the number of collection vehicles required.

2.4. Literature Summary

Firstly, IoT and cloud-edge collaborative technologies provide effective methods and technical frameworks for decision making and control of municipal waste management systems. However, to our knowledge, using two such methods for managing waste collection and transportation rarely has been discussed.

Secondly, in recent studies, waste collection and waste transportation have been treated as two systems with independent decision making, and few studies have focused on the study of linked decision making for waste collection and transportation systems in dynamic environments. Therefore, how to establish the integrated framework considering multi-scale and multi-stage state sensing and timely synchronized optimization is an urgent problem in the MSWCT system.

3. Problems Description

This section mainly introduces the operation process of the MSWCT system, and analyses the difficulties faced by the current system.

3.1. Operation Process of the MSWCT System

The operation process of the MSWCT system is shown in Figure 1, including "two stages and four steps". The two stages mainly refer to the collection stage and the transportation stage. The four units include the waste storage at the collection point, the recycling waste pick-up of collection vehicles, the waste transfer, and the waste transit. The entire system operation is triggered by pick-up requirements of the waste collection point. After going through the four steps in sequence, the waste at the collection point finally goes to the circular economy industrial park for final treatment.

3.2. Analysis of the Operation Process of the MSWCT System

During the operation process of the MSWCT system, each step is decided independently, but all steps are closely associated in operation. The collection fleet develops and executes the collection plan according to the pick-up requirements of the collection point and the internal resource allocation. The transit fleet develops and executes the transit plan according to the transit requirements of the transfer station and the internal resource configuration.

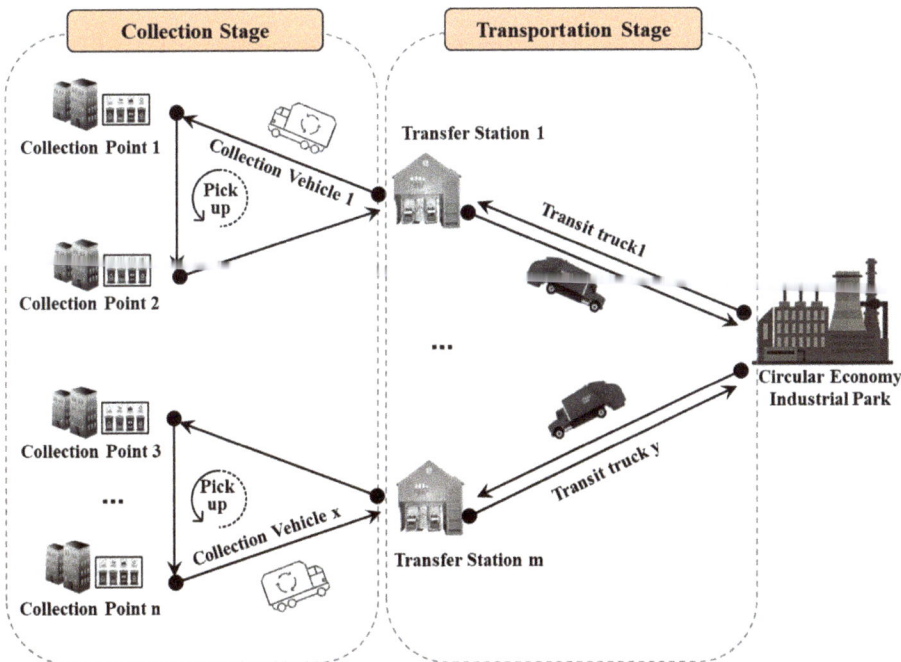

Figure 1. Operation process of the MSWCT system.

However, due to the random generation time of waste and the high uncertainty of the amount of waste generated, the collection and transportation requirements are constantly changing at the collection point. Moreover, the waste collection and transportation and transit process faces random disturbances from various internal and external factors such as vehicle failure, traffic jam, and bad weather. Regarding random changes in requirements and various disturbances, if the system decision is not made timely, the collection plan and the transit plan may fail to be executed normally. Additionally, there will be problems including overflowing trash bins, overfilled warehouses at transfer stations, and trash bin odors.

After analysis, we conclude three main reasons for the above problems:

(1) Failure to obtain the real-time information on the whole process of waste collection and transportation. There are two main parts: first, vertically speaking, the internal decision-making layer of each subsystem cannot truly understand the real-time operation status of the execution layer. Due to inaccurate underlying data or delayed data upload, decisions and processing cannot be made timely after the dynamics occur in the execution process. Second, horizontally speaking, each subsystem operates independently, and the data are not shared between subsystems, resulting in information silos.

(2) Insufficient real-time decision-making ability of the system to respond to dynamics. This mainly affects real-time decision-making from two aspects: on one hand, in the traditional IoT platform environment, the massive real-time data are uploaded to the cloud for processing. Its long delay may cause untimely decision-making. On the other hand, due to the lack of timely judgment on the dynamic level, dynamics that can be processed within the subsystem are also uploaded to the cloud for analysis and processing, and then no real-time decision-making is made.

(3) Failure of synchronization operation between subsystems. When the system is affected by dynamics, the system cannot quickly make the optimal decision as it lacks a dynamic level judgment and processing mechanism.

Therefore, the key technical challenges to resolve the above problems lie in how to obtain real-time data of the whole process, how to dynamically judge the process control requirements, and how to establish a synchronization decision-making mechanism between subsystems. These are the key points addressed in this paper.

4. Cloud-Edge-Terminal-Based Synchronized Decision-Making and Control System for Waste Collection and Transportation

To address the above three challenges, this paper extends the traditional IoT architecture and the cloud-side collaborative computing architecture to propose a multi-level computing based on "cloud-edge-terminal" synchronized decision-making and control system architecture for MSWCT. The following three aspects are introduced regarding the system architecture, equipment deployment, and system operation mechanism.

4.1. Introduction to the Framework and Modules of CET-SDCS for MSWCT

The overall architecture of the MSWCT system is divided into three layers, from bottom to top: terminal layer, edge layer, and cloud layer, as shown in Figure 2.

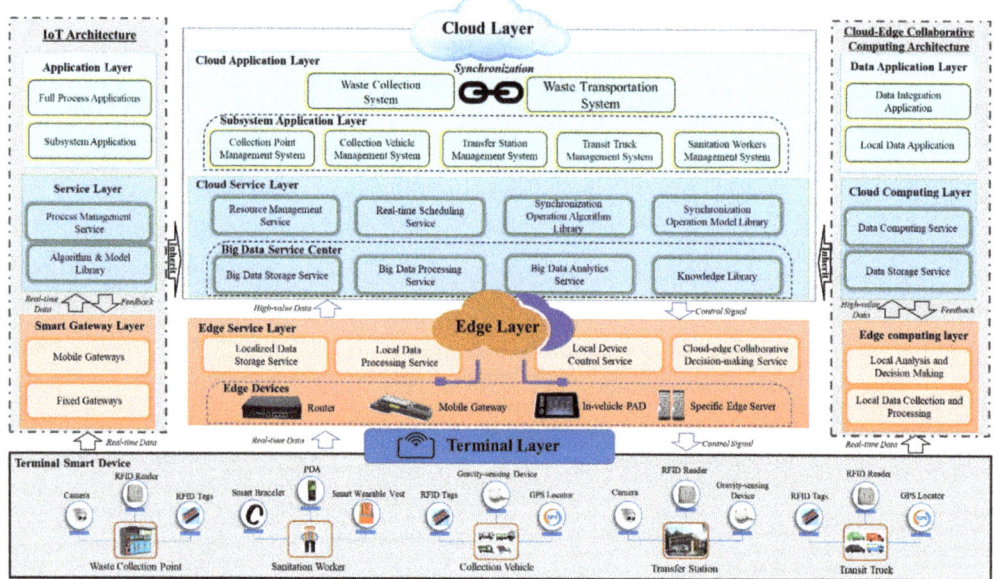

Figure 2. CET-SDCS architecture for MSWCT.

4.1.1. Terminal Layer

The terminal layer is the bottom smart device layer of CET-SDCS for MSWCT, which is also equivalent to the sensing layer of IoT.

Here, terminal smart devices refer to the installation of IoT devices (such as FRID tags, gravity sensors, RFID readers, cameras, bracelets, GPS locators, etc.) on traditional trash bins, waste collection kiosks, collection vehicles, transfer stations, transit trucks, and other equipment and facilities, so that these equipment and facilities have active/passive sensing functions and become terminal smart devices. The terminal smart devices also include smart bracelets and PDA that may be used by sanitation workers.

The main function of the terminal layer is responsible for real-time data collection and transmitting information to the edge layer. After the data are analyzed and decided by the system, the results are fed back to the terminal layer, and the terminal layer executes the decision instructions.

4.1.2. Edge Layer

The edge layer is the second layer of CET-SDCS for MSWCT, including the edge device layer and the edge service layer.

- Edge device layer

The main devices in the edge device layer are routers, mobile gateways, in-vehicle PAD, and specific edge servers. The router is mainly suitable for installation at waste collection points with waste collection kiosks, and is responsible for storing, processing and analyzing the video monitoring data of waste collection points, the status data of trash bins, and the interaction data of the collection vehicles for pick-up. The mobile gateway is mainly suitable for sanitation workers to carry out and complete data collection and processing at collection points without waste collection kiosks. The in-vehicle PAD is mainly placed on the collection vehicles and transit trucks to collect and process vehicle operation status data, location data, load data, etc. The specific edge server is mainly placed in the transfer station and used to handle the interactive collection of the transfer link, including the information of vehicle incoming and outgoing, the amount of waste unloaded by the collection vehicle, the status of the transfer box, and the transfer box incoming and outgoing.

- Edge service layer

The edge service layer is mainly services provided by edge devices, including the local data storage service, local data processing service, local device control service, and the cloud edge collaborative decision-making service. The edge service layer has the autonomy to make decisions in the local scope, and it can make decisions quickly by analyzing the data and determining that the dynamic situation is within the edge decision processing scope. The situation beyond the decision range is handled by the cloud edge collaborative decision service. The cloud edge collaborative decision means that the edge pre-analyzes the real-time data and predicts that the dynamic situation is beyond the decision authority; then, the pre-analyzed results are fed back to the cloud for further analysis, and the cloud finally feeds the final analysis and decision results to the edge.

The main function of the edge layer is to assist the cloud in staging and pre-processing the data collected in the first layer to improve data quality and reduce the upload of redundant data, as well as to make decisions on local issues while communicating control instructions to the lower layers.

4.1.3. Cloud Layer

The cloud layer is the uppermost layer of CET-SDCS for MSWCT, including the cloud service layer and the cloud application layer.

- Cloud service layer

The cloud service layer mainly includes the big data service center, resource management service, real-time scheduling service, synchronization operation algorithm library, and the synchronization operation model library.

The big data service center is mainly for big data storage, big data processing, and big data analysis of high-quality data and system historical decision data uploaded by the edge service layer, and forms a knowledge base that can be invoked by the system at any time. The data, algorithms, and models of the big data service center can also be invoked and support the operation of other services at any time.

The resource management service mainly refers to the visual management service for real-time traceability and status of system resources.

The real-time scheduling service is mainly for system resource work task issuance, task execution process control, and task adjustment.

The library of synchronized operational algorithms includes multidisciplinary design optimization (MDO), such as cooperative optimization (CO), analytic target cascade (ATC), and augmented Lagrangian coordination (ALC), as well as various types of heuristic optimization algorithms, such as genetic algorithms (GA), ant colony algorithms (ACO), and artificial neural networks (ANN).

The library of synchronized operation model mainly includes the waste collection stage path optimization model, the waste transportation stage path optimization model, the grade determination analysis model of system dynamics, the waste collection and transportation synchronized decision model, etc.

The main function of this layer is to provide service support for the cloud application layer and decision analysis service for the edge layer. The operation logic is to retrieve the necessary data from the data center according to the application requirements of specific scenarios in the upper layer, and combine and match resources, algorithms, and models to provide specific decision analysis for application scenarios.

- Cloud application layer

The cloud application layer includes the subsystem application layer and the synchronization application layer.

The application layer of the sub-system includes: (1) the waste collection point management system, which is mainly applicable to the community property or sanitation management department (such as street office). It is used for the management of trash bins and waste collection kiosk equipment resources at all collection points, including the registration, operation status, visualization of equipment and supervision of resident drop-off behavior, etc. (2) The management system of collection vehicles is mainly used by third-party collection companies for the registration, operation status, location, driving path optimization and driving record analysis of all collection vehicles, etc. New third-party collection and transportation companies must first register in the system before they can start business. (3) The management system of transfer stations is mainly used by government sanitation management departments (such as street offices). The transfer station management system is mainly applied to the relevant departments of government sanitation management or the collection company which has its own transfer station. It is used to manage the location, operation status and irregularities of all transfer stations. (4) The transit truck management system is mainly used by transit companies to manage the transfer business and the operation status, location, and driving path of transit trucks.

The synchronized application layer is mainly the synchronized operation between the MSWCT system, and also includes the synchronized operation between the MSWCT system internal subsystems. According to the core roles of different subsystems in different scenarios, it can be divided into collection synchronization transportation, transportation synchronization collection, and collection and transportation bi-directional synchronization. The related synchronization mechanism will be introduced in detail in the later contents.

The basic function of the cloud application layer is to provide application systems to meet the internal business needs of different participating entities in the MSWCT system; in addition to that, the most important thing is to provide application systems to support the synchronized operation between the subsystems.

4.2. CET-SDCS for MSWCT Endpoint Smart Device and Edge Computing Device Deployment

This section will show how to deploy terminal smart devices and edge computing devices to capture, collect, and process real-time data at each key point of waste collection and transportation. As shown in Figure 3, the main steps of the device deployment route are as follows.

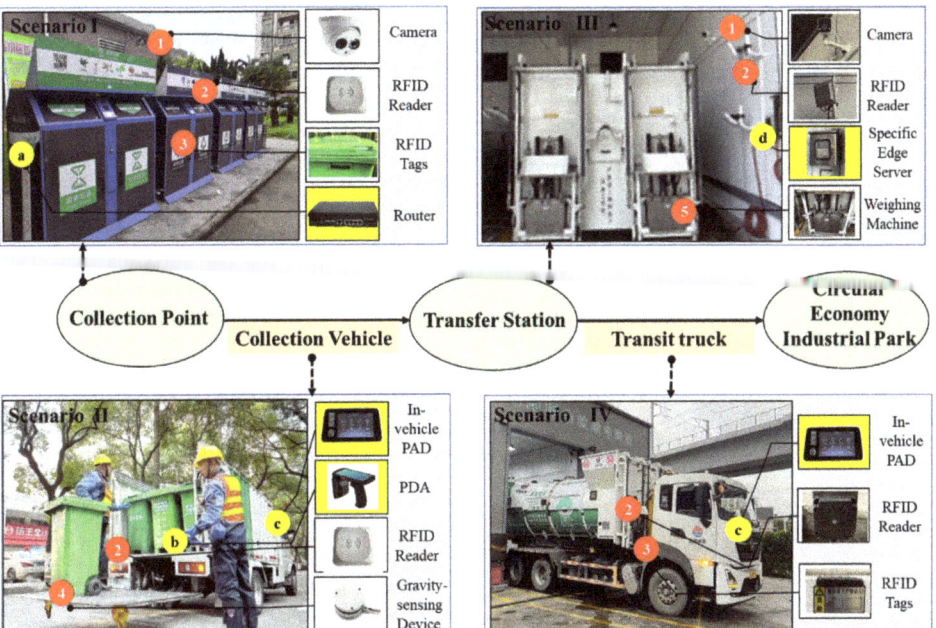

Figure 3. Deployment of devices at CET-SDCS for MSWCT.

4.2.1. Terminal Smart Device Deployment

Terminal smart device deployment at collection points: as shown in Scenario I in Figure 3, including a camera ①, RFID reader ② and RFID tag ③. (1) Camera deployment: mainly deployed at waste collection points for real-time monitoring of residents' irregularities, as well as the overflow of trash bins, and when abnormalities are found timely alerts will be issued. For sporadic distributed small waste points, from the perspective of realistic cost, the conditions can be installed: cameras for real-time monitoring, and no camera points can contact the collection fleet through the system cell phone app. (2) RFID reader deployment: the fixed RFID readers in collection points will be deployed to automatically bind new empty trash bins when they enter the collection point and record the point location and merchant information into the RFID tag. For sporadically distributed small waste points, the points information can be manually bound by equipping PDAs to the workers of the collection stage when the trash bin has reached its collection capacity. (3) RFID tag deployment: the trash bin is the most important monitoring target in the waste collection process, and each waste bin must be deployed with an RFID tag.

Terminal smart device deployment on collection vehicles: as shown in Scenario II in Figure 3, the devices deployed on each collection vehicle include the gravity-sensing device ④ and RFID readers ②. (1) The gravity-sensing device: the gravity-sensing devices are placed mainly at the rear of the collection vehicle, and the weight of each bin is recorded. (2) RFID readers: the RFID readers will record the merchant information of each trash bin and bind it with the weight information measured by the gravity-sensing device, and then transmit it to the on-board central control record.

Deployment of terminal smart devices in waste transfer stations: as shown in Scenario III in Figure 3, the waste transfer station is a key data transition point, which is an important link between waste collection and transportation. The IoT devices deployed are mainly cameras ①, RFID readers ②, and weighing machines ③. (1) The cameras are deployed mainly to monitor illegal dumping behavior, as well as the safety monitoring of workers and vehicles in the waste transfer station. (2) The RFID reader is mainly installed in the waste transfer station entrance and internal, where the transfer station entrance RFID reader is mainly used to read the information of vehicles in and out, and the station internal RFID reader is mainly used to read the information of large waste containers in and out. (3) After entering the station, the trash bins unloaded by the collection vehicles are weighed by the weighing machine and the merchants information of the trash bins are read; then, the trash bins are transported by conveyor belt to the large waste transit container for dumping. In addition to this, gas monitoring equipment and liquid level monitoring equipment are deployed to prevent odor and liquid spillage.

Terminal smart device deployment on transit truck: as shown in Scenario IV in Figure 3, RFID readers ② and RFID tags ③, the IoT sensing devices, are deployed on each transit truck. (1) The RFID reader is mainly used to read the category, station, weight, and other information of the transit container. (2) The RFID tag is mainly attached to transit containers to facilitate information recording in and out of transfer stations.

4.2.2. Edge Computing Device Deployment

Edge computing device deployment at the collection points: as shown in scenario I in Figure 3, the edge computing devices are mainly routers (a). All of the waste collection points have fixed network lines, and the routers can be deployed at the waste collection points to analyze and process the real-time video data.

Edge computing device deployment on the collection vehicles: as shown in scenario II in Figure 3, the deployed edge computing devices are mainly PDA (b) and in-vehicle PAD (c). (1) PDA is equivalent to a mobile gateway, mainly used for sanitation workers of the collection stage to write data on sporadic waste collection points and assist RFID readers to read and analyze data. (2) In-vehicle PAD is responsible for storing and analyzing real-time data of the collection vehicles. Real-time data, including vehicle travel speed, location, tire pressure, and loading capacity.

Edge computing device deployment on the waste transfer station: as shown in scenario III in Figure 3, the edge computing devices deployed are mainly specific edge servers (d) to store and process data of vehicles coming in and out, dumping waste volume, and containers coming in and out.

Edge computing device deployment on the transit truck: as shown in scenario IV in Figure 3, the in-vehicle PAD (c) is responsible for storing and analyzing real-time data of the transit truck, including the truck travel speed, position, tire pressure, and loading capacity.

In addition to the deployment of terminal smart devices and edge computing devices, it is also necessary to deploy related communication network equipment. The communication network is deployed using common 4G\5G, which is not described here, and can be deployed according to the actual demand.

4.2.3. System Process Reengineering

With the systematic deployment of smart devices and edge computing devices at each node of the MSWCT system and on transportation resources, an environment for real-time online decision making and control of the whole process of waste collection and transportation is created. The whole process of waste collection and transportation is redesigned to accommodate the intelligent environment.

The following highlights a few key operations in the reengineering process:

(1) The user of the waste collection point needs to send a demand for collection on the system's mobile app to trigger collection.

(2) The planner of the waste collection company planning department receives an order, develops the collection scheme, and sends the scheme to the collection fleet and waste transfer stations manager.

(3) The sanitation workers (driver) of the collection fleet download the collection scheme through the in-vehicle PAD, and drive to the collection point to collect the waste according to the scheme.

(4) When the collection vehicle arrives at the collection point, the empty trash bins are first unloaded, and bound to the collection point with a PDA. Then, the filled trash bins are put on the vehicle, weighed, and the collection point information read, which will be recorded in the in-vehicle PAD.

(5) When the collection vehicle arrives at the waste transfer station, it will be automatically sensed and recognized by the RFID reader. After completing the inbound registration, sanitation workers move into the designated position to unload the waste. The trash bins are first weighed by the weighing machine, and the synchronized RFID reader reads the RFID tag information of the trash bins, which is uploaded to the specific edge server of the transfer station for processing. Then, the waste is automatically dumped into the container by the lift, and then the sanitation workers clean the trash bin and label information is released. The collection vehicle loads the empty trash bin, registers to leave the transfer station, and accepts the next collection task.

(6) The waste transfer station sends transit demand to the transit fleet based on the collection scheme sent by collection company and the real-time storage situation of the container.

(7) The planning department of the transit company receives the transit order, develops the transit scheme, and sends it to the transit fleet.

(8) The sanitation workers of the transit fleet download the transit scheme through the in-vehicle PAD, and drive to the transfer station to transit the waste as planned.

(9) When the transit truck arrives at the transfer station, it will be automatically sensed and recognized by the RFID reader. After completed the inbound registration, the on-board RFID reader reads the transfer container information and adds the information to the transit truck on-board central control to make records. When the truck leaves the station and the registration is complete, the transit truck drives to the final waste treatment plant.

(10) The transit truck arrives at the final waste treatment plant. After completing the registration of entering the plant, the unloading of waste is carried out. After the waste is unloaded, the container is transported back to the transfer station. The sanitation workers confirm the completion of the whole transfer work on the vehicle-mounted integrated machine and accept the next transit task.

The above is the basic operation of the system process reengineering. In the actual operation process, the system often faces a variety of internal and external dynamic disturbances. Therefore, this paper further proposes a synchronous operation mechanism to deal with various dynamic disturbances faced by the system operation.

4.3. Operation Mechanism of CET-SDCS for MSWCT

This section follows the basic idea of synchronization operation proposed by Qu et al. [30,36] in the field of intelligent manufacturing, and extends its application to the field of waste management. A set of synchronization decision-making mechanisms for the MSWCT system is proposed, which includes two steps: firstly, the dynamics level of the system is classified and a set of classification rules for the dynamics level is established; secondly, a set of synchronization decision-making mechanisms is designed for different levels of dynamics.

4.3.1. The Dynamics Classification of the MSWCT System in Cloud-Edge-Terminal Architecture

The scope of the dynamics impact of the MSWCT system on the system or each unit is marked as R. The value of R is determined by the responsive threshold ($T[min,max]$) of the dynamics acting on the system and the state S_t at time T. Based on the value of R, the dynamics of the MSWCT system is classified into three levels, as follows:

First-level dynamics: When the impact of dynamic interference is less than the maximum responsive threshold for each unit within the MSWCT system (the collection point, the recycling waste pick-up of collection vehicles, the waste transfer, and the waste transit), i.e., when R is less than T_{max}, the dynamics can be eliminated by task readjustment within the units.

Second-level dynamics: When the impact of dynamic interference is more than the maximum responsive threshold for each unit, i.e., when R is more than T_{max}, the responsive ability of each unit is no longer able to respond to the dynamic impact on its own, and it needs to coordinate with other units to adjust tasks to deal with the dynamic impact.

Third-level dynamics: The impact of dynamic interference exceeds the responsive ability of multiple units collaboratively, i.e., the units cannot respond to the dynamic impact by readjusting tasks. At this time, it is necessary to call on external resources of the system, i.e., change the existing resource configuration (e.g., temporarily renting an external vehicle), to cope with the dynamic impact. (The third-level dynamics involves a game between the cost of bringing in external resources and the penalty cost for failure to fulfil orders. In this paper, the third-level dynamics is the case where the cost of calling in external resources is less than the penalty cost.)

According to the above classification rules for dynamics, examples of the dynamics encountered in the real operation of the MSWCT system and their levels are shown in Table 1.

Table 1. The example of dynamics classification of the MSWCT system.

Stages of Dynamic Generation	Dynamics	The Responses	Dynamics Classification
The waste storage at the collection point	Some of the bins at the collection point are full	Close the door of the full bin	First-synchronization
	The bins at the collection point are all full	Call the collection vehicle priority to pick up	Second-synchronization
	The bins at the collection point are all full	Collection vehicles are out of reach and external bins are brought in to replace full ones at the collection point	Third-synchronization
The recycling waste pick-up of collection vehicles	Traffic jams	Wait or reroute	First-synchronization
	Collection vehicle breakdown (with a spare vehicle to call)	Call the spare vehicle	Second-synchronization
	Collection vehicle breakdown (no spare vehicle to call)	Rental of external vehicles	Third-synchronization
The waste transfer	Some of the garbage transfer containers are full	Close container door	First-synchronization
	All the garbage transfer containers are full	Call the transfer truck to transfer, or call the collection vehicle to temporarily not enter the station	Second-synchronization
	All the garbage transfer containers are full	Rental of external transfer containers	Third-synchronization
The waste transit	Traffic jams	Wait or reroute	First-synchronization
	Transit truck breakdown (the fleet has idle truck calls)	Contact collection vehicles to unload at a less loaded transfer station	Second-synchronization
	Transit truck breakdown (the fleet has no idle truck calls)	Rental of external trucks	Third-synchronization

4.3.2. The Synchronization Decision-Making Mechanism of MSWCT System in Cloud-Edge-Terminal Architecture

The synchronization decision-making mechanism includes "three levels of synchronization, two stages of decision-making", referred to as the "three levels, two stages" decision-making mechanism, as shown in Figure 4 and described in detail below.

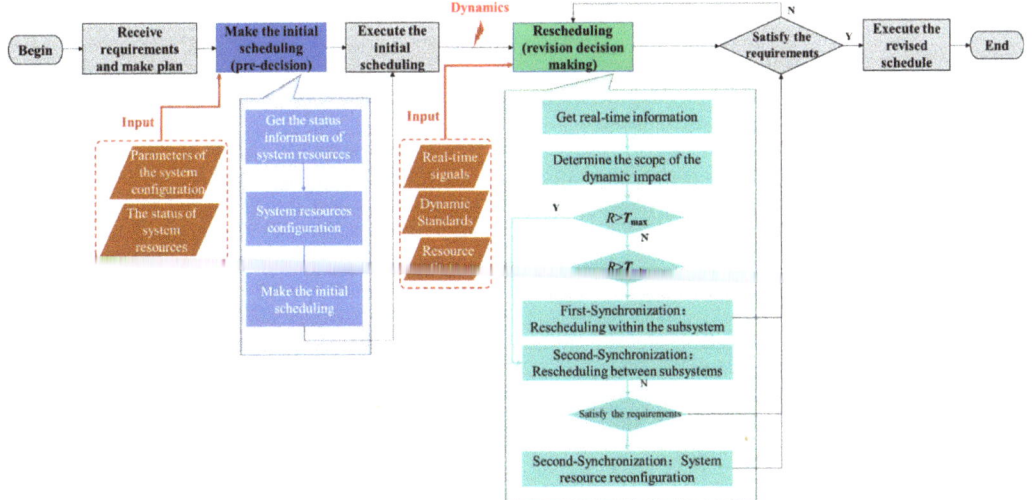

Figure 4. "Three levels, two stages" synchronization mechanism description.

- Three levels of synchronization

"Three levels of synchronization" is a three-level synchronization decision-making method, including first-, second- and third-synchronization, in response to the dynamics of three different levels.

First-synchronization: When the dynamic is a first-level dynamic, the terminal smart device can get accurate information about the unit operation in real time and send the information to the edge computing device within the unit for analysis. On top of guaranteeing normal operation within the unit, the edge computing server schedules and optimizes the unit tasks to eliminate the dynamic impact so as not to affect the normal operation of other decision-making units.

Second-synchronization: When the dynamic is a second-level dynamic, the terminal smart device takes the acquired real-time information and feeds it back to the edge computing devices for pre-processing. After the information pre-processing is completed, the edge server sends it to the cloud server for analysis. On the premise of guaranteeing each units' own interests, the cloud server can eliminate the dynamics by coordinating and changing the tasks and plans between the units to avoid affecting the stable operation at the system level.

Third-synchronization: When the dynamic is a third-level dynamic, the process of data collection, transmission, and pre-processing in the early stage is similar to that of second-synchronization processing, while the difference is the analytical processing in the cloud, where the algorithms and models of third-synchronization are more complex. After considering the full process optimization analysis, the system can eliminate the dynamics by re-scheduling system resources (e.g., vehicle scheduling between different collection companies) or adding new resources (e.g., temporarily renting or purchasing transportation and storage services).

- Two stages of decision-making

The two stages of decision-making includes two processes: initial scheduling (pre-decision) and rescheduling (revision decision making), as shown in Figure 4.

Initial scheduling: When the MSWCT system receives a collection order from a waste collection point, the synchronization service layer analyses, evaluates, and predicts the state of each subsystem component according to the requirements and constraints of the order, and determines the resource configuration, task assignment, and route planning according to the center of models to develop the waste collection and transit schemes. Then, the plan is transmitted to the main service systems. Each main service system proposes their own revisions after trade-offs and feedback to the synchronization service center of the system. This iteration is repeated until the system's optimal collection and transit scheduling (initial scheduling) is obtained.

Rescheduling: After receiving the initial scheduling, the waste collection and transit company organize the collection, transfer (temporary storage), and transit activities according to the instructions. In the real execution process, if the terminal device monitors the occurrence of dynamic interference and determines that the dynamic difference is more than the terminal device's predetermined degree, the dynamic response mechanism of the edge service layer is triggered first. If the dynamic difference exceeds the predetermined degree of the edge server, a request is made by the edge server to the cloud server, which determines the level of dynamics by analyzing. After determining the dynamics level, the cloud server analyzes and obtains the corresponding processing countermeasures and reformulates a revised planning scheme. Finally, the revised solution is obtained, and the instructions are transmitted to the terminal device layer for execution. The iteration is repeated until the end of the implementation task.

The "three levels, two stages" decision-making mechanism relying on the support of the cloud-edge-terminal architecture can quickly respond to the impact of the dynamics of the system and is the guarantee of the efficient operation of the system.

5. Case Study

This case takes the MSWCT system of a central street (Gongbei Street, Zhuhai City) in a key city node (a core city located on the west bank of China's Pearl River Estuary and a coastal tourist city) in the Guangdong-Hong Kong-Macao Greater Bay Area as the research object. Gongbei Street covers a total area of 10.32 square kilometers, with a permanent population of 230,000 and dense residential buildings. The street boasts a developed service and catering industry, producing an average of about 230 tons of waste per day. Gongbei Street is one of the pioneers in Zhuhai to apply the management mode of waste collection and transportation after classification.

The street currently has 420 registered waste collection points, 20 waste transfer stations, 9 waste collection companies, and 1 waste transit company. In total, 50 tons of kitchen waste and 170 tons of other waste are collected on a daily basis. Hazardous waste and recyclables are not collected every day, with an average daily collection volume of about 0.1 ton and 17 tons, respectively.

The "waste collection and transportation" process in Gongbei Street is under the unified supervision of the Urban Refinement Management Office (hereinafter referred to as the Refinement Office) under the Street Office. Initially, the units are required to fill in the paper documents manually for registration in a traditional way, and then the Refinement Office collect the paper documents and import them into the computer for statistical analysis. In this mode, due to the low data collection efficiency, low accuracy, and poor real-time data, various dynamic disturbances may occur in the actual operation process. When a disturbance occurs, the three parties, including the collection company, the transit company, and the Street Office, cannot obtain real-time data of the system to make timely adjustments.

In order to solve the above-mentioned management decision-making problems, the Street entrusted a third-party information system company to develop an IoT-based visual management system for waste classification. By placing RFID tags on trash bins, installing in-vehicle PDAs on waste trucks, and equipping sanitation workers and transfer stations with RFID tag readers, the platform aims to achieve online management of the MSWCT system. Here we present the details and challenges of the system operation.

5.1. The Operation of the MSWCT System and Its Challenges

With the help of the waste visual management system, the Gongbei Street Office has established a six-step operation process of the MSWCT system.

Step 1: The property management company (PMC) or merchant managing the collection points determine the daily waste collection and transportation requirements for a fixed period (for example, one month) based on the empirical value of its own waste collection volume (assuming the daily collection and transportation volume is equal). Then, they convert the collection and transportation requirement into an order, which is sent to the collection company.

Step 2: The waste collection company (WCC) develops the monthly collection and transportation scheme according to received orders, and sends it to the collection fleet (the driver is responsible for driving the collection vehicle and clearing the waste).

Step 3: The collection workers check the monthly collection scheme through the PDA. Based on the method of cyclic pick-up, they drive to the collection point with empty bins to collect waste with a fixed route every day.

Step 4: The empty bins are removed from the vehicle, and information regarding collection points and trash bin types are written into the RFID tag of the trash bin through handheld terminals. The full waste bins are put onto the vehicle, and driven to the next collection point after loading.

Step 5: The collection vehicles are loaded up and driven to the nearest transfer station to unload. Weighing by an intelligent weighbridge is the first part of the unloading process, and the RFID tag information of the bin is automatically read and bound before being uploaded to the system. After loading the empty bin at the transfer station, a new round of collection and transportation begins until the task is complete.

Step 6: The transfer station manager collects statistics on the current carrying capacity of the waste transfer station. When the transfer station reaches the preset transit threshold, a shipping request is sent to the transit company.

Step 7: After the waste transit company (WTC) receives the transportation request, it develops a transit scheme and, in turn, transits the waste from the waste transfer station to the waste final treatment plant. After the whole vehicle is weighed in the treatment plant, the data are fed back to the Street Office's Waste Classification Visualization Management System.

However, the street still faces three decision-making challenges: the acquisition of real-time data in the whole process, real-time dynamic decision making, and the synchronization of decision making among units.

Acquisition of real-time data in the whole process: The data currently obtained by the decision-making management of the Street Office are the execution results fed back by each subsystem. However, the real-time operation status data of trash bins, transfer stations, and transportation trucks involved in the whole process cannot be obtained.

Real-time dynamic decision-making: The current system adopts periodic decision making instead of real-time dynamic decision making. The actual implementation varies from day to day, and various dynamic disturbances are faced during the implementation process. When the system dynamic occurs, the system cannot monitor it, and can only take intervention measures after the dynamic impact results are produced.

Synchronization decision-making between units: Since there is no synchronization operation mechanism, the subsystems all make decisions independently. In the case of optimal operation of local subsystems, it is difficult to guarantee that the entire system works optimally because no synchronization relationship is established among units.

The main reasons for the above-mentioned challenges in the Gongbei Street Office are the lack of methods for acquiring real-time data during the whole process, methods for distributed data processing and decision making, and synchronization mechanisms and methods among system units. In response to these challenges, a project was launched with the support of Top Cloud Tech Co., Ltd., (Zhuhai, China) which provides system platform services for the Gongbei Street Office. By combining the ubiquitous perception architecture of IoT with the cloud-edge collaborative computing architecture, the project aims to build a synchronization system of real-time perception, multi-level collaborative computing and decision making for the whole process of waste collection and transportation. This project is highly aligned with the intelligent management strategy of waste classification promoted by the central government, and is a pilot project for the intelligent upgrading of waste classification in Zhuhai, which has won the recognition from the government department.

5.2. Re-Engineering Waste Collection and Transportation Operations

In order to adapt to the whole-process real-time perception and edge computing environment of IoT, the waste collection and transportation operation of the Gongbei Street Office was re-engineered with the help of CET-SDCS for MSWCT. Details are as shown in Figure 5 below.

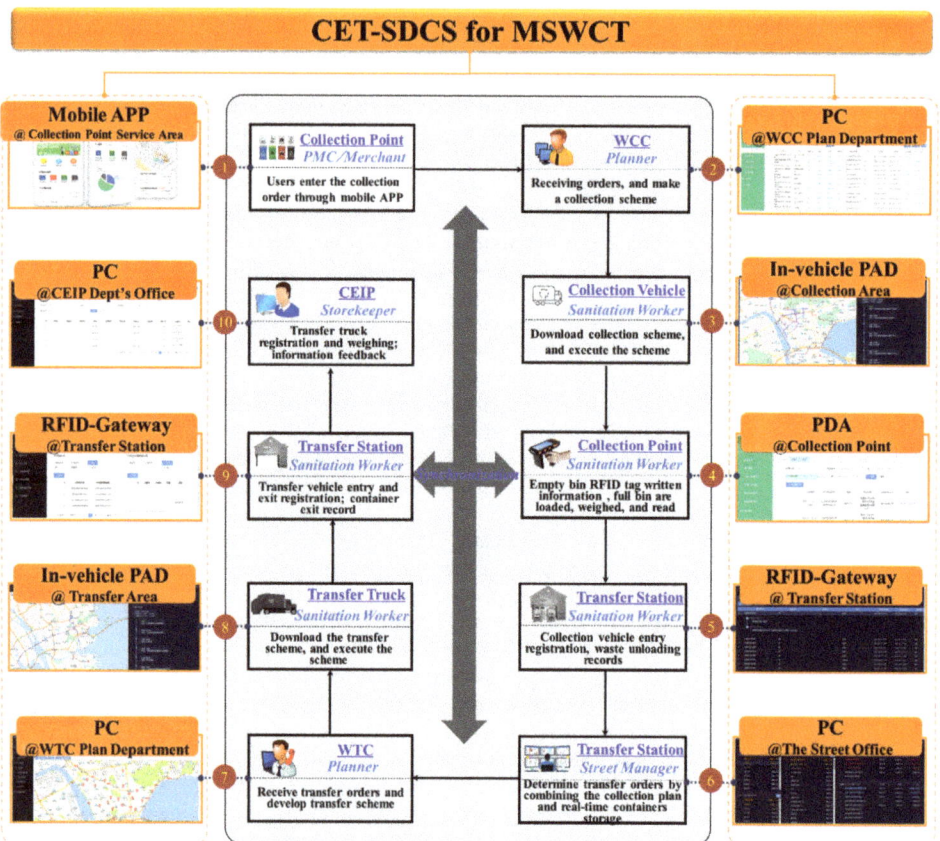

Figure 5. Re-engineered process with CET-SDCS for MSWCT.

(1) The management persons at the waste collection point (such as property management persons, and merchants) issue collection and transportation orders through the system mobile app. Therefore, some disturbances, such as urgent collection and transportation orders from merchants, can be handled in real time.

(2) The planner of the WCC's planning department receives an order, develops the collection and transportation plan according to the use of the company's resources, and sends the plan to the fleet. The collection and transportation plan determines the departure time, driving route, and transfer station location for unloading.

(3) The sanitation workers of the collection and transportation fleet download the collection and transportation scheme through the in-vehicle PAD, and go to the collection point to collect and transport the waste according to the scheme.

(4) When the collection vehicle arrives at the collection point, the empty trash bins are unloaded and bound to the collection point with a handheld mobile terminal/fixed RFID reader. The filled trash bin on put on the vehicle, weighed, and the collection point information read, which is be recorded in the in-vehicle PAD. If the weight is inconsistent with the planned amount, the in-vehicle PAD will send a signal of abnormal amount of waste to the system. After the vehicle is full, it drives to the nearest transfer station to unload. (As different types of waste have different characteristics, the collection and transportation forms are also different. For example, food waste is mostly transported with bins, which need to be changed. Bins are not required to be changed for other waste, but the basic process is the same. Take kitchen waste as an example in this paper.)

(5) When the collection vehicle arrives at the transfer station, it will be automatically sensed and recognized by the gate. After detection, the vehicle drives into the designated position to unload the waste. The waste is weighed, and the information of the trash bin is read and matched with the information that was recorded in the in-vehicle PAD. The operation process also includes dumping of the full waste trash bin, waste compression, empty bin cleaning, label information release, empty bin loading, and vehicle departure. The next cycle is started after completing the above operations.

(6) The waste transfer station downloads the collection and transportation scheme, and develops a waste transit order based on the actual waste volume. As such, some dynamic disturbances can be avoided.

(7) The planning department of the transit company receives the transit order, develops the transfer plan based on the internal vehicle status, and sends the transit plan to the transit fleet. The transit plan confirms the departure time of the transit truck, the sequence of the transit at the transfer station, and the driving route of the truck.

(8) The sanitation workers of the transit fleet download the transit plan through the in-vehicle PAD, and go to the transfer station to transit the waste as planned.

(9) When the transit truck arrives at the transfer station, it will be automatically sensed and recognized by the gate. After the detection, the transit truck enters the designated position to load the waste transfer box. The system automatically senses that the waste transfer box leaves the position, and the gate records the departure of the truck and the waste transfer box.

(10) The transit truck carries the waste transfer box to the final waste treatment plant. After the admission registration, the intelligent weighing device automatically reads the waste transfer box information, binds it with the weight information, and uploads the information to the system. The transit truck returns to the previous transfer station with the new empty transfer box and starts another round of transfer.

5.3. Benefits of CET-SDCS for MSWCT

Using the CET-SDCS for MSWCT, Gongbei Street can acquire real-time data of the whole process of waste collection and transportation and monitor the operation status in real time. At the same time, the real-time data collected by the terminal smart device is processed and analyzed through the edge computing device, which avoids redundant data uploading to the cloud, relieves the pressure on the network bandwidth and cloud data center, and greatly reduces the time delay of the system. It has improved the street's response speed to different levels of dynamics, and realized the synchronization of decision making among multiple units. It has also significantly improved the operating efficiency of the system, and reduced the operating costs of waste collection and transportation. The details are shown in Table 2.

Table 2. Efficiency and cost effectiveness of CET-SDCS for MSWCT.

Item	Year 2020	Year 2021	Change (%)
Daily collection weight per vehicle (taking kitchen waste collection as an example)	6 tons	18 tons	Increase by 200%
Total number of collection vehicle shifts per month	520 shifts	436 shifts	Decrease by 16.15%
Total cost of waste collection per year	6.24 million	5.232 million	Decrease by 16.15%
Annual operating costs of the transfer station	2.7 million	2 million	Decrease by 25.93%

In terms of the operating efficiency of the system, taking kitchen waste collection vehicles as an example, before the implementation of the project, the total collection volume of each vehicle per day was up to 6 tons, which increased to 18 tons after the implementation of the project. With the same number of vehicles, the transportation capacity of the collection and transportation fleet has been increased three-fold. In addition, the frequency of departures has also been reduced from 520 shifts per month before the implementation of the project to 436 shifts per month after the implementation, an average reduction of 84 shifts per month, with a year-on-year decrease of 16.15%.

In terms of cost saving, before the implementation of the project, the annual collection and transportation cost was CNY 6.24 million, and the operation and management cost of the transfer station was CNY 2.7 million. After the implementation, the annual collection and transportation cost is CNY 5.232 million, with a year-on-year decrease of 16.15%. The annual operation and management cost of the transfer station is CNY 2 million with a year-on-year decrease of 25.93%. The cumulative cost saving is CNY 1.708 million per year.

Although CET-SDCS has many of the above advantages, the initial investment cost of CET-SDCS is relatively large, and the main cost increase comes from the investment of a large number of edge computing devices. In the future, with the development and maturity of edge computing technology, the cost of CET-SDCS will gradually decrease.

6. Conclusions

This paper introduces the CET-SDCS for MSWCT, which can be applied by government sanitation departments and participating enterprises in different units involving waste classification. Both government departments and participating enterprises are faced with the challenges of acquiring real-time data during the whole process, dynamically judging process control requirements, and a lack of synchronized decision-making mechanism among subsystems in the operation of the MSWCT system. The entire waste collection and transportation scheme and progress are subject to many dynamic disturbances. Intelligent terminals and edge computing devices are systematically deployed at each key node of the MSWCT system to create an environment for real-time online decision making and control during the whole process of waste collection and transportation. Under an intelligent environment, the resources of the MSWCT system are transformed into intelligent objects that can be tracked. We can collect operating status data and perceive the occurrence of dynamics in real time. CET-SDCS for MSWCT supports the synchronized decision making and control of the system in a dynamic environment with real-time information. We developed a set of three-level dynamic hierarchical rules for the MSWCT system. Moreover, the cloud-edge-terminal multi-level computing architecture is used to collaboratively analyze and process different dynamics. We proposed a "three-level and two-stage" synchronized decision-making mechanism suitable for the MSWCT system. By implementing CET-SDCS for MSWCT system, we can not only improve the response speed of the system to dynamics of different levels in the operation process, and realize the synchronized decision making among multiple units, but we can also significantly improve system operating efficiency and cut operating costs.

This paper mainly explores the innovative applications of cloud-edge collaborative computing technologies and IoT technologies in the field of waste logistics operation management. Firstly, intelligent terminals and edge computing devices are systematically deployed to the key units of the MSWCT system, which realizes the acquisition of insensitive data during the whole process, and eliminates the phenomenon of non-sharing of information within and between units. Secondly, the dynamic disturbances affecting the operation of the MSWCT system are captured by IoT devices, and computed and analyzed through the cloud-edge collaborative computing architecture to establish the matching relationship between cloud-edge decision rights and different dynamic levels, and enable fast decision making for dynamics of different levels. Thirdly, the idea of synchronized operation is applied to the operation and management of waste logistics, which realizes the synchronized decision-making between the waste collection stage and the transportation stage, and the overall optimization of the system.

Future research work will answer the following questions. The first question is how to use the historical data of the system to establish a big data prediction model and a dynamic disturbance prediction model for the amount of waste generated, with an aim to prevent the dynamic occurrence in advance. The second question is how to achieve a better allocation of system resources under the synchronized operation environment. The third question is how to improve the convenience of introducing external resources of the system and achieve the business symbiosis of multi-stakeholders.

Author Contributions: Conceptualization, T.Q. and G.Q.H.; Data curation, X.Q., J.Z. and J.C.; Formal analysis, M.H. and X.Q.; Funding acquisition, T.Q. and J.C.; Investigation, M.W.; Methodology, M.W. and T.Q.; Project administration, M.W.; Resources, T.Q. and G.Q.H.; Writing—original draft, M.W.; Writing—review & editing, M.W. and M.H. All authors have read and agreed to the published version of the manuscript.

Funding: This paper was financially supported by the National Natural Science Foundation of China (51875251, 52205526), the National Key Research and Development Program of China (2021YFB3301701), the 2019 Guangdong Special Support Talent Program—Innovation and Entrepreneurship Leading Team (China) (2019BT02S593), the 2018 Guangzhou Leading Innovation Team Program (China) (201909010006), and the Science and Technology Development Fund (Macau SAR) (0078/2021/A). We also appreciate the sponsorships from the Zhuhai Top Cloud Tech Co., GBA and B&R International Joint Research Center for Smart Logistics, a provincial research lab sponsored by the Department of Science and Technology of Guangdong Province, thanks to which the international collaboration has been effectively conducted.

Institutional Review Board Statement: Not applicable.

Informed Consent Statement: Not applicable.

Data Availability Statement: Not applicable.

Conflicts of Interest: The authors declare no conflict of interest.

References

1. Zhang, A.; Wang, J.X.; Farooque, M.; Wang, Y.; Choi, T.M. Multi-dimensional circular supply chain management: A comparative review of the state-of-the-art practices and research. *Transp. Res. Pt. E-Logist. Transp. Rev.* **2021**, *155*, 102509. [CrossRef]
2. Zhou, M.H.; Shen, S.L.; Xu, Y.S.; Zhou, A.N. New policy and implementation of municipal solid waste classification in Shanghai, China. *Int. J. Environ. Res. Public Health* **2019**, *16*, 3099. [CrossRef] [PubMed]
3. Akhtar, M.; Hannan, M.A.; Begum, R.A.; Basri, H.; Scavino, E. Backtracking search algorithm in CVRP models for efficient solid waste collection and route optimization. *Waste Manag.* **2017**, *1*, 117–128. [CrossRef]
4. Yadav, V.; Karmakar, S. Sustainable collection and transportation of municipal solid waste in urban centers. *Sust. Cities Soc.* **2020**, *53*, 101937. [CrossRef]
5. Li, Y.P.; Huang, G.H.; Cui, L.; Liu, J. Mathematical Modeling for Identifying Cost-Effective Policy of Municipal Solid Waste Management under Uncertainty. *J. Environ. Inform.* **2019**, *34*, 55–67. [CrossRef]
6. Cleophas, C.; Cottrill, C.; Ehmke, J.F.; Tierney, K. Collaborative urban transportation: Recent advances in theory and practice. *Eur. J. Oper. Res.* **2019**, *273*, 801–816. [CrossRef]
7. Shao, S.; Xu, S.X.; Huang, G.Q. Variable neighborhood search and tabu search for auction-based waste collection synchronization. *Transp. Res. Pt. B-Methodol.* **2020**, *133*, 1–20. [CrossRef]
8. Anagnostopoulos, T.; Zaslavsky, A.; Kolomvatsos, K.; Medvedev, A.; Amirian, P.; Morley, J.; Hadjiefthymiades, S. Challenges and opportunities of waste management in IoT-enabled smart cities: A survey. *IEEE Trans. Sustain. Comput.* **2017**, *2*, 275–289. [CrossRef]

9. Thürer, M.; Pan, Y.H.; Qu, T.; Luo, H.; Li, C.D.; Huang, G.Q. Internet of Things (IoT) driven kanban system for reverse logistics: Solid waste collection. *J. Intell. Manuf.* **2019**, *30*, 2621–2630. [CrossRef]
10. Zhang, A.; Venkatesh, V.G.; Liu, Y.; Wan, M.; Qu, T.; Huisingh, D. Barriers to smart waste management for a circular economy in China. *J. Clean Prod.* **2019**, *240*, 118198. [CrossRef]
11. Pardini, K.; Rodrigues, J.J.P.C.; Kozlov, S.A.; Kumar, N.; Furtado, V. IoT-Based Solid Waste Management Solutions: A Survey. *J. Sens. Actuator Netw.* **2019**, *8*, 5. [CrossRef]
12. Salehi-Amiri, A.; Akbapour, N.; Hajiaghaei-Keshteli, M.; Gajpal, Y.; Jabbarzadeh, A. Designing an effective two-stage, sustainable, and IoT based waste management system. *Renew. Sust. Energ. Rev.* **2022**, *157*, 112031. [CrossRef]
13. Nabavi-Pelesaraei, A.; Bayat, R.; Hosseinzadeh-Bandbafha, H.; Afrasyabi, H.; Chau, K.W. Modeling of energy consumption and environmental life cycle assessment for incineration and landfill systems of municipal solid waste management-A case study in Tehran Metropolis of Iran. *J. Clean Prod.* **2017**, *148*, 427–440. [CrossRef]
14. Nabavi-Pelesaraei, A.; Bayat, R.; Hosseinzadeh-Bandbafha, H.; Afrasyabi, H.; Berrada, A. Prognostication of energy use and environmental impacts for recycle system of municipal solid waste management. *J. Clean Prod.* **2017**, *154*, 602–613. [CrossRef]
15. Mishra, M.; Hota, S.K.; Ghosh, S.K.; Sarkar, B. Controlling waste and carbon emission for a sustainable closed-loop supply chain management under a cap-and-trade strategy. *Mathematics* **2020**, *8*, 466. [CrossRef]
16. Nabavi-Pelesaraei, A.; Mohammadkashi, N.; Naderloo, L.; Abbasi, M.; Chau, K.W. Principal of environmental life cycle assessment for medical waste during COVID-19 outbreak to support sustainable development goals. *Sci. Total Environ.* **2022**, *827*, 154416. [CrossRef]
17. Jacobsen, R.; Willeghems, G.; Gellynck, X.; Buysse, J. Increasing the Quantity of Separated Post- consumer Plastics for Reducing Combustible Household Waste: The Case of Rigid Plastics in Flanders. *Waste Manag.* **2018**, *78*, 708–716. [CrossRef]
18. Li, Y.; Peyman, M.; Panadero, J.; Juan, A.A.; Xhafa, F. IoT Analytics and Agile Optimization for Solving Dynamic Team Orienteering Problems with Mandatory Visits. *Mathematics* **2022**, *10*, 982. [CrossRef]
19. Faccio, M.; Persona, A.; Zanin, G. Waste collection multi objective model with real time traceability data. *Waste Manag.* **2011**, *31*, 2391–2405. [CrossRef]
20. Mamun, M.A.; Hannan, M.A.; Hussain, A.; Basri, H. Theoretical model and implementation of a real time intelligent bin status monitoring system using rule based decision algorithms. *Expert Syst. Appl.* **2016**, *48*, 76–88. [CrossRef]
21. Yusof, N.M.; Zulkifli, M.F.; Yusof, M.; Azman, A.A. Smart Waste Bin with Real-time Monitoring System. *Int. J. Eng Technol.* **2018**, *7*, 725–729. [CrossRef]
22. Ramos, T.R.P.; de Morais, C.S.; Barbosa-Póvoa, A. The Smart Waste Collection Routing Problem: Alternative Operational Management Approaches. *Expert Syst. Appl.* **2018**, *103*, 146–158. [CrossRef]
23. Idwan, S.; Mahmood, I.; Zubairi, J.A.; Matar, I. Optimal Management of Solid Waste in Smart Cities Using Internet of Things. *Wirel. Pers. Commun.* **2020**, *110*, 485–501. [CrossRef]
24. Armbrust, M.; Fox, A.; Griffith, R.; Joseph, A.D.; Katz, R.; Konwinski, A.; Lee, G.; Patterson, D.; Rabkin, A.; Stoica, I. A view of cloud computing. *Commun. ACM* **2010**, *53*, 50–58. [CrossRef]
25. Shi, W.; Zhang, X.; Wang, Y.; Zhang, Q. Edge Computing: State-of-the-Art and Future Directions. *J. Comput. Res. Develop.* **2019**, *56*, 69–89.
26. Satyanarayanan, M. The emergence of edge computing. *Computer* **2017**, *50*, 30–39. [CrossRef]
27. Shi, W.; Cao, J.; Zhang, Q.; Li, Y.; Xu, L. Edge computing: Vision and challenges. *IEEE Internet Things J.* **2016**, *3*, 637–646. [CrossRef]
28. Yousefpour, A.; Fung, C.; Nguyen, T.; Kadiyala, K.; Jalali, F.; Niakanlahiji, A.; Kong, J.; Jue, J.P. All one needs to know about fog computing and related edge computing paradigms: A complete survey. *J. Syst. Architect.* **2019**, *98*, 289–330. [CrossRef]
29. Botta, A.; De Donato, W.; Persico, V.; Pescapé, A. Integration of cloud computing and internet of things: A survey. *Futur. Gener. Comp. Syst.* **2016**, *56*, 684–700. [CrossRef]
30. Qu, T.; Zhang, K.; Luo, H.; Wang, Z.; Jia, D.; Chen, X.; Huang, G.Q.; Li, X. Internet-of-things based dynamic synchronization of production and logistics: Mechanism, System and Case Study. *Chin. J. Mech. Eng.* **2015**, *51*, 36–44. [CrossRef]
31. Qu, T.; Lei, S.P.; Wang, Z.Z.; Nie, D.X.; Chen, X.; Huang, G.Q. IoT-based real-time production logistics synchronization system under smart cloud manufacturing. *Int. J. Adv. Manuf. Technol.* **2016**, *84*, 147–164. [CrossRef]
32. Luo, H.; Wang, K.; Kong, X.T.R.; Lu, S.; Qu, T. Synchronized production and logistics via ubiquitous computing technology. *Robot. Comput.-Integr. Manuf.* **2017**, *45*, 99–115. [CrossRef]
33. Noroozi, A.; Mazdeh, M.M.; Heydari, M.; Barzoki, M.R. Coordinating order acceptance and integrated production-distribution scheduling with batch delivery considering Third Party Logistics distribution. *J. Manuf. Syst.* **2018**, *46*, 29–45. [CrossRef]
34. Pan, Y.H.; Qu, T.; Wu, N.Q.; Qu, T.; Li, P.Z.; Zhang, K.; Guo, H.F. Digital Twin Based Real-time Production Logistics Synchronization System in a Multi-level Computing Architecture. *J. Manuf. Syst.* **2020**, *58*, 246–260. [CrossRef]
35. Ghiani, G.; Manni, A.; Manni, E.; Moretto, V. Optimizing a waste collection system with solid waste transfer stations. *Comput. Ind. Eng.* **2021**, *161*, 107618. [CrossRef]
36. Qu, T.; Zhang, K.; Li, C. Synchronized Decision-making and Control Method for Opti-state Execution of Dynamic Production Systems with Internet of Things. *Chin. J. Mech. Eng.* **2018**, *54*, 24–33. [CrossRef]

Article

Mathematical Formulations for Asynchronous Parallel Disassembly Planning of End-of-Life Products

Leilei Meng [1], Biao Zhang [1], Yaping Ren [2,*], Hongyan Sang [1], Kaizhou Gao [1] and Chaoyong Zhang [3]

1. School of Computer Science, Liaocheng University, Liaocheng 252000, China
2. Department of Industrial Engineering, School of Intelligent Systems Science and Engineering, Jinan University, Zhuhai 519070, China
3. State Key Lab of Digital Manufacturing Equipment and Technology, Huazhong University of Science and Technology, Wuhan 430074, China
* Correspondence: renyp1@163.com

Abstract: Disassembly is one of the most time-consuming and labor-intensive activities during the value recovery of end-of-life (EOL) products. The completion time (makespan) of disassembling EOL products is highly associated with the allocation of operators, especially in parallel disassembly. In this paper, asynchronous parallel disassembly planning (APDP), which avoids the necessity to synchronize disassembly tasks of manipulators during the parallel disassembly process, is studied to optimize the task assignment of manipulators for minimal makespan. We utilize four mixed integer linear programming (MILP) formulations to identify the optimal solutions. A set of different-sized instances are used to test and compare the performance of the proposed models, including some real-world cases. Finally, the proposed exact algorithm is further compared with the existing approach to solving APDP. Results indicate that a significant difference exists in terms of the computational efficiency of the MILP models, while three of four MILP formulations can efficiently achieve better solutions than that of the existing approach.

Keywords: demanufacturing; disassembly planning; asynchronous parallel disassembly; mixed integer linear programming; exact algorithm

MSC: 90B30

1. Introduction

As sustainable manufacturing and circular economy become popular in the industry, demanufacturing has recently attracted increasing attention. In demanufacturing, the first step is to disassemble end-of-life (EOL) products into components or parts and retrieve usable or repairable subassemblies. In addition to economic benefits, the disassembly of EOL products can bring environmental benefits due to the subsequent treatment of subassemblies (e.g., reuse, remanufacturing, and recycling) [1,2], especially toxic materials including solid, liquid, and gas. Disassembly planning (DP) aims to select the optimal disassembly sequence of an EOL product with maximum recovery value and/or processing efficiency [3].

According to the disassembly process, DP can be classified into two categories: (1) sequential disassembly, where parts are disassembled one by one; (2) parallel disassembly, where multiple parts can be disassembled by multiple manipulators simultaneously [4,5]. Sequential disassembly is a typical disassembly problem that has been studied for decades [6], in which only one part or component is disassembled at a time. Obviously, this one-by-one processing could incur a longer makespan to disassemble a product, especially for large or complex products. Parallel disassembly is thus developed that allows multiple manipulators to simultaneously perform disassembly operations. However, parallel disassembly must consider not only the precedence relationships among parts/disassembly operations but also the coordination among manipulators [4]. For parallel disassembly, two challenges need to be addressed: (1) which manipulator is selected for disassembling each part (allocation problem), (2) how to assign parts or disassembly tasks to each manipulator (sequencing problem). Therefore, parallel disassembly is more complicated than sequential disassembly, where sequential disassembly only involves a sequencing problem of disassembling parts/disassembly tasks.

To date, the existing literature on parallel disassembly largely focuses on synchronous manipulator processing, that is, synchronous parallel disassembly planning (SPDP) [3,7–9], which requires that the starting time of manipulators are synchronized in each parallel disassembly process. This synchronization simplifies parallel disassembly planning but increases the idle time of manipulators, which affects the disassembly efficiency. Recently, Ren et al. [4] presented a novel parallel disassembly, called asynchronous parallel disassembly, to eliminate the synchronous restriction and strengthen the collaboration among manipulators. Asynchronous parallel disassembly allows a manipulator to continuously work after completing a task as long as precedence (and other) constraints are not violated. In Ren et al.'s work, asynchronous parallel disassembly planning (APDP) was first studied and solved by an improved genetic algorithm (IGA). However, the authors did not describe APDP mathematically and there is no guarantee that the optimal disassembly solutions can be found by IGA. In order to make up for this shortcoming, this paper will make an improvement in terms of mathematical models and methodology based on [4]. Moreover, the proposed method in this work can solve the problems more optimally than the IGA in Ren et al.'s work.

This paper aims at developing an exact method based on the APDP, in which the minimum completion time (makespan) of disassembling a product can be identified. First, we propose a basic mathematical model (i.e., Model 1) for the APDP. Then, three extended models (i.e., Model 2, Model 3, and Model 4) are further developed. To evaluate the performance of the proposed models, a set of different-sized instances are tested. The results of these four formulations are presented and analyzed. Finally, the proposed approach is compared with the IGA used in [4]. Experimental results demonstrate that three of four MILP formulations outperform IGA, specifically, the solutions obtained from IGA are improved in 5 out of 11 test instances. In summary, the key contributions of this work can be summarized as follows:

(1) A nonlinear mathematical model is formulated to demonstrate the APDP.
(2) Four MILP formulations are developed based on the nonlinear model.
(3) The branch-and-cut algorithm of the CPLEX solver is employed to search for exact solutions. The results demonstrate that the exact solutions of three MILP models are able to improve the current best solutions in the test instances.

The remainder of this paper is organized as follows. Section 2 provides a literature review, primarily focusing on DP. Section 3 describes the APDP and Section 4 presents four MILP formulations for the APDP. Section 5 first presents the computational results of the models in terms of the problem complexity and the computational performance. Then, the computational results obtained from the proposed approach are compared with that of the existing IGA method. Finally, concluding remarks and future directions are covered in Section 4.

2. Literature Review

The DP is a combinatorial optimization problem and it can be solved by both exact algorithms and heuristic/metaheuristic approaches [10–14]. In terms of exact methods, branch-and-bound algorithms [5,15] and mathematical programming [16] are commonly used, especially the latter. For example, Johnson and Wang [17] established an integer linear programming model based on a two-commodity network flow formulation to find an optimal solution with maximum profit. Kang et al. [18] presented an integer programming model for disassembly sequence planning by modifying the shortest path problem. Lambert [19] formulated a binary integer linear programming approach to maximize profit by applying an AND/OR graph for enumerating the complete set of possible disassembly operations. Ren et al. [16] presented a MILP model to maximize the profit of a partial disassembly process. Edis et al. [20] proposed a MILP model for the disassembly line balancing problem. In addition, several extensions on the MILP model regarding line balancing, hazardousness and demand of parts, and direction changes are proposed.

The exact algorithms perform well when solving relatively small-sized problem instances [21]. However, with the increase in the problem size, their computational times grow exponentially. Therefore, approximate methods are widely used to solve DP problems [22]. Approximate methods mainly refer to heuristics and meta-heuristic algorithms. Smith and Hung [8] studied selective parallel disassembly planning and aimed to maximize product quality and minimize product cost and environmental impacts. Sanchez and Haas [23] studied building disassembly and designed a rule-based recursive method to obtain a near-optimal solution. Seo et al. [24] aimed to optimize the disassembly sequence considering economic and environmental aspects and proposed a genetic algorithm (GA). Kongar and Gupta [25] proposed a weighted multi-objective model to solve the DP problem with consideration of disassembly time, the penalty for direction changes, and the penalty for disassembly method changes. Tian et al. [26] studied the disassembly planning considering uncertainty and proposed a GA to minimize disassembly cost. Based on that, they proposed a hybrid intelligent algorithm that integrates fuzzy simulation and artificial bee colony [27]. Kheder et al. [28] designed a GA to optimize a disassembly process considering several criteria such as maintainability of components and disassembly direction changes. Ren et al. [3] proposed a hierarchical disassembly tree to model selective SPDP and a multi-objective evolutionary algorithm to simultaneously minimize disassembly time and maximize profit. Guo et al. [29] used a scatter search algorithm to simultaneously maximize disassembly profit and minimize time using the weighted coefficient method. Recently, Pistolesi and Lazzerini [9] studied a multi-objective SPDP and proposed a Tensorial Memetic Algorithm (TeMA) to maximize the degree of parallelism, the level of ergonomics, and the balance of workers' workload, while minimizing the disassembly time and the number of rotating the product.

Meta-heuristic approaches also include the artificial bee colony (ABC) algorithm [27,30–32], the particle swarm optimization (PSO) algorithm [33], the gravitational search algorithm (GSA) [16], and the discrete flower pollination algorithm [34]. They are highly dependent on solution encoding and decoding, parameter setting, and evolutionary operators [35]. On the other hand, it is difficult to guarantee both robustness and optimality of the solutions obtained from a meta-heuristic method [36].

From the literature review above, it is noted that (1) the meta-heuristic algorithms are commonly used to solve DPs, especially for large instances; (2) few studies are available on APDP. In particular, no work exists that models and solves APDP optimally. To fill these gaps, this work is focused on modeling and developing an efficient exact algorithm for APDP. Except for that, this work attempts to optimally solve APDP with medium-/large-sized instances.

3. Problem Description

3.1. Representation of DP

To model a DP problem, we first draw a disassembly precedence diagram to represent the prior relationships among disassembly operations/parts in a product. In a precedence diagram, each part of a product is indexed by j, $j = 0, 1, \ldots, N$. N is the number of parts and part 0 is a dummy part that denotes an initial point of the disassembly process. Figure 1 shows an example of the disassembly precedence diagram, in which there are 10 parts and a directed edge is used to represent the precedence relationship between pairwise adjacent parts. The edge can be viewed as a disassembly operation, which means that part j will be removed after traversing the edge pointing to it. In Figure 1, the disassembly operations are either solid lines (indicating AND precedence relationships) or dotted lines (indicating OR precedence relationships). A part that is an AND predecessor of part j

must be disassembled before removing part *j*. For example, part 7 is the AND predecessor of parts 5 and 6 so it has to be removed before part 5 or 6 can be disassembled. Before disassembling part *j*, not less than one of the parts that are OR predecessors of part *j* must be done. For example, part 3 is one of OR predecessors of parts 1 and the other is part 2, so either part 2 or part 3 has to be removed before part 1 can be disassembled.

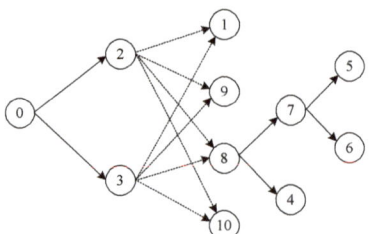

Figure 1. An example of the disassembly precedence diagram for a product.

3.2. Synchronous Parallel Disassembly and Asynchronous Parallel Disassembly

Here, we adapt the example in Figure 1 to differentiate synchronous and asynchronous disassembly processes, which are illustrated in Figure 2a,b, respectively. In Figure 2, the numbers labeled in the parentheses denote the indices of parts and the disassembly time of parts, respectively. Two manipulators are employed to perform the same disassembly sequences in both Figure 2a,b, that is, {2, 8, 7, 5} and {3, 10, 9, 1, 4, 6}. The projection of each rectangle denotes the disassembly time of the corresponding part. From Figure 2a, it is observed that the beginning time of disassembling parts of manipulators is synchronous and a manipulator cannot start a new disassembly task until all other manipulators complete their current ones. The makespan of the synchronous disassembly process is the sum of the maximum disassembly time among parts in each parallel disassembly, which are marked in shadows in Figure 2a. It can be seen that little idle time exists in the asynchronous disassembly process, that is, Figure 2b but a large amount of idle time occurs in synchronous manipulator processing, that is, Figure 2a.

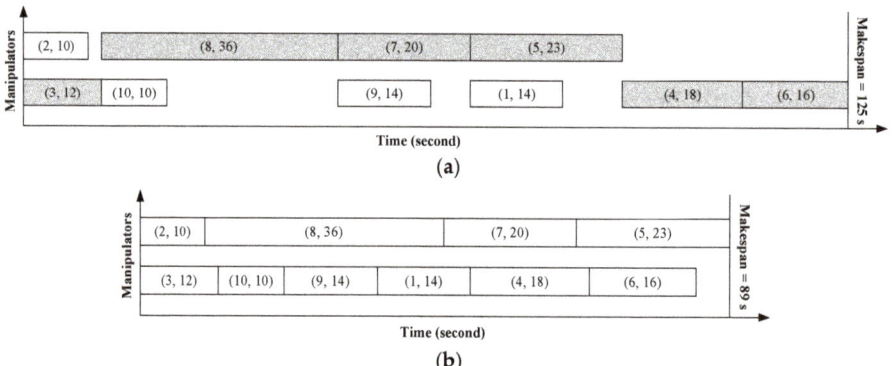

Figure 2. The comparison between two parallel disassembly processes. (**a**) Synchronous parallel disassembly process. (**b**) Asynchronous parallel disassembly process.

In this work, the following assumptions or specifications are considered:
- AND precedence and OR precedence relationships are ensured.
- Work area collisions among manipulators are considered.
- Once a part begins, it cannot be interrupted.
- Each part is exactly removed once by one manipulator.
- Disassembly times of parts are determined in advance.

- A manipulator can remove at most one part at the same time.

4. MILP Modeling of APDP

The notations are shown as follows:

N	the number of parts
i, j	part indices in a product, $i, j \in I = \{1, 2, \ldots, N\}$
p, p'	position indices of manipulators, where $p, p' \in P = \{1, 2, \ldots, N\}$
N_m	the number of manipulators
m	manipulator index, $m \in \{1, 2, \ldots, N_m\}$
t_i	the disassembly time of part i
$ANDP(i)$	index set of AND predecessors of part i
$ORP(i)$	index set of OR predecessors of part i
$W(i)$	index set of parts that have work area collisions with part i in the parallel disassembly process
M	a large positive number
$x_{i,m,p}$	a binary decision variable, $x_{i,m,p} = 1$, if part i occupies p^{th} position of the disassembly sequence of manipulator m; otherwise, $x_{i,m,p} = 0$
$x_{i,m}$	a binary decision variable, $x_{i,m} = 1$, if part i is removed by manipulator m; otherwise, $x_{i,m} = 0$
$u_{i,j,m}$	a binary decision variable, $u_{i,j,m} = 0$, if part i is removed immediately before part j by manipulator m; otherwise, $u_{i,j,m} = 0$
$y_{i,j}$	a binary decision variable, $y_{i,j} = 1$, if part i is removed before (adjacent or non-adjacent) part j; otherwise, $y_{i,j} = 0$, part j is removed before (adjacent or non-adjacent) part i
s_i	a continuous decision variable, the starting time of disassembling part i
$sm_{m,p}$	a continuous decision variable, the time when manipulator m starts to remove the pth part
C_{max}	a continuous decision variable, the maximum completion time (makespan) of the disassembly process

As shown in Equation (1), the objective of our APDP is to minimize the makespan of completely disassembling a product, in which the assignment of disassembly tasks and the sequence of removing parts are integrally determined for each manipulator. In the following, we will illustrate the MILP formulations of the APDP.

$$\min C_{max} \tag{1}$$

4.1. Model 1

As aforementioned, two subproblems, that is, the allocation problem and sequencing problem need to be addressed. Here, we introduce a binary decision variable $x_{i,m,p}$ that represents whether part i is the pth part removed by manipulator m. Moreover, two continuous decision variables, that is, s_i and C_{max}, are employed to denote the starting time of removing part i and the makespan of the disassembly process, respectively. The constraint sets of Model 1 are described in Equations (2)–(10):

$$\sum_{m=1}^{N_m} \sum_{p=1}^{N} x_{i,m,p} = 1, \forall i \tag{2}$$

$$\sum_{i=1}^{N} x_{i,m,p} \leq 1, \forall m, p \tag{3}$$

$$s_i x_{i,m,p+1} x_{j,m,p} \geq (s_j + t_j) x_{i,m,p+1} x_{j,m,p},$$
$$\forall i, j, m, p \in \{1, 2, \ldots, N-1\} \tag{4}$$

$$\sum_{i=1}^{N} x_{i,m,p} \geq \sum_{j=1}^{N} x_{j,m,p+1}, \ \forall m, \ p \in \{1, 2, \ldots, N-1\} \tag{5}$$

$$s_i \geq s_j + t_j, \ \forall i, j \in ANDP(i) \tag{6}$$

$$s_i \geq s_j + t_j, \ \forall i, \exists j \in ORP(i) \tag{7}$$

$$s_i \geq s_j + t_j \text{ or } s_j \geq s_i + t_i, \ \forall i, j \in W(i) \tag{8}$$

$$C_{max} \geq s_i + t_i, \ \forall i \tag{9}$$

$$s_i \geq 0, \forall i \tag{10}$$

Constraint (2) denotes that each part must be exactly removed once by one manipulator during the disassembly process. Constraint (3) denotes that a manipulator can remove at most one part simultaneously. Constraint (4) ensures that a manipulator can begin to disassemble the next part only after the current part is completely disassembled. To be more specific, if $x_{j,m,p}$ and $x_{i,m,p+1}$ are equal to 1, parts j and i are successively disassembled by manipulator m, which indicates that the completion time of removing part j is no more than the starting time of removing part i; otherwise, both sides of inequation (4) are equal to 0. Constraint (5) denotes that there is no idle position in each disassembly sequence until the last part of each disassembly sequence is removed by the manipulator. Constraint (6) and (7) guarantee the AND, and OR precedence relationships among parts, respectively. Constraint set (7) can also be formulated as $\sum_{j \in ORP(i)} s_i \geq s_j + t_j, \forall i$, among which $s_i \geq s_j + t_j$ returns 1 or 0. Constraint (8) excludes the work area collisions between manipulators when they work at the same time. Constraint (9) means that the makespan of a disassembly process must be more than the completion time of disassembling each part. Constraint (10) defines the decision variable s_i.

Equations (1)–(10) are linear except constraint (4). Constraint (4) includes the product of binary and continuous variables, which is typically non-convex and difficult to be solved. Here, we use the big M method to linearize formulation (4). Then, constraint (4) is converted to constraint (11). The MILP of Model 1 can be depicted by formulations (1)–(3) and (5)–(11).

$$s_i \geq s_j + t_j - M * (2 - x_{i,m,p+1} - x_{j,m,p}),$$
$$\forall i, j, m, p \in \{1, 2, \ldots, N-1\} \tag{11}$$

4.2. Model 2

Although constraint (11) is linear, it involves four indices (i.e., i, j, m, and p) and consists of a large number of constraints. This could incur an increase in the computational complexity of Model 1. To avoid the complex computation, we attempt to simplify constraint (11) in this segment.

First, a continuous variable $sm_{m,p}$ is defined that denotes the starting time of removing the pth part by manipulator m. With $x_{i,m,p}$, s_i, and $sm_{m,p}$, we can obtain the following equations:

$$sm_{m,p} = \sum_{i=1}^{N} s_i x_{i,m,p}, \forall m, p \tag{12}$$

$$sm_{m,p+1} \geq sm_{m,p} + \sum_{i=1}^{N} x_{i,m,p} t_i, \forall i, m, p \in \{1, 2, \ldots, N-1\} \tag{13}$$

Equation (12) illustrates the relationships among the decision variables, which denotes that if part i is the pth part removed by manipulator m, that is, $x_{i,m,p} = 1$, $sm_{m,p}$ must be equal to s_i. Constraint (13) is used to replace constraint (11), where the number of constraints becomes small. However, the right-hand side of Equation (12) is nonlinear. To linearize it, we formulate constraints (14)–(16), which are equivalent to constraint (12). To be more specific, if $x_{i,m,p} = 1$, constraint (14) enforces $sm_{m,p}$ to be no less than s_i and constraint (15) enforces $sm_{m,p}$ to be no more than s_i. Therefore, $sm_{m,p}$ is equal to s_i. If $x_{i,m,p} = 0$, constraint (14) and (15) are relaxed and holds, and constraint (16) guarantee that $sm_{m,p}$ is equal to 0.

$$sm_{m,p} \leq s_i + M(1 - x_{i,m,p}), \forall i, m, p \tag{14}$$

$$sm_{m,p} \geq s_i - M(1 - x_{i,m,p}), \forall i, m, p \tag{15}$$

$$sm_{m,p} \geq 0, \forall m, p \tag{16}$$

4.3. Model 3

Decision variable $x_{i,m,p}$ is indispensable and crucial in both Model 1 and Model 2. Here, $x_{i,m,p}$ is simplified to be $x_{i,m}$ to reduce the solution space and it determines whether part i is removed by manipulator m without considering the position p. Nevertheless, $x_{i,m}$ can only deal with the allocation problem of removal parts, and additional binary variable $y_{i,j}$ is thus introduced. If $y_{i,j}$ equals 1, part i is removed before part j; otherwise, part i is removed after part j, by which the disassembly sequence of parts can be determined.

The relationships among $x_{i,m}$, $y_{i,j}$, and s_i are formulated as:

$$\sum_{m=1}^{N_m} x_{i,m} = 1, \forall i \tag{17}$$

$$(s_j - s_i - t_i)x_{i,m}x_{j,m}y_{i,j} \geq 0, \forall m, i, j, i < j \tag{18}$$

$$(s_i - s_j - t_j)x_{i,m}x_{j,m}(1 - y_{i,j}) \geq 0, \forall m, i, j, i < j \tag{19}$$

Constraint (17) denotes that the disassembly task of each part must be exactly assigned to one manipulator. Constraints (18) and (19) are equivalent to constraint (11). Specifically, inequation (18) requires that the starting time of removing part j is later than the completion time of removing part i when $x_{i,m} = 1$, $x_{j,m} = 1$ and $y_{i,j} = 1$. Instead, inequation (19) denotes that the starting time of removing part i is later than the completion time of removing part j when $x_{i,m} = 1$, $x_{j,m} = 1$ and $y_{i,j} = 0$. Notably, constraints (18) and (19) are dual with respect to i and j. Hence, both indices can be subjected to $i < j$, which helps reduce the number of constraints in constraints (18) and (19).

Due to the nonconvexity and nonlinearity of constraints (18) and (19), we further transform them into constraints (20) and (21), respectively. The MILP of Model 3 is obtained by Equations (1), (6)–(10), (17), and (20)–(21).

$$s_j \geq s_i + t_i - M(3 - x_{i,m} - x_{j,m} - y_{i,j}), \forall m, i, j, i < j \tag{20}$$

$$s_j + t_j \leq s_i + M(2 - x_{i,m} - x_{j,m} + y_{i,j}), \forall m, i, j, i < j \tag{21}$$

4.4. Model 4

As presented in Model 3, $x_{i,m}$ is integrated with $y_{i,j}$ to address the allocation and sequencing problems of APDP. Herein, we combine $x_{i,m}$ and $y_{i,j}$ into a binary decision variable, i.e., $u_{i,j,m}$. Let $u_{i,j,m} = 1$ mean that part i is removed immediately before part j for the same manipulator m, and otherwise $u_{i,j,m} = 0$ [37]. Clearly, $u_{i,j,m}$ can simultaneously decide on the task assignment of manipulators and the disassembly sequence of parts. Furthermore, a dummy part, that is, part 0 is assumed to start and terminate each disassembly sequence. This implies that part 0 is disassembled twice by each manipulator, that is, the starting and the completion time of each disassembly sequence. It should be noted that the disassembly time of part 0 is zero.

Based on decision variables $u_{i,j,m}$, and s_i, Model 4 can be formulated as follows.

$$\sum_{i=0}^{N} \sum_{m=1}^{N_m} u_{i,j,m} = 1, \forall j \tag{22}$$

$$\sum_{i=0}^{N}\sum_{m=1}^{N_m} u_{i,j,m} = \sum_{i=0}^{N}\sum_{m=1}^{N_m} u_{j,i,m}, \forall j \in \{0,1,\ldots,N\} \tag{23}$$

$$\sum_{j=1}^{N} u_{0,j,m} \leq 1, \forall m \tag{24}$$

$$(s_j - s_i - t_i)\sum_{m=1}^{N_m} u_{i,j,m} \geq 0, \forall i,j \tag{25}$$

$$s_0 = 0 \tag{26}$$

Constraint (22) is equivalent to constraint (17), which indicates that each part has exactly one immediate predecessor that is disassembled by the same manipulator. Constraint (23) guarantees the equilibrium of in-degree and out-degree, that is, each part has exactly one immediate predecessor and follower in the disassembly sequence. Actually, the disassembly sequence of each manipulator is a tour that starts from part 0 and terminates at part 0. Constraint (24) is formulated to eliminate the subtour, that is, each manipulator can at most complete one disassembly sequence. Similar to constraint (4), constraint set (25) denotes that the immediate predecessor of each part must be earlier removed before it. Constraint (26) denotes that the starting time of part 0 is equal to zero.

Finally, inequation (25) is linearized to (27) using the big M method, and the MILP of Model 4 is formulated by Equations (1), (6)–(10), (22)–(24), and (26)–(27).

$$s_i + t_i \leq s_j + M(1 - \sum_{m=1}^{N_m} u_{i,j,m}), \forall i,j \tag{27}$$

5. Computational Results

The Branch-and-Cut (B&C) algorithm of IBM ILOG CPLEX 12.7.1 is used to solve the proposed MILP formulations. The B&C algorithm is embodied in the CPLEX software (i.e., IBM ILOG CPLEX 12.7.1, IBM International Business Machines Corporation, New York, NY, USA), which is very popular in solving mixed integer programming (MIP), especially for mixed integer linear programming (MILP). In this section, four product cases previously used in [4] are applied to test our models and evaluate the exact solutions found by the B&C. Except Case 1 with 10 parts as presented in Figure 1, others are real-world cases, that is, a valve cover head fixture with 22 parts (Case 2), an engine block with 35 parts (Case 3), and a five-speed mechanical transmission with 40 parts (Case 4). Also, the maximum CPU time (timelimit) used by the B&C is set to be 600 s and other configurations of the algorithm adopt the default settings in the CPLEX software. The algorithm is implemented on a desktop computer equipped with Intel Core i5-4460 CPU@3.20 GHz.

5.1. Comparisons of MILP Models

This subsection compares four MILP models in both size complexity and computational complexity. Three indicators are employed to evaluate the size complexity, that is, the number of binary decision variables (NBV), the number of constraints (NC), and the number of continuous decision variables (NCV). The performance of the MILP formulations is highly associated with NBV, NC, and NCV [38,39]. Like others, in this paper, the computational complexity is measured by the current solution (CS) found in the B&C, CPU time consumed by the B&C, Gap, and Opt. CPU time is equal to timelimit if the B&C algorithm cannot prove the optimal solution; otherwise, it is the time consumed for proving the optimal solution. Note that Gap is the relative tolerance between CS and BS, where BS is the lower bound obtained from the CPLEX solver, and Gap = |CS − BS|/CS% [40–43]. Opt represents the total number of problem instances solved to optimality by the B&C algorithm within 600 s.

5.1.1. Size Complexity

Table 1 summarizes the four MILP models, and Table 2 reports the detailed information on NBV, NC, and NCV of each model in the test instances. The first column of Table 2 denotes the number of manipulators employed in each case. It can be seen from Table 2 that Model 3 has the smallest NBV, Model 4 has the smallest NC, and Models 1, 3, and 4 have the smallest NCV. Model 1 has much more constraints than Model 2 since constraint (11) in Model 1 comprises of much more constraints than constraints (13)–(16) in Model 2. Due to decision variable $sm_{m,p}$, NCV in Model 2 is larger than that in Model 1. In Model 3, two-dimensional variables $x_{i,m}$ and $y_{i,j}$ replace the three-dimensional decision variables. Herein, the differences in the MILP models are analyzed with respect to decision variables and constraints, the following subsection will further discuss the relationships between the size complexity and the computational complexity.

Table 1. Summary of four MILP Models.

Models	Model 1	Model 2	Model 3	Model 4
Binary variables	$x_{i,m,p}$	$x_{i,m,p}$	$x_{i,m}$, $y_{i,j}$	$u_{i,j,m}$
Constraint sets	(2)–(3), (5)–(11)	(2)–(3), (5)–(10), (13)–(16)	(6)–(10), (17), (20)–(21)	(6)–(10), (22)–(24), (26)–(27)
Continuous variables	s_i, C_{max}	s_i, $sm_{m,p}$, C_{max}	s_i, C_{max}	s_i, C_{max}

Table 2. Comparison of size complexity.

Nm	Case	Model 1			Model 2			Model 3			Model 4		
		NBV	NC	NCV	NBV	NC	NCV	NBV	NC	NCV	NBV	NC	NCV
2	1	244	2504	12	244	610	34	79	262	12	288	190	13
	2	968	20,503	23	968	2197	67	275	1013	23	1056	622	24
	3	2458	83,593	36	2458	5331	106	673	2535	36	2598	1455	37
	4	3216	125,140	41	3216	6898	121	876	3302	41	3376	1867	42
3	1	365	3735	12	365	894	45	90	372	12	431	203	13
	2	1452	30,710	23	1452	3251	89	297	1475	23	1584	646	24
	3	3683	125,312	36	3683	7919	141	708	3725	36	3893	1492	37
	4	4816	187,619	41	4816	10,256	161	916	4862	41	5056	1909	42
4	1	486	4966	12	486	1178	56	101	482	12	574	216	13
	2	1936	40,917	23	1936	4305	111	319	1937	23	2112	670	24
	3	4908	167,031	36	4908	10,507	176	743	4915	36	5188	1529	37
	4	6416	250,098	41	6416	13,614	201	956	6422	41	6736	1951	42

5.1.2. Computational Complexity

This segment focuses on the analysis of computational complexity among the models and the comparison of the results is shown in Table 3. The first column of Table 3 denotes the number of manipulators employed in each case. It is observed that Model 1 performs worst in both the solution quality and the computational efficiency. It can only find the optimal solutions for 5 out of 12 instances and its Gap values are equal to 0 in 4 instances. For Case 3 and Case 4, Model 1 cannot even find any feasible solutions within 600 s. As described in Table 1, Model 1 includes a three-dimensional binary variable $x_{i,m,p}$ and a complex constraint (11), which results in poor computational performance.

Table 3. Comparisons of computational complexity.

Nm	Case	Model 1			Model 2			Model 3			Model 4		
		CS	CPU (s)	Gap	CS	CPU (s)	Gap	CS	CPU (s)	Gap	CS	CPU (s)	Gap
2	1	89	2.18	0	89	0.37	0	89	0.03	0	89	0.20	0
	2	25.5	600	29.41	20.5	484.26	0	20.5	1.67	0	20.5	1.61	0
	3	-	600	-	1727	600	16.33	1726	600	13.04	1726	600	16.28
	4	-	600	-	-	600	-	365	600	6.85	384	600	24.74
3	1	89	0.81	0	89	0.14	0	89	0.03	0	89	0.08	0
	2	20	600	10.0	20	179.28	0	20	0.91	0	20	0.27	0
	3	-	600	-	1445	169.65	0	1445	3.25	0	1445	548.67	0
	4	-	600	-	-	600	-	338	600	5.92	338	600	14.50
4	1	89	0.42	0	89	0.16	0	89	0.05	0	89	0.06	0
	2	18	346.31	0	18	50.5	0	18	0.20	0	18	0.25	0
	3	-	600	-	1445	204.92	0	1445	0.91	0	1445	345.54	0
	4	-	600	-	-	600	-	305	600	1.97	310	600	6.77
Mean			429.14	6.57		290.77	1.18		200.59	0.49		274.72	1.69
Opt			5			8			8			8	

In terms of computational performance, Model 2 is significantly better than Model 1. Firstly, Model 2 is able to optimally solve 8 out of 12 instances (i.e., Gap = 0). Secondly, its computational cost is much less than that of Model 1. By comparing their size complexities, we can find that constraint (11) is simplified to constraint (13) in Model 2, which highly reduces its complexity.

The Gap values of Models 2 and 3 show that the same instances can be optimally solved by both models. As seen in the CS values, Model 3 can obtain feasible or optimal solutions in each case within 600 s, whereas Model 2 cannot explore a feasible solution in 3 out of 12 instances within 600 s. This demonstrates that the computational efficiency of Model 3 is superior to that of Model 2. By comparing their decision variables in Table 1, we find that Model 3 does not involve a three-dimensional binary variable $x_{i,m,p}$ and a continuous variable $sm_{m,p}$. Furthermore, the constraints of Model 3 are much less than those of Model 2 according to the NC values in Table 2. Hence, the simplified decision variables and the reduced constraints might improve the computational performance of the models.

For Model 4, its CS values are slightly different from those of Model 3. Specifically, only two solutions are found in Model 4, which is a little inferior to Model 3 in all tests. On the other hand, the Gap values of Model 4 are significantly bigger than those of Model 3 when both cannot optimally solve the test instances. Therefore, Model 4 is not as good as Model 3 in terms of solution convergence.

The last two rows of Table 3 provide the mean CPU time, the mean Gap, and Opt of each model over all test instances. Notably, we only consider the instances that feasible solutions can be found within 600 s when computing the mean Gap. It is noted that Model 1 finds the least optimal solutions (i.e., Opt = 4), while the other models explore 8 optimal solutions within 600 s. Although Models 2, 3, and 4 have the same Opt, both the mean CPU time and the mean Gap of Model 3 significantly outperform those of Models 2 and 4. Therefore, Model 3 is the best, Models 2 and 4 are secondary, and Model 1 performs worst for solving the APDP.

Table 4 presents the best solutions for Cases 3 and 4 with N_m = 2, 3, and 4, respectively. Figures 3 and 4 present the Gantt charts of the best solutions for Cases 3 and 4, respectively.

As seen in Table 4, Figures 3 and 4, the makespan gets some extent improvement with the increase of manipulators. However, there exists a threshold with respect to N_m. In other words, the makespan of the disassembly process will not be reduced once the manipulators are redundant. For example, Case 3 with 3 and 4 manipulators are able to find the same optimal solution (i.e., 1445). This situation also usually happens in practice. Our proposed method can help decision-makers select the ideal manipulator configuration, where trade-offs have to be made between the makespan and the cost of manipulators. With regard to the case with considering unlimited manipulators, the four MILP mod-els can be seen in Appendix A.

Table 4. Best Solutions for Cases 3–4 with 2–4 Manipulators.

Case	N_m	Solution	C_{max}
3	2	M1:15,4,34,5,12,29,33,21,8,10,18,6,9,30,14 M2:1,13,31,16,35,24,20,7,11,19,26,17,23,25,32,22,3,2,27,28	1726
	3	M1:1,13,20,4,5,15,29,24,26,25,10,31,9,11,21,18,3,2,22,12,27,28 M2:34,35,32,17,30 M3:14,8,7,6,33,16,19,23	1445
	4	M1:34,33,24,29,25,16,13,4,5,3,2,22,27,28 M2:35,32,20,8,19,18,12,11,6 M3:15,21,14,7,30 M4:1,31,26,17,10,9,23	1445
4	2	M1:15,18,21,23,24,19,33,32,39,34,36,22,20,4,3,29,28,6,10,8,11 M2:16,17,2,25,26,5,37,40,35,38,31,7,9,27,30,14,13,1,12	365
	3	M1:17,22,2,19,21,5,31,37,38,7,9,28,1,10,8,12 M2:15,16,24,25,34,33,36,20,14,29,13 M3:18,26,23,40,35,32,39,4,27,30,6,3,11	338
	4	M1:15,2,26,25,5,34,38,7,9,30,29,6,10,8,12 M2:17,40,36,13 M3:18,24,20,32,31,39,22,14,3 M4:16,23,35,33,37,19,21,4,28,27,1,11	305

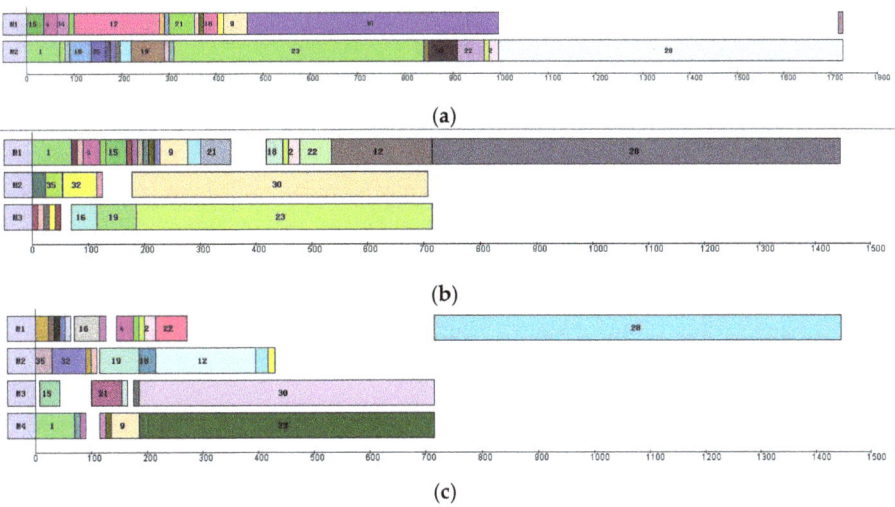

Figure 3. Gantt charts of Case 3 with 2–4 manipulators. (a) Case 3 with 2 manipulators ($C_{max} = 1726$). (b) Case 3 with 3 manipulators ($C_{max} = 1445$). (c) Case 3 with 4 manipulators ($C_{max} = 1445$).

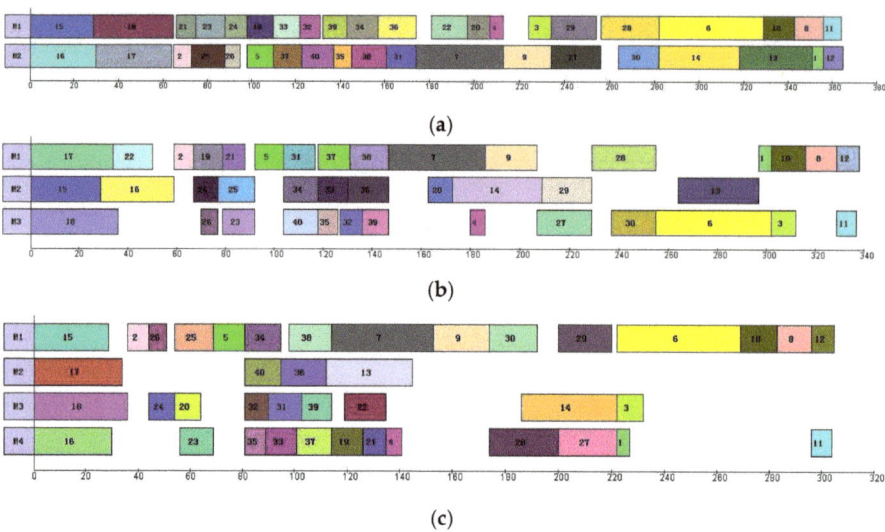

Figure 4. Gantt charts of Case 4 with 2–4 manipulators. (**a**) Case 4 with 2 manipulators ($C_{max} = 365$). (**b**) Case 4 with 3 manipulators ($C_{max} = 338$). (**c**) Case 4 with 4 manipulators ($C_{max} = 305$).

5.2. Result Comparisons with IGA

The exact solutions obtained from the proposed MILP models are compared with the solutions from the IGA in [4]. Table 5 shows the result comparisons, in which the best solution for each instance is highlighted. It can be seen that IGA can obtain seven best solutions in 12 test instances. Models 1–4 can identify 5, 9, 12, and 10 best solutions, respectively. Obviously, IGA outperforms Model 1, while it is not as good as Models 2–4. On the other hand, IGA cannot ensure that the same solution is obtained in each test, which can be demonstrated by the difference among the Best, Average and Worst values of IGA. Instead, the proposed method aims to solve the exact solutions of the APDP. Except for that, it can guarantee the robustness of the solution. In summary, three out of four proposed MILP models perform better than the IGA in both the quality and robustness of the solutions. This is because the IGA is one of the approximation algorithms, and it cannot guarantee obtaining the same solution within the same time limit. This is the commonness of most approximation algorithms. With regard to MILP formulation, it is solved by the exact Branch-and-Cut (B&C) algorithm of CPLEX, and the same solution within the same time limit can be obtained.

Table 5. Computational results of our MILP models and the IGA.

Case	Nm	IGA			Model 1	Model 2	Model 3	Model 4
		Best	Average	Worst				
1	2	89	90.3	93	89	89	89	89
	3	89	89	89	89	89	89	89
	4	89	89	89	89	89	89	89
2	2	20.5	20.8	21	25.5	20.5	20.5	20.5
	3	20	20	20	20	20	20	20
	4	18	18	18	18	18	18	18
3	2	1728	1731.9	1736	-	1727	1726	1726
	3	1505	1516.6	1525	-	1445	1445	1445
	4	1445	1454.9	1467	-	1445	1445	1445
4	2	400	414.8	426	-	-	365	384
	3	342	350.5	357	-	-	338	338
	4	306	312.8	317	-	-	305	310

The best values are marked in bold.

6. Conclusions

This paper is focused on exploring the exact solutions of asynchronous parallel disassembly planning (APDP) with minimal makespan during the disassembly process. A basic nonlinear mathematical model is presented to demonstrate the APDP. To improve the basic model, four MILP models are further developed using linearization or relaxation techniques. We employ the branch-and-cut algorithm embedded in CPLEX to solve the models. In the experimental tests, the four MILP models are analyzed from the perspective of size complexity. Then, the computational performance of each model is evaluated and compared by solving a set of instances. The obtained results indicate that Model 3 performs best, Models 2 and 4 are secondary, and the worst is Model 1. Finally, the obtained exact solutions are compared with the existing solutions from an improved genetic algorithm (IGA). The comparison demonstrates that three out of four proposed models can obtain better solutions than the IGA.

In this paper, only 12 tests are done to evaluate the differences of different MILP models. We welcome related researchers to use our MILP formulations to solve more different-sized instances and find more differences between different MILP models. It is undeniable that the efficiency of IGA (approximation algorithm) will be much higher than the MILP model for solving large-sized instances, this has been proved by much existing research for solving other combinatorial optimization problems [21,40]. This is because, with the increase of the size of the instance, the solution space, the number of decision variables, and the number of constraints will enlarge exponentially, which will result in difficult branching and finding new low bounds of the B&C algorithm.

In future studies, other important factors such as the recovered profit of EOL products and the manipulator configuration will be considered as the objective for APDP, which could help find much better optimal solutions that involve the balance between disassembly efficiency, cost, and profit.

Author Contributions: L.M.: Writing—Original draft, methodology. B.Z.: conceptualization. Y.R.: validation, supervision. H.S.: formal analysis. K.G.: validation. C.Z.: editing. All authors have read and agreed to the published version of the manuscript.

Funding: This research is supported by the Funds for National Natural Science Foundation of China [grant numbers 52205529, 52205526 and 62173356], the Natural Science Foundation of Shandong Province [grant numbers ZR2021QE195 and ZR2021QF036], the Basic and Applied Basic Research

Foundation of Guangdong Province of China (Grant No. 2019A1515110399) and Guangyue Youth Scholar Innovation Talent Program support received from Liaocheng University [LCUGYTD2022-03].

Institutional Review Board Statement: Not applicable.

Informed Consent Statement: Not applicable.

Data Availability Statement: The data that support the findings of this study are available from the corresponding author, upon reasonable request.

Conflicts of Interest: The authors declare no conflict of interest.

Appendix A

With regard to the case considering unlimited manipulators, the four MILP models are as follows. Model 1 is subjected to constraint sets (A1)–(A8), Model 2 is subjected to constraint sets (A1)–(A12), Model 3 is subjected to constraint sets (A4)–(A8) and (A13)–(A14), and Model 4 is subjected constraint sets (A4)–(A8) and (A15)–(A18).

$$\sum_{p=1}^{N} x_{i,p} = 1, \forall i \tag{A1}$$

$$\sum_{i=1}^{N} x_{i,p} \leq 1, \forall p \tag{A2}$$

$$\sum_{i=1}^{N} x_{i,p} \geq \sum_{j=1}^{N} x_{j,p+1}, \forall p \in \{1,2,\ldots,N-1\} \tag{A3}$$

$$s_i \geq s_j + t_j, \forall i,j \in ANDP(i) \tag{A4}$$

$$s_i \geq s_j + t_j, \forall i, \exists j \in ORP(i) \tag{A5}$$

$$s_i \geq s_j + t_j \text{ or } s_j \geq s_i + t_i, \forall i, j \in W(i) \tag{A6}$$

$$C_{max} \geq s_i + t_i, \forall i \tag{A7}$$

$$s_i \geq 0, \forall i \tag{A8}$$

$$sm_{p+1} \geq sm_p + \sum_{i=1}^{N} x_{i,p} t_i, \forall i, p \in \{1,2,\ldots,N-1\} \tag{A9}$$

$$sm_p \leq s_i + M(1 - x_{i,p}), \forall i, p \tag{A10}$$

$$sm_p \geq s_i - M(1 - x_{i,p}), \forall i, p \tag{A11}$$

$$sm_p \geq 0, \forall p \tag{A12}$$

$$s_j \geq s_i + t_i - M(1 - y_{i,j}), \forall m, i, j, i < j \tag{A13}$$

$$s_j + t_j \leq s_i + My_{i,j}, \forall m, i, j, i < j \tag{A14}$$

$$\sum_{i=0}^{N} u_{i,j} = 1, \forall j \tag{A15}$$

$$\sum_{i=0}^{N} u_{i,j} = \sum_{i=0}^{N} u_{j,i}, \forall j \in \{0,1,\ldots,N\} \tag{A16}$$

$$\sum_{j=1}^{N} u_{0,j} \leq 1 \tag{A17}$$

$$s_0 = 0 \tag{A18}$$

References

1. Ren, Y.; Zhang, C.; Zhao, F.; Tian, G.; Lin, W.; Meng, L.; Li, H. Disassembly line balancing problem using interdependent weights-based multi-criteria decision making and 2-Optimal algorithm. *J. Clean. Prod.* **2018**, *174*, 1475–1486. [CrossRef]
2. Colledani, M.; Battaïa, O. A decision support system to manage the quality of End-of-Life products in disassembly systems. *CIRP Ann. Manuf. Technol.* **2016**, *65*, 41–44. [CrossRef]
3. Ren, Y.; Tian, G.; Zhao, F.; Yu, D.; Zhang, C. Selective cooperative disassembly planning based on multi-objective discrete artificial bee colony algorithm. *Eng. Appl. Artif. Intell.* **2017**, *64*, 415–431. [CrossRef]
4. Ren, Y.; Zhang, C.; Zhao, F.; Xiao, H.; Tian, G. An asynchronous parallel disassembly planning based on genetic algorithm. *Eur. J. Oper. Res.* **2018**, *269*, 647–660. [CrossRef]
5. Zhang, X.F.; Zhang, S.Y. Product cooperative disassembly sequence planning based on branch-and-bound algorithm. *Int. J. Adv. Manuf. Technol.* **2010**, *51*, 1139–1147. [CrossRef]
6. Kara, S.; Pornprasitpol, P.; Kaebernick, H. Selective Disassembly Sequencing: A Methodology for the Disassembly of End-of-Life Products. *CIRP Ann. Manuf. Technol.* **2006**, *55*, 37–40. [CrossRef]
7. Xiu, F.Z.; Gang, Y.; Zhi, Y.H.; Cheng, H.P.; Guo, Q.M. Parallel disassembly sequence planning for complex products based on fuzzy-rough sets. *Int. J. Adv. Manuf. Technol.* **2014**, *72*, 231–239.
8. Smith, S.; Hung, P.-Y. A novel selective parallel disassembly planning method for green design. *J. Eng. Des.* **2015**, *26*, 283–301. [CrossRef]
9. Pistolesi, F.; Lazzerini, B. TeMA: A Tensorial Memetic Algorithm for Many-Objective Parallel Disassembly Sequence Planning in Product Refurbishment. *IEEE Trans. Ind. Inform.* **2019**, *15*, 3743–3753. [CrossRef]
10. Ren, Y.; Zhang, C.; Zhao, F.; Triebe, M.J.; Meng, L. An MCDM-Based Multiobjective General Variable Neighborhood Search Approach for Disassembly Line Balancing Problem. *IEEE Trans. Syst. Man Cybern. Syst.* **2020**, *50*, 3770–3783. [CrossRef]
11. Feng, Y.; Zhou, M.; Tian, G.; Li, Z.; Zhang, Z.; Zhang, Q.; Tan, J. Target Disassembly Sequencing and Scheme Evaluation for CNC Machine Tools Using Improved Multiobjective Ant Colony Algorithm and Fuzzy Integral. *IEEE Trans. Syst. Man Cybern. Syst.* **2019**, *49*, 2438–2451. [CrossRef]
12. Hsu, H.-P. A Fuzzy Knowledge-Based Disassembly Process Planning System Based on Fuzzy Attributed and Timed Predicate/Transition Net. *IEEE Trans. Syst. Man Cybern. Syst.* **2016**, *47*, 1800–1813. [CrossRef]
13. Tang, Y. Learning-Based Disassembly Process Planner for Uncertainty Management. *IEEE Trans. Syst. Man Cybern. Part A Syst. Hum.* **2008**, *39*, 134–143. [CrossRef]
14. Tang, Y.; Zhou, M. Fuzzy-Petri-net based disassembly planning considering human factors. *IEEE Trans. Syst. Man Cybern. A Syst.* **2004**, *26*, 718–726. [CrossRef]
15. Güngör, A.; Gupta, S.M. Disassembly sequence plan generation using a branch-and-bound algorithm. *Int. J. Prod. Res.* **2001**, *39*, 481–509. [CrossRef]
16. Ren, Y.; Yu, D.; Zhang, C.; Tian, G.; Meng, L.; Zhou, X. An improved gravitational search algorithm for profit-oriented partial disas-sembly line balancing problem. *Int. J. Prod. Res.* **2017**, *55*, 7302–7316. [CrossRef]
17. Johnson, M.R.; Wang, M.H. Economical evaluation of disassembly operations for recycling, remanufacturing and reuse. *Int. J. Prod. Res.* **1998**, *36*, 3227–3252. [CrossRef]
18. Kang, J.-G.; Lee, D.-H.; Xirouchakis, P.; Persson, J.-G. Parallel Disassembly Sequencing with Sequence-Dependent Operation Times. *CIRP Ann.* **2001**, *50*, 343–346. [CrossRef]
19. Lambert, A. Optimizing disassembly processes subjected to sequence-dependent cost. *Comput. Oper. Res.* **2007**, *34*, 536–551. [CrossRef]
20. Edis, E.B.; Ilgin, M.A.; Edis, R.S. Disassembly line balancing with sequencing decisions: A mixed integer linear programming model and extensions. *J. Clean. Prod.* **2019**, *238*, 117826. [CrossRef]
21. Meng, L.; Zhang, C.; Shao, X.; Ren, Y.; Ren, C. Mathematical modelling and optimisation of energy-conscious hybrid flow shop scheduling problem with unrelated parallel machines. *Int. J. Prod. Res.* **2018**, *57*, 1119–1145. [CrossRef]
22. Pistolesi, F.; Lazzerini, B.; Mura, M.D.; Dini, G. EMOGA: A Hybrid Genetic Algorithm with Extremal Optimization Core for Multi-objective Disassembly Line Balancing. *IEEE Trans. Ind. Inform.* **2018**, *14*, 1089–1098. [CrossRef]
23. Sanchez, B.; Haas, C. A novel selective disassembly sequence planning method for adaptive reuse of buildings. *J. Clean. Prod.* **2018**, *183*, 998–1010. [CrossRef]
24. Seo, K.-K.; Park, J.-H.; Jang, D.-S. Optimal Disassembly Sequence Using Genetic Algorithms Considering Economic and Environmental Aspects. *Int. J. Adv. Manuf. Technol.* **2001**, *18*, 371–380. [CrossRef]
25. Kongar, E.; Gupta, S.M. Disassembly sequencing using genetic algorithm. *Int. J. Adv. Manuf. Technol.* **2005**, *30*, 497–506. [CrossRef]
26. Tian, G.; Zhou, M.; Chu, J. A Chance Constrained Programming Approach to Determine the Optimal Disassembly Sequence. *IEEE Trans. Autom. Sci. Eng.* **2013**, *10*, 1004–1013. [CrossRef]
27. Tian, G.; Zhou, M.; Li, P. Disassembly Sequence Planning Considering Fuzzy Component Quality and Varying Operational Cost. *IEEE Trans. Autom. Sci. Eng.* **2017**, *15*, 748–760. [CrossRef]
28. Kheder, M.; Trigui, M.; Aifaoui, N. Disassembly sequence planning based on a genetic algorithm. *Proc. Inst. Mech. Eng. Part C: J. Mech. Eng. Sci.* **2014**, *229*, 2281–2290. [CrossRef]
29. Guo, X.; Liu, S.; Zhou, M.; Tian, G. Dual-Objective Program and Scatter Search for the Optimization of Disassembly Sequences Subject to Multiresource Constraints. *IEEE Trans. Autom. Sci. Eng.* **2017**, *15*, 1091–1103. [CrossRef]

30. Kalayci, C.B.; Gupta, S.M. Artificial bee colony algorithm for solving sequence-dependent disassembly line balancing problem. *Expert Syst. Appl.* **2013**, *40*, 7231–7241. [CrossRef]
31. Lu, Q.; Ren, Y.; Jin, H.; Meng, L.; Li, L.; Zhang, C.; Sutherland, J.W. A hybrid metaheuristic algorithm for a profit-oriented and ener-gy-efficient disassembly sequencing problem. *Robot. Cim. Int. Manuf.* **2020**, *61*, 101828. [CrossRef]
32. Tian, G.; Ren, Y.; Feng, Y.; Zhou, M.; Zhang, H.; Tan, J. Modeling and Planning for Dual-Objective Selective Disassembly Using and/or Graph and Discrete Artificial Bee Colony. *IEEE Trans. Ind. Inform.* **2018**, *15*, 2456–2468. [CrossRef]
33. Li, W.; Xia, K.; Gao, L.; Chao, K.-M. Selective disassembly planning for waste electrical and electronic equipment with case studies on liquid crystaldisplays. *Robot. Comput. Manuf.* **2013**, *29*, 248–260. [CrossRef]
34. Wang, K.; Li, X.; Gao, L.; Garg, A. Partial disassembly line balancing for energy consumption and profit under uncertainty. *Robot. Comput. Manuf.* **2019**, *59*, 235–251. [CrossRef]
35. Zhang, B.; Pan, Q.-K.; Gao, L.; Li, X.; Meng, L.-L.; Peng, K.-K. A multiobjective evolutionary algorithm based on decomposition for hybrid flowshop green scheduling problem. *Comput. Ind. Eng.* **2019**, *136*, 325–344. [CrossRef]
36. Meng, L.; Zhang, C.; Shao, X.; Ren, Y. MILP models for energy-aware flexible job shop scheduling problem. *J. Clean. Prod.* **2018**, *210*, 710–723. [CrossRef]
37. Castro, P.M.; Grossmann, I.E. Generalized Disjunctive Programming as a Systematic Modeling Framework to Derive Scheduling Formulations. *Ind. Eng. Chem. Res.* **2012**, *51*, 5781–5792. [CrossRef]
38. Meng, L.; Zhang, C.; Shao, X.; Zhang, B.; Ren, Y.; Lin, W. More MILP models for hybrid flow shop scheduling problem and its extended problems. *Int. J. Prod. Res.* **2019**, *58*, 3905–3930. [CrossRef]
39. Pan, C.-H. A study of integer programming formulations for scheduling problems. *Int. J. Syst. Sci.* **1997**, *28*, 33–41. [CrossRef]
40. Meng, L.; Zhang, C.; Ren, Y. Mathematical Modeling and Optimization of Energy-Conscious Flexible Job Shop Scheduling Problem with Worker Flexibility. *IEEE Access* **2019**, *7*, 68043–68059. [CrossRef]
41. Castro, P.M.; Zeballos, L.J.; Méndez, C.A. Hybrid time slots sequencing model for a class of scheduling problems. *AIChE J.* **2011**, *58*, 789–800. [CrossRef]
42. Meng, L.; Zhang, C.; Ren, Y.; Zhang, B.; Lv, C. Mixed-integer linear programming and constraint programming formulations for solving distributed flexible job shop scheduling problem. *Comput. Ind. Eng.* **2020**, *142*, 106347. [CrossRef]
43. Meng, L.; Gao, K.; Ren, Y.; Zhang, B.; Sang, H.; Zhang, C. Novel MILP and CP Models for Distributed Hybrid Flowshop Scheduling Problem with Se-quence-Dependent Setup Times. *Swarm Evol. Comput.* **2022**, *71*, 101058. [CrossRef]

Article

Energy-Efficient Hybrid Flowshop Scheduling with Consistent Sublots Using an Improved Cooperative Coevolutionary Algorithm

Chengshuai Li [1], Biao Zhang [1,*], Yuyan Han [1,*], Yuting Wang [1], Junqing Li [2] and Kaizhou Gao [3]

1 School of Computer Science, Liaocheng University, Liaocheng 252059, China
2 School of Computer Science, Shandong Normal University, Jinan 252000, China
3 Macau Institute of Systems Engineering, Macau University of Science and Technology, Taipa, Macau 999078, China
* Correspondence: zhangbiao@lcu-cs.com (B.Z.); hanyuyan@lcu-cs.com (Y.H.); Tel.: +86-13863565273 (B.Z.); +86-18864974734 (Y.H.)

Abstract: Energy conservation, emission reduction, and green and low carbon are of great significance to sustainable development, and are also the theme of the transformation and upgrading of the manufacturing industry. This paper concentrates on studying the energy-efficient hybrid flowshop scheduling problem with consistent sublots (HFSP_ECS) with the objective of minimizing the energy consumption. To solve the problem, the HFSP_ECS is decomposed by the idea of "divide-and-conquer", resulting in three coupled subproblems, i.e., lot sequence, machine assignment, and lot split, which can be solved by using a cooperative methodology. Thus, an improved cooperative coevolutionary algorithm (vCCEA) is proposed by integrating the variable neighborhood descent (VND) strategy. In the vCCEA, considering the problem-specific characteristics, a two-layer encoding strategy is designed to represent the essential information, and a novel collaborative model is proposed to realize the interaction between subproblems. In addition, special neighborhood structures are designed for different subproblems, and two kinds of enhanced neighborhood structures are proposed to search for potential promising solutions. A collaborative population restart mechanism is established to ensure the population diversity. The computational results show that vCCEA can coordinate and solve each subproblem of HFSP_ECS effectively, and outperform the mathematical programming and the other state-of-the-art algorithms.

Keywords: hybrid flowshop scheduling; energy efficiency; consistent sublots; collaborative coevolutionary algorithm; variable neighborhood descent

MSC: 90B30

1. Introduction

With the changing climate and environment, green development, energy saving, and emission reduction become the themes of transformation and upgrading of the manufacturing industry. Advanced production scheduling technology can effectively improve production efficiency and reduce energy consumption in the manufacturing industry, enhancing the core competitiveness of enterprises. As a branch of scheduling problems, the hybrid flowshop scheduling problem (HFSP) [1] has a very strong industrial application background, such as microelectronics, furniture, textile, petrochemical, and pharmaceutical fields [2–5]. In HFSP, a group of jobs need to go through a series of processing stages in succession and each stage has multiple identical machines. The goal of the HFSP is to determine the job sequence and machine assignment of these jobs at each stage with considering production constraints. The problem is a very complex combinatorial optimization problem [6], and even on a very small scale, it proves to be NP-hard [1]. In the most research on the HFSP [7], each job is treated as a whole, and the job cannot proceed to the next stage before the completion of the processing at a given stage [8]. In the actual production scenario [9,10], a job, called a lot in the following, usually consists of a number of identical items. When the lot is large, items already processed completely on a machine need to wait a long time in the output buffer of this machine, whereas the downstream machine may be idle. This scenario will have a negative impact on the production efficiency and lead to unnecessary energy consumption. Therefore, it is very important to develop a scheduling methodology suitable for this scenario to enhance the energy efficiency and core competitiveness of such factories.

In this paper, we introduce the technique of lot streaming into the HFSP, resulting in a novel problem, i.e., lot streaming HFSP. The lot streaming, first introduced by Reiter [11] in the context of job shop scheduling, is preferable for implementing the time-based strategy and widely adopted by top-notch companies to improve their customer service. Lot streaming is the process of splitting a large lot into several sublots and scheduling those sublots in an overlapping fashion to accelerate progress [12]. That is, the lot streaming is used to divide a lot with a large number of items into several sublots with a small number of items. Each sublot can be transported to the downstream stage for processing immediately after its completion at the upstream stage and does not have to wait for the completion of the entire lot. This method can effectively reduce the production cycle and improve production efficiency so that products can be delivered to customers faster, and more orders can be accepted within a limited time. Moreover, this method can effectively increase machine utilization, reduce machine idle time, and thus reduce energy consumption.

According to the lot streaming studies, the lot division methods [13] are equal sublots, consistent sublots, and variable sublots. With equal sublots, a lot can be divided into several sublots with equal size, i.e., each sublot contains the same number of items, and the number and size of sublots remain unchanged throughout the processing process. Consistent sublots mean that a lot is divided into several sublots that may have different sizes, and the number and size of sublots remain unchanged throughout the processing process. Equal sublots can also be understood as a specific case of consistent sublots. Unlike consistent sublots, in variable sublots [14], the number and size of sublots may change throughout the processing process. In real production, variable sublots are rarely used because their diverse nature seriously increases the difficulty of production management. Moreover, its comprehensive cost performance is not high for most enterprises. In contrast, consistent sublots are often used in most enterprises' actual production.

In sum, the energy-efficient HFSP with consistent sublots (HFSP_ECS) is the focus of our study. To solve the problem, three coupled subproblems must be addressed, i.e., lot sequence, machine assignment, and lot split. Thus, the HFSP_ECS is much more complex than the classical HFSP, and obviously NP-hard. With its NP-hard property, the metaheuristics are suggested to solve the problem. In addition, when using the metaheuristics, in order to obtain a globally optimal solution, the three subproblems must be coevolved and addressed simultaneously [15,16]. It is therefore natural to employ the cooperative coevolutionary algorithm (CCEA) [17]. Its design is inspired by the natural phenomenon that the coexisting species promote each other and coevolve. The algorithm adopts the strategy of "divide and conquer", which decomposes an optimization problem into several subproblems. In addition, the whole problem is optimized by a reciprocal evolutionary mechanism driven by cooperative or competitive interactions between subproblems [18]. The local search strategy also plays an important role in CCEA. This paper develops an improved cooperative coevolutionary algorithm (vCCEA) by integrating the variable neighborhood descent (VND) strategy [19]. The vCCEA can solve the whole problem by evolving the subproblems simultaneously and interacting between the subproblems. In addition, considering the problem-specific characteristics, a two-layer encoding strategy is designed to represent the solution information and a novel collaborative model is proposed to realize the interaction between subproblems. Special neighborhood structures are designed for different subproblems and two kinds of enhanced local disturbance strategies are proposed to search for potential promising solutions. This algorithm mainly contains four processes, i.e., initialization process, cooperative coevolutionary process, VND processes, and population restart processes. First, an archive that holds several complete solutions is initialized and two populations based on these solutions are built in the initialization process. Then, the two populations and archive coevolve through the collaborative model in the coevolutionary process. While in the cooperative coevolutionary process, the VND process is used to generate a new solution. With the evolution proceeding, the population restart process can be triggered to ensure the population diversity.

The main contributions of this study are as follows. (1) An energy-efficient hybrid flowshop scheduling problem with consistent sublots (HFSP_ECS) is studied and a mathematical model is developed for it. (2) An improved cooperative coevolutionary algorithm based on the idea of "divide-and-conquer" is proposed by integrating the VND strategy. (3) A novel collaborative model suitable for the specific characteristics of HFSP_ECS is designed to realize the interaction between the populations and the archive. (4) Two kinds of enhanced local neighborhood structures are proposed to search for potential promising solutions.

The remaining of the paper is organized as follows. A brief literature review is provided in Section 2. Section 3 describes HFSP_ECS in detail and a linear integer programming model (MILP) is established for a better representation of this problem. Section 4 introduces the algorithm process of vCCEA and improvement strategies in detail. In Section 5, the experimental study design is presented and the results are analyzed. Finally, some conclusions are given and future research prospects are outlined in Section 6.

2. Literature Review

Although HFSP has been studied for several decades, little research has been carried out on energy-efficient HFSP with lot streaming. Most of the existing studies have been conducted with the objective of minimizing the production cycle to optimize HFSP with lot streaming, and little attention has been paid to the energy consumption in the production process. The following is a first review of the HFSP with lot streaming in detail, and then the existing research results on green scheduling are analyzed. Finally, the characteristics of the research problem in this paper are summarized.

With the development of a multi-species small-scale production model in recent years, more and more scholars are focusing on the HFSP with lot streaming. Depending on the number of lots, the lot streaming HFSP can be divided into two main categories, i.e., single-lot HFSP and multiple-lot HFSP. The single-lot HFSP means that only one lot needs to be processed, and how to divide lots and how to sort sublots are two major problems, i.e., sublot size and sublot sequence. Zhang et al. [12] studied a special two-stage HFSP with single-lot that the first stage has multiple identical machines and the second stage only has one machine. They first formulated the problem as an MILP considering the equal sublots, and proposed a heuristic to reach an effective solution. For the same problem, Liu [20] used linear programming and rotation methods to solve the sublot sequence and sublot size, respectively. Moreover, an effective heuristic rule is proposed for the general HFSP with equal sublots. Cheng et al. [21] studied a two-stage HFSP that the first stage only has one machine and the second stage has two parallel machines. Assuming that the number of sublots are known, the closed-form expressions are used to obtain the best sublot sizes. Then, according to the best sublot sizes, the upper bound of the sublot quantities is defined, and an algorithm combining closed-form expressions is used to obtain the global optimal solution. In addition, a heuristic is proposed for the case where the number of sublots is unknown.

Compared with the single-lot HFSP, more research focuses on multiple-lot HFSP. Potts and Baker [22] first showed how to use equal sublots in the one-job model and analyzed equal-sized sublots as a heuristic procedure. After that, they cited some difficulties in multiple-lot scheduling. Kalir and Sarin [23] studied a multiple-lot HFSP with small equal sublots, and proposed a heuristic called bottleneck minimal idleness with the objective of minimizing the maximum completion time. Naderi and Yazdani [24] studied a multiple-lot HFSP with setup time constraints. Assuming that the number of sublots were known, an MILP was established and an imperialist competitive algorithm was proposed. Zhang et al. [25] studied the HFSP with equal sublots, and a discrete fruit fly optimization algorithm was developed for solving this problem, where two main search procedures were designed to balance the exploration and exploitation abilities of the algorithm. For the same problem, Zhang et al. [26] proposed an effective migrating birds optimization algorithm with the objective of minimizing the total flow time, and a heuristic rule was introduced to address the case that the sublots from different lots have the changes to reach the downstream stage at the same time.

The multiple-lot HFSP studied above were all with equal sublots, and this means that sublots from the same lot have the equal size. When the sublots from the same lot are not equal in size, the multiple-lot HFSP is called HFSP with consistent sublots. For example, Ming Cheng and Sarin [13] studied a two-stage HFSP where the first stage only had one machine and the second stage had two identical machines. They used some conclusions from the single-lot scheduling problem, and proposed a mathematical programming-based heuristic method for this problem. Zhang et al. [27] studied a special two-stage HFSP where the first stage had multiple identical machines and the second stage only had a single machine. Additionally, two heuristic strategies were proposed to solve two subproblems, i.e., lot sequence, and lot split. Nejati et al. [28] studied a multiple-lot k-stage HFSP with a specific production scenario. They improved the genetic algorithm and simulated an annealing algorithm for this particular problem, and the effectiveness of the improved strategy was verified. Lalitha et al. [29] studied a special k-stage HFSP where the front k-1 stages only had one machine per stage and the last stage had multiple machines. An MILP was developed and some small-scale problems were solved by the optimizer. A two-stage heuristic algorithm was proposed to solve medium–large scale problems, hierarchically. Zhang et al. [30] studied an HFSP with consistent sublots and considered the setup and transportation operations. A collaboration operator was proposed and a collaborative variable neighborhood descent algorithm was developed based on this operator.

Green development, energy saving, and emission reduction are of great significance to sustainable development. Qin et al. [31] studied an HFSP with an energy-saving criterion, and considered blocking constraints. A mathematical model for HFSP with blocking constraints and energy-efficient criterion was developed and an improved iterative greedy algorithm based on the swap operator was proposed. Duan et al. [32] studied a heterogeneous multi-stage HFSP with energy-efficient for large metal component manufacturing, and an improved NSGA-II combined with the moth-flame optimization algorithm (NSGA-II–MFO) with the objective of minimizing the maximum completion time and carbon emission was proposed. Dong et al. [33] studied a distributed two-stage re-entrant green HFSP, a two-level mathematical model and an improved hybrid slap swarm and NSGA-III algorithm with the objectives of minimum completion time, total carbon emission and total energy consumption was proposed. Geng et al. [34] studied an energy-efficient re-entrant HFSP with considering customer order constraints under Time-of-Use (TOU) electricity price, and a memetic algorithm with an energy saving strategy was proposed to solve this problem.

In summary, both the lot streaming HFSP and the green HFSP have had a certain number of research results. Compared with these studies, the characteristics of our study can be summarized as follows. A k-stage energy-efficient HFSP with consistent sublots is studied in this paper, and the number of machines per stage is not limited. While Ming Cheng and Sarin [13] and Wei Zhang et al. [27] studied the special two-stage HFSP, and Lalitha et al. [29] studied a special k-stage HFSP that the first k-1 stages only have one machine at each stage and the last stage has multiple machines. Compared with these studies, the HFSP_ECS studied in this paper has a wider scope of application. In study of Ming Cheng and Sarin [13] and Naderi and Yazdani [24], the sublots from different lots can be mixed and cross-processed, but they are prohibited in our research. This is because in real production, the machine needs to be adjusted accordingly before processing different products. Assuming that sublots are allowed to be mixed, the machine will be in a state of frequent adjustment, which has a serious impact on productivity and increases unnecessary energy consumption. Additionally, in the above studies on lot streaming, the research focuses on minimizing the completion time without considering the energy consumption in the process. However, in the actual production, energy consumption is a non-negligible factor. In our study, all machines were turned on and off uniformly, and there was a positive correlation between energy consumption and minimized completion time.

3. Problem Description

The HFSP_ECS addressed can be described as follows. A set of lots J is to be consecutively processed in a series of K stages. Each stage k has $M_i \geq 1$ identical parallel machines and at least one stage has the number of machines greater than one, i.e., $M_i > 1$. Each lot to be processed is made up of a group of identical items. The consistent sublots is employed to split a lot to several sublots with assuming that the maximum sublot quantities are limited. Each sublot contains a certain number of items, and the number of the items contained in a sublot is defined as the sublot size. The number and size of the sublots do not change during the K processing stages. At the same stage, different sublots from the same lot are processed continuously on the same machine. Similarly, the items from the same sublot need to be processed continuously. The sublots can proceed to the next stage immediately after its completion of the previous stage. The processing time of a sublot is the product of the sublot size and the item processing time. The processing energy consumption of the sublot is the product of the unit energy consumption and processing time. The idle energy consumption of a machine is the product of unit idle energy and idle time, the idle time, and the idle energy consumption per unit. The scheduling task of the HFSP_ECS is to solve the three subproblems' lot sequence, machine assignment, and lot split, and its objective is to minimize the energy consumption. The assumptions are summarized as follows:

- All machines are available at time 0, and all machines turn off uniformly at the end of the process.
- Assume an infinite buffer between stage and allow the machine to be idle.
- Each lot must be processed through all stages, and only one machine can be selected at the same stage, and interrupt and preemption are not allowed during processing.
- One machine can at most process only one item at the same time, and the items from the same sublot need to be processed continuously.
- Each lot is divided into several sublots and the sublot quantities are limited by a maximum value.
- The sublots of each lot can be processed at the next stage immediately after the completion of the previous stage.
- The first sublot can be started as soon as it arrives at this stage. After the remaining sublots reach the stage, it also needs to wait for the previous sublots to complete processing before it can be processed.
- Sublots from different lots are not allowed to be mixed during processing; if two lots are processed on the same machine, the later lot will not be processed until all the sublots of the previous lot have been processed.
- Machine setup and transport operations are included in the machining process.

With the above description and assumptions, to better describe and solve this problem, an MILP [30] is established, the notations and constraints are described as follows:

Objective:

$$Minimize(E_{\max}) \tag{1}$$

Constraints:

$$C_{\max} \geq C_{K,j,L} \quad \forall j \in \{1,2,\ldots,J\} \tag{2}$$

$$\sum_{i=1}^{M_k} D_{k,j,i} = 1 \quad \forall k \in \{1,2,\ldots,M_k\}, \forall j \in \{1,2,\ldots,J\} \tag{3}$$

$$\sum_{e=1}^{L} N_{j,e} = T_j \quad \forall j \in \{1,2,\ldots,J\}, \forall e \in \{1,2,\ldots,L\} \tag{4}$$

$$N_{j,e} \geq 0 \quad \forall j \in \{1,2,\ldots,J\}, \forall e \in \{1,2,\ldots,L\} \tag{5}$$

$$N_{j,e} + (1 - W_{j,e}) \times G \geq 1 \quad \forall j \in \{1,2,\ldots,J\}, \forall e \in \{1,2,\ldots,L\} \tag{6}$$

$$N_{j,e} - W_{j,e} \times G \leq 0 \quad \forall j \in \{1,2,\ldots,J\}, \forall e \in \{1,2,\ldots,L\} \tag{7}$$

$$W_{j,e} \geq W_{j,e+1} \quad \forall j \in \{1,2,\ldots,J\}, \forall e \in \{1,2,\ldots,L-1\} \tag{8}$$

$$S_{1,j,1} \geq 0 \quad \forall j \in \{1,2,\ldots,J\} \tag{9}$$

$$C_{k,j,e} = S_{k,j,e} + P_{k,j} \times N_{j,e} \quad \forall k \in \{1,2,\ldots,K\}, \forall j \in \{1,2,\ldots,J\}, \forall e \in \{1,2,\ldots,L\} \tag{10}$$

$$S_{k+1,j,e} - C_{k,j,e} \geq 0 \quad \forall k \in \{1,2,\ldots,K-1\}, \forall j \in \{1,2,\ldots,J\}, \forall e \in \{1,2,\ldots,L\} \tag{11}$$

$$S_{k,j,e+1} - C_{k,j,e} \geq 0 \quad \forall k \in \{1,2,\ldots,K\}, \forall j \in \{1,2,\ldots,J\}, \forall e \in \{1,2,\ldots,L-1\} \tag{12}$$

$$Y_{k,j,j1,i} + Y_{k,j1,j,i} \leq D_{k,j,i} \quad \forall k \in \{1,2,\ldots,K\}, \forall j! = j1, j \in \{1,2,\ldots,J\}, j1 \in \{1,2,\ldots,J\}, \\ \forall e \in \{1,2,\ldots,L-1\}, i \in \{1,2,\ldots,M_k\} \tag{13}$$

$$Y_{k,j,j1,i} + Y_{k,j1,j,i} \leq D_{k,j1,i} \quad \forall k \in \{1,2,\ldots,K\}, \forall j! = j1, j \in \{1,2,\ldots,J\}, \\ j1 \in \{1,2,\ldots,J\}, i \in \{1,2,\ldots,M_k\} \tag{14}$$

$$Y_{k,j,j1,i} + Y_{k,j1,j,i} \geq D_{k,j,i} + D_{k,j1,i} - 1 \quad \forall k \in \{1,2,\ldots,K\}, \forall j! = j1, j \in \{1,2,\ldots,J\}, \\ j1 \in \{1,2,\ldots,J\}, i \in \{1,2,\ldots,M_k\} \tag{15}$$

$$S_{k,j,1} - C_{k,j1,L} + G \times (3 - Y_{k,j1,j,i} - D_{k,j,i} - D_{k,j1,i}) \geq 0 \quad \forall k \in \{1,2,\ldots,K\}, \forall j! = j1, \\ j \in \{1,2,\ldots,J\}, j1 \in \{1,2,\ldots,J\}, i \in \{1,2,\ldots,M_k\} \tag{16}$$

$$E_{process} = \sum_{k=1}^{K} \sum_{j=1}^{J} \sum_{e=1}^{L} N_{j,e} \times EP_{k,j} \tag{17}$$

$$E_{idle} = \sum_{k=1}^{K} \sum_{i=1}^{M_k} (C_{max} - \sum_{j=1}^{J} T_j \times P_{k,j} \times D_{k,j,i}) \times EI_k \tag{18}$$

$$E_{max} = E_{process} + E_{idle} \tag{19}$$

Equation (1) indicates that the optimization objective minimizes the energy consumption E_{max}. Equation (2) requires C_{max} to be greater than or equal to the completion time of the last sublot of all lots in the last stage. Equation (3) requires that only one processing machine can be selected for each lot at the same stage. Equation (4) indicates that the sum of the items contained in all sublots from the same lot must equal the number of items contained in this lot. Equation (5) defines that the number of items contained in each sublot of lots is greater than or equal to 0. Equations (6) and (7) represent the value of $W_{j,e}$. Equation (8) shows that the nonempty sublot in the lots is expected to precede the empty sublot. Equation (9) make sure the start processing time is a non-negative number. Equation (10) shows the calculation method of completion time. In Equation (11), the sublot is required to complete the processing of the previous stage before starting the next stage of processing. Equation (12) expresses that the sublots from the same lot are processed in numbered order at each stage. Equation (13) defines $Y_{k,j,j1,i}$ and $Y_{k,j1,j,i}$. They cannot take the value of 1 at the same time. Equations (14) and (15) are dual constraints, similar to Equation (13), emphasize that the machine can only process one lot at a time. Equation (16) indicates that at the same machine, the later lot can be processed only after the previous lot has been processed; otherwise, the equation does not work. Equations (17) and (18) give the calculation method of total process energy and total idle energy, respectively. Equation (19) shows that the total energy consumption is equal to the sum of the total process energy consumption and the total idle energy consumption.

4. Improved vCCEA for Solving HFSP_ECS Problem

The proposed vCCEA is developed in this section. First, the design motivation and the algorithm framework are illustrated. After that, the components of vCCEA, involving solution encoding and decoding strategies, initialization strategy, cooperative coevolutionary strategy, VND strategy, and the population restart mechanism, are described in detail. Finally, the whole algorithm procedure is given.

4.1. The Motivations and Framework of vCCEA

The HFSP_ECS is a highly complex combinatorial optimization problem. Recall that when solving the HFSP_ECS, three subproblems must be addressed simultaneously: lot sequence, machine assignment and lot split. These subproblems are not independent but highly coupled. That is, if only one subproblem is optimized, the global optimal solution is almost impossible to be obtained. Therefore, the CCEA is employed, which uses the idea of "divide and conquer" to achieve global optimization by optimizing each subproblem as well as implementing the interaction between subproblems. Among three subproblems, the machine assignment is generally addressed by the proposed heuristic rules [35]. This paper still uses heuristic rules to solve this subproblem, and this rule is incorporated into the decoding strategy. For the other two subproblems, two populations are set up, each of which corresponds to a subproblem. These two populations are lot sequence population and lot split population, which represent lot sequence subproblem and lot split subproblem, respectively. In addition, an archive is also created, where a number of references or complete solutions are stored. It aims to establish collaborative relationships among the individuals from lot sequence and lot split populations in the collaborative coevolutionary process.

The whole algorithm consists of an initialization process, cooperative coevolutionary process of two populations, VND processes, and population restart processes. First, the archive and the two populations are initialized. Then the novel cooperative model was used to control the populations for the cooperative coevolution. In the cooperative coevolutionary process, each individual from the population collaborates with one reference randomly selected from the archive to construct a complete solution. This complete solution is perturbed by the VND process to generate new individuals for updating the population and archive. In this process, different neighborhood structures are designed for individuals from different populations. Moreover, a restart strategy is designed for the individuals who have not been updated for several generations in the population to prevent the algorithm falling into local optima. The vCCEA framework is shown in Figure 1.

4.2. Ending and Decoding

4.2.1. Solution Encoding

Recall that this problem contains three subproblems: lot sequence, machine assignment, and lot split. Based on the problem specific characteristics, a two-layer encoding strategy is adopted in this paper. The first layer uses a permutation $\Pi_J = \{\pi_1, \pi_2 \ldots \pi_j \ldots \pi_J\}$ to represent the scheduling order of the lots. Where π_j indicates the lot index and J represents the total number of the lots. Note that a legitimate permutation requires that each lot only appears once [36]. The lot that appears in advance in the permutation is given higher processing priority, and the scheduling order of lots in subsequent stages is determined by the heuristic rules mentioned in the solution decoding. The second layer uses a matrix $Z_{J \times L}$ with J rows and L columns to represent the lot split, where each row represents the segmentation information of a lot. A complete solution consists of two parts: lot permutation and lot split matrix, which can be expressed as $\langle \Pi_J, Z_{J \times L} \rangle$.

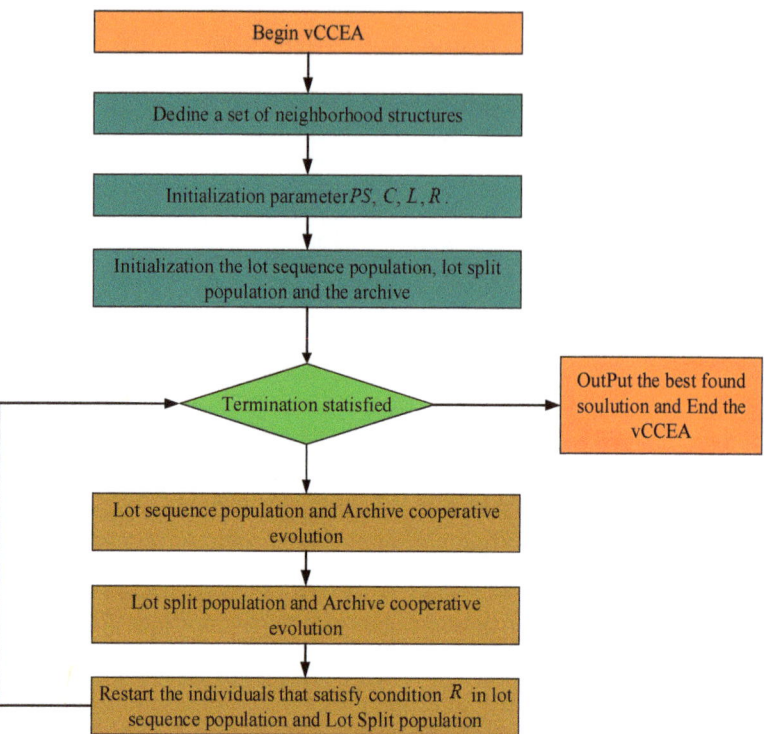

Figure 1. The framework of vCCEA.

Here, a simple illustrative example is given for illustrating the solution encoding. In this example, there are five lots and two stages. The first stage has two parallel machines, i.e., M1 and M2, and the second stage contains three parallel machines, i.e., M3, M4, and M5. The unit idle energy consumption of machines M1 and M2 is 2, and the unit idle energy consumption of machines M3, M4, and M5 also is 2. Lot size, sublot size, item processing time and other specific production data are given in Table 1. According to the above encoding strategy, the encoding for this simple example can be expressed as $\langle \Pi_5, Z_{5\times 3} \rangle$, where the first layer is a legal permutation-based encoding vector $\Pi_5 = \{3, 5, 1, 4, 2\}$. This permutation indicates that the current scheduling order is 3,5,1,4,2. In other words, lot 3 was processed first, followed by lot 5, lot 1, lot 4, and lot 2. The matrix $Z_{5\times 3}$ serves as the second layer, and is shown in Equation (20). Using lot 5 as an example, the lot 5 is divided into three sublots. The first sublot size is 1, the second sublot size is 1, and the third sublot size is 2.

$$Z_{5\times 3} = \begin{bmatrix} 1 & 2 & 2 \\ 2 & 3 & 3 \\ 2 & 2 & 2 \\ 1 & 2 & 2 \\ 1 & 1 & 2 \end{bmatrix} \quad (20)$$

Table 1. Illustrative example of HFSP_ECS.

Lot	Lot Size	Sublot Size			Single Item Process Time		Energy Consumption Per Unit Time	
		Sublot1	Sublot2	Sublot3	Stage1	Stage2	Stage1	Stage2
Lot1	5	1	2	2	1	2	3	2
Lot2	8	2	3	3	1	1	4	3
Lot3	6	2	2	2	2	2	2	4
Lot4	5	1	2	2	2	2	3	3
Lot5	4	1	1	2	1	2	1	2

4.2.2. Solution Decoding

The solution decoding can transform the solution into a feasible schedule, and it mainly solves two problems, lot sequence and machine assignment. For machine assignment, we give priority to idle machines, thus, the "first available machine" rule (FAM) [37] is adopted in this paper. Regarding the lot sequence, the lot scheduling order at stage is determined by the permutation $\Pi_J = \{\pi_1, \pi_2 \ldots \pi_j \ldots \pi_J\}$, while the lot sequence of subsequent stages is determined by the "first-come–first-served" rule. That is, the lot completed earlier at the previous stage is given priority to be scheduled at the following stages. In HFSP_ECS, the sublot of a lot can be immediately transported to the downstream stage for processing when the sublot completes the processing at the current stage. Based on this feature, the "first-come–first-served" rule based on sublot preemption is adopted, i.e., the lot whose first sublot completes the processing at the previous stage first has higher priority at the downstream stage. Under this rule, if the completion time of the first sublots of some lots at the previous stage is equal, the completion time of their second sublots is compared, and so on.

According to the above encoding and decoding strategies, the Gantt chart of the schedule for the illustrative example in Section 4.2.1 is shown in Figure 2. Here, the (a, b) represents a sublot, where a is the lot number, b is the sublot number, and then the minimum energy consumption is 555.

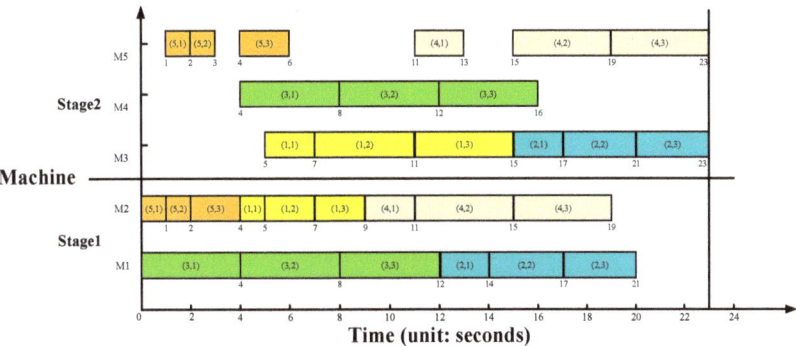

Figure 2. The schedule Gantt chart for the illustrative example.

4.3. Algorithm Initialization

At the beginning of the algorithm, an archive and two collaborative populations need to be initialized. The archive $\left\{ \left\langle \Pi^{R[1]}, Z^{R[1]} \right\rangle, \left\langle \Pi^{R[1]}, Z^{R[1]} \right\rangle, \ldots, \left\langle \Pi^{R[PS]}, Z^{R[PS]} \right\rangle \right\}$ is made up of PS combinations. Each combination $\left\langle \Pi^{R[ind]}, Z^{R[ind]} \right\rangle$, $ind = 1 \ldots PS$ represents a complete solution, where $\Pi^{R[ind]}$ represents the lot sequence for solution ind. Similarly, $Z^{R[ind]}$ represents the lot split for solution ind. When the archive is initialized, the two components of each solution are initialized in two different ways. The lot sequence is initialized by a random way, while the lot split is determined by the uniform initialization method [38]. The uniform initialization procedure is described as follows.

Procedure Uniform initialization

Step1. Each lot is evenly divided into several sublots. For the jth lot, the size of each sublot is $N_{j,e} = \lfloor T_j/L \rfloor$, where $\lfloor \ \rfloor$ means the nearest integer that is smaller than T_j/L.

Step2. For the jth, the remaining size r_j is obtained that $r_j = T_j - \sum_{e=1}^{L} N_{j,e}$.

Step3. For the jth, r_j is added to any sublot randomly.

The two populations are the lot sequence population and the lot split population. The lot sequence population consists of PS individuals, i.e., $\{\Pi^{[1]}, \Pi^{[2]}, \ldots, \Pi^{[PS]}\}$. That is, each individual only represents the lot sequence of a solution, this population is initialized with the lot sequences of the solutions in the archive, i.e., $\Pi^{[ind]} = \Pi^{R[ind]}$ for $ind = 1, 2, \ldots, PS$. Obviously, the individuals in lot sequence population are indeed not the complete solutions, such that they cannot be evaluated directly. To evaluate each $\Pi^{[ind]}$, a collaborator must be identified to build an evaluable solution. Here, the lot split individual $Z^{R[ind]}$ is determined as the collaborator, and the index of this collaborator is recorded by $Col_1[ind] = ind$, where $ind = 1, 2, \ldots, PS$. The individual $\Pi^{[ind]}$ and its collaborator $Z^{[Col_1[ind]]}$ construct a complete solution $\langle \Pi^{[ind]}, Z^{[Col_1[ind]]} \rangle$. The energy consumption value of the solution is also that of the individual $\Pi^{[ind]}$. Similarly, the lot split population consists of PS lot split matrix initially, i.e., $\{Z^{[1]}, Z^{[2]}, \ldots, Z^{[PS]}\}$ where $Z^{[ind]}$ for $ind = 1, 2, \ldots, PS$. The individual $\Pi^{R[ind]}$ is determined as the collaborator for $\{Z^{[1]}, Z^{[2]}, \ldots, Z^{[PS]}\}$, and the index of this collaborator is recorded by $Col_2[ind] = ind$, where $ind = 1, 2, \ldots, PS$. Individual $Z^{[ind]}$ in this population and a lot sequence collaborator $\Pi^{[Col_2[ind]]}$ comprise a new solution $\langle \Pi^{[Col_2[ind]]}, Z^{[ind]} \rangle$. The energy consumption value of the solution is also that of the individual $Z^{[ind]}$.

4.4. Cooperative Coevolution Process

The whole cooperative coevolutionary process can be divided into two parts: evolution of the lot sequence population and evolution of the lot split population. The evolution of the lot sequence population is first performed. Through this process, individuals in the lot sequence population are updated on the one hand, and certain solutions in the archive can obtain better information of lot sequences on the other hand. Then, the evolution of the lot split population is performed. This process aims to update individuals in the lot split population and ensures that solutions in the archive can obtain better lot split information. Through the above two processes, the evolution of both populations is achieved and the solutions in the archive are also updated during the evolution process. The two processes are described in detail below.

4.4.1. Evolution of the Lot Sequence Population

In the evolution process of the lot sequence population, a complete solution is first constructed by individual $\Pi^{[ind]}$ from lot sequence population and its collaborator Z in the archive. To maintain the diversity of the population and to avoid premature convergence, the last collaborator $Z^{R[Col_1[ind]]}$ of $\Pi^{[ind]}$ that is pointed by the index is not used. Instead, the lot split matrix $Z^{R[rand]}$ is randomly selected from the archive as the current collaborator, where $rand$ is a randomly generated integer between 1 and PS. The combined solution here can be expressed as $\langle \Pi^{[ind]}, Z^{R[rand]} \rangle$. Then, the VND process is performed on lot sequence $\Pi^{[ind]}$ of the combined solution. A new lot sequence individual $\Pi'^{[ind]}$ is generated by individual $\Pi^{[ind]}$, and the solution $\langle \Pi^{[ind]}, Z^{R[rand]} \rangle$ comes to $\langle \Pi'^{[ind]}, Z^{R[rand]} \rangle$.

According to the VND characteristics [39], as long as a new individual $\Pi'^{[ind]}$ is generated, the performance of the new solution $\left\langle \Pi'^{[ind]}, Z^{[rand]} \right\rangle$ needs to be evaluated first. If the objective value of $\left\langle \Pi'^{[ind]}, Z^{[rand]} \right\rangle$ is better than $\left\langle \Pi^{[ind]}, Z^{[rand]} \right\rangle$, then the archive and the population will be updated by a new solution $\left\langle \Pi'^{[ind]}, Z^{[rand]} \right\rangle$. Otherwise, the VND process continues. If the whole VND process fails to find a good $\Pi'^{[ind]}$, then the evolution of the individual is ended for this time.

The process of updating the archive and lot sequence population can be described as follows. If the objective value of the new solution $\left\langle \Pi'^{[ind]}, Z^{R[rand]} \right\rangle$ is better than $\left\langle \Pi^{[ind]}, Z^{R[Col_1[ind]]} \right\rangle$, the solution $\left\langle \Pi^{[ind]}, Z^{R[Col_1[ind]]} \right\rangle$ will be updated by the new solution $\left\langle \Pi'^{[ind]}, Z^{R[rand]} \right\rangle$, i.e., $\Pi^{[ind]} = \Pi'^{[ind]}$, $Col_1[ind] = rand$. Note that the last collaborator $Z^{R[Col_1[ind]]}$ may have been changed in the evolutionary process of the lot split population. At the same time, the archive is attempted to be updated. If the objective value of the new solution $\left\langle \Pi'^{[ind]}, Z^{R[rand]} \right\rangle$ is better than $\left\langle \Pi^{R[rand]}, Z^{R[rand]} \right\rangle$, then the individual $\Pi^{R[rand]}$ will be updated by individual $\Pi'^{[ind]}$, i.e., $\Pi^{R[rand]} = \Pi'^{[ind]}$. The above process is repeated from $ind = 1$ to $ind = PS$. Given the above, the coevolutionary process for the individuals $\Pi^{[ind]}$ in the lot sequence population is shown in Figure 3.

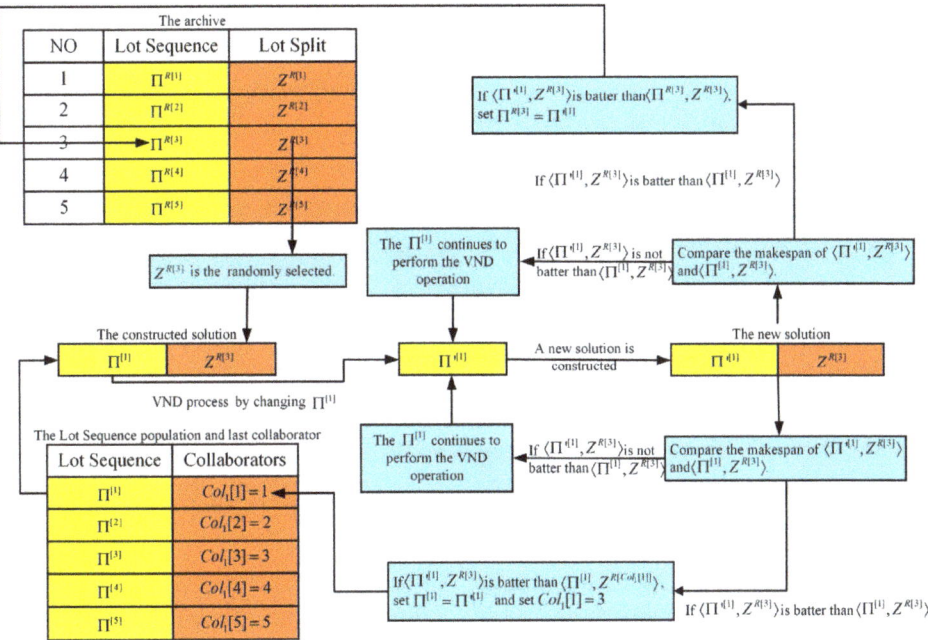

Figure 3. Evolution process of the lot sequence population.

An efficient neighborhood structure plays a key role in the whole algorithm. To design a good neighborhood structure, the problem characteristics must be exploited. When the lot sequence population evolves, the neighborhood structure only works on the lot sequence. That is, a new individual $\Pi'^{[ind]}$ is formed by perturbing the individual $\Pi^{[ind]}$ in the neighborhood structure. Therefore, to obtain a better lot sequence, three neighborhood structures are specially designed based on a solution encoding strategy, and the VND process is used to switch the neighborhoods. Two of these neighborhood structures are the insert and swap operations that are widely used in HFSP problems, referred to as lot insertion and lot swap. However, when solving the large-scale problems, a single insertion or swap may not effectively perturb the current solution. Therefore, a lot swap operation with a large search range is proposed by improving the lot swap, called the Enhanced lot swap in this instance. The lot insertion is not enhanced here since its high time complexity. The three neighborhood structures for lot sequence are described below: (1) Lot insertion. A new lot sequence is formed by taking a random lot from the lot sequence and inserting it into a randomly different position. (2) Lot swap. Take two lots at random from the lot sequence and exchange their positions in the sequence. (3) Enhanced lot swap. Perform l times of the lot swap, where l is dynamically determined by the number of lots in the lot sequence. We set l as $L \times J$, where L is a real number between 0 and 1, and J is the number of lots. Additionally, the detailed process of lot sequence population evolution is shown in Algorithm 1.

Algorithm 1 Evolution of the lot sequence population

1: Define a set of neighborhood structures $N^1_k, k = 1, \ldots, k_{max}$
2: **for** $ind = 1$ to PS
3:      $rand \leftarrow$ generate a random integer in $[1 - PS]$
4:      $\langle \Pi^{[ind]}, Z^{R[rand]} \rangle \leftarrow$ constitute a complete solution
5:      Define $\Pi \leftarrow \Pi^{[ind]}$
6:      Let $k \leftarrow 1$, $Count \leftarrow 0$
7:      **while** $k \leq k_{max}$ **do**
8:         **while** $Count < C$ **do**
9:            $\Pi'^{[ind]} \leftarrow Neighborhood(\Pi, N^1_k)$
10:            **if** $\langle \Pi'^{[ind]}, Z^{R[rand]} \rangle$ better than $\langle \Pi, Z^{R[rand]} \rangle$
11:               $Count \leftarrow 0$, $k \leftarrow 1$, $\Pi \leftarrow \Pi'^{[ind]}$
12:               **if** $\langle \Pi'^{[ind]}, Z^{R[rand]} \rangle$ better than $\langle \Pi^{[ind]}, Z^{R[Col_1[ind]]} \rangle$ or $Z^{R[Col_1[ind]]}$ was changed
13:                  $\Pi^{[ind]} \leftarrow \Pi'^{[ind]}$, $Col_1[ind] = rand$
14:               **end if**
15:               **if** $\langle \Pi'^{[ind]}, Z^{R[rand]} \rangle$ better than $\langle \Pi^{[rand]}, Z^{R[rand]} \rangle$
16:                  $\Pi^{[rand]} \leftarrow \Pi'^{[ind]}$
17:               **end if**
18:            **else**
19:               $Count ++$
20:            **end if**
21:         **end while**
22:         $k++$
23:      **end while**
24: **end for**

4.4.2. Evolution of the Lot Split Population

Similar to the evolution process of the lot sequence population, a complete solution is constructed by individual $Z^{[ind]}$ from lot split population and its collaborator $\Pi^{R[rand]}$ in the archive, where $rand$ is a randomly generated integer in the range $[1, PS]$. The constructed solution here can be expressed as $\langle \Pi^{R[rand]}, Z^{[ind]} \rangle$. After that, the VND procedure is executed on the solution $\langle \Pi^{R[rand]}, Z^{[ind]} \rangle$, and the neighborhood structure here only works on the lot split. Through the VND process, $Z^{[ind]}$ becomes $Z'^{[ind]}$, and thus, the solution $\langle \Pi^{R[rand]}, Z^{[ind]} \rangle$ comes to $\langle \Pi^{R[rand]}, Z'^{[ind]} \rangle$. In the process, as long as a new solution $\langle \Pi^{R[rand]}, z'^{[ind]} \rangle$ is generated, the new solution $\langle \Pi^{R[rand]}, Z'^{[ind]} \rangle$ is evaluated. If $\langle \Pi^{R[rand]}, Z'^{[ind]} \rangle$ is better than $\langle \Pi^{R[rand]}, Z^{[ind]} \rangle$, then the solution $\langle \Pi^{R[rand]}, Z'^{[ind]} \rangle$

is used to update the archive and lot split population. Otherwise, the VND process continues to find a potentially better solution. The process of updating the archive and lot split population can be described as follows: If the solution $\langle \Pi^{R[rand]}, Z'^{[ind]} \rangle$ is better than $\langle \Pi^{R[Col_2[ind]]}, Z^{[ind]} \rangle$, then the $Z^{[ind]}$ and the $Col_2[ind]$ will be updated by $Z'^{[ind]}$ and $\Pi^{R[rand]}$, i.e., $Z^{[ind]} = Z'^{[ind]}$, $Col_2[ind] = rand$. It should also be noted that $\Pi^{R[Col_2[ind]]}$ may have been changed as the lot sequence population evolves. At the same time, if the objective value of the solution $\langle \Pi^{R[rand]}, Z'^{[ind]} \rangle$ is better than $\langle \Pi^{R[rand]}, Z^{R[rand]} \rangle$, set $Z^{R[rand]} = Z'^{[ind]}$. This process is shown in Figure 4.

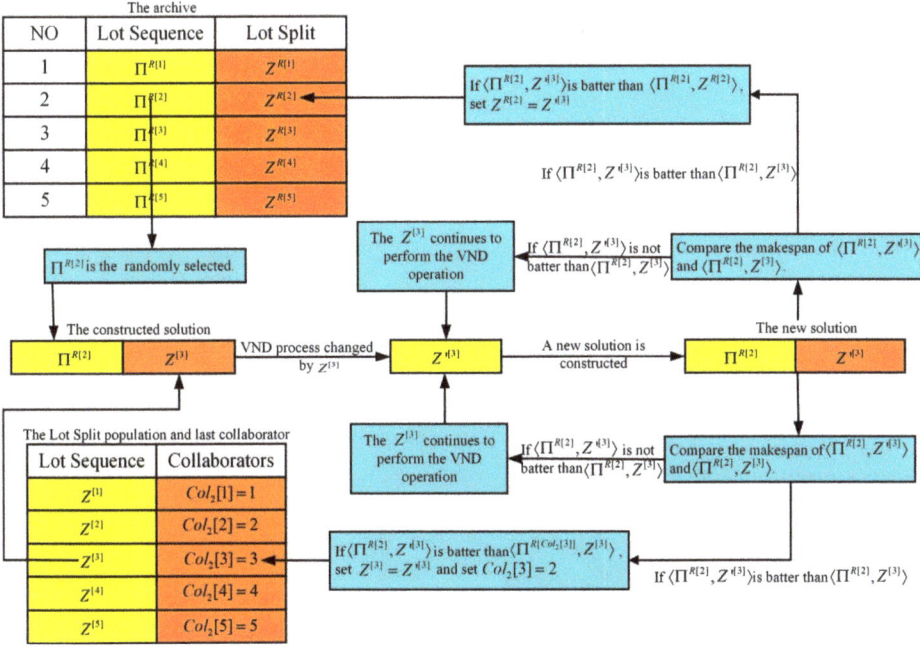

Figure 4. Evolution process of the lot split population.

In the evolution process of the lot split population, to obtain high-quality individuals $Z'^{[ind]}$, three neighborhood structures acting only on the lot split part are specially designed, and the VND process is used to switch the neighborhood. The three perturbation strategies for lot split are described below: (1) Lot split mutation. As shown in Figure 5, from the lot split matrix, a lot with two or more sublots are randomly selected. Reduce a random number in distribution U [1,5] from the size of one sublot and add the number to the size of another sublot. (2) Enhanced lot split mutation. Perform l times lot split mutation, where l is dynamically determined by the number of lots. We set l as $L \times J$, where L is a real number between 0 and 1, and J is the number of lots. (3) Stochastic splits. All lots are redivided into sublots in a random manner. The procedure of the evolution of the lot split population is given in Algorithm 2.

Algorithm 2 Evolution of the lot split population

1: Define a set of neighborhood structures $N^2_k, k = 1, \ldots, k_{max}$
2: **for** $ind = 1$ to PS
3:    $rand \leftarrow$ generate a random integer in $[1 - PS]$
4:    $\left\langle \Pi^{R[rand]}, Z^{[ind]} \right\rangle \leftarrow$ constitute a complete solution
5:    Define $Z \leftarrow Z^{[ind]}$
6:    Let $k \leftarrow 1, Count \leftarrow 0$
7:    **while** $k \leq k_{max}$ **do**
8:       **while** $Count < C$ **do**
9:          $Z'^{[ind]} \leftarrow Neighborhood(Z, N^2_k)$
10:          **if** $\left\langle \Pi^{R[rand]}, Z'^{[ind]} \right\rangle$ better than $\left\langle \Pi^{R[rand]}, Z \right\rangle$
11:             $Count \leftarrow 0, k \leftarrow 1, Z \leftarrow Z'^{[ind]}$
12:             **if** $\left\langle \Pi^{R[rand]}, Z'^{[ind]} \right\rangle$ better than $\left\langle \Pi^{R[Col_2[ind]]}, Z^{[ind]} \right\rangle$ or $\Pi^{R[Col_2[ind]]}$ was changed
13:                $Z^{[ind]} \leftarrow Z'^{[ind]}, Col_2[ind] = rand$
14:             **end if**
15:             **if** $\left\langle \Pi^{R[rand]}, Z'^{[ind]} \right\rangle$ better than $\left\langle \Pi^{R[rand]}, Z^{R[rand]} \right\rangle$
16:                $Z^{[rand]} \leftarrow Z'^{[ind]}$
17:             **end if**
18:          **else**
19:             $Count++$
20:          **end if**
21:       **end while**
22:    $k++$
23:    **end while**
24: **end for**

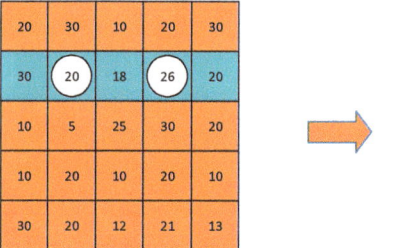 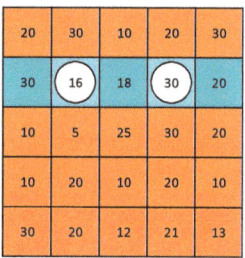

Figure 5. Illustrations of the lot split mutation.

4.5. Coevolutionary Population Restart

With the evolving of the algorithm, the diversity of the two populations might be reduced. In this case, the efficiency of the population coevolution may be poor. To avoid the algorithm falling into the local optimality, two different restart strategies are adopted for the populations. For the lot sequence population, an individual $\Pi^{[ind]}$ is reinitialized if it has not been improved in a predetermined number of R consecutive generations. The novel individual should contain valuable information about the original individual and remain somewhat different from the original individual. For this purpose, a two-point crossover (TPX) method was used, as illustrated in Figure 6. Where two parent lot sequences are randomly selected from the archive because good solutions are stored in an archive. For the lot split population, an individual $Z^{[ind]}$ is also reinitialized if it has not been updated in a predetermined number of R consecutive generations. Due to the lot split matrix is different from the regular sequence, the classical TPX might produce infeasible schedules. Therefore, a cooperative selection operator is proposed. When determining the split information for one lot, two solutions are selected at random from the archive and compared based on their objective values, and the split information for this lot comes from the better one. The process is repeated from the first lot to the last lot. Here, we use $Z_j^{[ind]}$ to represent the lot split information for lot j in individual ind, and this process is shown in Algorithm 3.

Algorithm 3 Lot split population restart

1: **for** $j = 1$ to $j = J$
2:     Randomly select two solutions in archive $\langle \Pi^a, Z^a \rangle$ and $\langle \Pi^b, Z^b \rangle$
3:     **if** $\langle \Pi^a, Z^a \rangle$ better than $\langle \Pi^b, Z^b \rangle$
4:         $Z_j^{[ind]} \leftarrow Z_j^a$
5:     **else**
6:         $Z_j^{[ind]} \leftarrow Z_j^b$
7:     **end if**
8: **end for**

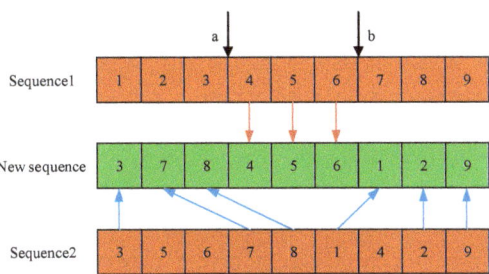

Figure 6. Illustration of TPX for a lot sequence.

4.6. The Algorithm Procedure

With the above description, the whole vCCEA is displayed in Algorithm 4. Where the $UpdateBestSolution(\langle \Pi, Z \rangle)$ means update the optimal solution using solution $\langle \Pi, Z \rangle$, and the $Age(\langle \Pi, Z \rangle)$ represents the number of consecutive update failures of the solution composed of individual Π (or Z) and their collaborators.

Algorithm 4 Lot split population restart

1: Initialize algorithm parameters, including PS, C, L, R.
2: Define the termination criterion T.
3: Define a set of neighborhood structures $N_k^1, k = 1, \ldots, k_{max}$ and $N_k^2, k = 1, \ldots, k_{max}$
4: Initialize archive and two populations
5: Find the best solutions $\langle \Pi^{best}, Z^{best} \rangle$ in archive
6: **while** T is not satisfied **do**
7:     **for** $ind = 1$ to PS
8:         $rand \leftarrow$ generate a random integer in $[1 - PS]$
9:         $\langle \Pi^{[ind]}, Z^{R[rand]} \rangle \leftarrow$ constitute a complete solution
10:        Define $\Pi \leftarrow \Pi^{[ind]}$
11:        Let $k \leftarrow 1$, $Count \leftarrow 0$
12:        **while** $k \leq k_{max}$ **do**
13:            **while** $Count < C$ **do**
14:                $\Pi'^{[ind]} \leftarrow Neighborhood(\Pi, N_k^1)$
15:                **if** $\langle \Pi'^{[ind]}, Z^{R[rand]} \rangle$ better than $\langle \Pi, Z^{R[rand]} \rangle$
16:                   $UpdateBestSolution(\langle \Pi'^{[ind]}, Z^{R[rand]} \rangle)$
17:                   $Count \leftarrow 0, k \leftarrow 1, \Pi \leftarrow \Pi'^{[ind]}$
18:                **if** $\langle \Pi'^{[ind]}, Z^{R[rand]} \rangle$ better than $\langle \Pi^{[ind]}, Z^{R[Col_1[ind]]} \rangle$

19:                          $\Pi^{[ind]} \leftarrow \Pi'^{[ind]}$, $Col_1[ind] = rand$
20:                          $Age\left(\left\langle \Pi^{[ind]}, Z^{R[Col_1[ind]]} \right\rangle\right) \leftarrow 0$
21:                  else
22:                          $Age\left(\left\langle \Pi^{[ind]}, Z^{R[Col_1[ind]]} \right\rangle\right) + +$
23:                  end if
24:                  if $\left\langle \Pi'^{[ind]}, Z^{R[rand]} \right\rangle$ better than $\left\langle \Pi^{[rand]}, Z^{R[rand]} \right\rangle$
25:                      $\Pi^{[rand]} \leftarrow \Pi'^{[ind]}$
26:                  end if
27:              else
28:                  $Count + +$
29:              end if
30:          end while
31:          $k + +$
32:          end while
33:      end for
34:      for $ind = 1$ to PS
35:          $rand \leftarrow$ generate a random integer in $[1 - PS]$
36:          $\left\langle \Pi^{R[rand]}, Z^{[ind]} \right\rangle \leftarrow$ constitute a complete solution
37:          Define $Z \leftarrow Z^{[ind]}$
38:          Let $k \leftarrow 1$, $Count \leftarrow 0$
39:          while $k \leq k_{max}$ do
40:              while $Count < C$ do
41:                  $Z'^{[ind]} \leftarrow Neighborhood(Z, N^2_k)$
42:                  if $\left\langle \Pi^{R[rand]}, Z'^{[ind]} \right\rangle$ better than $\left\langle \Pi^{R[rand]}, Z \right\rangle$
43:                      $UpdateBestSolution\left(\left\langle \Pi^{R[rand]}, Z'^{[ind]} \right\rangle\right)$
44:                      $Count \leftarrow 0$, $k \leftarrow 1$, $Z \leftarrow Z'^{[ind]}$
45:                      if $\left\langle \Pi^{R[rand]}, Z'^{[ind]} \right\rangle$ better than $\left\langle \Pi^{R[Col_2[ind]]}, Z^{[ind]} \right\rangle$
46:                          $Z^{[ind]} \leftarrow Z'^{[ind]}$, $Col_2[ind] = rand$
47:                          $Age\left(\left\langle \Pi^{R[Col_2[ind]]}, Z^{[ind]} \right\rangle\right) \leftarrow 0$
48:                      else
49:                          $Age\left(\left\langle \Pi^{R[Col_2[ind]]}, Z^{[ind]} \right\rangle\right) + +$
50:                      end if
51:                      if $\left\langle \Pi^{R[rand]}, Z'^{[ind]} \right\rangle$ better than $\left\langle \Pi^{R[rand]}, Z^{R[rand]} \right\rangle$
52:                          $Z^{[rand]} \leftarrow Z'^{[ind]}$
53:                      end if
54:                  else
55:                      $Count + +$
56:                  end if
57:              end while
58:              $k + +$
59:          end while
60:      end for
61:      for $ind = 1$ to PS
62:          if $Age\left(\left\langle \Pi^{[ind]}, Z^{R[Col_1[ind]]} \right\rangle\right) > R$
63:              $Restart1(\Pi^{[ind]})$, $Age\left(\left\langle \Pi^{R[Col_2[ind]]}, Z^{[ind]} \right\rangle\right) \leftarrow 0$
64:          end if
65:          if $Age\left(\left\langle \Pi^{R[Col_2[ind]]}, Z^{[ind]} \right\rangle\right) > R$
66:              $Restart2(Z^{[ind]})$, $Age\left(\left\langle \Pi^{R[Col_2[ind]]}, Z^{[ind]} \right\rangle\right) \leftarrow 0$
67:          end if
68:      end for
69: end while
70: Output the best solution $\left\langle \Pi^{best}, Z^{best} \right\rangle$.

5. Experimental Analyses

In this section, the performance of the proposed vCCEA is evaluated by experimental design and results analysis. The simulation experiment environment of this paper is a PC with 3.60 GHz Intel Core i7 processor and 32 GB RAM. The vCCEA and all compared algorithms are written in the Visual Studio 2019 C++, and run on the release x64 platform. In the algorithm test, the maximum running time is used as the algorithm termination to ensure fairness. In addition, it is considered that the algorithm has practical significance only when it can solve the problem in an acceptable time. Therefore, the termination condition is set as $t \times J \times K$ milliseconds, where J indicates the number of lots and K represents the number of stages, respectively. Referring to the literature [30], t is set as 80.

5.1. Experimental Dataset and Performance Indicators

In this paper, two benchmark sets β_1 and β_2 are designed to verify the validity of the vCCEA. Where 48 small-scale instances are designed in β_1 to study the difference between the MILP and the vCCEA in solving HFSP_ECS, and 100 medium–large scale instances solved by the metaheuristic algorithm are designed in β_2 to verify the performance of vCCEA. In β_1, the number of lots is J comes from $\{6, 8, 10, 12, 14\}$, and the number of stages S comes from $\{3, 5, 8\}$. Thus, there are 15 different combinations of $J \times S$ that can be obtained. In β_2, the number of lots in J comes from $\{20, 40, 60, 80, 100\}$, and the number of stages is S comes from $\{3, 5, 8, 10\}$. Similarly, there are 20 different combinations in β_2. For β_1, only one instance is randomly generated per combination. For β_2, five instances are randomly generated per combination. Thus, there are 15 small scale instances and 100 medium–large scale instances in β_1 and β_2, respectively. In β_1 and β_2, the number of parallel machines at each stage is randomly generated from the range $[1, 5]$. In addition, the number of items for each lot is obtained from a uniform distribution $U[50, 100]$, the processing time of items at each stage is randomly sampled from the uniform distribution $U[1, 10]$, the processing energy consumption per unit time is obtained from the range $[2, 5]$, the energy consumption per idle unit of the machine takes a value in the range $[1, 3]$, and the maximum number of sublots is set as 5. In this study, time is measured in seconds, and energy consumption is measured in joules, and the relative percentage increase (RPI) is used as the performance metric. The RPI is calculated as in Equation (21).

$$RPI = \frac{E_{avg} - E_{best}}{E_{best}} \times 100 \qquad (21)$$

where E_{avg} is the average energy consumption of an instance solved by the given algorithm independently performed several times, and E_{best} is the best result obtained by all the compared algorithms. Algorithms with smaller RPI values will have better performance.

5.2. Parameter Setting

Appropriate parameters are very important to the metaheuristics, which can effectively improve their efficiency and robustness. There are four parameters in the vCCEA proposed in this paper, including the number of solutions in the archive (PS), the maximum number of consecutive failures in a neighborhood during the VND process (C), the parameters (L) that control the number of executions in the two enhanced neighborhood structures and the maximum number of successive generations (R) of updating the individual in two populations unsuccessfully. We first determine the value level of each parameter through preliminary experiments, where the details of value levels are shown in Table 2. To verify the influence of each parameter and its value at different levels, an orthogonal array $L16$ is designed using the Taguchi experimental method to determine their combinations and is displayed in Table 3. For the combinations in Table 3, five instances with different scale problems are selected from benchmark set β_2, and the five different problem scales are 20×5, 40×5, 60×5, 80×5, and 100×5. Each instance is run independently 20 times, and the RPI value of each instance is calculated. Then, as shown in Table 3, the average RPI value of the five instances in each combination is collected as the response value.

Table 2. Parameter level factor.

Parameters	The Level of Parameter			
	1	2	3	4
PS	5	10	15	20
C	5	10	15	20
L	0.1	0.2	0.3	0.4
R	50	100	150	200

Table 3. Orthogonal array and response values.

Combination	Parameter				Response (RPI)
	PS	C	L	R	
1	5	5	0.1	50	0.084
2	5	10	0.2	100	0.0711
3	5	15	0.3	150	0.0384
4	5	20	0.4	200	0.0653
5	10	5	0.2	150	0.0688
6	10	10	0.1	200	0.0766
7	10	15	0.4	50	0.0406
8	10	20	0.3	100	0.0480
9	15	5	0.3	200	0.0806
10	15	10	0.4	150	0.0601
11	15	15	0.1	100	0.0884
12	15	20	0.2	50	0.0623
13	20	5	0.4	100	0.0706
14	20	10	0.3	50	0.0664
15	20	15	0.2	200	0.0748
16	20	20	0.1	150	0.0803

The trend of the parameter level is shown in Figure 7, and Table 4 gives the significance rank of each parameter of the vCCEA. According to Figure 7 and Table 4, it can be concluded that parameter L has the greatest impact on the algorithm among these parameters. This is because the parameter L is related to the VND strategy. In the process of VND, the good or bad neighborhood structure has an important influence on the algorithm. A good neighborhood structure can promote the exploration ability of the algorithm and speed up the convergence. For parameter PS, a larger population size can accommodate more potential solutions and help the algorithm search globally. However, it does not support longitudinal and deep search in a limited running time. Too small a population size is not conducive to global search. For parameter C, a too small value will not make full use of each neighborhood perturbation strategy and a too large value will waste the computational time. For parameter R, if the value is set too small, the good information of advanced individuals in the two populations cannot be fully utilized, and if the value is set too large, the diversity of the population cannot be guaranteed and the algorithm may converge prematurely. Therefore, the appropriate parameters are critical for vCCEA. Through the above parameter experiment and analysis, the best parameter combination we can obtain is $PS = 10$, $C = 15$, $L = 0.3$ and $R = 150$. This parameter combination is used in the following experiments.

5.3. Evaluation of the Algorithm Components and Strategies

In this subsection, the algorithm components and strategies are validated and analyzed for effectiveness. Our algorithm contains the VND process, collaborative model, and two enhanced neighborhood structures, and these three strategies are not independent but highly coupled. To verify the effect of each of the three components and the cooperation between them, three other versions of vCCEA are constructed, vCCEA_1, vCCEA_2, and vCCEA_3, where the vCCEA_1 is the vCCEA that removes the VND process. The vCCEA2 is used to verify the validity of the collaboration model. The VCCEA_3 is the vCCEA that remove the two enhanced neighborhood structures during the VND process. And the β_2 is used to verify vCCEA and the other three versions of vCCEA. For each instance in β_2, the four algorithms are independently run 20 times. For each algorithm, the RPI value of each instance is obtained first. Then, the average RPI of five instances from the same scale problem is calculated and represented by the average RPI values (ARPI). The results are shown in Table 5.

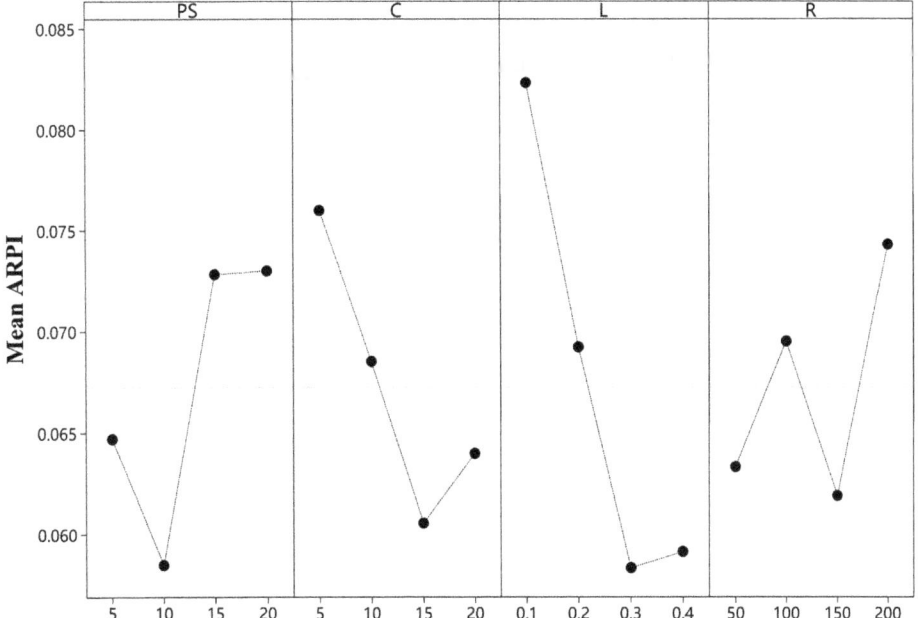

Figure 7. The trend of the parameter level.

Table 4. The average RPI response values.

Level	PS	C	L	R
1	0.0647	0.0760	0.0823	0.0633
2	0.0585	0.0686	0.0693	0.0695
3	0.0729	0.0606	0.0584	0.0619
4	0.0730	0.0640	0.0592	0.0743
Delta	0.0145	0.0155	0.0240	0.0124
Rank	3	2	1	4

From Table 5, we can clearly see that the whole vCCEA is the best performer. In the other three versions of the vCCEA, the vCCEA_1 is the worst one. In the cooperative coevolutionary process, the VND process is used to generate new individuals Π(or Z). With the same perturbation strategy, the result of neighborhood switching using VND process is obviously better than that of traditional neighborhood perturbation. Thus, the VND process is crucial to the algorithm. Among these 20 problems with different sizes, the vCCEA_2 is worse than the vCCEA. It can be seen that the collaborative model proposed in this paper is effective. By comparing vCCEA_3 and vCCEA, the validity of the two enhanced neighborhood structures is proven. These two enhanced neighborhood structures can enlarge the search area of the VND process, and it is beneficial for the vCCEA to find the potential promising solution in a larger solution space.

Table 5. Comparison of vCCEA components.

ARPI	vCCEA	vCCEA_1	vCCEA_2	vCCEA_3
20_3	0.0716	0.4028	0.5022	0.2135
20_5	0.0328	0.111	0.0713	0.1105
20_8	0.0283	0.0671	0.0195	0.0553
20_10	0.0052	0.0617	0.0226	0.0487
40_3	0.0251	0.0841	0.0776	0.0988
40_5	0.02	0.0961	0.0766	0.1121
40_8	0.0195	0.0523	0.0148	0.056
40_10	0.0167	0.0501	0.0886	0.0578
60_3	0.0049	0.0379	0.0186	0.0431
60_5	0.0068	0.0582	0.0272	0.0597
60_8	0.0148	0.0623	0.0668	0.0707
60_10	0.0083	0.0571	0.017	0.0506
80_3	0.0032	0.0297	0.0085	0.0273
80_5	0.0142	0.0556	0.038	0.0549
80_8	0.0104	0.044	0.0141	0.0438
80_10	0.0193	0.0479	0.0321	0.0465
100_3	0.0141	0.0672	0.041	0.0649
100_5	0.0204	0.0631	0.0444	0.0532
100_8	0.0192	0.0773	0.0318	0.0749
100_10	0.0189	0.0416	0.0278	0.0371
Mean	0.0187	0.0784	0.062	0.069

5.4. Evaluation of the vCCEA on the Small-Scale Instances

This section focuses on the differences between vCCEA and MILP when solving the small-scale problems. We use the Gurobipy 9.1.2 optimizer to run the MILP on the instances in β_1, and the maximum running time is limited to 3600 s. In addition, the vCCEA is used to solve the instances in β_1, and the termination condition is set to $80 \times J \times K$. The results are shown in Table 6.

Table 6. The validation results of MILP.

Problem	MILP			vCCEA		
	Objective	Time (s)	RPI	Objective	Time (s)	RPI
6_3	48,421	4.36	0	48,421	1.453	0
6_5	169,894	8.13	0	169,894	2.406	0
6_8	364,151	10.13	0	364,151	3.844	0
8_3	104,164	20.06	0	104,164	1.921	0
8_5	220,119	154.4	0	220,119	3.203	0
8_8	369,027	46.73	0	369,027	5.125	0
10_3	122,068	17.41	0	122,068	2.406	0
10_5	223,049	3600	0	223,049	4	0
10_8	612,361	3600	0	612,361	6.406	0
12_3	222,509	3600	0	222,509	2.906	0
12_5	311,630	3600	0	311,630	4.813	0
12_8	612,660	3600	0	612,660	7.688	0
14_3	237,372	3600	0	237,372	3.375	0
14_5	281,607	3600	3.678	271,617	5.609	0
14_8	684,055	3600	0.1826	683,506	8.984	0

From Table 6, it can be concluded that for small-scale instances, both the MILP and vCCEA can find optimal solutions. The MILP and vCCEA find the same results for the first 13 instances in β_1. In addition, for instances 14_5 and 14_8, the vCCEA revealed better results. As the complexity of the problem increases, the effectiveness of the MILP is gradually inferior to the vCCEA. For large-scale instances, the MILP model has difficulty in providing a good solution in a short time. As we know that time is a non-negligible factor in actual production, thus the near-optimal solutions are required in an acceptable time. Therefore, with the increasing size of the instances, the advantages of vCCEA become more and more obvious.

5.5. Evaluation of vCCEA on the Medium–Large Scale Instances

Next, the performance of the proposed vCCEA is evaluated on the medium–large scale instances in β_2. Here, we collected five metaheuristic algorithms for comparisons, namely, CVND [30], GA [40], GAR [24], VMBO [41], and DABC [42], which are those presented for the HFSP in the literature most recently and have been proven to have excellent performance. For the HFSP_ECS, three highly coupled subproblems need to be solved, i.e., lot sequence, machine assignment, and lot split. Due to the specificity of the problem, we retain the original characteristics of each comparison algorithm and modify it to adapt to our problem. All algorithms use the same double-layer encoding and decoding strategies as proposed in this paper, and select the corresponding lot split operator from this article. As these comparison algorithms have been partially changed for adapting to our problem, their parameters are also optimized and adjusted on the original basis by using the DOE method to ensure that these algorithms can play with better performance. For each instance in β_2, each algorithm is run independently 20 times, and the average energy consumption and the ARPI of five instances from the same scale problem are calculated. The experimental results are given in Table 7. Additionally, to more visually demonstrate the differences between these six algorithms, the means and 95% least significant difference (LSD) confidence intervals [43] were analyzed. Figure 8 shows the confidence interval comparisons between vCCEA and each algorithm, and Figure 9 shows the confidence interval comparison among all algorithms, where the X-axis represents the various algorithms and the Y-axis is the ARPI value.

Table 7. Comparison results of vCCEA and other algorithms on β_2.

Problem	vCCEA		CVND		GA		GAR		VMBO		DABC	
	AVG	RPI	AVG	RPI	AVG	RPI	AVG	RPI	AVG	RPI	AVG	RPI
20_3	104,859.2	0.0716	105,168.8	0.367	105,241.6	0.4366	105,622.4	0.8	105,118.9	0.3194	105,380.9	0.5695
20_5	286,304.1	0.0328	286,558.3	0.1216	286,650.9	0.154	287,162.9	0.3329	286,555.6	0.1207	286,341.3	0.0458
20_8	556,484.2	0.0376	556,780.2	0.0908	556,746.2	0.0847	557,223.5	0.1705	556,616.3	0.0614	556,421	0.0262
20_10	674,734.2	0.0135	675,111.7	0.0695	675,225	0.0863	675,640	0.1478	674,985.4	0.0507	674,824.4	0.0269
40_3	249,561.5	0.0251	249,702.6	0.0817	249,803.9	0.1223	250,206.8	0.2838	249,746.1	0.0991	249,831.4	0.1333
40_5	435,346.9	0.024	435,831.7	0.1353	435,944.6	0.1613	436,981.2	0.3994	435,847.7	0.139	436,000.1	0.1741
40_8	1,040,283	0.0228	1,040,946	0.0865	1,041,001	0.0918	1,042,108	0.1982	1,040,757	0.0683	1,040,905	0.0825
40_10	1,150,216	0.0186	1,151,282	0.1113	1,151,477	0.1282	1,153,416	0.2969	1,151,298	0.1127	1,151,912	0.1661
60_3	406,475.4	0.0049	406,556.5	0.0348	406,668.4	0.0524	406,839.1	0.0943	406,672.4	0.0533	406,640	0.0454
60_5	772,749.8	0.0068	772,993.9	0.0384	773,326.6	0.0815	773,701.2	0.1299	773,183	0.0629	773,111.7	0.0536
60_8	1,272,264	0.0205	1,272,954	0.0747	1,273,432	0.1123	1,277,052	0.3969	1,273,614	0.1266	1,275,208	0.2519
60_10	1,781,242	0.0082	1,782,288	0.0669	1,782,747	0.0927	1,784,128	0.1703	1,782,522	0.0801	1,782,387	0.0725
80_3	538,223.9	0.0032	538,356.1	0.0278	538,429.4	0.0414	538,612.1	0.0753	538,420.2	0.0397	538,330.7	0.0231
80_5	1,105,906	0.0143	1,106,629	0.0796	1,106,944	0.1081	1,107,842	0.1893	1,106,768	0.0922	1,107,026	0.1155
80_8	1,666,493	0.0105	1,668,307	0.1193	1,667,385	0.064	1,668,484	0.13	1,667,195	0.0526	1,667,606	0.0772
80_10	2,381,343	0.0193	2,382,087	0.0506	2,382,973	0.0878	2,385,528	0.1951	2,382,764	0.079	2,383,807	0.1228
100_3	647,384.2	0.0141	647,558.7	0.041	647,756.7	0.0716	648,072.5	0.1204	647,836.8	0.084	647,836.7	0.084
100_5	1,225,888	0.0203	1,226,310	0.0548	1,226,695	0.0862	1,228,023	0.1946	1,226,821	0.0965	1,227,563	0.1571
100_8	2,474,499	0.0179	2,477,750	0.1493	2,476,969	0.1178	2,477,487	0.1387	2,475,958	0.0769	2,476,269	0.0895
100_10	2,907,226	0.0188	2,908,332	0.0569	2,908,726	0.0704	2,910,371	0.127	2,908,690	0.0692	2,910,773	0.1409
Mean	1,083,874	0.0202	1,084,575	0.0924	1,084,707	0.1126	1,085,725	0.2296	1,084,568	0.0942	1,084,909	0.1229

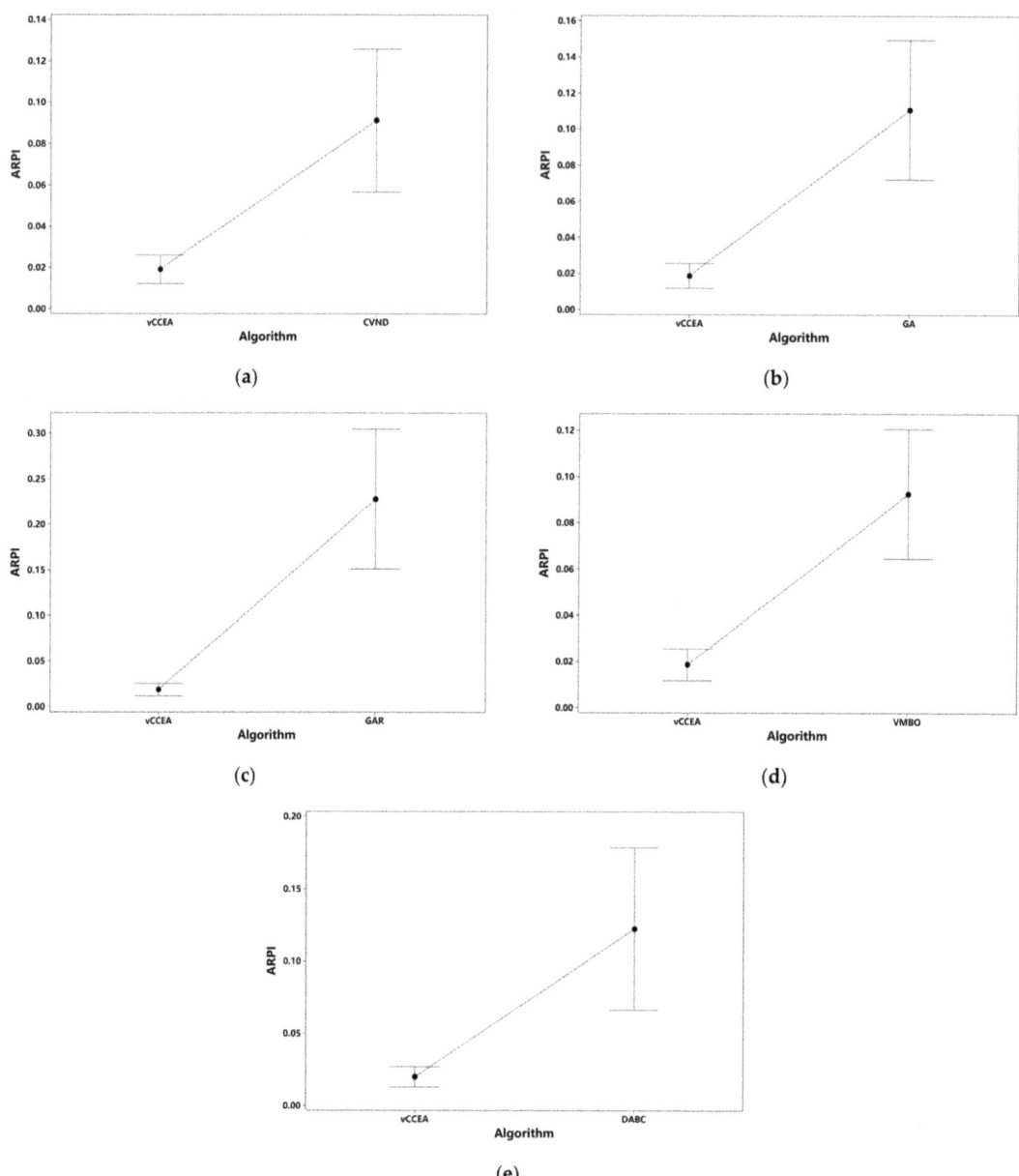

Figure 8. Confidence interval graph. (**a**) Confidence intervals of vCCEA and CVND; (**b**) confidence intervals of vCCEA and GA; (**c**) confidence intervals of vCCEA and GAR; (**d**) confidence intervals of vCCEA and VMBO; (**e**) confidence intervals of vCCEA and DABC.

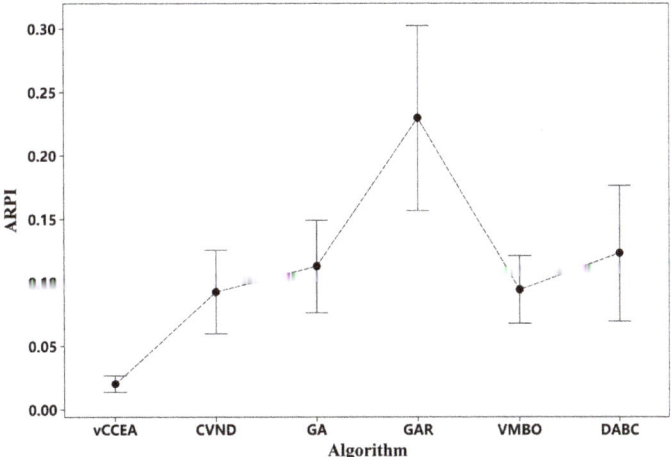

Figure 9. Confidence interval graph for these six algorithms.

As seen in Table 7, the vCCEA is the best one among these algorithms, which obtains best results for 19 of the 20 different problems in β_2. The DABC algorithm finds the optimal solution for the remaining one scale problem, with the scale being 20 × 8. The last row of Table 7 gives the average energy consumption and average RPI for all instances. It is obvious that vCCEA has the best results among all the algorithms. In addition, according to the confidence intervals shown in Figures 8 and 9, it can clearly be seen that the performance of the proposed vCCEA is obviously better than that of the other five algorithms. To further evaluate the performance of the algorithm, we analyze the convergence of the algorithm, and the convergence curves of these algorithms on two examples are given. These two examples are from 40 × 5 and 80 × 10, respectively, and the convergence curves are shown in Figures 10 and 11. The X-axis represents the running time of the algorithm, and the Y-axis represents the energy consumption value.

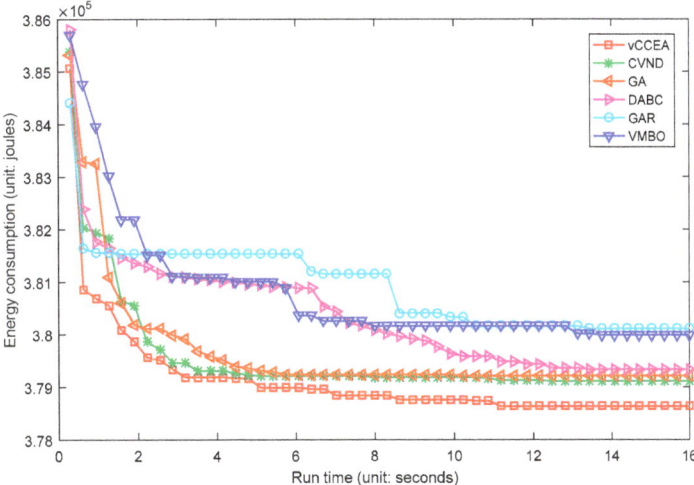

Figure 10. The convergence curve for instances of 40 × 5.

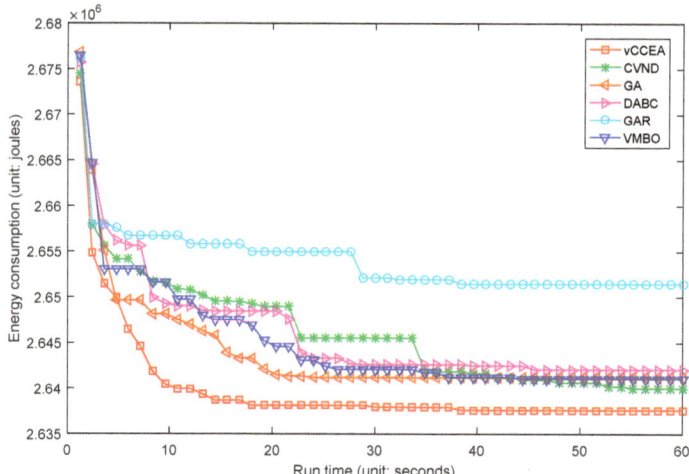

Figure 11. The convergence curve for instances of 80 × 10.

From Figures 10 and 11, the convergence speed of vCCEA is the fastest, and the convergence degree is also better than that of the other algorithms. This is closely related to the cooperative coevolutionary strategy and VND process in the proposed vCCEA. Two populations in the algorithm evolve separately using the VND process specifically designed for them and constantly interacting with the archive. As well as with the population restart strategy, the local search capability of the vCCEA can be ensured, and it also balances the diversity and density of the populations, which further improves the algorithm performance.

Therefore, through the above analysis, the conclusion can be drawn that the vCCEA can effectively solve HFSP_ECS and the robustness of the vCCEA can be guaranteed.

6. Conclusions

In this paper, the energy-efficient flowshop scheduling problem with consistent sublots (HFSP_ECS) is studied, and it supports the overlap of successive operations within a multi-stage manufacturing system. This is a highly complex combinatorial optimization problem that consists of three highly coupled subproblems. We use the minimized energy consumption as the optimization objective. By limiting the maximum number of sublots, a linear integer programming model (MILP) of the addressed problem is established and its validity is verified by the Gurobi optimizer. An improved cooperative coevolutionary algorithm (vCCEA) is proposed by integrating the variable neighborhood decent (VND) strategy. In vCCEA, with the consideration of the problem-specific characteristics, a two-layer encoding strategy is designed, and a novel collaborative interaction model is proposed. Additionally, to ensure the local search ability of the algorithm, different neighborhood structures are designed for different subproblems, and two kinds of enhanced local neighborhood structures are proposed to search for potential promising solutions. To avoid trapping into the local optima, a population restart mechanism is designed. Moreover, through a large number of experiments on different benchmark sets, the effectiveness of the proposed strategies is proved. The experimental results show that vCCEA is significantly better than the mathematical programming and the other algorithms in solving the HFSP_ECS.

For the HFSP_ECS, the maximum sublot quantities is limited in this paper, so in the future, how to divide the lots and the number of sublots is a direction of our research. At the same time, we will consider more production constraints in the future, such as setup, blocking, transportation, and delivery time. In addition, the realistic manufacturing processes always have multi-objective characteristics and variability. This requires us to consider more optimization objectives and weigh the relationship between multiple objective functions. Furthermore, the possible emergencies during production are also required and studied to derive useful dynamic and rescheduling strategies.

Author Contributions: C.L.: conceptualization, methodology, data curation, software, validation, writing—original draft. B.Z.: conceptualization, methodology, software, validation, writing—original draft. Y.H.: conceptualization, methodology, software, validation, writing—original draft. Y.W.: conceptualization, methodology, supervision, writing—original draft. J.L.: conceptualization, methodology, visualization, investigation. K.G.: conceptualization, methodology, writing—review and editing. All authors have read and agreed to the published version of the manuscript.

Funding: This work was supported by the National Natural Science Foundation of China under grant numbers 61803192, 61973203, 62106073, 62173216, and 62173356. We are grateful for Guangyue Youth Scholar Innovation Talent Program support received from Liaocheng University, the Youth Innovation Talent Introduction and Education Program support received from the Shandong Province Colleges and Universities, and the Natural Science Foundation of Shandong Province under grant numbers ZR2021QE195.

Institutional Review Board Statement: Not applicable.

Informed Consent Statement: Not applicable.

Data Availability Statement: The data that support the findings of this study are available from the corresponding author, upon reasonable request.

Conflicts of Interest: The authors declare that they have no conflict of interest.

Abbreviations

Notations
- K Total number of stages.
- k Index of stages, $k \in \{1, 2, \ldots, K\}$.
- J Total number of lots.
- j Index of lots, $j \in \{1, 2, \ldots, J\}$.
- M_k Number of parallel machines at stage k.
- i Index of machines at stage k, $i \in \{1, 2, \ldots, M_k\}$.
- T_j Total number of items of lot j.
- L Maximum number of sublots of each lot.
- e Index of the sublots, $e \in \{1, 2, \ldots, L\}$.
- $P_{k,j}$ Item processing time of lot j at stage k.
- $EP_{k,j}$ The energy consumption per unit time when lot j is processed on stage k.
- EI_k The energy consumption per unit time when the machine on stage k is idle.
- G A positive large number.

Decision variables
- $N_{j,e}$ Number items of sublot e of lot j.
- $S_{k,j,e}$ Beginning time of sublot e of lot j at stage k.
- $C_{k,j,e}$ Ending time of sublot e of lot j at stage k.
- $W_{j,e}$ A binary variable. The value is 1 if items in the sublot e of lot j is greater than 0, and 0 otherwise.
- $D_{k,j,i}$ A binary variable. The value is 1 if lot j is scheduled on machine i at stage k, and 0 otherwise.
- $Y_{k,j,j1,i}$ A binary variable. When lot j and lot $j1$ are scheduled on the same machine at stage k, the value is 1 if lot j is processed before lot $j1$, and 0 otherwise.
- C_{max} Completion processing time for all lots.
- $E_{process}$ Total energy consumption for all machine processing.
- E_{idle} Total energy consumption of all machines when they stay in the idle.
- E_{max} The total energy consumption.

References

1. Ruiz, R.; Vázquez-Rodríguez, J.A. The Hybrid Flow Shop Scheduling Problem. *Eur. J. Oper. Res.* **2010**, *205*, 1–18. [CrossRef]
2. Huang, Y.-Y.; Pan, Q.-K.; Gao, L. An Effective Memetic Algorithm for the Distributed Flowshop Scheduling Problem with an Assemble Machine. *Int. J. Prod. Res.* **2022**. [CrossRef]
3. Peng, K.; Pan, Q.-K.; Gao, L.; Zhang, B.; Pang, X. An Improved Artificial Bee Colony Algorithm for Real-World Hybrid Flowshop Rescheduling in Steelmaking-Refining-Continuous Casting Process. *Comput. Ind. Eng.* **2018**, *122*, 235–250. [CrossRef]
4. Shao, W.; Shao, Z.; Pi, D. Multi-Local Search-Based General Variable Neighborhood Search for Distributed Flow Shop Scheduling in Heterogeneous Multi-Factories. *Appl. Soft Comput.* **2022**, *125*, 109138. [CrossRef]
5. Wu, X.; Cao, Z. An Improved Multi-Objective Evolutionary Algorithm Based on Decomposition for Solving Re-Entrant Hybrid Flow Shop Scheduling Problem with Batch Processing Machines. *Comput. Ind. Eng.* **2022**, *169*, 108236. [CrossRef]
6. Gro, M.; Krumke, S.O.; Rambau, J. *Online Optimization of Large Scale Systems*; Springer Science & Business Media: Berlin/Heidelberg, Germany, 2001; pp. 679–704.
7. Neufeld, J.S.; Schulz, S.; Buscher, U. A Systematic Review of Multi-Objective Hybrid Flow Shop Scheduling. *Eur. J. Oper. Res.* **2022**. [CrossRef]
8. Missaoui, A.; Ruiz, R. A Parameter-Less Iterated Greedy Method for the Hybrid Flowshop Scheduling Problem with Setup Times and Due Date Windows. *Eur. J. Oper. Res.* **2022**, *303*, 99–113. [CrossRef]
9. Gong, D.; Han, Y.; Sun, J. A Novel Hybrid Multi-Objective Artificial Bee Colony Algorithm for Blocking Lot-Streaming Flow Shop Scheduling Problems. *Knowl.-Based Syst.* **2018**, *148*, 115–130. [CrossRef]
10. Daneshamooz, F.; Fattahi, P.; Hosseini, S.M.H. Scheduling in a Flexible Job Shop Followed by Some Parallel Assembly Stations Considering Lot Streaming. *Eng. Optim.* **2022**, *54*, 614–633. [CrossRef]
11. Reiter, S. A System for Managing Job-Shop Production. *J. Bus.* **1966**, *39*, 371–393. [CrossRef]
12. Zhang, W.; Liu, J.; Linn, R.J. Model and Heuristics for Lot Streaming of One Job in M-1 Hybrid Flowshops. *Int. J. Oper. Quant. Manag.* **2003**, *9*, 49–64.
13. Cheng, M.; Mukherjee, N.J.; Sarin, S.c. A Review of Lot Streaming. *Int. J. Prod. Res.* **2013**, *51*, 7023–7046. [CrossRef]
14. Wang, W.; Xu, Z.; Gu, X. A Two-Stage Discrete Water Wave Optimization Algorithm for the Flowshop Lot-Streaming Scheduling Problem with Intermingling and Variable Lot Sizes. *Knowl.-Based Syst.* **2022**, *238*, 107874. [CrossRef]
15. Borndörfer, R.; Danecker, F.; Weiser, M. A Discrete-Continuous Algorithm for Globally Optimal Free Flight Trajectory Optimization. In Proceedings of the 22nd Symposium on Algorithmic Approaches for Transportation Modelling, Opti-mization, and Systems 2022, Potsdam, Germany, 8–9 September 2022.
16. Maristany de las Casas, P.; Sedeño-Noda, A.; Borndörfer, R. An Improved Multiobjective Shortest Path Algorithm. *Comput. Oper. Res.* **2021**, *135*, 105424. [CrossRef]
17. Shi, M.; Gao, S. Reference Sharing: A New Collaboration Model for Cooperative Coevolution. *J. Heuristics* **2017**, *23*, 1–30. [CrossRef]
18. Pan, Q.-K.; Gao, L.; Wang, L. An Effective Cooperative Co-Evolutionary Algorithm for Distributed Flowshop Group Scheduling Problems. *IEEE Trans. Cybern.* **2022**, *52*, 5999–6012. [CrossRef]
19. Mladenović, N.; Hansen, P. Variable Neighborhood Search. *Comput. Oper. Res.* **1997**, *24*, 1097–1100. [CrossRef]
20. Liu, J. Single-Job Lot Streaming in M−1 Two-Stage Hybrid Flowshops. *Eur. J. Oper. Res.* **2008**, *187*, 1171–1183. [CrossRef]
21. Cheng, M.; Sarin, S.C.; Singh, S. Two-Stage, Single-Lot, Lot Streaming Problem for a $1+2$ $1 + 2$ Hybrid Flow Shop. *J. Glob. Optim.* **2016**, *66*, 263–290. [CrossRef]
22. Potts, C.N.; Baker, K.R. Flow Shop Scheduling with Lot Streaming. *Oper. Res. Lett.* **1989**, *8*, 297–303. [CrossRef]
23. Kalir, A.A.; Sarin, S.C. A Near-Optimal Heuristic for the Sequencing Problem in Multiple-Batch Flow-Shops with Small Equal Sublots. *Omega* **2001**, *29*, 577–584. [CrossRef]
24. Naderi, B.; Yazdani, M. A Model and Imperialist Competitive Algorithm for Hybrid Flow Shops with Sublots and Setup Times. *J. Manuf. Syst.* **2014**, *33*, 647–653. [CrossRef]
25. Zhang, P.; Wang, L.; Wang, S. A Discrete Fruit Fly Optimization Algorithm for Flow Shop Scheduling Problem with Intermingling Equal Sublots. In Proceedings of the 33rd Chinese Control Conference, Nanjing, China, 28–30 July 2014; pp. 7466–7471.
26. Zhang, B.; Pan, Q.; Gao, L.; Zhang, X.; Sang, H.; Li, J. An Effective Modified Migrating Birds Optimization for Hybrid Flowshop Scheduling Problem with Lot Streaming. *Appl. Soft Comput.* **2017**, *52*, 14–27. [CrossRef]
27. Zhang, W.; Yin, C.; Liu, J.; Linn, R.J. Multi-Job Lot Streaming to Minimize the Mean Completion Time in m-1 Hybrid Flowshops. *Int. J. Prod. Econ.* **2005**, *96*, 189–200. [CrossRef]
28. Nejati, M.; Mahdavi, I.; Hassanzadeh, R.; Mahdavi-Amiri, N.; Mojarad, M. Multi-Job Lot Streaming to Mini-mize the Weighted Completion Time in a Hybrid Flow Shop Scheduling Problem with Work Shift Con-straint. *Int. J. Adv. Manuf. Technol.* **2014**, *70*, 501–514. [CrossRef]
29. Lalitha, J.L.; Mohan, N.; Pillai, V.M. Lot Streaming in [N-1](1)+N(m) Hybrid Flow Shop. *J. Manuf. Syst.* **2017**, *44*, 12–21. [CrossRef]
30. Zhang, B.; Pan, Q.-K.; Meng, L.-L.; Zhang, X.-L.; Ren, Y.-P.; Li, J.-Q.; Jiang, X.-C. A Collaborative Variable Neighborhood Descent Algorithm for the Hybrid Flowshop Scheduling Problem with Consistent Sublots. *Appl. Soft Comput.* **2021**, *106*, 107305. [CrossRef]
31. Qin, H.-X.; Han, Y.-Y.; Zhang, B.; Meng, L.-L.; Liu, Y.-P.; Pan, Q.-K.; Gong, D.-W. An Improved Iterated Greedy Algorithm for the Energy-Efficient Blocking Hybrid Flow Shop Scheduling Problem. *Swarm Evol. Comput.* **2022**, *69*, 100992. [CrossRef]

32. Duan, J.; Feng, M.; Zhang, Q. Energy-Efficient Collaborative Scheduling of Heterogeneous Multi-Stage Hybrid Flowshop for Large Metallic Component Manufacturing. *J. Clean. Prod.* **2022**, *375*, 134148. [CrossRef]
33. Dong, J.; Ye, C. Green Scheduling of Distributed Two-Stage Reentrant Hybrid Flow Shop Considering Distributed Energy Resources and Energy Storage System. *Comput. Ind. Eng.* **2022**, *169*, 108146. [CrossRef]
34. Geng, K.; Ye, C. A Memetic Algorithm for Energy-Efficient Distributed Re-Entrant Hybrid Flow Shop Scheduling Problem. *IFS* **2021**, *41*, 3951–3971. [CrossRef]
35. Qiao, Y.; Wu, N.; He, Y.; Li, Z.; Chen, T. Adaptive Genetic Algorithm for Two-Stage Hybrid Flow-Shop Scheduling with Sequence-Independent Setup Time and No-Interruption Requirement. *Expert Syst. Appl.* **2022**, *208*, 118068. [CrossRef]
36. Fan, J.; Li, Y.; Xie, J.; Zhang, C.; Shen, W.; Gao, L. A Hybrid Evolutionary Algorithm Using Two Solution Representations for Hybrid Flow-Shop Scheduling Problem. *IEEE Trans. Cybern.* **2021**. [CrossRef] [PubMed]
37. Guinet, A.; Solomon, M.M.; Kedia, P.K.; Dussauchoy, A. A Computational Study of Heuristics for Two-Stage Flexible Flowshops. *Int. J. Prod. Res.* **1996**, *34*, 1399–1415. [CrossRef]
38. Zhang, B.; Pan, Q.; Meng, L.; Lu, C.; Mou, J.; Li, J. An Automatic Multi-Objective Evolutionary Algorithm for the Hybrid Flowshop Scheduling Problem with Consistent Sublots. *Knowl.-Based Syst.* **2022**, *238*, 107819. [CrossRef]
39. Lan, S.; Fan, W.; Yang, S.; Pardalos, P.M. A Variable Neighborhood Search Algorithm for an Integrated Physician Planning and Scheduling Problem. *Comput. Oper. Res.* **2022**, *147*, 105969. [CrossRef]
40. Keskin, K.; Engin, O. A Hybrid Genetic Local and Global Search Algorithm for Solving No-Wait Flow Shop Problem with Bi Criteria. *SN Appl. Sci.* **2021**, *3*, 1–15. [CrossRef]
41. Zhang, X.; Zhang, B.; Meng, L.; Ren, Y.; Meng, R.; Li, J. An Evolutionary Algorithm for a Hybrid Flowshop Scheduling Problem with Consistent Sublots. *Int. J. Autom. Control.* **2022**, *16*, 19–44. [CrossRef]
42. Pan, Q.-K.; Gao, L.; Li, X.-Y.; Gao, K.-Z. Effective Metaheuristics for Scheduling a Hybrid Flowshop with Sequence-Dependent Setup Times. *Appl. Math. Comput.* **2017**, *303*, 89–112. [CrossRef]
43. Balande, U.; Shrimankar, D. A Modified Teaching Learning Metaheuristic Algorithm with Opposite-Based Learning for Permutation Flow-Shop Scheduling Problem. *Evol. Intel.* **2022**, *15*, 57–79. [CrossRef]

Disclaimer/Publisher's Note: The statements, opinions and data contained in all publications are solely those of the individual author(s) and contributor(s) and not of MDPI and/or the editor(s). MDPI and/or the editor(s) disclaim responsibility for any injury to people or property resulting from any ideas, methods, instructions or products referred to in the content.

Article

A Multi-Objective Optimization Method for Flexible Job Shop Scheduling Considering Cutting-Tool Degradation with Energy-Saving Measures

Ying Tian [1,2], Zhanxu Gao [1,2,*], Lei Zhang [3,4,*], Yujing Chen [1,2] and Taiyong Wang [1,2]

1. Key Laboratory of Mechanism Theory and Equipment Design of Ministry of Education, Tianjin University, Tianjin 300072, China
2. School of Mechanical Engineering, Tianjin University, Tianjin 300072, China
3. School of Mechanical Engineering, Tianjin University of Commerce, Tianjin 300134, China
4. Tianjin Tianshen Intelligent Equipment Co., Ltd., Tianjin 300300, China
* Correspondence: gzx_22@tju.edu.cn (Z.G.); zhgraceli@tjcu.edu.cn (L.Z.)

Abstract: Traditional energy-saving optimization of shop scheduling often separates the coupling relationship between a single machine and the shop system, which not only limits the potential of energy-saving but also leads to a large deviation between the optimized result and the actual application. In practice, cutting-tool degradation during operation is inevitable, which will not only lead to the increase in actual machining power but also the resulting tool change operation will disrupt the rhythm of production scheduling. Therefore, to make the energy consumption calculation in scheduling optimization more consistent with the actual machining conditions and reduce the impact of tool degradation on the manufacturing shop, this paper constructs an integrated optimization model including a flexible job shop scheduling problem (FJSP), machining power prediction, tool life prediction and energy-saving strategy. First, an exponential function is formulated using actual cutting experiment data under certain machining conditions to express cutting-tool degradation. Utilizing this function, a reasonable cutting-tool change schedule is obtained. A hybrid energy-saving strategy that combines a cutting-tool change with machine tool turn-on/off schedules to reduce the difference between the simulated and actual machining power while optimizing the energy savings is then proposed. Second, a multi-objective optimization model was established to reduce the makespan, total machine tool load, number of times machine tools are turned on/off and cutting tools are changed, and the total energy consumption of the workshop and the fast and elitist multi-objective genetic algorithm (NSGA-II) is used to solve the model. Finally, combined with the workshop production cost evaluation indicator, a practical FJSP example is presented to demonstrate the proposed optimization model. The prediction accuracy of the machining power is more than 93%. The hybrid energy-saving strategy can further reduce the energy consumption of the workshop by 4.44% and the production cost by 2.44% on the basis of saving 93.5% of non-processing energy consumption by the machine on/off energy-saving strategy.

Keywords: cutting-tool degradation; machine tool turning-on/off schedule; hybrid energy-saving strategy; multi-objective optimization; flexible job shop scheduling

MSC: 90B30; 90B35

1. Introduction

In the current industrial environment, the manufacturing industry, as an important part, consumes a lot of energy and resources in the process of product manufacturing [1]. The report on power consumption released by the China Electricity Council in 2022 showed that China's industrial electricity consumption accounted for 64.5% of the total social electricity consumption in the first 10 months of 2022, while manufacturing electricity consumption accounted for 76% of industrial electricity consumption. In addition, research shows that 99% of environment-related problems in mechanical processes are due to electrical energy consumption [2]. Therefore, the establishment of an energy-saving machining system is an urgent requirement to reduce environmental impacts and every manufacturing enterprise needs to focus on it.

Energy-saving strategies using new materials and technologies may require enterprises to transform and invest a lot in existing manufacturing systems, therefore enterprises are usually inclined to carry out energy-saving scheduling and management [3]. Through scientific matching of production tasks and machine tools, more accurate calculation of tasks sequencing, reduce idle time of machine tools, and reasonable selection of machine tools on/off time can improve energy efficiency [4]. Additionally, Guzman et al. indicated that a gap still exists in developing mathematical models to deal with scheduling problems. Novel modeling approaches should be developed to address and associate the parameters related to production and sustainability [5], among which Feng et al. integrated multiple optimization algorithms and apply edge artificial intelligence (AI) to smart green scheduling of sustainable flexible shop floors [6]. Guzman et al. provided a mixed integer linear programming (MILP) model to address the multi-machine CLSD-BPIM (a capacitated lot-sizing problem with sequence-dependent setups and parallel machines in a bi-part injection molding) [7]. Mula et al. proposed a matheuristic algorithm to optimize the job-shop problem, which combines a genetic algorithm with a disjunctive mathematical model to cut computational times, and the Coin-OR Branch and Cut open-source solver is employed [8]. Rakovitis et al. developed a novel mathematical formulation for the energy-efficient flexible job-shop scheduling problem using the improved unit-specific event-based time representation and proposed a grouping-based decomposition approach to efficiently solve large-scale problems [9]. Knowing that approximately 80% of the energy consumption of machine tools is attributed to non-processing operations, whereas the actual energy consumed by processing operations accounts for less than 20% [10]. If only relying on advanced algorithms to achieve further energy saving in the workshop, the effect is limited. Wu and Sun realized energy saving by changing the turning on/off time of machine tools and choosing different machining speeds [11]. Gong et al. effectively reduced the number of machine restarts and total energy consumption by changing the start time of operations on different machines [12]. Cheng et al. proposed machine tool on/off criterion criteria, speed-scaling policy and transportation optimization strategy, and applied them to manufacturing unit scheduling problems to achieve overall energy saving [13]. An et al. proposed a worn cutting-tool maintenance strategy that reduced the impact of cutting-tool degradation and the total energy consumption of cutting-tool maintenance in manufacturing workshops [14]. Setiawan et al. studied a shop rescheduling problem caused by the failure or reduced service life of cutting tools [15].

As can be seen from the aforementioned literature, on the one hand, most energy-saving scheduling problems start from the perspective of improving the performance of the algorithm, which makes the optimization calculation of shop energy consumption more accurate. However, on the other hand, from the perspective of workshop system management to achieve energy saving, in order to further realize the energy saving of the manufacturing system, it is important to consider the contribution of the coupling relationship between the energy consumption of individual equipment and the energy consumption of the system to the actual production and optimization objectives; however, this was almost ignored in previous studies. As the basic energy consumption equipment in the manufacturing process [16], the energy consumption caused by machine tools cannot be ignored. However, accurate estimation of energy consumption is the basis for improving energy efficiency. In recent years, different modeling methods for machine tool energy consumption have been proposed, such as those by He et al. and He et al., who combined the tool machining path with the energy consumption model to improve machining efficiency [17,18]. Shailendra et al. established an empirical model between cutting parameters and energy consumption of end turning by experiments [19]. Haruhiko et al. proposed an empirical model for predicting machine tool power consumption based on the power function between specific energy consumption and material removal rate [20]. In addition, as the direct implementer of machine tool cutting, tool changing and maintenance will directly affect the production schedule, in order to avoid the tool suddenly reaching the end of life, resulting in the conflict of resources, energy consumption increase and the extension of the makespan and other problems. T. Mikołajczyk et al. and Sun et al. established the prediction model of tool residual life based on the historical data of tool wear [21,22]. M. Castejo'n et al. and P.J. Bagga et al. constructed a tool wear image dataset to predict tool life using cluster analysis and an exponential model [23,24]. Shi et al., Zhang et al. and Muhammad et al. introduced tool wear into the energy consumption model to achieve accurate energy consumption modeling, which laid a foundation for the integration of tool life prediction and energy consumption model [25–27]. Figure 1 summarizes the above literature.

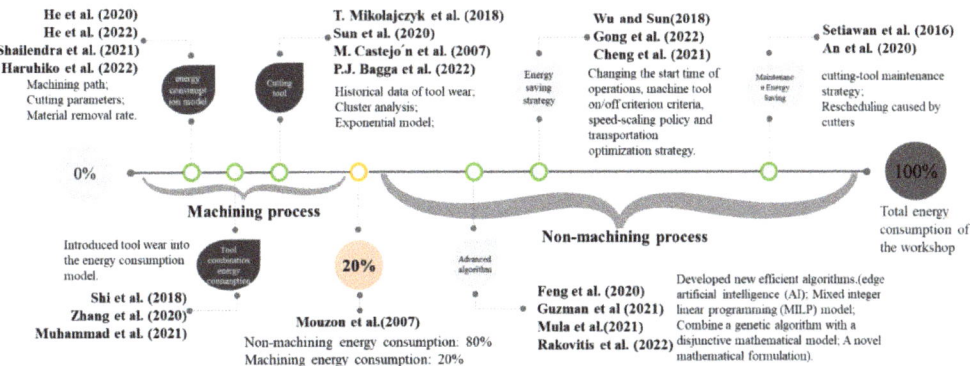

Figure 1. Analysis of energy-saving scheduling research status.

In summary, few researchers combine shop scheduling under low-carbon production with single-machine tool energy consumption and tool life prediction. This paper analyzes the coupling relationship between shop scheduling, single-machine tool energy consumption and tool life prediction, and organically integrates the three to achieve deeper shop consumption reduction. Firstly, the machining power model and the tool life model of the machine tool were established through the tool wear-cutting experiment. Then, the two models were integrated into the shop scheduling system to obtain the machining power of each production procedure and the tool change time of each machine tool in the shop scheduling process, so as to realize the precise modeling of energy consumption at the system level. In addition, on the basis of the machine tool turn-on/off strategy of the workshop, considering the relationship between the tool change time and the turn-on/off time of the machine tool, the tool change time is adjusted to further reduce the machining power and the makespan of the workshop, so as to reduce the production energy consumption of the workshop, as shown in Figure 2.

The remainder of the paper is organized as follows. Section 2 describes the FJSP, cutting-tool degradation model, and hybrid energy-saving strategy of cutting-tool change and machine tool turn-on/off. In Section 3, a multi-objective optimization model of flexible job shop scheduling is established that considers tool degradation and energy-saving measures. Section 4 introduces the proposed NSGA-II algorithm and its specific improvements. Section 5 sets the optimization model parameters through data collection and the analysis of actual cases. The rationality, effectiveness, and practical effects of the proposed model and algorithm are analyzed through verification experiments. Section 6 presents the conclusions and directions for future study.

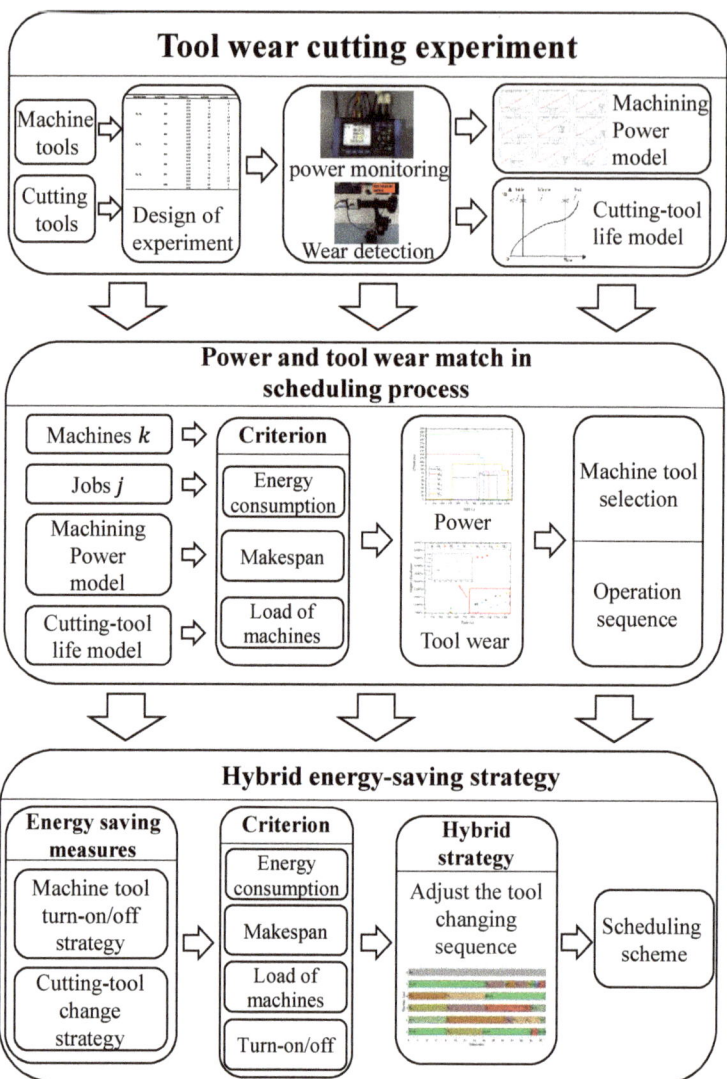

Figure 2. Energy-saving scheduling research route.

2. Problem Description

The relevant symbols are provided in this section. Then, the FJSP that considers cutting-tool degradation with energy-saving measures (FJSP–CTD–ESM) is described. First, the FJSP is described. Then, the calculation method of the cutting-tool life, dynamic machining power, and the hybrid energy-saving strategy of cutting-tool change and machine tool turn-on/off is proposed, which combines the cutting-tool degradation and machine tool turn-on/off effects.

2.1. FJSP Description

In the FJSP, there are n kinds of jobs $J = \{J_i\}_{i=1,2,\ldots,n}$ and k machine tools $M = \{M_m\}_{m=1,2,\ldots,k}$, and each job J_i has S_i preset sequence of operations $O = \{o_{i,j}\}_{j=1,2,\ldots,S_i}$

(Li et al., 2012). At least one operation $o_{i,j}$ in O can be processed by different machine tools, with a corresponding difference in the processing time and efficiency for the same operation.

The following conditions should be met in the FJSP: (1) A machine tool cannot be assigned to two or more operations simultaneously. (2) Each job has the same processing priority: initially, all jobs can be processed. (3) There is no constraint relationship between different jobs. (4) The optional machine tools for the job have no priority relationship. (5) All job processing tasks are non-preemptive. (6) The processing power of the machine tool and degree of cutting-tool wear obey the law of tool degradation. (7) Once a process begins, it cannot be interrupted before completion. Changing the cutting tool and turning the machine tool on/off cannot be inserted into the machining process. (8) The conversion time between different jobs with the same machine tool as well as the transportation time between different stages of the same job are ignored.

The symbols used in this paper are defined in Table 1.

Table 1. The symbols used in this paper.

Symbol	Descriptions
i, h	The index for jobs, $i, h = 1, 2, \ldots, n$
j, g	The index for operations, $j, g = 1, 2, \ldots, max\{S_i, S_g\}$
m	The index for machine tools, $m = 1, 2, \ldots, k$
r	The index for the machine tool's processing task, $r = 1, 2, \ldots, l_m$
l_m	The number of processing tasks for the machine tool M_m
S_i	The number of operations for job J_i
n	The number of jobs
k	The number of machine tools
J_i	The $i-th$ job
$o_{i,j}$	The $j-th$ operation of the job J_i
M_m	The $m-th$ machine tool
P_m	The total power of the machine tool M_m
P_{ijm}	The power of operation $o_{i,j}$ which is on the machine tool M_m
P_{dm}	The dynamic power of the machine tool M_m
P_{sm}	The static power of the machine tool M_m
P_{ctm}	The cutting-tool changing power of the machine tool M_m
P_{Add}	The additional power of the workshop
$a_1 - a_8$	The exponential parameters between each cutting parameter and the dynamic power
K_1, K_2	The coefficients of the dynamic power model
$b_1 - b_4$	The exponential parameters between each cutting parameter and the cutting-tool life
K_3	The coefficients of the tool life model
n_v	The spindle speed
f	The feed speed
a_p	The cutting depth
a_e	The cutting width
t_m	The used time of the cutting tool of the machine tool M_m
T_m	The cutting-tool life of the machine tool M_m
t_{ctm}	The cutting-tool changing time of the machine tool M_m
PT	The processing time of an operation
PT_{ij}	The processing time of the operation $o_{i,j}$
PT_{ijm}	The processing time of the operation which is on the machine tool M_m
ST_{ij}	The start time of the operation $o_{i,j}$
ST_{mr}	The start time of the $r-th$ processing task of the machine tool M_m
CT_{ij}	The end time of the operation $o_{i,j}$
CT_{mr}	The end time of the $r-th$ processing task of the machine tool M_m
T_{Rm}	The no-load balance time of the machine tool
H_m	The on/off security threshold time of the machine tool M_m
RT_{mean}	The actual average turning-on/off machine tool time
W_m	The degree of tool wear

Table 1. Cont.

Symbol	Descriptions
E_{total}	The total energy consumption of the workshop
E_c	The processing energy consumption of machine tools
E_{Re}	The energy consumption of turning on/off machine tools
E_{Rem}	The energy consumed by a single on/off of the machine tool
E_{ct}	The total energy consumption of changing the cutting tool
E_s	The standby energy consumption of machine tools
E_{Add}	The additional energy consumption of the workshop
RTE_{mean}	The actual average energy consumption of turning on/off the machine tool
C_{max}	The makespan
G	The total number of turning-on/off machine tools and changing cutting tools
WL	The total load of machine tools
CF_m	The coefficient of cutting tool capacity of the machine tool M_m
DW	The degree of reduction in processing capacity of the cutting tool
$COST$	The production cost
SF_m	The additional coefficient of turning on/off the machine tool M_m
ω_e	Unit energy cost
ω_m	The unit operating cost of the machine tool
ω_t	Machine tool turn on/off loss cost
ω_l	Cost per unit of labor time
x	The number of tasks that cutting-tool changing operation can be advanced
$\gamma_{ijmr}/\gamma_{hgmr}$	$\gamma_{ijmr}/\gamma_{hgmr} = 1$, if the operation $o_{i,j}$ is the $r - th$ processing task of M_m, $\gamma_{ijmr}=1$; otherwise $\gamma_{ijmr}/\gamma_{hgmr} = 0$
η_{mr}	$\eta_{mr} = 1$, if the machine tool M_m is turned on/off before its $r - th$ processing task; otherwise, $\eta_{mr} = 0$
λ_{mr}	$\lambda_{mr} = 1$, if the machine tool M_m changes the cutting tool before its $r - th$ processing task; otherwise, $\lambda_{mr} = 0$
δ_m	$\delta_m = 1$, if the machine tool M_m turns on/off twice or more; otherwise, $\delta_m = 0$

2.2. Cutting-Tool Degradation Model

In the FJSP, the degradation of the cutting tool reduces its machining capacity, leading to an increase in the machining power and the interruption of the process caused by the blunt cutting tool. If the cutting-tool wear is considered in advance during the scheduling process, the change in machining power caused by cutting-tool wear can be accurately predicted. This not only improves processing efficiency and reduces energy consumption but also prevents the cutting tool from becoming blunt.

This section introduces the machining power model and cutting-tool life model derived from the tool degradation model.

(1) Machining power model

From the point of view of the working state of the machine tool, the machine tool power P_m in the workshop production process can be divided into two parts, as shown in Equation (1). The first part is the dynamic machining power of the machine tool P_{dm}, which includes the spindle power of the machine tool in the workpiece-cutting process. The second part is the static power P_{sm} of the machine tool, including the no-load power of the motor and the power of the numerical control, lighting, and cooling systems.

$$P_m = P_{dm} + P_{sm}, \qquad (1)$$

P_{sm} exhibits little change in the machining process; hence, it is regarded as a constant value.

The dynamic power model [28,29] proposed by Tian et al. and Tian et al. is divided into two parts: the initial dynamic power without tool wear, and the additional dynamic power caused by tool wear, as shown in Equation (2):

$$P_{dm} = K_1 n_v^{a_1} f^{a_2} a_p^{a_3} a_e^{a_4} + K_2 t_m n^{a_5} f^{a_6} a_p^{a_7} a_e^{a_8} \qquad (2)$$

(2) Cutting-tool life model

To determine the relationship between the cutting-tool life and different cutting parameters, a type of cutting-tool failure should be selected as the criterion. According to ISO 8688-2:1989 *Tool life testing in milling-part 2: end milling* (1989), the wear of an end milling cutter can be divided into rake-face wear and flank-face wear [30]. Because the flank-face wear is easy to measure, the blunt standard of the tool wear is often set according to the maximum allowable value of the flank-face wear (usually expressed as VB). In this study, the end of the end milling cutting tool's life was defined as having a maximum VB of 0.3 mm in one of all teeth ($VB_{max} = 0.3$). The cutting-tool life model of Tian et al. and Sun et al. is shown in Equation (3) [22,29]:

$$T_m = K_3 \cdot n_v^{b_1} f^{b_2} a_e^{b_3} a_e^{b_4} \tag{3}$$

As we all know, tool wear is produced in complex mechanical and thermal environments, and there will be different dullness criteria for different processing objects or different quality requirements. In this paper, according to the dullness criterion mentioned in the ISO standard, in other application scenarios with higher cutting quality requirements, this part of modeling needs to establish a dullness criterion that meets the quality requirements and build models under these standards. This article only provides such a solution.

2.3. The Hybrid Energy-Saving Strategy

Section 2.2 shows that the cutting-tool life is not only related to the material and specifications of the cutting tool but also to the cutting parameters. Therefore, the cutting tool remaining useful life (RUL) cannot be calculated directly from the processing time of different operations. This results in a unique tool-changing schedule that affects the makespan and machine tool turn-on/off schedule.

Three measures are proposed to solve this problem.

(1) The cutting-tool change strategy

In this study, the cutting tool is changed before it is damaged to ensure that it meets processing quality requirements, reduces the risk of accidents, and improves the reliability of the processing system. Therefore, if the remaining service life of the cutting tool is insufficient to support the next processing task in the schedule, the cutting tool is considered unavailable and changed before the start of the next processing task, as expressed by Equation (4).

$$T_m - t_m < PT \tag{4}$$

Owing to the different cutting-tool lives under different cutting parameters, the cutting-tool service time cannot be added directly. A normalized approach is adopted to deal with this problem, that is, the increase in cutting-tool wear caused by the processing task is obtained using the processing task time/cutting-tool life under the cutting parameters of the task. Then, the total cutting-tool wear W_m is used to determine whether the cutting tool has reached the end point of its service life, as expressed by Equation (5).

$$W_m + PT/T_m < 1 \tag{5}$$

Equation (5) defines that cutting-tool wear must be less than 1.

(2) The machine tool turn-on/off strategy

During the production process, if a machine tool remains idle for some time, it is sensible to turn it off to avoid wasting energy and reduce carbon emissions. Turning machine tools on/off leads to additional energy consumption and could also damage their performance and service life. Therefore, the no-load balance time T_{Rm} should be set to control when to turn the machine tool on/off, as expressed by Equation (6). Meanwhile, to reduce the damage caused by turning the machine tool on/off, the interval between on/off times is controlled by setting the on/off security threshold time H_m, as expressed by Equation (7) [11].

$$ST_{mr} - CT_{m(r-1)} \geq T_{Rm}\eta_{mr} \tag{6}$$

$$\left|\eta_{mr}CT_{m(r-1)} - \eta_{mr'}ST_{mr'}\right| \geq H_m\delta_m, \ r > r' \tag{7}$$

Equation (6) shows that if the time interval between two subsequent processing tasks is greater than the no-load balancing time, the machine tool should be turned off. Equation (7) shows that if the machine tool is turned on/off twice or more, the interval between the time the machine tool is turned on and the next turn-off must exceed the on/off security threshold time of the machine tool.

(3) Hybrid energy-saving strategy of cutting-tool change and machine tool turn-on/off

If the cutting-tool change operation is separated from the machine tool turn-on/off operation, the single cutting-tool change operation not only increases the makespan but also the standby energy consumption of the machine tool. Sacrificing a small amount of cutting-tool processing capacity by advancing the timing of the cutting-tool change will shorten the makespan and reduce energy consumption. Here, we set a reasonable coefficient CF_m of the cutting-tool capacity to control when to change the cutting tool. Equation (8) ensures that the reduced processing capacity of the machine tool M_m is within an acceptable range. The cutting-tool change operation can be carried out before x tasks to realize energy savings.

$$CF_m \geq 1 - W_m + \sum_{r=0}^{x}(\lambda_{mr}PT_{mr}/T_m) \tag{8}$$

3. Formulation of FJSP–CTD–ESM

In this section, the energy footprint model is defined. Then, the optimization model of the FJSP–CTD–ESM is established.

3.1. Energy Footprint Model

The total energy consumption E_{total} of the workshop consists of five parts, as shown in Equation (9). Figure 3 shows the energy consumption of the machine tool at different stages [1].

$$E_{total} = E_C + E_{Re} + E_{ct} + E_S + E_{Add} \tag{9}$$

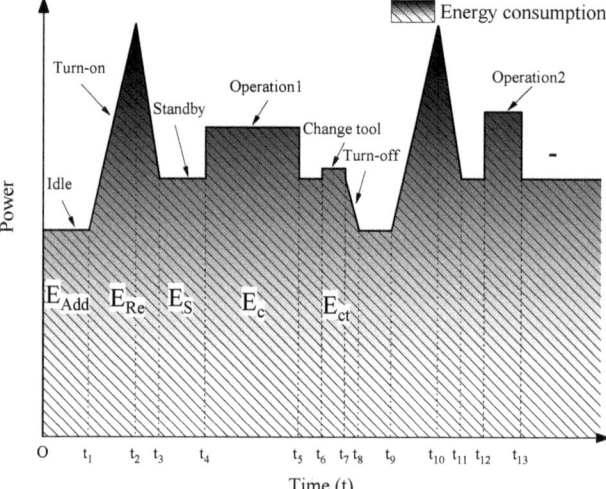

Figure 3. Schematic diagram of energy consumption distributions for different running states.

The energy consumption of each part is analyzed in detail below.

(1) Processing energy consumption E_c of machine tools

The processing energy consumption E_c of process $o_{i,j}$ is closely related to the cutting time PT_{ijm} and the machine tool power P_{ijm}, which varies with the machine tool type, cutting parameters, and cutting-tool wear. The energy consumption of cutting is calculated as Equation (10).

$$E_c = \sum_{m=1}^{k} \sum_{i=1}^{n} \sum_{j=1}^{S_i} \sum_{r=1}^{l_m} \gamma_{ijmr} P_{ijm} PT_{ijm} \tag{10}$$

(2) Energy consumption E_{Re} of turning machine tools on/off

The energy consumption when turning the machine tool on/off E_{Re} is influenced by the type and performance of the machine tool; it has no relation with the processing operation. Thus, the energy consumption of turning the machine tool on/off E_{Rem} once was set as a constant value. The energy consumption of machine tool turn-on/off is calculated as Equation (11).

$$E_{Re} = \sum_{m=1}^{k} \sum_{r=1}^{l_m} \eta_{mr} E_{Rem} \tag{11}$$

(3) Total energy consumption E_{ct} of changing the cutting tool

As the processing time increases, it is necessary to change the cutting tool before it becomes blunt. The energy consumption of cutting-tool change is calculated as Equation (12).

$$E_{ct} = \sum_{m=1}^{k} \sum_{r=1}^{l_m} \lambda_{mr} P_{ctm} t_{ctm} \tag{12}$$

(4) Standby energy consumption E_s

When the machine tool is idle and kept on between two processes, it consumes energy while on standby, which is expressed as:

$$E_s = \sum_{m=1}^{k} \sum_{r=1}^{l_m} P_{sm}(1 - \eta_{mr})\left(ST_{mr} - CT_{m(r-1)}\right) \tag{13}$$

(5) Additional energy consumption E_{Add} of the workshop

The energy consumption of the workshop results not only from machine tool-related processes but also from lighting, computer utilization, and other sources. In this study, the additional energy consumption is not examined in detail; hence, it is set to a constant and calculated as Equation (14).

$$E_{Add} = P_{Add} * C_{max} \tag{14}$$

where $P_{Add} = 9.65\ Kw$.

3.2. Formulation of the FJSP–CTD–ESM Optimization Model

In actual production, the total energy consumption is not the only indicator; the makespan, total load of the machine tool, and the total number of times the machine tool is turned on/off and cutting tools are changed also need to be considered. Therefore, the multi-objective optimization model proposed in this paper has four objectives: the makespan f_1 (min), the total energy consumption of f_2 (Kw·min), the total load of machine tools f_3 (min), and the total number of times the machine tools are turned on/off and cutting tools are changed f_4 (time), expressed as Equations (15)–(35).

$$\min F = [f_1, f_2, f_3, f_4] \tag{15}$$

where

$$f_1 = C_{max} = \max_{m,r} CT_{mr} \tag{16}$$

$$f_2 = E_{total} = E_c + E_{Re} + E_{ct} + E_s + E_{Add}$$

$$= \begin{cases} \sum_{m=1}^{k}\sum_{i=1}^{n}\sum_{j=1}^{S_i}\sum_{r=1}^{l_m} \gamma_{ijmr} P_{ijm} PT_{ijm} + \\ \sum_{m=1}^{k}\sum_{r=1}^{l_m} \eta_{mr} E_{Rem} + \\ \sum_{m=1}^{k}\sum_{r=1}^{l_m} \lambda_{mr} P_{ctm} t_{ctm} + \\ \sum_{m=1}^{k}\sum_{r=1}^{l_m} P_{sm}(1-\eta_{mr})\left(ST_{mr} - CT_{m(r-1)}\right) + P_{Add} * C_{max} \end{cases} \quad (17)$$

$$f_3 = WL = \sum_{m=1}^{k}\sum_{i=1}^{n}\sum_{j=1}^{S_i}\sum_{r=1}^{l_m} \gamma_{ijmr} PT_{ijm} \quad (18)$$

$$f_4 = G = \sum_{m=1}^{k}\sum_{r=1}^{l_m} (\eta_{mr} + \lambda_{mr}) \quad (19)$$

Subject to

$$CT_{ij} - PT_{ij} \geq CT_{i(j-1)} \quad (20)$$

$$\begin{cases} ST_{m(r+1)} - ST_{mr} > 0 \\ ST_{m(r+1)} - CT_{mr} \geq 0 \end{cases} \quad (21)$$

$$\sum_{m=1}^{k} \gamma_{ijmr} = 1 \quad (22)$$

$$ST_{mr} - CT_{m(r-1)} \geq T_{Rm} \eta_{mr} \quad (23)$$

$$\left| \eta_{mr} CT_{m(r-1)} - \eta_{mr'} ST_{mr'} \right| \geq H_m \delta_m, \ r > r' \quad (24)$$

$$W_{mr} < 1 \quad (25)$$

$$ST_{mr} - CT_{m(r-1)} \geq t_{ctm} \lambda_{mr} \quad (26)$$

$$CF_m \geq 1 - W_m + \sum_{r=0}^{x} (\lambda_{mr} PT_{mr} / T_m) \quad (27)$$

$$\gamma_{ijmr} = \begin{cases} 1, & \text{if the operation } o_{i,j} \text{ is the r th processing task of the machine tool } M_m \\ 0, & \text{otherwise} \end{cases} \quad (28)$$

$$\eta_{mr} = \begin{cases} 1, & \text{if the machine tool } M_m \text{ is turned on/off before its r th processing task} \\ 0, & \text{otherwise} \end{cases} \quad (29)$$

$$\lambda_{mr} = \begin{cases} 1, & \text{if the machine tool } M_m \text{ changes the cutting tool before its r th processing task} \\ 0, & \text{otherwise} \end{cases} \quad (30)$$

$$\delta_m = \begin{cases} 1, & \text{if the machine tool } M_m \text{ is turned on/off twice or more} \\ 0, & \text{otherwise} \end{cases} \quad (31)$$

$$ST > 0 \quad (32)$$

$$CT > 0 \quad (33)$$

$$PT > 0 \quad (34)$$

$$i \in [1,n], j \in [1,s], m \in [1,k], r \in [1,l_m] \quad (35)$$

Constraint [20] indicates that an operation cannot begin unless the preceding operation was completed. Constraint [21] confirms that a machine tool cannot be assigned to two or more processes simultaneously. Constraint [22] ensures that the same process cannot be conducted by two or more machine tools. Constraint [23] states that the machine tool turn-on/off does not overlap with the processing task, and the on/off time must exceed the no-load balance time. If it is the first round of processing, $CT_{ijm0} = 0$; otherwise, $CT_{ijm0} = CT_{ijml_m}$. Constraint [24] indicates that the interval between the time the machine tool is turned on and the next turn-off must exceed the machine tool on/off security threshold time M_m. Constraint [25] implies that the actual degree of tool wear W_{mr} must be less than 1. Constraint [26] requires that the cutting-tool change does not overlap with the processing task, and the time interval between the two processes is greater than the defined cutting-tool change time. Constraint [27] shows that the cutting-tool change of M_m is carried out in advance to achieve energy savings under the reduced processing capacity of the machine tool within an acceptable range. Constraints [28–35] are the constraints of decision variables.

4. Proposed NSGA-II

In this section, a general framework to solve the FJSP–CTD–ESM is proposed; the NSGA-II is briefly introduced, and the motivation behind the NSGA-II to optimize the FJSP–CTD–ESM is analyzed. Specific improvement measures of the NSGA-II algorithm are also described.

4.1. Framework

The optimization method of integrating the cutting-tool degradation, hybrid energy-saving strategy, and production scheduling determines the cutting-tool capability and the order and priority of production tasks by combining machine tools and scheduling. The scheduling scheme is implemented in two steps: First, the machining power model and cutting-tool life model based on tool degradation were added to the fast and elitist multi-objective genetic algorithm (NSGA-II) scheduling algorithm [31] to generate an initial scheduling scheme, which includes the cutting-tool change. Second, through the scheduling mechanism, the cutting-tool change and machine tool turn-on/off were arranged to generate the final scheduling scheme to achieve the goal of energy conservation.

4.2. Details and Improvements in NSGA-II

4.2.1. Scheduling Mechanisms

In the FJSP–CTD–ESM, processing energy consumption is mainly determined by machining power, which is also affected by cutting parameters and machine tool type. Non-machining energy consumption is mainly determined by the running state of machine tools. Because the cutting parameters were determined, the allocation of the appropriate machine tool to the operation and choosing the suitable machine tool turn-on/off and cutting-tool change times are the main considerations of the scheduling scheme. Two scheduling mechanisms are proposed:

(1) Cutting-tool degradation mechanism

During the processing operation, the cumulative processing time of the cutting tool is calculated in advance and the machining power P_m and degree of cutting-tool wear W_m of machine tool M_m are then calculated using the tool degradation model. When the degree of cutting-tool wear is expected to be greater than 1 ($W_m > 1$) after the machine tool completes the next operation, the cutting tool will be changed before processing ($\lambda_{mr} = 1$), and the machining power P_m is recalculated. The cutting-tool degradation mechanism is shown in Figure 4.

(2) Hybrid mechanism of cutting-tool change and machine tool turn-on/off

Based on the scheduling algorithm, the hybrid mechanism of cutting-tool change and machine tool turn-on/off is added to determine when to turn the machine tool on/off and change the cutting tool, as shown in Figure 5.

Step 1: According to the start and end time of the processing task, determine whether the non-processing time is greater than the no-load balancing time T_{Rm}. If so, go to Step 2; otherwise, end.

Step 2: Determine whether there is an on/off operation before this non-processing stage. If so, go to Step 3. Otherwise, turn off the machine tool in this non-processing stage and go to Step 5.

Step 3: Compare whether the time difference between the start of the non-processing stage and the last turn-on time of the machine tool is greater than the defined on/off security threshold time H_m. If the difference exceeds H_m, turn off the machine tool at the beginning of the non-processing stage and go to Step 5; otherwise, go to Step 4.

Step 4: Set the last turn-on time of the machine tool to t_1 and the start time of the non-processing stage to t_2. If $t_2 - t_1 - H_m > T_{Rm}$, turn off the machine tool at $(t_1 + H_m)$ and go to Step 5; otherwise, end.

Step 5: Check whether the machine tools have both cutting-tool change and turn-on/off operations. If so, go to Step 6; otherwise, end.

Step 6: Determine whether the degree of tool wear W_m at the nearest machine tool on/off position before the cutting-tool change operation is greater than the difference between 1 and the cutting-tool capacity coefficient. If so, combine the cutting-tool change and machine tool turn-on/off operations, and recalculate the optimization target value; otherwise, end.

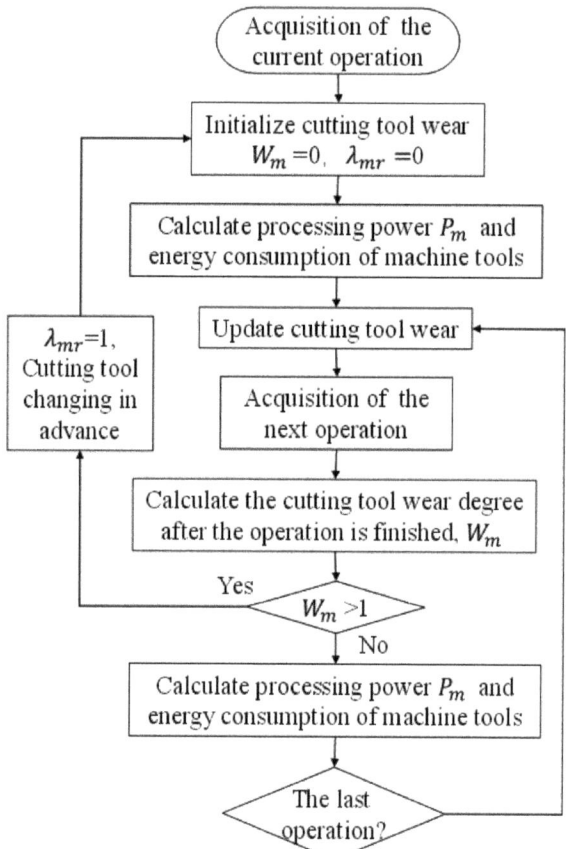

Figure 4. Cutting-tool degradation mechanism.

Input: Initial Schedulingscheme, k, T_{Rm}, CF_m #See original NSGA-II Deb et al. (2002) and Section 4.2.2.
1: **for** i in range (k):
2:    Tst_i = TurnonTime(Schedulingscheme) #The turn on start time set of M_i.
3:    St_i = StandbyTime(Schedulingscheme) #The standby time set of M_i.
4:    Sst_i = StandbystartTime(Schedulingscheme) #The standby start time set of M_i.
5:    **for** j in range(len(St_i)):
6:       **if** $St_i[j] > T_{Rm}$:
7:          Less_list = [o for o, x in enumerate(Tst_i) if x < $Sst_i[j]$]]
9:          **if** Lese_list != []:
9:             **if** $Sst_i[j]$ - max(Less_list) >= H_m:
10:               Schedulingscheme = ChangeScheme1(Schedulingscheme, Tst_i, St_i, Sst_i) #Modify the scheduling scheme to change the standby state to the turn off state and Section 4.2.2.
11:            **elif** $St_i[j]$ - max(Less_list) - H_m + $Sst_i[j] > T_{Rm}$:
12:               Schedulingscheme = ChangeScheme2(Schedulingscheme, Tst_i, St_i, Sst_i) #Modify the scheduling scheme to change the standby state to the turn off state from max(Less_list) + H_m and Section 4.2.2.
13:         **else:**
14:            Schedulingscheme = ChangeScheme1(Schedulingscheme, Tst_i, St_i, Sst_i)
15: **for** i in range (k):
16:    CTt_i = ChangetoolTime(Schedulingscheme) #The change tool time set of M_i.
17:    $CTst_i$ = ChangetoolTime(Schedulingscheme) #The change tool start time set of M_i.
18:    Tt_i = Turnon/offTime(Schedulingscheme) #The turn on/off time set of M_i.
18:    Tst_i = TurnonTime(Schedulingscheme) #The turn on start time set of M_i.
19:    **if** CTt_i != [] and Tt_i != []:
20:       **for** j in range(len($CTst_i$)):
21:          W_m = ObtainWear($Tst_i[j]$, $CTst_i[j]$) #Obtain tool wear at the nearest turn-on/off position before the cutting tool change
22:          **if** (1-W_m) < CF_m and Tt_i >= CTt_i:
23:             Schedulingscheme = ChangeScheme3(Schedulingscheme, CTt_i, $CTst_i$, Tt_i, Tst_i) #Modify the scheduling scheme to combine the cutting tool changing with the turn-on/off and Section 4.2.2.
24:          **elif** (1-W_m) < CF_m and $Tt_i < CTt_i$:
25:             Schedulingscheme = ChangeScheme4(Schedulingscheme, CTt_i, $CTst_i$, Tt_i, Tst_i) #Modify the scheduling scheme to delete the turn-on/off and bring the cutting tool changing to this position in advance and Section 4.2.2.
Output: Schedulingscheme.

Figure 5. Hybrid mechanism algorithm form of cutting-tool change and machine tool turn-on/off.

4.2.2. Encoding and Decoding with Changing Cutting and Turn-on/off

In the FJSP, encoding and decoding are expressed in the form of chromosomes, which are divided into the process chromosome and the machine tool chromosome. We utilize the encoding and decoding methods proposed by Zhang et al. [32], as shown in Figure 6.

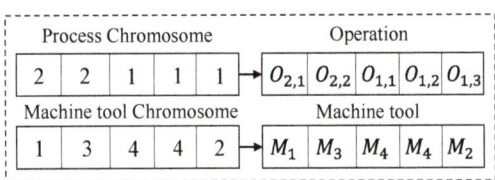

Figure 6. Chromosome encoding process.

In addition, changing the cutting tool and turning the machine tool on/off affects the scheduling scheme, including the following six scenarios. (1) Scenario 1: If the machine tool M_m needs to be turned off before $o_{i,j+1}$, the non-processing time and the last turn-on time of M_m should be considered. When the non-processing time is greater than the no-load balancing time T_{Rm}, and the difference between the start time CT_{mr} of the non-processing time and the last turn-on time $ST_{mr'}$ of M_m is greater than the defined on/off security threshold time H_m, the machine tool is directly turned off between CT_{mr} and $ST_{m(r+1)}$, as shown in Figure 7. (2) Scenario 2: If $CT_{mr} - ST_{mr'} < H_m$ and $ST_{m(r+1)} - ST_{mr'} - H_m > T_{Rm}$, turn off M_m between $(ST_{mr'} + H_k)$ and $ST_{m(r+1)}$, as shown in Figure 8. (3) Scenario 3. If machine tool M_m needs a cutting-tool change before $o_{i,j+1}$, the non-processing time must be considered. If $(ST_{m(r+1)} - CT_{mr})$ is greater than the cutting-tool change time t_{ctm}, change the cutting tool in CT_{mr}, as shown in Figure 9. (4) Scenario 4: If the machine tool M_m needs a cutting-tool change before $o_{i,j+1}$ and $ST_{m(r+1)} - CT_{mr} < t_{ctm}$, $ST_{m(r+1)}$ needs to move to the right to $ST'_{m(r+1)}$ to make $ST'_{m(r+1)} - CT_{mr} = t_{ctm}$, as shown in Figure 10. (5) Scenario 5: If the cutting-tool change and machine tool turn-on/off occurs in sequence, these should be combined, as shown in Figure 11. (6) Scenario 6: If the conditions of scheduling mechanism 2 are met, two cases will occur. Case 1: the cutting-tool change is incorporated into the machine tool turn-on/off. Case 2: Advance the cutting-tool change and eliminate the machine tool turn-on/off, as shown in Figure 12.

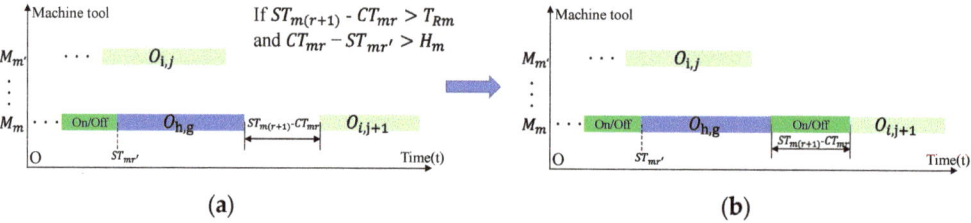

Figure 7. Scenario 1: (**a**) Initial Gantt chart; (**b**) Adjusted Gantt chart.

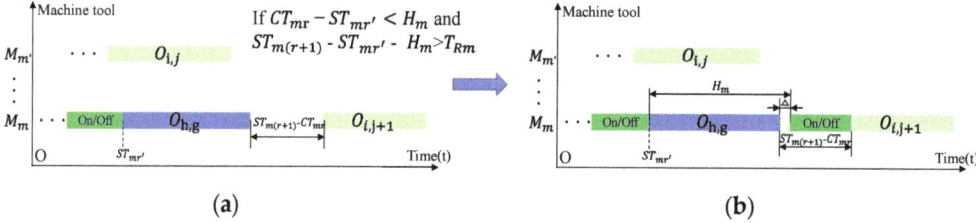

Figure 8. Scenario 2: (**a**) Initial Gantt chart; (**b**) Adjusted Gantt chart.

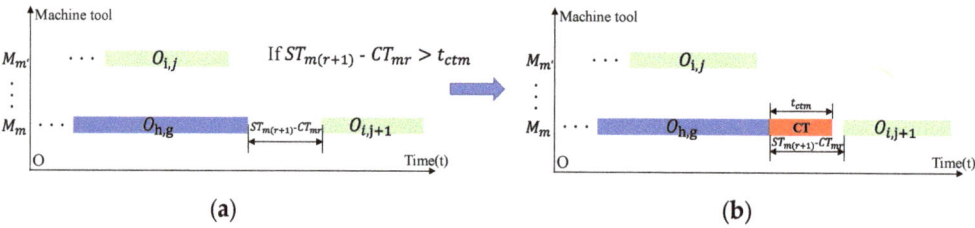

Figure 9. Scenario 3: (**a**) Initial Gantt chart; (**b**) Adjusted Gantt chart.

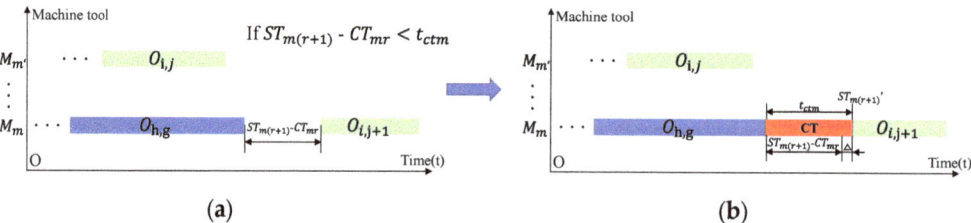

Figure 10. Scenario 4: (**a**) Initial Gantt chart; (**b**) Adjusted Gantt chart.

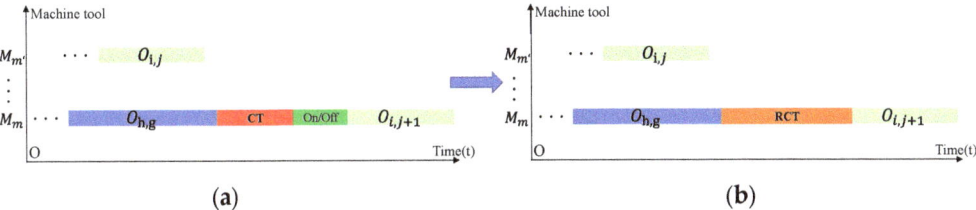

Figure 11. Scenario 5: (**a**) Initial Gantt chart; (**b**) Adjusted Gantt chart.

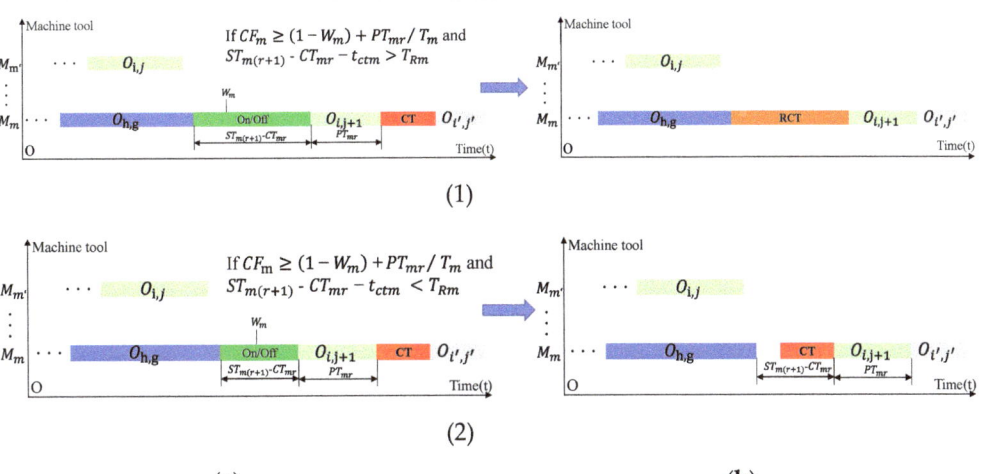

Figure 12. Scenario 6: (**1**) Sufficient machine-off time; (**2**) Insufficient machine-off time. (**a**) Initial Gantt chart; (**b**) Adjusted Gantt chart.

4.2.3. Crossover

A crossover is used to maintain population diversity and explore a new solution space. In the parent population, two types of crossover were performed according to chromosome types [32], with the crossover of the process chromosome occurring in odd positions, while that of the machine tool chromosome occurring in even positions, as shown in Figure 13.

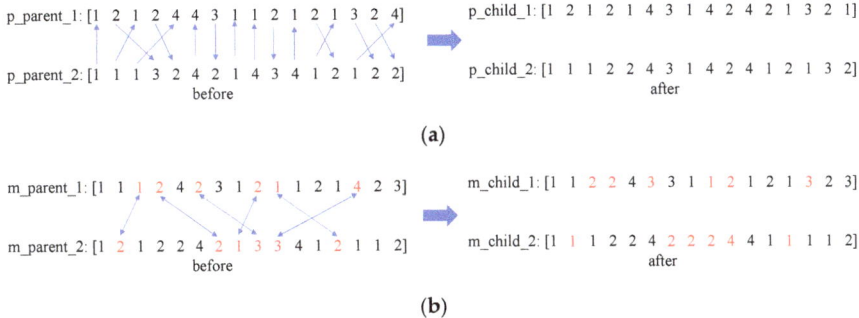

Figure 13. Crossover: (**a**) Crossover of the process chromosome; (**b**) Crossover of the machine tool chromosome.

4.2.4. Mutation

A mutation is the use of the solution space to generate different neighborhood solutions through different mutations to prevent the population from falling into a local optimum during the process of population evolution convergence and increase the diversity of the population. The mutation can be divided into the process chromosome mutation and the machine tool chromosome mutation [32]. In the process chromosome mutation, gene I at a random mutation site on a random parental chromosome is mutated into the random gene I'. At the same time, one of the genes I' on the other sites of this chromosome is randomly selected to become gene I, and the corresponding machine tool chromosome is changed accordingly. In the machine tool chromosome mutation, the genes at two random mutation sites on a random parental chromosome are mutated into any gene within the allowed mutation range, as shown in Figure 14.

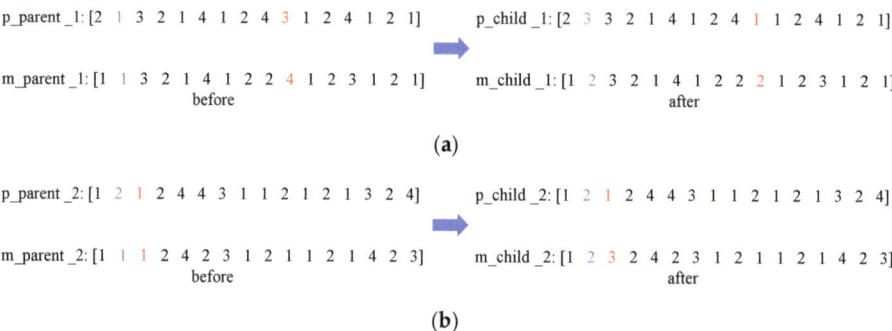

Figure 14. Mutation: (**a**) Crossover of the process chromosome; (**b**) Crossover of the machine tool chromosome.

5. Case Study

In this section, the parameter determination method in FJSP–CTD–ESM is briefly described, and the comparison experiment based on the FJSP is designed. In addition, to provide enterprises with a better basis for selecting scheduling schemes, this paper integrates production functional resources with job-shop scheduling and provides production cost indicators to evaluate scheduling schemes. Thereafter, the rationality and effectiveness of the cutting-tool degradation model and hybrid energy-saving strategy of cutting-tool change and machine tool turn-on/off are illustrated by the example results.

5.1. Design of Experiments

5.1.1. Environment Setting

All the algorithms were run in Python 2.7 on a personal computer with an Intel (R) Core (TM) i7-9750H, 2.6 GHz CPU and 8 GB RAM.

5.1.2. Model Parameter Determination

To obtain stable machining power and tool wear data, the workpiece (i.e., 45# steel with dimensions 60 × 60 × 35 mm) was processed by milling. The cutting mode was straight-line face milling. The cutting path of the experimental workpiece is shown in Figure 15. The basic properties of the machine tool and tool used in the experiment are shown in Table 2. To establish the relationship between the machining power of machine tools and machining parameters, and that between the tool life and machining parameters, the machining power of machine tools and tool life under different cutting parameters were obtained by an orthogonal experiment. By referring to the Concise Manual of Cutting Parameters, it is found that in general, when the high-speed end milling cutter face-milling 45 steel, the recommended cutting speed is 21~40 m/min, and the recommended range of feed per tooth is 0.12~0.2 mm. Therefore, within the recommended range, we consider the workpiece conditions, machine conditions, test costs and other factors, and through a large number of tests select the cutting parameters, as shown in Table 3 for the experiment. All the power data of a single milling cutter in a stable cutting period were collected for each group of experiments. The experimental devices are shown in Figure 16.

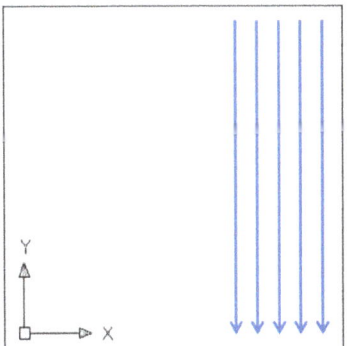

Figure 15. The tool cutting path.

Table 2. Basic parameters of experimental devices.

Machine Tools	Machine Tools Type (Model)	Cutting-Tool Type	Diameter of Milling Cutter Edge (mm)	Milling Cutter Material	Number of Milling Cutter Edges	Length of Milling Cutter Edge (mm)	Length of Milling Cutter (mm)	Cutting Fluid	Anti-wear Coating
M_1, M_2	Three-axis CNC machining center(TSIM-VMA8050V4)	End Mill	φ10	M2AI high-speed steel	4	25	66	Water	No
M_3, M_4	Three-axis CNC machining center (TSIM-VMC1580)	End Mill	φ12	M2AI high-speed steel	4	35	85	Water	No
M_5, M_6	Five-axis CNC machining center (TSIM-VMA210V)	End Mill	Φ8	M2AI high-speed steel	4	22	66	Water	No

Table 3. Experimental cutting parameters table.

Machine Tools	n_v (r/min)	f (mm/r)	a_p (mm)	a_e (mm)
M_1, M_2	700	0.15	0.8	1
		0.16	1	1.5
		0.17	1.2	2
	800	0.15	1	2
		0.16	1.2	1
		0.17	0.8	1.5
	900	0.15	1	1.5
		0.16	0.8	2
		0.17	1.2	1

Table 3. Cont.

Machine Tools	n_v (r/min)	f (mm/r)	a_p (mm)	a_e (mm)
M_3, M_4	600	0.17	0.8	1
		0.18	1	1.5
		0.19	1.2	2
	700	0.17	1	2
		0.18	1.2	1
		0.19	0.8	1.5
	800	0.17	1	1.5
		0.18	0.8	2
		0.19	1.2	1
M_5, M_6	850	0.13	0.8	1
		0.14	1	1.5
		0.15	1.2	2
	950	0.13	1	2
		0.14	1.2	1
		0.15	0.8	1.5
	1050	0.13	1	1.5
		0.14	0.8	2
		0.15	1.2	1

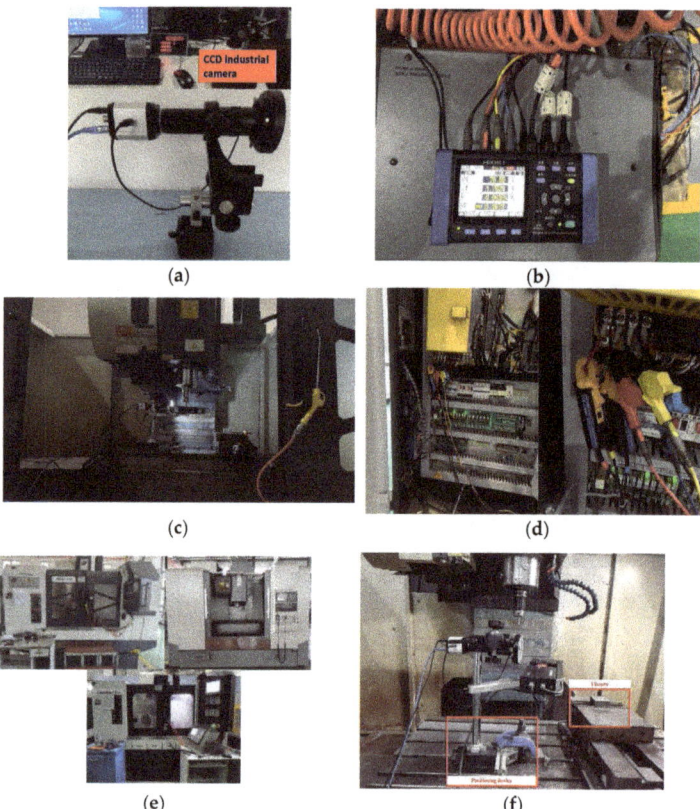

Figure 16. Experimental device: (**a**) Tool wear detection device; (**b**) Clamp on power logger (PW3360A982-04); (**c**) Tool wear detection process; (**d**) Power acquisition wiring diagram; (**e**) CNC machining center ($M_{1/2}, M_{3/4}, M_{5/6}$); (**f**) Positioning device and fixture.

During the milling process, cutting-tool wear was detected once per ten cuts according to the cutting route. When the end point of the cutting-tool wear was reached, machining was stopped and the tool was changed. Photos of the detected partial cutting-tool wear are shown in Figure 17.

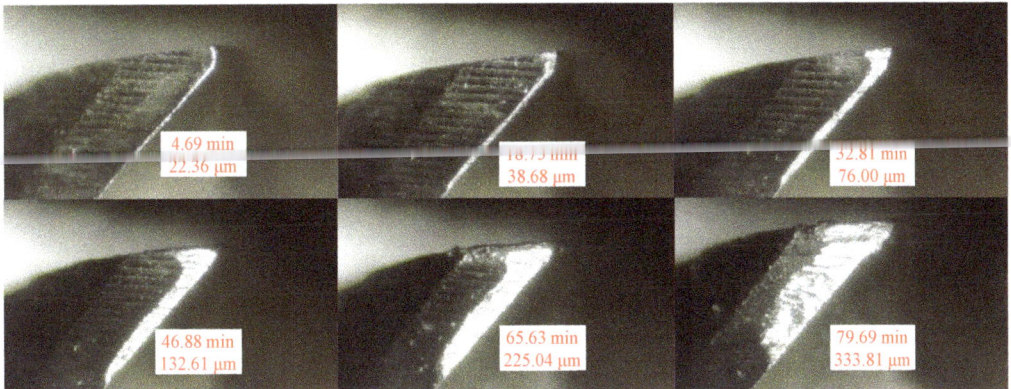

Figure 17. Partial tool wear detection photos.

The multivariate linear regression method [33] was used to determine the parameters in the cutting-tool degradation model, as shown in Figure 18. The machining power and cutting-tool life models are shown in Table 4.

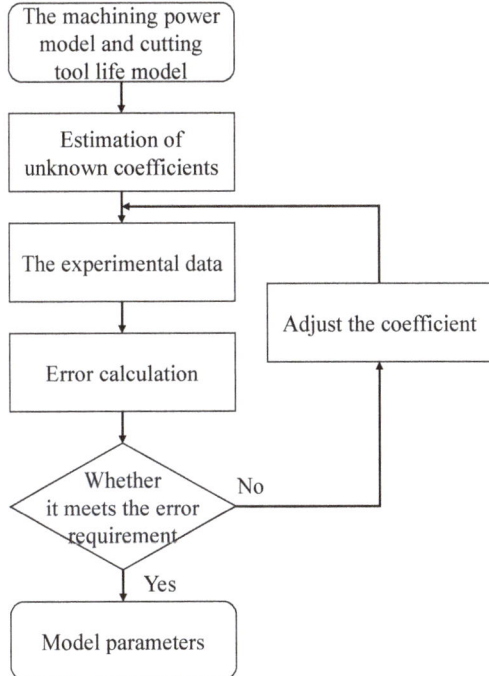

Figure 18. Multivariate linear regression method.

Table 4. Cutting-tool degradation model.

Machine Tools	Model
M_1, M_2	$P_d = 0.9442 n_v^{0.6385} f^{0.1416} a_p^{0.3255} a_e^{0.2693} + 4.24 \times 10^{-5} t_m n_v^{1.6716} f^{1.2510} a_p^{0.9296} a_e^{0.7356}$ $T = 10.0048 n_v^{-0.3821} f^{-2.44733} a_p^{0.59782} a_e^{-0.26984}$
M_3, M_4	$P_d = 1.0400 n_v^{0.6580} f^{-0.2245} a_p^{0.1842} a_e^{0.0789} + 2.24 \times 10^{-5} t_m n^{2.2058} f^{3.0474} a_p^{0.0977} a_e^{0.4933}$ $T = 23.3873 n_v^{-0.1448} f^{-1.2645} a_p^{0.7309} a_e^{-0.0774}$
M_5, M_6	$P_d = 1.7413 n_v^{0.5870} f^{0.1269} a_p^{0.1231} a_e^{0.0932} + 1.15 \times 10^{-5} t_m n_v^{0.3816} f^{-2.5387} a_p^{-0.5164} a_e^{0.2689}$ $T = 25.5911 n_v^{0.1248} f^{-0.0842} a_p^{0.0048} a_e^{-0.0726}$

The no-load balance time T_{Rm} of the machine tool was determined by measurement experiments and the on/off security threshold time H_m was obtained from the equipment manual.

The no-load balance time T_{Rm} must meet the following condition:

$$\begin{cases} T_{Rm} \geq RT_{mean} \\ T_{Rm} = \frac{RTE_{mean}}{P_{sm}} * SF_m \end{cases} \tag{36}$$

where $SF_m = 1.2$.

5.1.3. Job and Workshop Configuration Information

The flexible job shop has six machine tools and five types of workpieces. The machining process information on the machine tools and workpieces are listed in Tables 5 and 6, respectively. The axonometric drawing of the five workpieces is shown in Figure 19.

Table 5. Machine tool information.

Machine Tools	The No-Load Balance Time (T_R^m/s)	The on/off Security Threshold Time (H_k/s)	Cutting-Tool Change Time (t_{ct}/s)/Power (P_{ct}/W)	Static Power (P_{sm}/W)
M_1, M_2	48	100	60/195	520
M_3, M_4	45	90	80/295	420
M_5, M_6	32	60	40/156	325

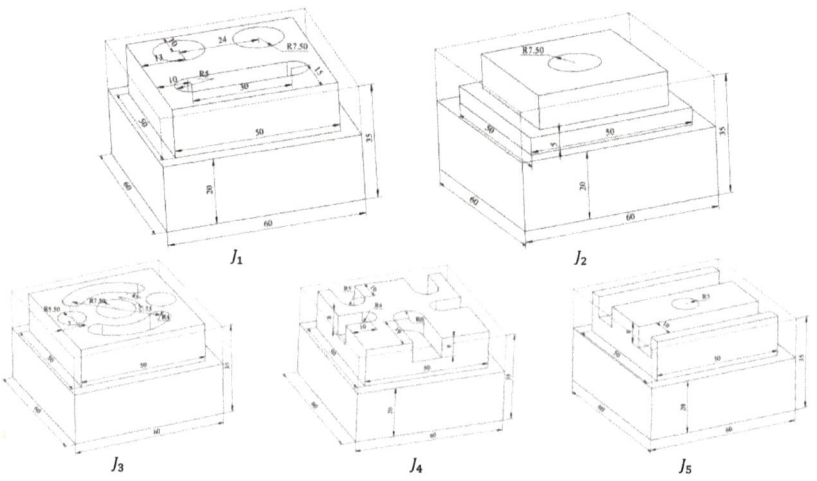

Figure 19. Three-dimensional model drawing of the five workpieces.

Table 6. Workpiece information.

Job Number	Operations		Optional Machine Tools	Processing Time (min)	Cutting Parameters (n_v, f, a_p, a_e)
J_1	$O_{1,1}$	Milling 50 × 50 × 15 convex platform	M_1, M_2 M_3, M_4	16.34 8.16	900,0.17,3,2.5 800,0.19,3,5
	$O_{1,2}$	Milling 30 × 10 × 15 slot	M_1, M_2	2.68	700,0.16,1.5,2
	$O_{1,3}$	Enlarge holes 2 × Ø12 × 15 → 2 × Ø15 × 15	M_1, M_2 M_5, M_6	3 4	700,0.15,1.5,1.5 850,0.13,1.5,1.5
J_2	$O_{2,1}$	Milling 50 × 50 × 15 convex platform	M_1, M_2 M_3, M_4	16.34 8.16	900,0.17,3,2.5 800,0.19,3,5
	$O_{2,2}$	Milling 40 × 40 × 10 convex platform	M_1, M_2 M_5, M_6	12.45 14.8	900,0.15,2.5,2.5 1050,0.13,2,2.5
	$O_{2,3}$	Enlarge hole Ø12 × 15 → Ø15 × 15	M_5, M_6	2	850,0.13,1.5,1.5
J_3	$O_{3,1}$	Milling 50 × 50 × 15 convex platform	M_1, M_2 M_3, M_4	16.34 8.16	900,0.17,3,2.5 800,0.19,3,5
	$O_{3,2}$	Milling 2 × 27 × 8 × 8 slots	M_5, M_6	4	850,0.13,1,2
	$O_{3,3}$	Enlarge hole Ø12 × 15 → Ø15 × 15	M_1, M_2 M_5, M_6	1.5 2	700,0.15,1.5,1.5 850,0.13,1.5,1.5
	$O_{3,4}$	Enlarge holes 2 × Ø10 × 15 → 2 × Ø11 × 15	M_5, M_6	2.56	850,0.13,1,0.5
J_4	$O_{4,1}$	Milling 50 × 50 × 15 convex platform	M_1, M_2 M_3, M_4	16.34 8.16	900,0.17,3,2.5 800,0.19,3,5
	$O_{4,2}$	Milling 19 × 12 × 8 slot	M_3, M_4	1.49	600,0.17,1,2
	$O_{4,3}$	Milling 2×10×10 × 8 slots	M_1, M_2	1.53	700,0.15,1,2
	$O_{4,4}$	Milling 2 × 10 × ×8 × 8 slots	M_5, M_6	1.45	850,0.13,1,2
J_5	$O_{5,1}$	Milling 50 × 50 × 15 convex platform	M_1, M_2 M_3, M_4	16.34 8.16	900,0.17,3,2.5 800,0.19,3,5
	$O_{5,2}$	Milling 2 × 50 × 10 × 8 slots	M_1, M_2	7.62	700,0.15,1,2
	$O_{5,3}$	Enlarge hole Ø9 × 15 → Ø10 × 15	M_5, M_6	0.85	850,0.13,1,0.5

5.1.4. Establishment of Production Cost Indicator

Reducing cost plays an important role in the profitability, survival and development of an enterprise. How to get the maximum benefit with the minimum cost is an important topic that enterprises and even the whole society face and need to study and solve. To provide a better basis for selecting scheduling schemes, this paper establishes a mathematical model of production cost to evaluate scheduling schemes [34,35], as shown in Equation (36).

$$COST = \omega_e E_{total} + \omega_m WL + \omega_t G + \omega_l C_{max} \tag{37}$$

Table 7 shows the specific unit cost components in the production cost indicator, which includes unit energy cost, unit operating cost of machine tool, machine tool turn-on/off loss cost and cost per unit of labor time.

Table 7. Related unit costs.

Unit Energy Cost (CNY/KW·h)	Unit Operating Cost of Machine Tool (CNY/h)	Machine Tool Turn on/off Loss Cost (CNY/time)	Cost Per Unit of Labor Time (CNY/h)
0.725	9	1	30

5.2. Evaluation

5.2.1. Experiment Results

(1) Hybrid mechanism of cutting-tool change and machine tool turn-on/off

It can be seen from Section 2.3 that machining power is not only related to tool wear but also related to cutting parameters. Therefore, to reflect and highlight the relationship between machining power variations and tool wear, the relationship between machining power and tool wear and the accuracy of the power model was analyzed by using actual and simulation data under the premise of certain cutting parameters.

It can be seen from the model that the machining power is linearly related to the tool utilization time. By comparing the actual collected power data with the tool utilization time and power data predicted by regression, it was found that the errors were all within a controllable range. The maximum error of the M_1, M_2; M_3, M_4; and M_5, M_6 models are 6.44%, 3.36%, 4.67%, respectively, as shown in Figure 20.

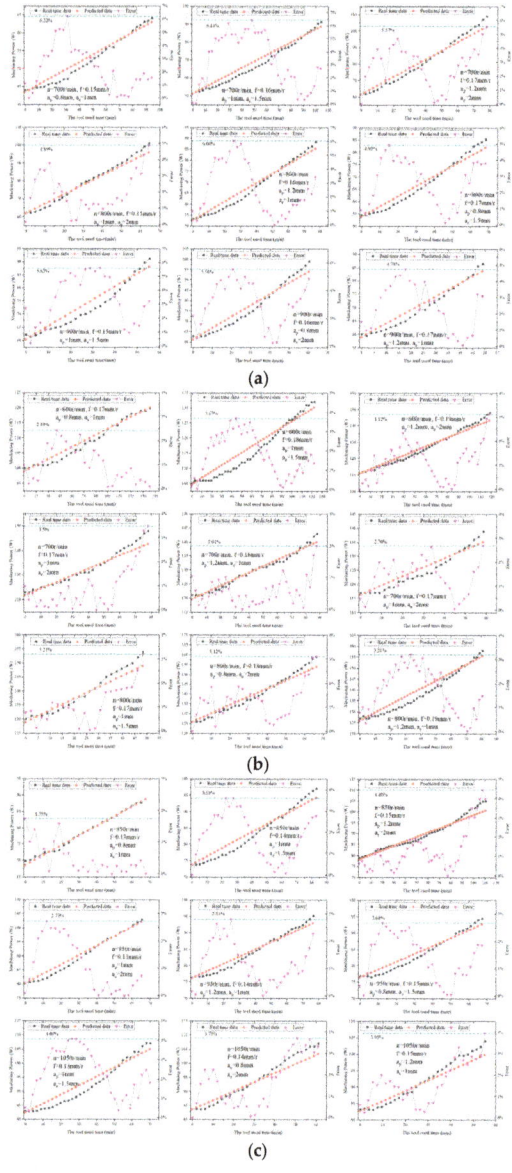

Figure 20. Comparison of machining power and tool utilization time data: (**a**) M_1, M_2; (**b**) M_3, M_4; (**c**) M_5, M_6.

(2) Scheduling algorithm results

To reflect the performance of the improved NSGA-II (INSGA-II), scheduling solutions were generated under the premise that the degrees of cutting-tool wear of machine tools M_1-M_6 are 60%, 70%, 50%, 50%, 70% and 60%, respectively. Table 8 summarizes the experimental results and shows the number of Pareto solutions, target values (C_{max}, E_{total}, WL, and G) and production cost indicator for each Pareto solution. The production cost is between CNY 36 and 40. The Pareto solution of the example is shown in Figure 21, where the X-, Y-, and Z-axis represents the WL, C_{max}, and E_{total}, respectively; the color represents G. As seen in Figure 21, the solution space is sufficient and the Pareto front is well distributed. The makespan is between 27 and 31 min, the total energy consumption of the workshop is between 319 and 350 $Kw\cdot min$, the total machine tool load is 80–90 min, and the total number of times machine tools were turned on/off and cutting tools were changed is from five to nine times. The above data show that the INSGA-II algorithm can balance the four target values. The decision-maker can choose the optimal compromise using the multicriteria decision-making method.

Table 8. Cutting-tool degradation model.

Pareto Numbers	Pareto Solutions (C_{max}(min),E_{total}(Kw·min), WL(min),G (time))	Production Cost (CNY)
15	(29.60,337.46,81.93,7), (28.95,329.10,84.78,8), (27.18,319.5,90.61,8), (28.95,331.36,81.93,8),(28.95,331.32,82.43,9), (27.18,317.67,92.96,8), (28.95,329.10,84.78,8), (28.95,329.34,84.28,9),(28.96,329.01,85.78,8), (28.95,331.36,81.93,8), (27.79,325.47,90.11,8), (28.96,334.26,93.96,7), (29.47,335.72,82.43,6), (31.18,349.53,85.78,5), (29.60,334.64,85.78,6)	37.17, 38.17, 38.04, 37.77, 38.84, 38.37, 38.17, 39.10, 38.32, 37.77, 38.34, 38.61, 36.16, 36.68, 36.71

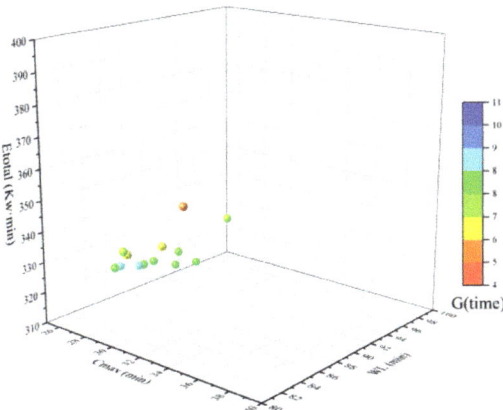

Figure 21. Pareto solutions.

Figure 22 is a Gantt chart of Pareto solutions for this example. The X-axis represents the time, the Y-axis represents the machine number, and each block represents an operation. O denotes the machine tool processing operation, e.g., the first block $O_{5,1}$ of M_3 indicates that the first process of J_3 was processed on M_3. CT denotes the cutting-tool change. *Idle* indicates that the machine tool is not in use, e.g., the gray block on M_6. *On/Off* indicates that the machine tool is turned off, e.g., the green block on M_1. R_C_T indicates that the machine tool is off; however, the cutting tool will be changed at the beginning or end of this period, e.g., the gray-green block on M_2. S indicates that the machine tool is on standby, e.g., the light blue block on M_5. The scheduling scheme can provide the appropriate cutting-tool change time and turn off the machine tools on standby when necessary to save energy.

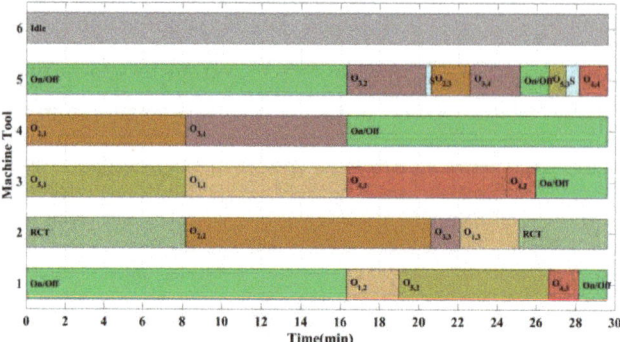

Figure 22. Gantt chart of an instance.

5.2.2. Assessing the Effects of the Cutting-Tool Degradation Model

In this section, based on the cutting-tool degradation model, multi-objective scheduling optimization is conducted starting with new cutting tools. Five schemes are selected from the Pareto optimal solutions for comparison, as follows: Scheme 1 includes the minimum sum of the four target values (C_{max}, E_{total}, WL, and G) with the weight of [0.3, 0.1, 0.5, and 0.1], and its four target values and cost are CNY (26.64, 309.7, 92.96, and 7) and 37.01. Scheme 2 includes the minimum makespan, and its four target values and cost are CNY (26.64, 309.7, 92.96, and 7) and 37.01. Scheme 3 includes the minimum total energy consumption of the workshop, and its four target values and cost are CNY (26.64, 309.7, 92.96, and 7) and 37.01. Scheme 4 includes the minimum total load of machine tools, and its four target values and cost are CNY (28.95, 328.13, 81.93, and 7) and 36.73. Scheme 5 includes the least number of times that the machine tools are turned on/off and cutting tools are changed, and its four target values and cost are CNY (36.82, 408.87, 90.61, and 5) and 40.94. Figure 23 shows the Gantt chart of production scheduling of Scheme 1. Figures 24 and 25 show the simulation power curve and degree of cutting tool wear curve of each machine tool, respectively, in the production process of Scheme 1. These reflect the change in the machining power of each machine tool with the processing operation, verify the influence of the cutting-tool degradation model on the total energy consumption of machine tools, and highlight the necessity of the tool degradation model.

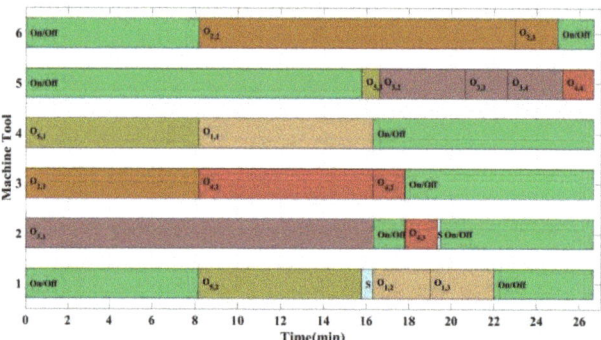

Figure 23. Gantt chart of scheme 1.

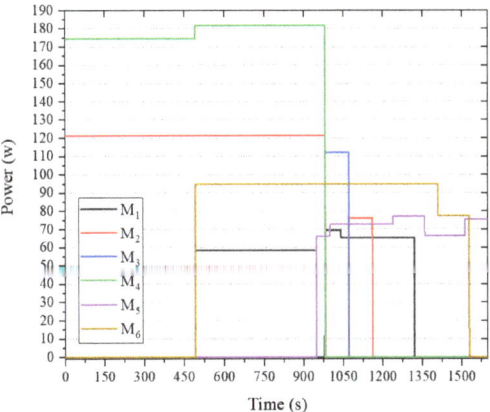

Figure 24. Simulation machining power curve.

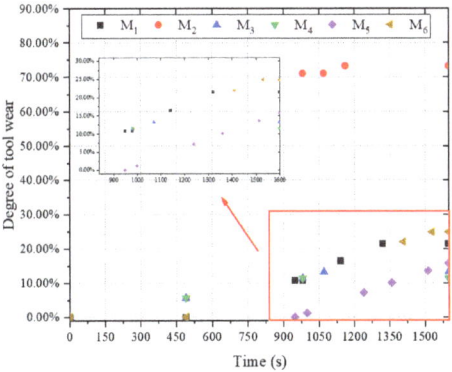

Figure 25. Scatter chart of tool wear.

From the cutting-tool degradation model, all machine tools can provide feedback on the real power condition of the machining process. Taking machine tool M_1 as an example, the curve of simulated and actual machining power can be obtained after actual machining, as shown in Figure 26. The simulated and actual average machining power of the three processes are 58.46 W, 69.49 W, and 65.24 W; and 56.7 W, 68.9 W, and 69.5 W, respectively. The power errors of the three processes are 3.15%, 0.85%, and 6.14%, respectively. The main reason for the considerable fluctuation in the actual machining power is that the cutting direction is not constant during machining. Changes in the cutting direction lead to an instantaneous power decrease because no cutting occurs at that moment, and the spindle generates a large amount of instantaneous power when it just touches the workpiece. The reason for the large error in the simulation results of the third process is that during hole enlargement, the actual cutting width is larger than the given cutting width (1.5 mm) because the actual processing path is circumferential; this makes the actual machining power larger than the simulation power. However, overall, the errors are all within the acceptable range and the cutting-tool degradation model can be applied in scheduling planning. This is conducive to making the simulation closer to the actual production, making the scheduling scheme and scheduling results more practical, and it plays a key role in predicting the machining power of machine tools.

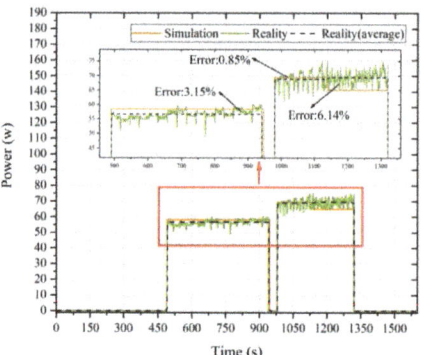

Figure 26. Comparison curve between simulated power and actual machining power.

5.2.3. Assessing the Effects of the Energy-Saving Strategies

Comparing the results of the five scheduling schemes in Section 2.3 shows that adopting the machine tool turn-on/off measure reduced the average total machine standby time in the five schemes by over 99.2%: from 77.18 min to 35.40 s. The total energy consumption of turning machine tools on/off increased from 0 $Kw·min$ to 1.744 $Kw·min$, whereas the standby energy consumption of the machine tools decreased from 31.891 $Kw·min$ to 2.044 $Kw·min$. In addition, the cost of energy consumption decreased by about CNY 0.36. Although the machine tool turn-on/off strategy slightly increased the energy consumption when these are turned on/off, it significantly reduced the standby energy consumption, as shown in Figure 27. Therefore, it can be concluded that the machine tool turn-on/off energy-saving strategy is very effective.

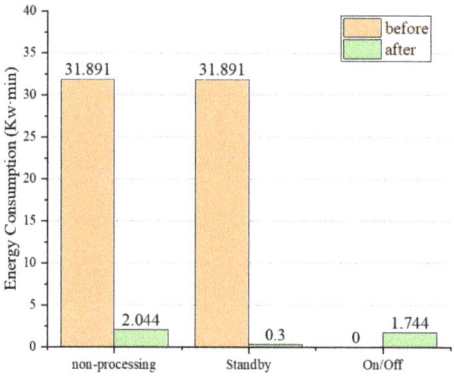

Figure 27. Influence of the machine tool on/off strategy on non-processing energy consumption.

To assess the effects of the hybrid energy-saving strategy, we compared the energy consumption and makespan distinction before and after its adoption. Figure 28 shows the scheduling scheme changes before and after the hybrid energy-saving measure was applied. The four target values and cost before and after optimization are CNY 30.47, 347.18, 89.93, 10 and 39.92 and CNY 28.95, 331.76, 89.93, 10 and 38.97, respectively. It can be seen from the Gantt chart that after adopting the energy-saving strategy, the cutting-tool change of M_3 was performed before $O_{5,1}$, resulting in a 3.95% reduction in the makespan from 30.14 min to 28.95 min, a 4.44% reduction in the total energy consumption of the workshop from 347.18 $kW·min$ to 331.76 $kW·min$ and a 2.44% reduction in the production cost from CNY 39.92 to 38.97, equivalent to CNY 47.3 saved every 24 h. However, the cutting-tool life of

M_3 was calculated as 143.002 min using the cutting-tool life model, while the processing time of $O_{5,1}$ was 8.16 min, thus reducing the processing capacity of the cutting tool DW by 5.7%, as shown in Figure 29.

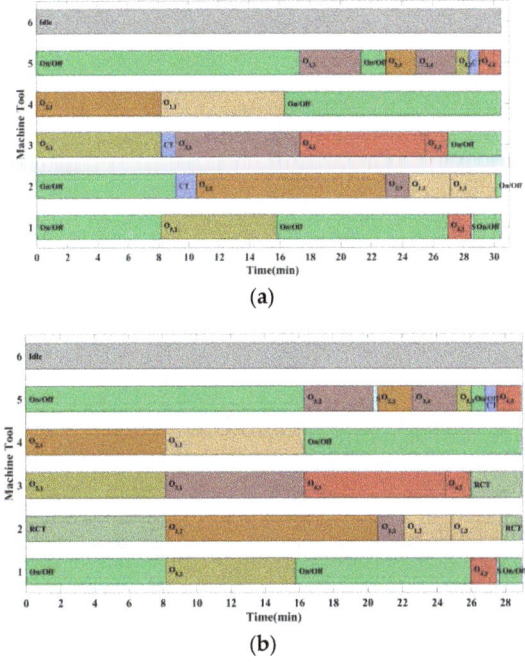

Figure 28. Comparison of scheduling schemes before and after the hybrid energy-saving strategy: (a) Before the hybrid energy-saving strategy; (b) After the hybrid energy-saving strategy.

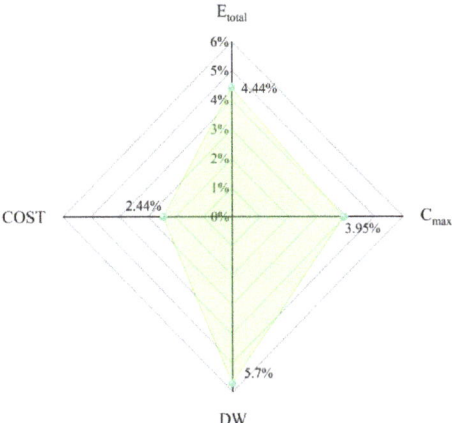

Figure 29. Total impact of the hybrid energy-saving strategy.

The energy-saving strategy mainly reduced the energy consumption of the workshop by changing the timing of the cutting-tool change while reducing the makespan; the total machine tool load and the total number of times the machine tools were turned on/off and cutting tools were changed were not affected. The changes in the total energy consumption of the workshop were analyzed, as shown in Figure 30. In the solutions before and after optimization, the additional energy consumption of the workshop E_{Add} was the highest. This is because the energy consumption of a large number of additional equipment such as lighting, air pumps, and air conditioners in the actual workshop was far greater than that of the machine tools. Because this equipment is continuously operated, its energy consumption is positively correlated with time. As shown in Figure 31, the power consumption of M_3 changed when the cutting tool was changed in advance. The red and green parts represent the energy consumed before and after optimization, respectively. On the whole, the processing energy consumption E_c of the optimized solution decreased.

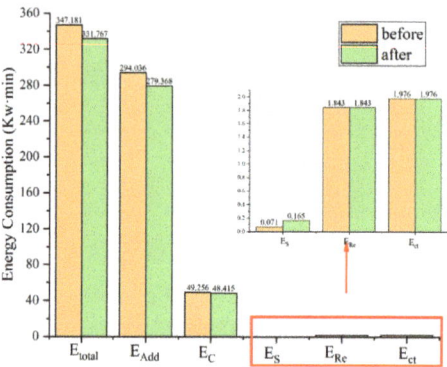

Figure 30. Effect of the hybrid energy-saving strategy on energy consumption.

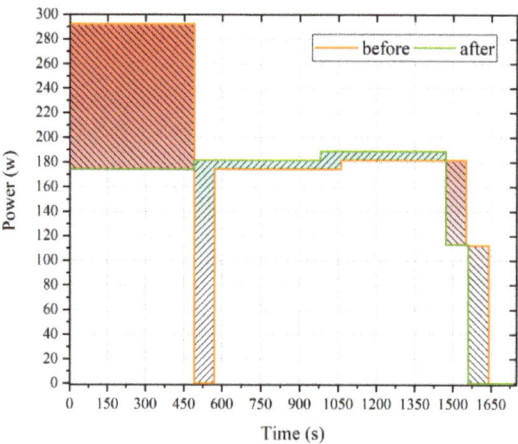

Figure 31. Power contrast curve of M_3 after adopting the hybrid energy-saving strategy.

However, the reduction in E_c is much smaller than that in E_{Add} in terms of energy consumption and has little influence on the total energy consumption. The decrease in E_{Add} is mainly attributed to the integration of the cutting-tool change and machine tool turn-on/off processes, which leads to the reduction in the makespan, thus reducing the energy consumption of additional equipment. However, the cutting-tool change and machine tool turn-on/off processes were not eliminated; hence, their energy consumption did not change. In summary, the hybrid energy-saving strategy effectively reduced energy consumption and optimized the makespan, making it vital within the acceptable degree of reduction in the cutting-tool processing capacity.

6. Conclusions

Production planning and scheduling are usually the most critical activities in intelligent manufacturing enterprises. In the manufacturing process, manufacturers not only need to use the minimum resources to meet the production demand with as little energy consumption and in as short a time as possible but also face the challenge of the lack of mutual responsibility between the scheduling system and the single machine, which often leads to a large deviation between the scheduling optimization results and the actual application. Therefore, a new FJSP–CTD–ESM method is proposed in this paper to provide strong support for intelligent manufacturing enterprises to reduce the time and energy consumption in the production process. Through analyzing the coupling relationship between shop scheduling, single-machine tool energy consumption and tool life prediction, and organically integrating the three to achieve deeper shop consumption reduction. The resulting effect is as follows:

(1) Cutting-tool degradation during shop scheduling was analyzed. Based on the experimental data, exponential regression models of the dynamic power and cutting-tool life were established under certain machining conditions, with an error of approximately 6.5%. (2) A dynamic cutting-tool change strategy by monitoring the RUL was proposed to change the cutting tool before it becomes blunt. This makes the optimization model closer to the real machining situation. (3) Oriented towards low-carbon production objectives, the conventional machine tool turn-on/off schedule can reduce the non-processing energy consumption by 93.5%. Integrating the cutting-tool change strategy into the conventional machine tool turn-on/off schedule further reduces the total energy consumption by 4.44% and production cost by 2.44%. It was proved that this hybrid energy-saving strategy effectively reduces the energy consumption of workshops and has great application prospects.

In terms of the defects in this study, the proposed model does not consider the constraints of transport, clamping, and assembly on shop scheduling. In addition, the establishment of the machining power model and the tool life model of each machine tool in the workshop needs to spend a lot of time on the cutting wear experiment (about 45 h), which brings a lot of work to the preparation of the early production. When the shop changes the machine tool or changes a different type of tool, the models need to be rebuilt. Based on the above limitations, some suggestions are recommended as follows: (1) To explore a fast method to obtain the machining power model and the tool life model and make these models have a certain universal applicability. (2) To integrate more practical constraints such as transport, clamping, assembly, random breakdown or rush orders into the optimization model. (3) To design an efficient solution algorithm to solve multi-objective and many-objective optimization problems.

Author Contributions: Conceptualization, Y.T. and Z.G.; methodology, Y.T. and Z.G.; software, Z.G.; validation, Z.G.; formal analysis, Z.G.; investigation, Y.T., Z.G., L.Z., Y.C. and T.W.; resources, Y.T., L.Z. and T.W.; data curation, Z.G. and Y.C.; writing—original draft preparation, Y.T. and Z.G.; writing—review and editing, Y.T., Z.G. and T.W.; visualization, Z.G.; supervision, Y.T. and Z.G.; project administration, Y.T., L.Z. and Z.G.; funding acquisition, Y.T. All authors have read and agreed to the published version of the manuscript.

Funding: This research was funded by the National Natural Science Foundation of China, grant number 51975407.

Data Availability Statement: Not applicable.

Acknowledgments: The authors would like to thank the editors and anonymous reviewers whose comments helped greatly improve this paper. The work is supported by the National Natural Science Foundation of China (Grant No.51975407).

Conflicts of Interest: The authors declare no conflict of interest.

References

1. Zhou, L.; Li, J.; Li, F.; Meng, Q.; Li, J.; Xu, X. Energy consumption model and energy efficiency of machine tools: A comprehensive literature review. *J. Clean. Prod.* **2016**, *112*, 3721–3734. [CrossRef]
2. Danil, Y.P.; Mozammel, M.; Munish, K.G.; Álisson, R.M.; Giuseppe, P.; Deepak, R.U.; Navneet, K.; Aqib, M.K.; Ítalo, T.; Szymon, W.; et al. Resource saving by optimization and machining environments for sustainable manufacturing: A review and future prospects. *Renew. Sustain. Energy Rev.* **2022**, *166*, 112660.
3. Bi, Z.M.; Wang, L.H. Optimization of machining processes from the perspective of energy consumption: A case study. *J. Manuf. Syst.* **2012**, *31*, 420–428. [CrossRef]
4. Zeng, L.L.; Zhou, F.X.; Xu, X.H.; Gao, Z. Dynamic scheduling of multi-task for hybrid flow-shop based on energy consumption. In Proceedings of the 2009 International Conference on Information and Automation, Zhuhai/Macau, China, 22–24 June 2009; pp. 478–482.
5. Guzman, E.; Andres, B.; Poler, R. Models and algorithms for production planning, scheduling and sequencing problems: A holistic framework and a systematic review. *J. Ind. Inf. Integr.* **2022**, *27*, 100287. [CrossRef]
6. Feng, Y.; Hong, Z.; Li, Z.; Zheng, H.; Tan, J. Integrated intelligent green scheduling of sustainable flexible workshop with edge computing considering uncertain machine state. *J. Clean. Prod.* **2020**, *246*, 119070. [CrossRef]
7. Guzman, E.; Andres, B.; Poler, R. Matheuristic algorithm for job-shop scheduling problem using a disjunctive mathematical model. *Computers* **2021**, *11*, 1. [CrossRef]
8. Mula, J.; Díaz-Madroñero, M.; Andres, B.; Poler, R.; Sanchis, R. A capacitated lot-sizing model with sequence-dependent setups, parallel machines and bi-part injection moulding. *Appl. Math. Model.* **2021**, *100*, 805–820. [CrossRef]
9. Rakovitis, N.; Li, D.; Zhang, N.; Li, J.; Zhang, L.; Xiao, X. Novel approach to energy-efficient flexible job-shop scheduling problems. *Energy* **2022**, *238*, 121773. [CrossRef]
10. Mouzon, G.; Yildirim, M.B.; Twomey, J. Operational methods for minimization of energy consumption of manufacturing equipment. *Int. J. Prod. Res.* **2007**, *45*, 4247–4271. [CrossRef]
11. Wu, X.; Sun, Y. A green scheduling algorithm for flexible job shop with energy-saving measures. *J. Clean. Prod.* **2018**, *172*, 3249–3264. [CrossRef]
12. Gong, G.; Chiong, R.; Deng, Q.; Gong, X.; Lin, W.; Han, W.; Zhang, L. A two-stage memetic algorithm for energy-efficient flexible job shop scheduling by means of decreasing the total number of machine restarts. *Swarm Evol. Comput.* **2022**, *75*, 101131. [CrossRef]
13. Cheng, L.; Tang, Q.; Zhang, L.; Meng, K. Mathematical model and enhanced cooperative co-evolutionary algorithm for scheduling energy-efficient manufacturing cell. *J. Clean. Prod.* **2021**, *326*, 129248. [CrossRef]
14. An, Y.; Chen, X.; Zhang, J.; Li, Y. A hybrid multi-objective evolutionary algorithm to integrate optimization of the production scheduling and imperfect cutting tool maintenance considering total energy consumption. *J. Clean. Prod.* **2020**, *268*, 121540. [CrossRef]
15. Setiawan, A.; Wangsaputra, R.; Martawirya, Y.Y.; Halim, A.H. An FMS Dynamic Production Scheduling Algorithm Considering Cutting Tool Failure and Cutting Tool Life. *IOP Conf. Ser. Mater. Sci. Eng.* **2016**, *114*, 012052. [CrossRef]
16. Liu, F.; Wang, L.Q.; Liu, G.J. Content architecture and future trends of energy efficiency research on machining systems. *J. Mech. Eng.* **2013**, *49*, 87–94. [CrossRef]
17. He, Y.; Tian, X.; Li, Y.; Wang, S.; John, W. Modeling machining energy consumption including the effect of toolpath. *Procedia CIRP* **2020**, *90*, 573–578. [CrossRef]
18. He, Y.; Tian, X.; Li, Y.; Wang, Y.; Wang, Y.; Wang, S. Modeling and analyses of energy consumption for machining features with flexible machining configurations. *J. Manuf. Syst.* **2022**, *62*, 463–476. [CrossRef]
19. Shailendra, P.; Girish, K.G.; Srikanta, R. Modelling of Variable Energy Consumption for CNC Machine Tools. *Procedia CIRP* **2021**, *98*, 247–251.
20. Haruhiko, S.; Tetsuo, S. Energy Efficiency in Machining Systems Based on Power-Law Model for Specific Energy Consumption. *Procedia CIRP* **2022**, *107*, 931–936.
21. Mikołajczyk, T.; Nowicki, K.; Bustillo, A.; Pimenov, D.Y. Predicting tool life in turning operations using neural networks and image processing. *Mech. Syst. Signal Process.* **2018**, *104*, 503–513. [CrossRef]
22. Sun, H.; Liu, Y.; Pan, J.; Zhang, J.; Ji, W. Enhancing cutting tool sustainability based on remaining useful life prediction. *J. Clean. Prod.* **2020**, *244*, 118794. [CrossRef]
23. Castejón, M.; Alegre, E.; Barreiro, J.; Hernández, L.K. On-line tool wear monitoring using geometric descriptors from digital images. *Int. J. Mach. Tools Manuf.* **2007**, *47*, 1847–1853. [CrossRef]
24. Bagga, P.J.; Bajaj, K.S.; Makhesana, M.A.; Patel, K.M. An online tool life prediction system for CNC turning using computer vision techniques. *Mater. Today Proc.* **2022**, *62*, 2689–2693. [CrossRef]
25. Shi, K.; Zhang, D.; Liu, N.; Wang, S.; Ren, J.; Wang, S. A novel energy consumption model for milling process considering tool wear progression. *J. Clean. Prod.* **2018**, *184*, 152–159. [CrossRef]
26. Zhang, X.; Yu, T.; Dai, Y.; Qu, S.; Zhao, J. Energy consumption considering tool wear and optimization of cutting parameters in micro milling process. *Int. J. Mech. Sci.* **2020**, *178*, 105628. [CrossRef]
27. Muhammad, Y.; Syed, J.; Ashfaq, K.; Mushtaq, K. Development and analysis of tool wear and energy consumption maps for turning of titanium alloy (Ti6Al4V). *J. Manuf. Process.* **2021**, *62*, 613–622.

28. Tian, C.; Zhou, G.; Zhang, J. Optimization of cutting parameters considering tool wear conditions in low-carbon manufacturing environment. *J. Clean. Prod.* **2019**, *226*, 706–719. [CrossRef]
29. Tian, Y.; Shao, W.; Wang, T. Energy Footprint Modeling and Parameter Optimization in Workshop Manufacturing Process. *China Mech. Eng.* **2021**, *33*, 1–10. (In Chinese)
30. *ISO 8688-2: 1989*; Tool Life Testing in Milling-Part 2: End Milling. IX-ISO: Geneva, Switzerland, 1989.
31. Deb, K.; Pratap, A.; Agarwal, S.; Meyarivan, T. A fast and elitist multiobjective genetic algorithm: NSGA-II. *IEEE Trans. Evol. Comput.* **2002**, *6*, 182–197. [CrossRef]
32. Zhang, G.; Gao, L.; Li, P.; Zhang, C. Improved Genetic Algorithm for the Flexible Job-shop Scheduling Problem. *J. Mech. Eng.* **2009**, *45–47*, 145–151. [CrossRef]
33. Leng, J.; Gao, X.; Zhu, J. The application of multivariate linear regression forecast model. *J. Stat. Decis.* **2016**, *7*, 82–85. (In Chinese)
34. Chu, H.; Dong, K.; Li, R.; Cheng, Q.; Zhang, C.; Huang, K.; Yang, C.; Zheng, Y. Integrated modeling and optimization of production planning and scheduling in hybrid flow shop for order production mode. *Comput. Ind. Eng.* **2022**, *174*, 108741. [CrossRef]
35. Ramya, G.; Chandrasekaran, M.; Arulmozhi, P. Optimization of production cost for integrating job shop scheduling with production resources. *Mater. Today Proc.* **2021**, *37*, 1839–1844. [CrossRef]

Disclaimer/Publisher's Note: The statements, opinions and data contained in all publications are solely those of the individual author(s) and contributor(s) and not of MDPI and/or the editor(s). MDPI and/or the editor(s) disclaim responsibility for any injury to people or property resulting from any ideas, methods, instructions or products referred to in the content.

Article

Optimal Design of Reverse Logistics Recycling Network for Express Packaging Considering Carbon Emissions

Jia Mao [1], Jinyuan Cheng [1], Xiangyu Li [1], Honggang Zhao [2,*] and Ciyun Lin [1]

1 School of Transportation, Jilin University, Changchun 130022, China
2 College of Chemical Engineering, Xinjiang Normal University, Urumqi 830054, China
* Correspondence: 10762199701000z@xjnu.edu.cn

Abstract: With the development of China's express delivery industry, the number of express packaging has proliferated, leading to many problems such as environmental pollution and resource waste. In this paper, the process of reverse logistics network design for express packaging recycling is given as an example in the M region, and a four-level network containing primary recycling nodes, recycling centers, processing centers, and terminals is established. A candidate node selection model based on the K-means algorithm is constructed to cluster by distance from 535 courier outlets to select 15 candidate nodes of recycling centers and processing centers. A node selection model based on the NSGA-II algorithm is constructed to identify recycling centers and processing centers from 15 candidate nodes with minimizing total cost and carbon emission as the objective function, and a set of Pareto solution sets containing 43 solutions is obtained. According to the distribution of the solution set, the 43 solutions are classified into I, II, and III categories. The results indicate that the solutions corresponding to Class I and Class II solutions can be selected when the recycling system gives priority to cost, Class II and Class III solutions can be selected when the recycling system gives priority to environmental benefits, and Class III solutions can be selected when the society-wide recycling system has developed to a certain extent. In addition, this paper also randomly selects a sample solution from each of the three types of solution sets, conducts coding interpretation for site selection, vehicle selection, and treatment technology selection, and gives an example design scheme.

Keywords: express packaging; green reverse logistics; reduce carbon emissions; K-means algorithm; bi-objective model; NSGA-II algorithm

MSC: 93-10

1. Introduction

In recent years, to promote the high-quality development of green couriers, green transportation, green consumption, and other areas, the concept of saving has been deeply rooted in people's hearts; green low-carbon mode of production and lifestyle is accelerating the formation. The report of the 20th National Congress of the Communist Party of China proposed to "accelerate the green transformation of the development mode", and such measures are especially evident in the express delivery industry. The 2021 government work report clearly pointed out that we should strengthen the construction of urban and rural circulation systems, especially to speed up e-commerce and express into the countryside, and expand consumption at the county and township level, which is the eighth time "express" was included in the government work report. According to the National Bureau of Statistics data, China's 2011–2021 express business volume increased significantly (see Figure 1). At the same time, along with the in-depth implementation of the new development pattern strategy, China's express industry will certainly enter a new stage of development shortly, bringing a new round of growth in the volume of express business and its revenue [1–4].

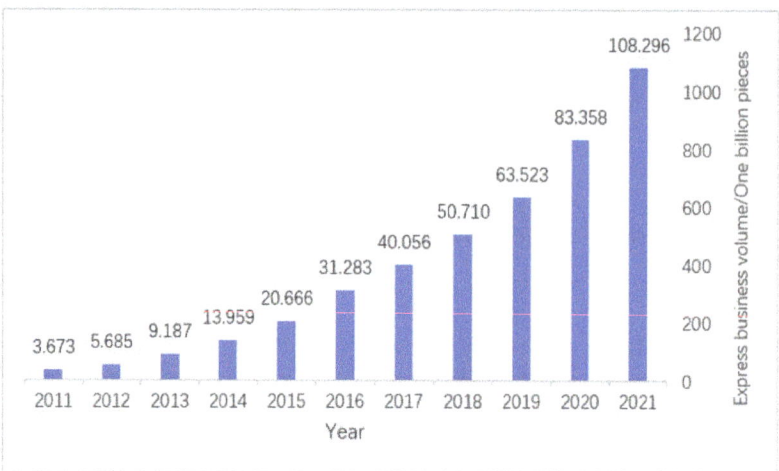

Figure 1. The 2011–2021 express business volume.

The monitoring data of the State Post Bureau showed that the country received 569 million express parcels on the Double Eleven, an increase of 28.54% year-on-year. However, the rapid development of the express industry has also brought about many social and environmental problems; especially the environmental pollution, management chaos, and waste of resources caused by express packaging waste are increasingly obvious [5–7]. Data show that in China's megacities, the increment of express packaging waste has accounted for 93% of the increment of domestic waste, and in some large cities 85% to 90%. How to effectively manage courier waste has become an urgent environmental problem to be solved. The main problems are manifested in the following areas.

(1) The phenomenon of excessive packaging of express products. The problem is more common in the current courier industry because the first impression of consumers on the courier packaging directly affects the entire shopping experience, and the contribution of consumer shopping satisfaction is greater, so e-commerce merchants in the delivery of goods based on basic protective protection, usually increase the protective measures to avoid damage and other situations in transit [8–10].

(2) Some of the courier packaging used in the production of materials with poor environmental performance, resulting in packaging waste that is difficult to naturally degrade. The common airbag foam padding, tape, and black bags made of PVC and other materials in courier packaging degrade slowly under natural conditions and produce a lot of toxic and harmful substances when incinerated [11].

(3) The existing courier packaging has a low degree of standardization and a low reuse rate. The development of express packaging standards involves many aspects, such as packaging materials, filler materials, size specifications, plastic sealing methods, marking, and inspection methods. Low standardization will, on the one hand, reduce logistics efficiency, reduce the management level and quality of logistics services, and increase unnecessary costs, and on the other hand, reduce packaging mobility, narrow the scope of application, increase the difficulty of coordinating the use of express packaging, and make the overall recycling rate lower [12].

(4) The overall recycling rate of express packaging is low. A related research study shows that the actual recycling rate of cardboard and recyclable plastic in China in a year is less than 10%, and the overall courier packaging recycling rate is less than 20%. In some densely populated cities, the incremental amount of courier packaging waste accounts for more than 90% of the total incremental amount of domestic waste.

(5) The reverse logistics system of express packaging recycling is not sound, and systematic scientific planning guidance is missing, manifested by the lagging work of express packaging classification, the confusion of social recycling channels and the low degree of specialization of treatment methods, the inadequacy of institutional mechanisms of relevant enterprises and government departments, the lack of laws and regulations and policy support, and the low enthusiasm of consumer participation in recycling [13–16].

Promoting the green transformation of express packaging, solving the bottlenecks faced by the industry, and achieving the sustainable development of the express industry is a complex and long-term systemic project that requires the participation and joint efforts of experts from different fields and different industry sectors [17]. In response to the above-mentioned problems in the express delivery industry, scholars have studied express packaging recycling from different perspectives.

In terms of site selection, Harsaj proposed a fuzzy multi-objective optimization model that quantifies three aspects simultaneously: economic, environmental, and social, and solved it using an improved particle swarm algorithm (PSO), and finally validated the model with a medical syringe recycling system [18]. Gao proposed a reverse logistics network design scheme based on a forward logistics network, and constructed an optimization model based on a multi-objective scenario with the objective functions of maximizing the expected total monetary profit, minimizing the expected total carbon emission cost, and maximizing the expected total job creation, and transformed it into a single-objective model to finally obtain the Pareto-optimal solution, and finally validated the effectiveness by using tires as an example [19]. Nie studied the supply chain configuration problem, constructed a mixed integer linear programming model with minimizing carbon emissions as the objective function, solved it using dynamic programming algorithms, and finally carried out an example verification to achieve a balance between economic and social benefits [20]. Guo studied fresh food distribution, built a two-stage model, considered the total system cost and vehicle path, and solved using a genetic algorithm and particle swarm algorithm, which effectively reduced carbon emissions and total cost [21]. Reddy constructed a multi-level multi-period mixed integer linear programming model with profit maximization as the objective function, considering the effects of facility location, vehicle type, and return rate, and finally gave an example analysis [22].

From the perspective of recycling model selection research, Liang used the Internet as a bridge to realize the design of a virtual APP and recycling device from the perspective of consumer psychology, real consumption situation, and the current situation of packaging recycling, to form a complete express packaging recycling system [2]. Yang constructed a multi-agent express packaging waste recycling system including the government, individuals, and enterprises. Based on differential game theory, the behavioral characteristics of individuals and the optimal strategies of government and enterprises under the market-driven recycling model, government-driven recycling model, and cooperative-driven recycling model were explored [23]. Based on previous studies by scholars, the main research contributions of this paper are as follows [24].

- From the concept of reducing carbon emission and environmental pollution, this paper gives the process of designing the reverse logistics network for express packaging recycling, taking the M region as an example, and establishes a four-level network containing primary recycling nodes, recycling centers, processing centers, and terminals.
- Construct a candidate node selection model based on the K-means algorithm, cluster by distance from 535 express outlets, and use the obtained basic data to calculate the distance between each node, the express volume of each node, etc.
- Construct a node selection model based on the NSGA-II algorithm, with the objective function of minimizing the total cost and carbon emission, and consider the effects of different locations of the selected nodes, different types of vehicles between nodes, and different processing technologies adopted by the processing centers.

2. Problem Description

In this paper, according to the economic development and administrative division of Changchun, seven district administrative units under Changchun are selected as the area under study (hereinafter collectively referred to as M area), including Nanguan District, Kuancheng District, Chaoyang District, Erdao District, Lvyuan District, Shuangyang District, and Jiutai District (not considering Gongzhuling District). In this paper, we design the reverse logistics network for express packaging in region M. The regional map of region M is shown in Figure 2.

Figure 2. Regional map of M area.

According to the relevant data from Changchun Bureau of Statistics, this paper obtains the 2018–2020 population figures for the seven administrative regions mentioned above, as shown in Appendix A Table A1.

The proportion of the population of each district to the total population of Changchun was obtained (see Appendix A Table A2), in which the average proportion of the municipal districts to the total population of the city from 2018 to 2020 was the weighted average, and the weights of each year from 2018 to 2020 were 0.5, 0.3, and 0.2 according to the principle that the closer the year, the greater the weight.

In this paper, Baidu map API was used to obtain the original data of the latitude and longitude of courier points in the M area of Changchun and obtain 535 final valid data points after eliminating individual invalid data points, including 99 in Nanguan District, 81 in Kuancheng District, 107 in Chaoyang District, 103 in Erdao District, 81 in Lvyuan District, 17 in Shuangyang District, and 47 in Jiutai District. The latitude and longitude of express points in Nanguan District are shown in Appendix A Table A3, and the rest of the areas are omitted.

The relevant statistical information of Changchun Postal Administration was checked to obtain the express business volume in Changchun from 2013 to 2020, as shown in Table 1.

Table 1. The 2013–2020 express business statistics table in Changchun.

Year	Express Business Volume/Million Pieces	Year	Express Business Volume/Million Pieces
2013	27.1409	2017	98.9954
2014	41.3411	2018	129.7255
2015	52.3329	2019	161.9971
2016	78.6633	2020	237.2633

To meet the design requirements of the subsequent recycling network, the data in Table 1 need to be used to forecast the express business volume of Changchun in the next few years and select the appropriate value as the design value. In this paper, the least squares method is used to fit a linear function and an exponential function to the express business volume data of Changchun from 2013 to 2020, and the obtained functional relationships are shown in Equations (1) and (2).

$$y = 2242.9x - 540.05 \quad (1)$$

$$y = 2183e^{0.2971x} \quad (2)$$

In the above Equations (1) and (2), $x = $ Year $- 2012$. The fitted image is shown in Figure 3, and it can be visually seen that the fitting effect of Equation (2) is better than the fitting effect of Equation (1). Using Equations (1) and (2), the prediction of express business volume for 2013–2020 and 2021–2025 is shown in Table 2 and Figure 3.

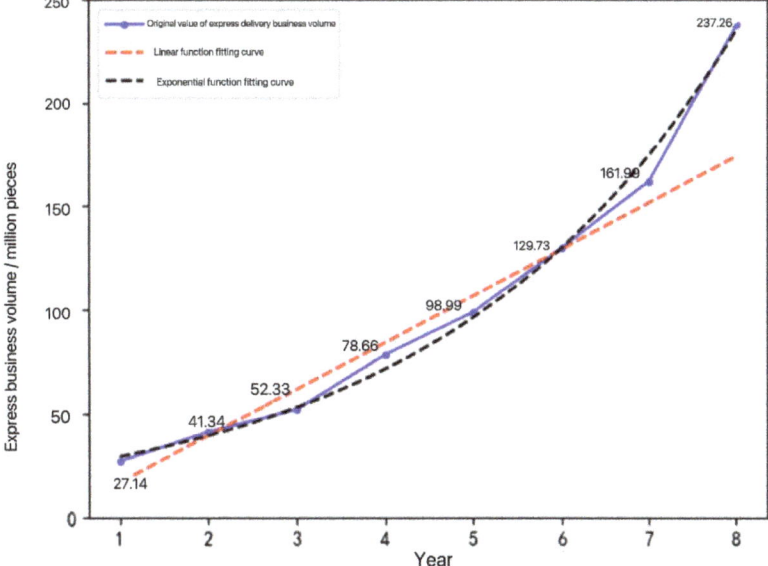

Figure 3. Fitting graph of express business volume.

Table 2. Express business volume forecast.

Serial Number	Actual Value/ Million Pieces	Linear Forecast Value/Million Pieces	Error	Index Forecast Value/Million Pieces	Error
1	27.1409	17.0285	37.26%	29.38209	8.26%
2	41.3411	39.4575	4.56%	39.54682	4.34%
3	52.3329	61.8865	18.26%	53.22803	1.71%
4	78.6633	84.3155	7.19%	71.64226	8.93%
5	98.9954	106.7445	7.83%	96.4269	2.59%
6	129.7255	129.1735	0.43%	129.7858	0.05%
7	161.9971	151.6025	6.42%	174.6851	7.83%
8	237.2633	174.0315	26.65%	23511.74	0.90%
9	/	196.4605	/	316.4563	/
10	/	218.8895	/	425.9343	/
11	/	241.3185	/	573.2863	/
12	/	263.7475	/	771.6146	/
13	/	286.1765	/	1038.555	/

As we can see in Table 3, the prediction effect of Equation (2) is better than that of Equation (1), so the express volume of 103,855,000 pieces in 2025 (x = 13) predicted by Equation (2) is selected as the design value.

Table 3. The parameters given in this paper and their values.

$M = 6000$ kg	$c = 4000$ kg/m^2
$m_0 = 0.3$ kg	$c_{ar1} = 0.00800$ kg/m^2
$V_{max} = 30,000,000$ pieces	$c_{ar2} = 0.00804$ kg/m^2
$V_{max} m_0 = 9,000,000$ kg	$c_{ar3} = 0.00808$ kg/m^2
$C_1 = 1200$ CNY/m^2	$a_1 = 1.2500$ CNY/kg
$C_2 = 900$ CNY/m^2	$a_2 = 1.2400$ CNY/kg
$C_3 = 850$ CNY/m^2	$a_3 = 1.2300$ CNY/kg
$C_4 = 800$ CNY/m^2	$\alpha = 0.5, \beta = 0.2, \gamma = 0.3$

3. Algorithm Introduction

3.1. Introduction to K-Means Algorithm

3.1.1. Principle of K-Means Algorithm

The K-means algorithm belongs to unsupervised machine learning and is a common classical clustering algorithm with the advantages of simplicity, efficiency, and ease of implementation, but it is sensitive to the selection of the initial clustering centers, which can affect the accuracy and speed of convergence if not selected properly. The K-means problem in a general sense can be described as follows: given a dataset containing N elements, each of which is an M-dimensional real vector, the objective is to select K points as clustering centers and divide the N elements into K sets, where each set corresponds to a clustering center so that the sum of the squared distances of all elements to the corresponding clustering center is minimized, at which point the clustering center of each set is the mean point of each set element [25].

3.1.2. K Value Determination Method

(1) Select-on-demand method: This means that the number of classification groups of data is determined according to the actual demand.
(2) Elbow method: error squared and SSE is a function of the number of clusters K, SSE becomes smaller with the increase of K, and when K increases to a certain value, the rate of change of SSE will rapidly become smaller; that is, as the value of K continues to increase and tends to level off, so that the relationship between K and SSE graph is similar to the elbow, the inflection point of the elbow is the optimal number of clusters K.

(3) Contour coefficient method: the contour coefficient of a certain data point of a cluster is the difference between the average distance (cohesion) of the data and the data of the same cluster and the average distance (separation) of all data of the nearest cluster and the ratio of the larger of the two. After finding the data, the contour coefficient of the rest of the data in the same cluster is obtained, and the average value is the average contour coefficient of the data in the group. The larger the average contour coefficient, the better the clustering effect, the corresponding K value is the optimal number of clusters.

(4) Gap Statistics method: in the sample area in accordance with the uniform distribution of randomly generated and the original sample number of random samples, and these random samples and K-means clustering, calculate the loss of random samples and the actual sample loss of the difference between the maximum value of the corresponding K is the optimal number of clusters.

3.2. Introduction of NSGA-II Algorithm

3.2.1. Introduction to Multi-Objective Optimization Algorithms

When there are two or more objective functions, it is called multi-objective optimization.

The general form of multi-objective optimization is shown in Equation (3).

$$minF = [f_1(x), f_2(x), f_3(x), \ldots f_m(x)]^T \tag{3}$$

In the above equation, $F(x)$ is the multi-objective optimization result, $f_1(x), f_2(x), f_3(x), \ldots f_m(x)$ is the objective component, and m is the objective dimension.

3.2.2. Introduction to NSGA-II Algorithm

NSGA-II algorithm is a commonly used multi-objective genetic algorithm with the advantages of lower computational complexity and better population goodness and diversity. Its core is the introduction of fast non-dominated sorting, crowding degree, and elite strategy, as shown below [26].

(1) Introduction to the fast non-dominated sorting method.

Let n_i denote the number of individuals dominating individual in the population, and S_i is the set of individuals dominated by individual i. Find all individuals with $n_i = 0$ in the population, i.e., the number of individuals dominating individual i is 0, i.e., individual i is not dominated, and deposit the eligible individual i into the non-dominated set R1, which means the subdominated rank is 1.

For all individuals j in the current non-dominated set R1, iterate through the set S_j of the individuals it dominates. Since the individuals j dominating individual t have been deposited in the current non-dominated set R1, the n_t of each individual t in the set S_j is subtracted by 1. That is, the number of individuals governing the solution of individual t is reduced by 1. If $n_t - 1 = 0$ is satisfied, then individual t is deposited in the set H.

R1 is used as the first level of the set of non-dominated individuals, and the individuals in this set are only dominated by other individuals and not by any other individuals, and all individuals in this set are assigned the same non-dominated ranking level, and then the above grading operation is continued for the set H, and the corresponding ranking level is also assigned, until all individuals are graded, i.e., all individuals are assigned the corresponding ranking level.

(2) Crowding degree profile.

The crowding degree i_d denotes the density of individuals around a given point in a population of a given generation, and in practice, it is measured by the length of the largest rectangle around individual i that contains individual i but not other individuals, where the crowding degree of individuals on each rank boundary is $+\infty$. According to the definition of crowding degree, it can be seen that the larger the crowding degree is, the better the individuals are. The specific algorithm text is not repeated.

(3) Introduction to the elite strategy.

The elite strategy is to prevent the elimination of good individuals in the population in each generation, and to mix all individuals in the parent and child generations, and then select them according to the rank of non-dominance sorting and the size of crowding degree to get the new generation population that meets the population size requirement, effectively avoiding the loss of good individuals in the parent population, and the execution process is shown in Figure 4 [27].

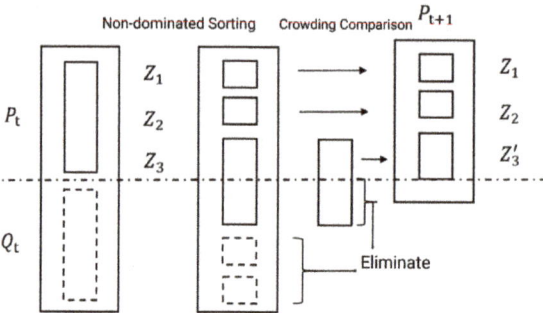

Figure 4. Elite strategy diagram.

As shown above, firstly, the parents P_t and Q_t are merged to obtain a new population with two times the original population size, and the individuals in the new population are sorted non-dominantly and selected according to the rank of non-dominant rank from smallest to largest until the selection reaches the rank of Z_i, so that the number of selected individuals plus the number of individuals in this rank is greater than the original population size for the first time, and then the Z_i is calculated. Z_i rank in the crowding degree of individuals, and according to the size of the crowding degree from the largest to the smallest selection, until the population number requirement is met, so that the new generation of parents P'_t.

4. Model Building

4.1. Modeling of Reverse Logistics Network in M Region

This paper determines the third-party logistics-centered express packaging model considering government participation, i.e., in the subsequent design of this paper, it is assumed that a third-party logistics enterprise specializing in express packaging recycling will carry out unified recycling and processing of express packaging of each courier company.

4.1.1. Network Level and Node Analysis

According to the development status of the M region, this paper designs a four-layer recycling network, and the schematic diagram of express packaging reverse logistics network layers and nodes in the M region is shown in Figure 5.

Among them, the first level is the primary recycling layer; the nodes of this level are the 535 courier points acquired, responsible for the recovery of express packaging directly from consumers, mainly by the consumers themselves to return express packaging, supplemented by door-to-door service for recycling. The second level is the recycling level; the node of this level is the recycling center, which is responsible for collecting and storing the express packaging recovered by the courier points within a certain area and connects to the primary recycling level with the relevant carriers leased or purchased, and the transportation process is short-distance transportation. The third level is the processing layer; the node of this level is the processing center, which is responsible for classifying the express packaging recovered by each recycling center and carrying out different technical treatments according to different categories, mainly including reuse treatment and transport to each recycling center, transport to the paper mill, and transport to landfill, with the relevant carrier leased or purchased to connect the recycling layer and the terminal layer, the transport process is medium and long-distance transport compared with the transport process of the first and second levels. The transportation process is medium to long distance compared to the first and second levels. The fourth level is the terminal level, the nodes of this level are the paper mill and the landfill, which are responsible for accepting the express packaging after sorting in the processing center, the longitude and latitude of the paper mill and the landfill are (43.910551° N, 125.420776° E) and (43.964575° N, 125.358692° E), and they are connected to the processing level by the relevant carriers leased or purchased. The process is also medium to long distance.

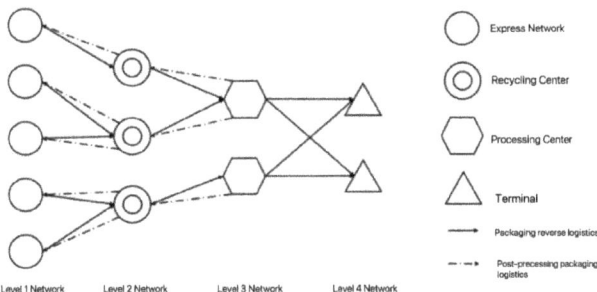

Figure 5. Schematic diagram of express packaging reverse logistics network hierarchy and nodes in M region.

4.1.2. Determination of Candidate nodes Based on the K-Means Algorithm

- Basic assumptions

(1) Euclidean distance is used in this paper to calculate the distance between the data and the center of clusters (center of mass).

(2) It is assumed that the influence of the Earth's surface on the distance calculation is negligible in the range of M region.

- Symbol Description

Symbols	Meaning
SSE	Clustering error of all sample data.
V	New cluster center and old cluster center error.
K	Number of cluster centers K_i set of values, $K = \{1, 2, \cdots, N-1, N\}$.
K_0	Number of clustering centers, $K_0 \in K$.
μ_i	The ith clustering center (center of mass), $1 \leq i \leq K$ and i is an integer.
S_i	The center of clustering (center of mass) is the ith data set of μ_i, $1 \leq i \leq K$ and i is an integer.
x_j	The jth data, $x_j \in S_i$

- Model Building

$$SSE = \sum_{i=1}^{K} \sum_{x_j \in S_i} ||x_j - \mu_i||^2 \quad (4)$$

$$minV = \sum_{i=1}^{K_0} \sum_{x_j \in S_i} ||x_j - \mu_i||^2 \quad (5)$$

- K-means clustering algorithm steps

(1) Determine K_0 (see Figure 6)

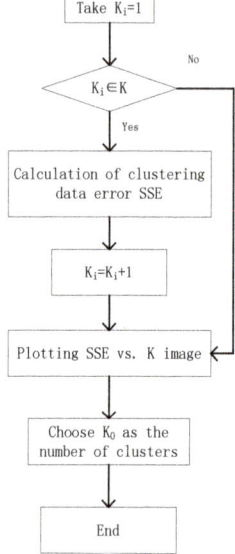

Figure 6. Determining K_0 in the K-means algorithm.

(2) K-means clustering (see Figure 7)

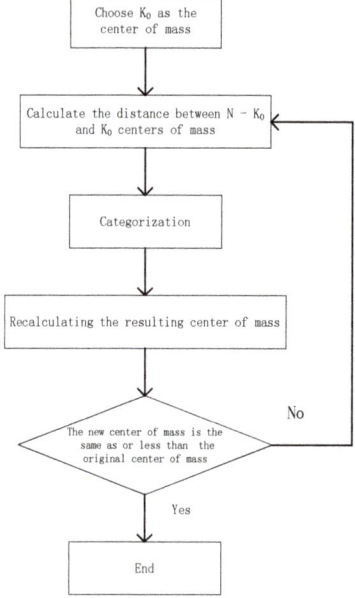

Figure 7. K-means algorithm specific steps.

4.2. NSGA-II Algorithm-Based Node Siting Modeling

1. Basic assumptions
   (1) The calculation cycle is one year.
   (2) Each recycling center can only be handled by one processing center.
   (3) The ratio of inflow to the outflow of express business is 1:1, and the recycling rate is 50%.
   (4) The recycled products are single, all are cartons.
   (5) Straight line approximation instead of actual distance.
   (6) The available vehicles are sufficient, and vehicle path planning and scheduling problems are not considered.
   (7) When the vehicle is from the recycling center to the processing center, only one model can serve, and vice versa, two processes can be served by different models (there are four models 1, 2, 3 and 4, the last two of which are battery-driven), each model has the same rated mass, and the corresponding data are solved according to the full-load state in the calculation.
   (8) The processing center is for rental use.
   (9) Expenses such as equipment purchase, maintenance, and workers' wages are included in the unit processing costs.
   (10) No consideration is given to inventory costs, landfill costs, etc.
   (11) Other parameters such as fixed construction costs for different types of areas are known.
   (12) The express packaging after processing will be transported to each recycling center, and then by each recycling center to each first-level network.
   (13) Only the transportation cost between the recycling center, treatment center, landfill, and paper mill and the carbon emission of the transportation process and treatment process is considered.

- Symbol Description

Symbols	Meaning
F	Total cost
f_1	Shipping cost
f_2	Processing cost
f_3	Construction cost
N	Number of candidate nodes
d_{ji}	The straight-line distance between the jth candidate node and the ith candidate node
V_{ji}	Packing volume between the jth candidate node transported to the ith candidate node
V_i	Amount of packaging recycling at the ith node
V_{max}	The ith node can carry the maximum recycling volume
m_0	Mass equivalent per courier package
t_{rk}	Freight rate for the kth vehicle unit, k = 1, 2, 3, 4
a_j	Processing cost using the jth technology unit (j = 1,2,3)
C_k	Regional k unit construction costs, k = 1, 2, 3, 4
c	Unit storage capacity
g_1	CO_2 emissions during transportation
g_2	CO_2 emissions from the treatment process
c_{trk}	The kth vehicle unit carbon emission factor, k = 1, 2
c_{trk}	Carbon emission factor per unit for the kth vehicle, k = 3, 4
L_k	Fuel consumption per unit distance for the kth vehicle, k = 1, 2
L_k	Electricity consumption per unit distance for the kth vehicle, k = 3, 4
L_k^*	The fuel consumption per unit distance of the kth vehicle, when fully loaded, k = 1, 2
L_k^*	The electricity consumption per unit distance of the kth vehicle, when fully loaded, k = 3, 4

Symbols	Meaning
L_k^0	The fuel consumption per unit distance of the kth vehicle, when unloaded, k = 1, 2
L_k^0	Electricity consumption per unit distance for the kth vehicle, at no load, k = 3, 4
m	The kth load capacity
M	The kth rated capacity
c_{arj}	CO_2 emissions per unit mass of packaging treated with the jth technology, (j = 1,2,3)
α	Reuse rate
β	Percentage of packaging that is disposed of and transported to landfill
γ	Percentage of packaging shipped to paper mills after processing

- Objective function

In this paper, the objective function is set from two perspectives: economic and environmental.

(1) Economic perspective: Since the revenue source of reverse logistics is complicated, government subsidies and profit distribution need to be considered, so only cost minimization is considered in this paper.
(2) Environmental perspective: to minimize the emissions of CO_2, one of the greenhouse gases [28–31].

$$minF = f_1 + f_2 + f_3 \tag{6}$$

$$minG = g_1 + g_2 \tag{7}$$

$$f_1 = \sum_{i=1}^{N}\sum_{j=1}^{N} X_i X_{ji} d_{ji} V_{ji} m_0 t_{rk} + \sum_{i=1}^{N} X_i d_{im} V_{im} m_0 t_{rk} + \sum_{i=1}^{N} X_i d_{in} V_{in} m_0 t_{rk} + \sum_{i=1}^{N}\sum_{j=1}^{N} X_i X_{ij} d_{ij} V_{ij} m_0 t_{rk} \tag{8}$$

$$f_2 = \begin{cases} a_j V_i m, & V_i m \le V_{max} m_0 \\ +\infty, & V_{max} m_0 < V_i V_i \end{cases} \tag{9}$$

$$f_3 = \begin{cases} \sum_{i=1}^{N} X_i V_i m C_1, & i \in \{1,2,3\} \\ \sum_{i=1}^{N} X_i V_i m C_2, & i \in \{4,5,6\} \\ \sum_{i=1}^{N} X_i V_i m C_3, & i \in \{7,8,9,10,11,12,13\} \\ n \sum_{i=1}^{N} X_i V_i m C_4, & i \in \{14,15\} \end{cases} \tag{10}$$

$$g_1 = \sum_{i=1}^{N}\sum_{j=1}^{N} X_i X_{ji} d_{ji} V_{ji} m_0 L_k c_{trk} + \sum_{i=1}^{N} X_i d_{im} V_{im} m_0 L_k c_{trk} + \sum_{i=1}^{N} X_i d_{in} V_{in} m_0 L_k c_{trk} + \sum_{i=1}^{N}\sum_{j=1}^{N} X_i X_{ij} d_{ij} V_{ij} m_0 L_k c_{trk} \tag{11}$$

$$L_k = L_k^0 + \frac{L_k^* - L_k^0}{N} m_0 \tag{12}$$

$$g_2 = V_1 m_0 c_{arj} \tag{13}$$

- Constraints

$$X_i = \begin{cases} 1, & \text{The ith candidate node is selected as the processing center} \\ 0, & \text{The ith candidate node is selected as the recycling center} \end{cases} \quad (14a)$$

$$X_{ji} = \begin{cases} 1, & \text{The jth candidate node is assigned to the ith candidate node} \\ 0, & \text{The jth candidate node is not assigned to the ith candidate node} \end{cases} \quad (14b)$$

$$0 \le V_i \le V_{max} \quad (15a)$$

$$V_i = V_{ii} + V_{ji} \quad (15b)$$

$$V_i = V_{im} + V_{in} \quad (15c)$$

Equation (6) represents the cost, including transportation cost, construction cost, and treatment cost, in which, transportation cost includes three parts from recycling center to treatment center, treatment center to landfill and paper mill, and treatment center back to the recycling center, construction cost considers four types of areas A, B, C, and D and the cost per unit construction area is different for candidate nodes in different areas, and treatment cost considers alternative of three technologies, and the treatment cost of different technologies is different. Equation (7) represents carbon emissions, including carbon emissions from the transportation process and carbon emissions from the treatment process, where carbon emissions from the transportation process include three parts from recycling center to treatment center, from treatment center to landfill and paper mill, and from treatment center back to the recycling center, and carbon emissions from treatment process consider the three alternative technologies, and the carbon emissions generated by different technologies are different. The above Equation (15a) indicates that the storage volume of node i takes a range of values, Equation (15b) indicates that node i is equal to its storage volume plus the volume transported from point j to point i, Equation (15c) indicates that the volume transported out of node i is not greater than the storage volume of node i. Equations (15a) and (15b) indicate that the above two equations indicate the conservation of flow, the way to achieve each of the above constraints, especially the capacity constraint through the constraint matrix.

According to the relevant information and combined with the actual situation, the following values of the relevant parameters are given in this paper. The values of each variable are as follows in Table 3.

Take fuel consumption per unit distance at no load $L_1^0 = 0.11$ L/km, $L_1^* = 0.15$ L/km at full load, carbon emission factor per unit fuel consumption $c_{tr1} = 2.5$ kg/L, freight per unit $t_{r1} = 0.001$ CNY/km/kg in vehicle type 1, fuel consumption per unit distance at no load $L_2^0 = 0.1$ L/km, $L_2^* = 0.15$ L/km at full load. The carbon emission factor per unit of fuel consumption c_{tr2} is 2.8 kg/L, the freight cost per unit t_{r2} is 0.0008, and the electricity consumption per unit distance L_3^0 is 0.1 in vehicle type 2. When vehicle type 3 is empty, $L_3^* = 0.3$, when fully loaded, the carbon emission factor per unit of electricity consumption c_{tr3} is 0.8, the freight cost per unit t_{r3} is 0.0015, and the electricity consumption per unit distance $L_4^0 = 0.1$. When vehicle type 4 is empty, $L_4^* = 0.3$ when fully loaded, the carbon emission factor per unit of electricity consumption $c_{tr4} = 0.1$, unit freight t_{r4} is 0.0012.

5. Algorithm Design
5.1. NSGA-II Algorithm Description

(1) Chromosome coding

In this paper, we set each generation of the population containing n individuals, and each individual has only one chromosome, using a repeatable integer coding method, and the total length of the chromosome is 75. From the perspective of corresponding functions, each chromosome can be divided into five parts, and the length of each part is 15. Specifically, the first part indicates the site selection code, the second part indicates the vehicle type selection code from the recycling center to the treatment center, the third part indicates the vehicle selection code from the processing center to the recycling center, the fourth part indicates the vehicle selection type code from the processing center to the paper mill and the landfill, and the fifth part is the processing technology selection code.

- First part: site selection code

    For a generational population, the first part of the chromosome of the ith ($1 \leq I \leq n$, and i is an integer, the same below) individual, the jth ($1 \leq j \leq 15$, and j is an integer, the same below) position indicates j candidate nodes and the value k corresponding to the jth position indicates that the jth candidate node is assigned to node k, and k becomes the processing center, where $k \in \{1 \leq k \leq 15$, and k is an integer$\}$.

    For example, Figure 8I represents the first part of the chromosome of the first individual of a generation population, whose length is 15, and the value corresponding to the first position is 1, indicating that node 1 is assigned to node 1, i.e., node 1 is selected as a processing center by the candidate node, and so on, and the value corresponding to the 15th position is 15, indicating that node 15 is assigned to node 15, i.e., node 15 is selected as a processing center.

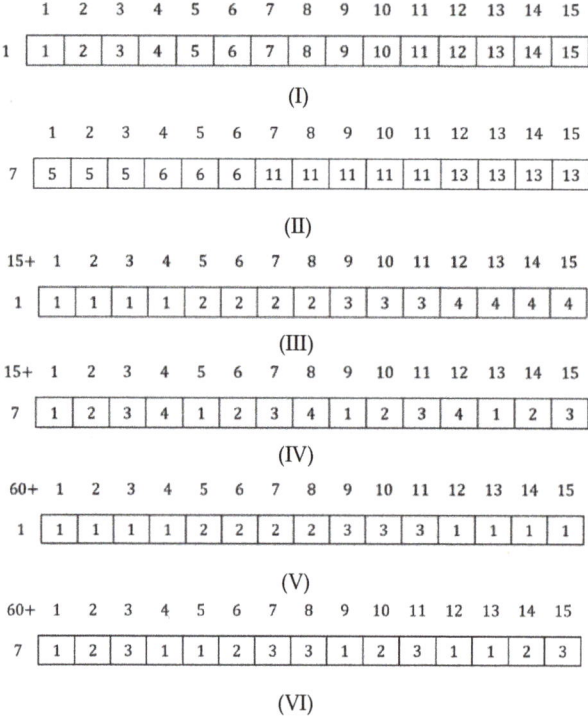

Figure 8. (I,II) indicate the site selection code, (III,IV) indicate the vehicle type selection code from the recycling center to the processing center, the vehicle selection code from the processing center to the recycling center and the vehicle type selection code from the processing center to the paper mill and landfill, (V,VI) are the processing technology selection code.

Figure 8II represents the first part of the chromosome of the 7th individual of this generation population, whose length is 15, and the 1st, 2nd, and 3rd positions correspond to values all of 5, indicating that nodes 1, 2, and 3 are assigned to node 5, i.e., node 5 is selected as a processing center by the candidate node, and accordingly, nodes 1, 2, and 3 are selected as a recycling center by the candidate node, and so on, and the 12th, 13th, 14th, and 15th positions correspond to the value 13, indicating that nodes 12, 13, 14, and 15 are assigned to node 13, i.e., node 13 is selected as the processing center by the candidate node, and nodes 12, 14, and 15 are selected as the recycling center by the candidate node.

- Second, third, and fourth parts.

For the second part of the ith ($1 \leq i \leq n$ and i is an integer, same below) individual chromosome of a generational population, the value l corresponding to the jth ($16 \leq j \leq 30$ and j is an integer, same below) position indicates the type of transport vehicle between the $(j-15)$th candidate node and the kth node corresponding to the $(j-15)$th position in the first part, where $l \in \{1 \leq l \leq 4$ and l is an integer $\}$ and $k \in \{1 \leq k \leq 15$ and k is an integer$\}$.

For example, Figure 8III represents the second part of the chromosome of the first individual of a generational population which is the same population as the population of Figure 8I with a length of 15. The 16th position corresponds to a value of 1, indicating that the type of the transport vehicle between the first candidate node and the first candidate node corresponding to the first position in the first part is type 1, and so on, and the 30th position corresponds to the value of 4 indicates that the type of the transport vehicle between the 15th candidate node and the 15th candidate node corresponding to the 15th position in the first part is type 4.

Figure 8IV represents the chromosome of the 7th individual of this generation population with a length of 15, and the values corresponding to the 16th, 20th, 24th, and 28th positions are all 1, indicating that the type of transport vehicle between the 1st, 5th, 9th, and 13th candidate nodes and the 5th, 6th, 11th, and 13th candidate nodes corresponding to the first part is all type 1, and the values corresponding to the 17th, 21st, 25th, and 29th positions are 2, indicating that the vehicle types of the transport vehicles between the 2nd, 6th, 10th, and 14th candidate nodes and the corresponding 2nd, 6th, 10th, and 14th candidate nodes in the first part are all of type 2, and the remaining cases and so on.

- Fifth part.

For the ith ($1 \leq i \leq n$, i is an integer, the same below) individual chromosome of the fifth part of a generational population, the value p corresponding to the jth ($61 \leq j \leq 75$, j is an integer, the same below) position denotes the pth technique chosen for the kth node corresponding to the $j-15$th position of the first part, where $p \in \{1 \leq l \leq 3$ and p is an integer$\}$ and $k \in \{1 \leq k \leq 15$ and k is an integer$\}$. For example, Figure 8V represents the fifth part of the chromosome of the first individual of a generational population (this population is the same population as the population in Figure 8), whose length is 15, and the 61st position corresponds to a value of 1, indicating the j60th candidate node, i.e., the first candidate node uses technology 1, and so on, and the 75th position corresponds to a value of 1, indicating the j60th candidate node i.e., the 15th candidate node also adopts technique 1.

Figure 8VI represents the chromosome of the seventh individual of this generation population with a length of 15, and the values corresponding to the 61st, 64th, 65th, 69th, 72nd, and 73rd positions are all 1, indicating that the 1st, 4th, 5th, 9th, 12th, and 13th candidate nodes corresponding to the first part adopt technology 1, and the values corresponding to the 62nd, 66th, 70th, and 74th positions are all 2, indicating that the 2nd, 6th, 10th, and 14 candidate nodes adopt technique 2, and the values corresponding to the 63rd, 67th, 68th, 71st, and 75th positions are all 3, indicating that the 3rd, 7th, 8th, 11th, and 15th candidate nodes adopt technique 3.

(2) Population initialization

According to the above coding method, in this paper, let there be $n = 50$ individuals per generation of population, each individual has only one chromosome, and the length of each chromosome is 75, i.e., m = 75, the first part corresponds to the candidate processing center coding, each position randomly generates a repeatable integer k ($1 \leq k \leq 15$), the second, third, and fourth parts correspond to the vehicle type coding, each position randomly generates a repeatable integer l ($1 \leq l \leq 4$), the fifth part corresponds to the type of technology used, $p \in \{1 \leq l \leq 3,$ and p is an integer$\}$.

(3) Adaptation degree function

In this paper, the fitness of each individual is calculated according to the rank size and crowding degree of the non-dominated stratum, specifically, the parents and children are merged, the new population after the merger is non-dominated stratified, and the crowding degree is calculated for all individuals, and finally, the individuals are selected according to the principle that priority is given to individuals with small non-dominated stratification rank and priority is given to individuals with large crowding degree in the same stratum until the population number is satisfied requirements, the method has a slightly different logic from the classical NSGA-II algorithm, but is identical in purpose and fully equivalent in effect [32–34].

(4) Crossover operation [35]

In this paper, the simulated binary crossover method is used to perform crossover operations on population chromosomes. Assuming that the children generated by the crossover of parents x_a and x_b are y_a and y_b, then for the kth position of children y_a and y_b we have.

$$y_a(k) = \frac{1}{2}[(1+\beta)x_a(k) + (1-\beta)x_b(k)] \tag{16}$$

$$y_b(k) = \frac{1}{2}[(1-\beta)x_a(k) + (1+\beta)x_b(k)] \tag{17}$$

Among them,

$$\beta = \begin{cases} 2r^{\frac{1}{1+\eta}}, r \leq 0.5 \\ (2-2r)^{-\frac{1}{1+\eta}}, r > 0.5 \end{cases} \tag{18}$$

In the above equation, $r \sim U[0,1]$, η is a custom parameter, and the larger the value, the closer the offspring is to the parent.

In this paper, we take $\eta = 20$, and for crossover, the first half of individuals and the second half of individuals in each generation of the population are combined two by two, and when the number of individuals is odd, the last individual does not participate in the crossover.

(5) Variation operation

In this paper, the polynomial variation method is used to perform various operations on population chromosomes; specifically, the variation form is,

$$v'_k = v_k + \delta(u_k - l_k) \tag{19}$$

Among them,

$$\delta = \begin{cases} \left[2u + (1-2u)(1-\delta_1)^{\eta_m+1}\right]^{\frac{1}{\eta_m+1}} - 1, u \leq 0.5 \\ 1 - \left[2(1-u) + 2(u-0.5)(1-\delta_2)^{\eta_m+1}\right]^{\frac{1}{\eta_m+1}}, u > 0.5 \end{cases} \tag{20}$$

In the above equation, $\delta_1 = (v_k - l_k)/(u_k - l_k)$, $\delta_2 = (v_k - v_k)/(u_k - l_k)$, u is a random number in the interval $[0,1]$, η_m is a custom parameter, and this paper takes $\eta_m = 20$.

5.2. NSGA-II Algorithm Steps

Step 1: encoding by repeatable integer coding.
Step 2: initialize the population and generate a population containing m individuals, each containing one chromosome, at this point, set as the initial population.
Step 3: non-dominated stratification of the individuals of the initial population.
Step 4: calculate the fitness of the individuals of the initial population based on the results of the non-dominated stratification in step 3.

Step 5: select a certain number of individuals in the initial population as the evolutionary generation 0 according to the calculation result in step 4, and all individuals of the initial population are selected as generation 0 in this paper.

Step 6: start evolution, take generation i ($i \in \{0 \leq i < 50$ and k is an integer$\}$) as the parent, perform crossover and mutation operations on the individuals of the parent to generate the children corresponding to the parent of generation i, and fuse the individuals of the parent and children of generation i.

Step 7: decode the fused individuals from step 6 and calculate the objective function values of the fused individuals.

Step 8: non-dominated stratification of the fused individuals from step 6 and calculation of their crowding degree.

Step 9: according to the calculation result of step 8, select m individuals as the $(i+1)th$ generation according to the non-dominated stratification level from the lowest to the highest and when the same level according to the crowding degree from the largest to the smallest, and return to step 6 if the required number of evolutionary iterations is not satisfied.

Step 10: the $(i+1)th$ generation of individuals has been noted as the Pareto solution and the corresponding solution is the Pareto frontier solution [36–38].

The algorithm terminates.

The basic flow chart of the algorithm is shown in the following Figure 9.

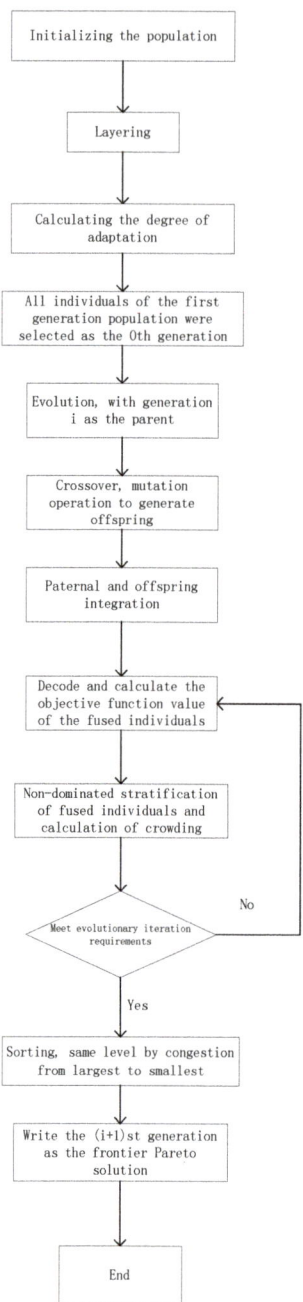

Figure 9. The basic process of mutation operation.

6. Analysis of Results

6.1. Candidate Points

(1) Execution of the algorithm yields the SSE versus K plot, as shown in Figure 10.

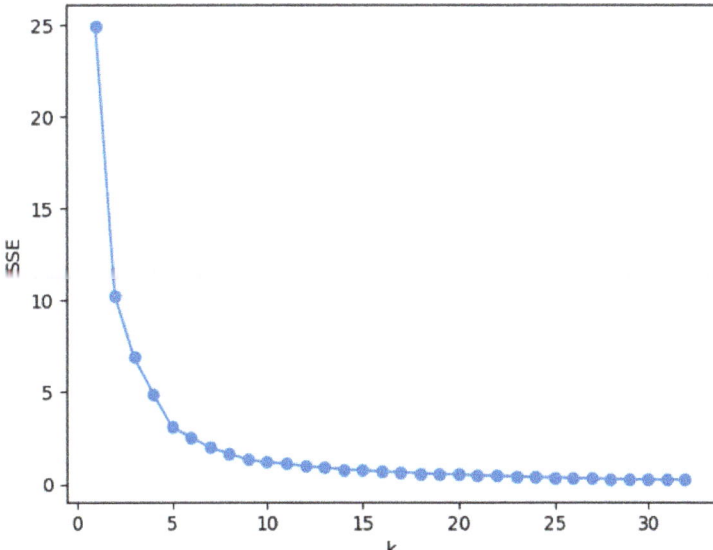

Figure 10. SSE versus K.

From the above Figure 8, it can be seen that the inflection point appears between K = 5 and K = 10. It is known from the rule of elbow law that $K_0 = 15$ should satisfy $5 \leq K_0 \leq 10$, but considering the actual demand, K_0 can be expanded appropriately by the rule of on-demand selection law, and $K_0 = 15$ is taken in this paper.

(2) Take $K_0 = 15$, execute K-means algorithm, get 15 clustering centers, and use them as candidate processing centers, whose latitude and longitude information is shown in Table 4, and the location schematic is shown in Figure 11.

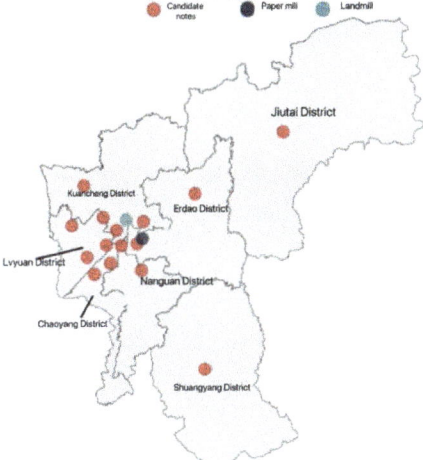

Figure 11. Schematic diagram of the location of the candidate nodes, paper mill, and landfill.

Table 4. Latitude and longitude of candidate nodes.

Serial Number	Latitude/°N	Longitude/°E	Serial Number	Latitude/°N	Longitude/°E
1	44.20957	125.9666	9	43.89134	125.3411
2	43.85894	125.2093	10	43.97082	125.2716
3	43.54504	125.6638	11	43.9477	125.1507
4	43.84200	125.2989	12	43.95960	125.4261
5	44.05939	125.1975	13	44.03693	125.6269
6	43.82241	125.4182	14	43.89649	125.4009
7	43.89262	125.2839	15	43.81163	125.2380
8	43.93453	125.3227			

6.1.1. Classification of Candidate Nodes in Region M

Considering the economic development status of seven districts, this paper delineates four categories of regions A, B, C, and D, as shown in Figure 12.

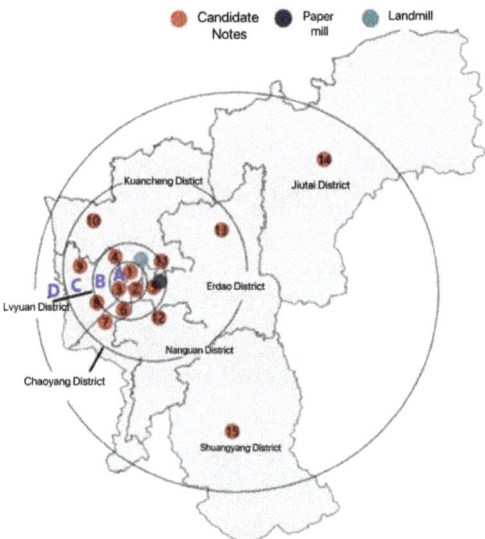

Figure 12. Schematic diagram of candidate node sub-region location.

According to the above classification results, the regions to which each candidate node belongs are shown in Table 5.

Table 5. Classification regions and administrative regions to which each candidate node belongs.

Candidate Nodes	Classification Area	Administrative District	Candidate Nodes	Classification Area	Administrative District
1	A	Kuancheng District	9	C	Lvyuan District
2	A	Nanguan District	10	C	Kuancheng District
3	A	Lvyuan District	11	C	Kuancheng District
4	B	Lvyuan District	12	C	Nanguan District
5	B	Erdao District	13	C	Erdao District
6	B	Chaoyang District	14	D	Jiutai District
7	C	Chaoyang District	15	D	Shuangyang District
8	C	Lvyuan District			

6.1.2. Determination of The Distance between Candidate Nodes

The latitude and longitude of 15 nodes can be known from Table 3, and the distance between any two points (L_1, N_1) and (L_2, N_2) is calculated using Equation (20) to obtain the distance between each candidate node, as shown in Table 6.

$$d = \sqrt{[111(N_1 - N_2)]^2 + \{111[E_1 \cos(N_1) - E_2 \cos(N_2)]\}^2} \qquad (21)$$

Table 6. Distance between candidate nodes.

Serial Number	1	2	3	4	5	6	7	8
23.86859	0	40.23685	12.67707	23.22249	44.70217	29.2916	73.10302	13.03013
16.60001	40.23685	0	29.87562	18.59793	6.318052	10.96083	113.3377	27.81905
13.40235	12.67707	29.87562	0	11.51298	33.4658	19.47316	84.28883	3.378439
3.75025	23.22249	18.59793	11.51298	0	21.95307	9.150016	95.73491	10.19329
20.84032	44.70217	6.318052	33.4658	21.95307	0	16.03422	117.6109	31.87447
6.106751	29.2916	10.96083	19.47316	9.150016	16.03422	0	102.3944	17.09786
96.87778	73.10302	113.3377	84.28883	95.73491	117.6109	102.3944	0	85.74007
11.22128	13.03013	27.81905	3.378439	10.19329	31.87447	17.09786	85.74007	0
39.59672	63.28908	23.0548	52.68995	41.21885	19.52163	34.00031	136.3915	50.81169
4.792569	19.34723	20.89395	10.23743	6.236652	25.49322	9.973975	92.44419	7.36417
8.717617	16.11011	24.30006	9.500052	9.929159	29.18902	13.34816	89.14593	6.131975
35.19108	48.15778	30.43948	45.10163	38.93564	35.71272	30.90118	114.8546	41.757
16.30645	30.78207	18.70151	25.93917	20.0393	25.01903	13.35269	101.709	22.63918
7.435185	27.15075	14.28599	19.15585	11.17926	20.04865	4.903537	99.99842	16.22207
0	23.86859	16.60001	13.40235	3.75025	20.84032	6.106751	96.87778	11.22128

Serial Number	9	10	11	12	13	14	15
1	63.28908	19.34723	16.11011	48.15778	30.78207	27.15075	23.86859
2	23.0548	20.89395	24.30006	30.43948	18.70151	14.28599	16.60001
3	52.68995	10.23743	9.500052	45.10163	25.93917	19.15585	13.40235
4	41.21885	6.236652	9.929159	38.93564	20.0393	11.17926	3.75025
5	19.52163	25.49322	29.18902	35.71272	25.01903	20.04865	20.84032
6	34.00031	9.973975	13.34816	30.90118	13.35269	4.903537	6.106751
7	136.3915	92.44419	89.14593	114.8546	101.709	99.99842	96.87778
8	50.81169	7.36417	6.131975	41.757	22.63918	16.22207	11.22128
9	0	43.94864	47.30247	39.51704	38.13702	36.7922	39.59672
10	43.94864	0	3.958057	35.54501	16.25327	8.920409	4.792569
11	47.30247	3.958057	0	35.63389	16.58221	11.11113	8.717617
12	39.51704	35.54501	35.63389	0	19.29206	27.75662	35.19108
13	38.13702	16.25327	16.58221	19.29206	0	9.082896	16.30645
14	36.7922	8.920409	11.11113	27.75662	9.082896	0	7.435185
15	39.59672	4.792569	8.717617	35.19108	16.30645	7.435185	0

6.1.3. Determination of the Candidate Node Express Volume

According to the previous data, the design values were weighted according to the average ratio of the population in the seven districts of the M region to the total population of Changchun, and the results are shown in Table 7.

The classification results of the candidate nodes, Nanguan District has one class A and C regional nodes, respectively, candidate nodes 2 and 12, known from Table 1 Nanguan District express the business volume of 103,352,300 pieces. This paper assumes that the ratio of A and C regional nodes express business volume in Nanguan District is 7: 3, then the express business volume of candidate nodes 2 and 12 are 7234.65967 and 3100.56843 million pieces. According to the above rules, the express business volume of each candidate node is shown in Table 8.

Table 7. Express business volume by district.

Administrative District	Express Business Volume/Million Pieces
Nanguan District	103.3523
Kuancheng District	90.56302
Chaoyang District	103.4675
Erdao District	79.95588
Lvyuan District	90.23914
Shuangyang District	50.62379
Jiutai District	92.637

Table 8. Express the business volume of each candidate node.

Candidate Nodes	Express Business Volume/Million Pieces	Candidate Nodes	Express Business Volume/Million Pieces
1	54.33781	9	9.023914
2	72.3466	10	18.1126
3	45.11957	11	18.1126
4	27.07174	12	31.00568
5	47.97353	13	31.98235
6	62.08048	14	50.62379
7	41.38699	15	92.637
8	9.023914		

6.2. Number of Iterations, Crossover Variance Probability Selection

In this paper, we use Python 3.8.5 for algorithm implementation, in which some sub-functions directly call the functions of the Geatpy library, such as selection sub-functions and crossover sub-functions.

In this paper, we set the number of population individuals m = 100 and M = 3000, in the actual problem, the number of iterations will have a large impact on the performance of the whole algorithm, so in this paper, the two single objectives of total cost and carbon dioxide total emission, as shown in Figure 13, where the blue line indicates the average value and the red line indicates the minimum value, it can be seen that both the average value and the minimum value decrease gradually with the increase of the number of generations and tend to be stable, and both objective functions show good convergence, so it is feasible to take M = 3000.

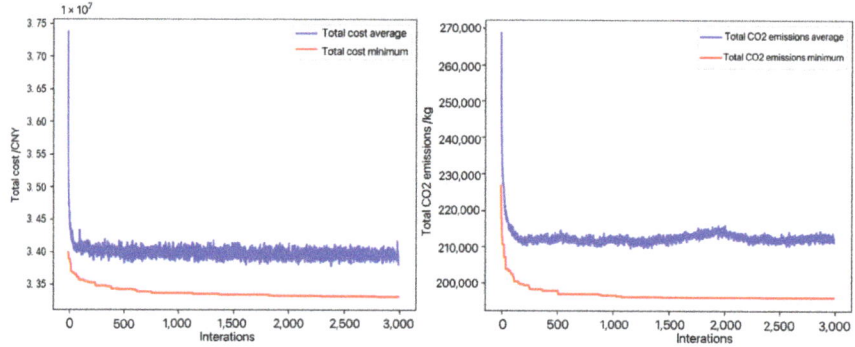

Figure 13. Plot of the total cost–number of iterations, total carbon dioxide emissions–number of iterations c (M = 3000).

In this paper, we compare and analyze the relevant indicators for four cases with cross-variance probabilities of 0.9, 0.8, 0.7, and 0.6. Total cost vs. total carbon dioxide emissions relationship diagram (cross-variance probability is 0.9, 0.8, 0.7, 0.6) as shown in Figure 14A–D and Table 9.

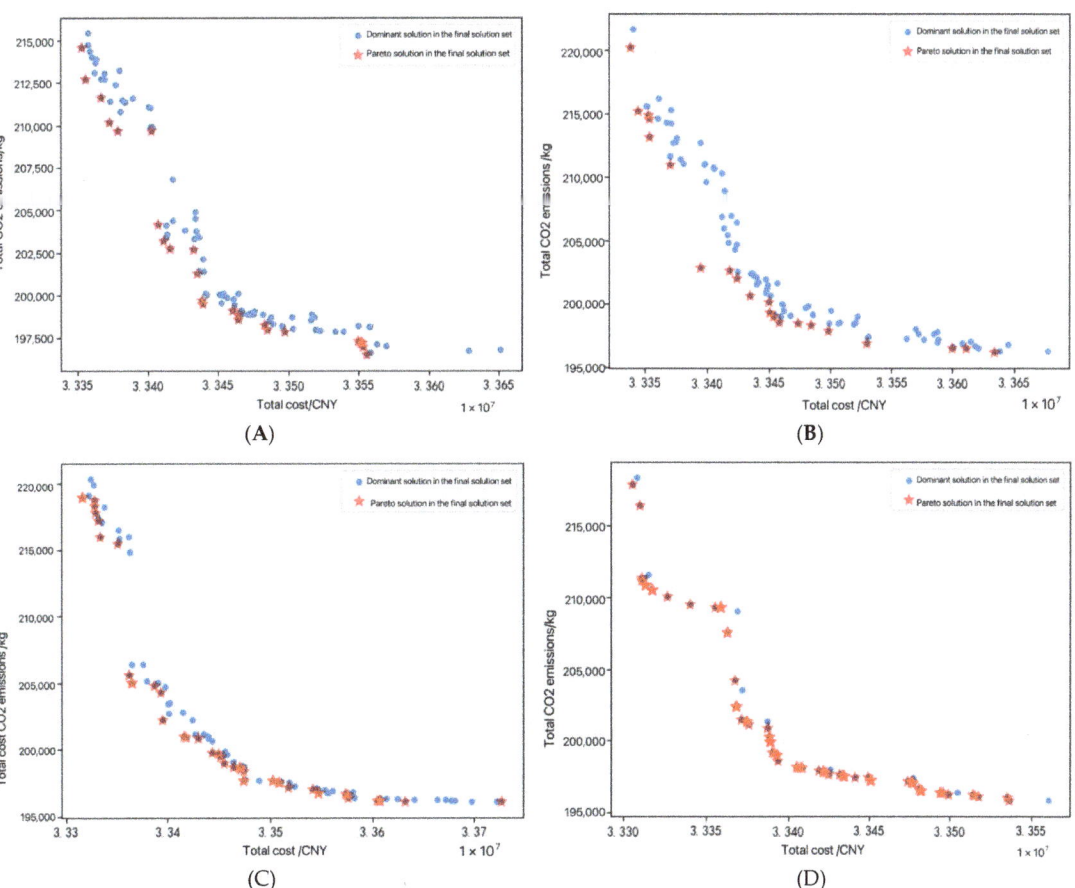

Figure 14. (**A**) Total cost vs. total carbon dioxide emissions relationship diagram (cross-variance probability is 0.9). (**B**) Total cost and total carbon dioxide emissions relationship diagram (cross-variance probability is 0.8). (**C**) Total cost versus total carbon dioxide emissions relationship diagram (cross-variance probability is 0.7). (**D**) Total cost and total carbon dioxide emissions relationship diagram (cross-variance probability is 0.6).

Table 9. Correlation indicators.

Cross-Variance Probabilities	Indicator Name	Percentage of Non-Dominated Solutions	HV	Spacing
0.9	Numerical value	0.24	0.016768	3312.822067
0.8	Numerical value	0.21	0.019379	3649.327564
0.7	Numerical value	0.43	0.019267	2713.471153
0.6	Numerical value	0.88	0.017934	3232.380758

Note: After testing, each index fluctuates somewhat during repeated calculations, and the best value in each calculation process is taken.

Integrating the three indicators of non-dominated solution percentage, HV, and Spacings, and the final three generated images, this paper selects the case of M = 3000 and the probability of cross-variance is 0.7 for analysis, and pools the analysis results to give management suggestions. According to the results of the selection of the number of iterations, this paper runs the procedure at M = 3000 and the cross-variance probability is 0.7, and a total of 43 Pareto solutions are obtained, as shown in Figure 15, which can be more clearly seen in the Pareto frontier solutions [39,40].

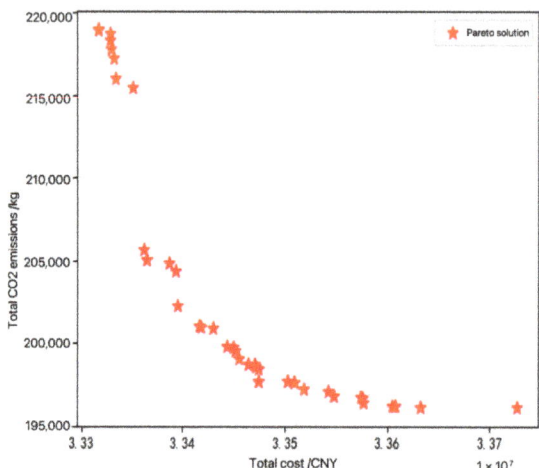

Figure 15. Total cost and carbon dioxide emissions Pareto solution set.

For further analysis, the obtained Pareto solution sets can be classified into I, II, and III, as shown in Figure 16.

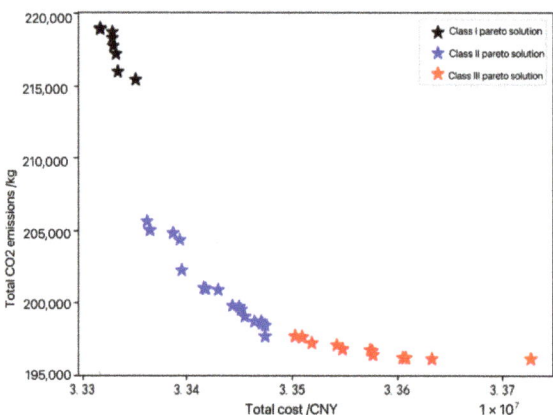

Figure 16. Classification of total cost and total carbon dioxide emissions (M = 3000) Pareto solution set.

Among them, the total cost of class I is at a low level and carbon emission is at a high level, the total cost and carbon emission of class II are both at a medium level, and the total cost of class III is at a high level and carbon emission is at a low level. For different development stages of recycling system construction and development, different solution sets of different regions can be selected as design solutions under the consideration of total cost and carbon emission only. When the whole society's recycling system has developed to a certain extent, Region III can be chosen.

In this paper, one point from each of the three categories I, II, and III is randomly selected for analysis, and the selected points are shown in Figure 17.

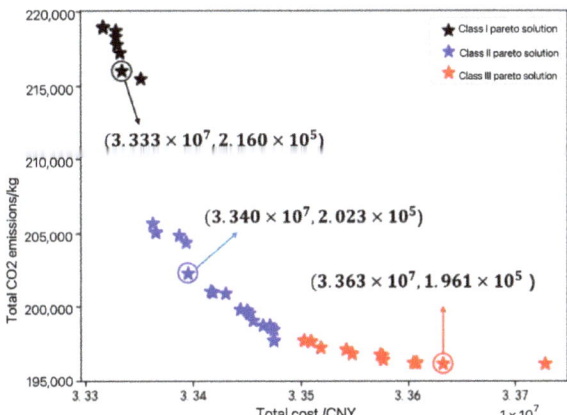

Figure 17. Schematic diagram of sample solution selection for the Pareto solution of total cost and total carbon dioxide emissions (M = 3000).

The coordinates of the point selected for Class I are $(3.333 \times 10^7, 2.160 \times 10^5)$, which is noted as the sample solution for Class I, i.e., the total cost is 3.333×10^7 CNY and carbon emission is 2.160×10^5 kg. The first, second, third, and fourth parts of the chromosome corresponding to this point are coded as

$$\begin{bmatrix} 14 & 10 & 4 & 7 & 11 & 7 & 4 & 14 & 5 & 14 & 14 & 13 & 13 & 12 & 14 \end{bmatrix}$$
$$\begin{bmatrix} 2 & 1 & 1 & 2 & 3 & 4 & 2 & 4 & 4 & 1 & 3 & 4 & 4 & 2 & 4 \end{bmatrix}$$
$$\begin{bmatrix} 2 & 2 & 3 & 1 & 2 & 1 & 2 & 2 & 4 & 2 & 2 & 1 & 2 & 1 & 2 \end{bmatrix}$$
$$\begin{bmatrix} 3 & 3 & 1 & 2 & 3 & 1 & 3 & 4 & 3 & 2 & 4 & 2 & 3 & 4 & 4 \end{bmatrix}$$
$$\begin{bmatrix} 2 & 3 & 2 & 1 & 3 & 2 & 3 & 3 & 1 & 1 & 3 & 3 & 3 & 3 & 3 \end{bmatrix}$$

According to the algorithm design rules, the above code is decoded to obtain the recycling center responsible for each processing center, the model used, and the technology used, as shown in Table 10 (for convenience, Table 11 notes the recycling center to the processing center as Section 1, the processing center back to the recycling center as Section 2, and the processing center to the landfill and paper mill as Section 3, the same as the following table). The location of each node is shown in Figure 18A.

Table 10. Class I sample solution analysis.

Processing Center	Recycling Center in Charge	Road Section 1	Road Section 2	Road Section 3	Technical Processing
4	3	1	3	1	1
5	9	4	4	3	1
7	4, 6	2, 4	1, 1	2, 1	1, 2
10	2	1	2	3	3
11	5	3	2	3	3
12	14	2	1	4	3
13	12, 13	4, 4	1, 2	2, 3	3, 3
14	1, 8, 10, 11, 15	2, 4, 1, 3, 4	2, 2, 2, 2, 2	3, 4, 2, 4, 4	2, 3, 1, 3, 3

Table 11. Class II sample solution analysis.

Processing Center	Recycling Center in Charge	Road Section			Technical Processing
		1	2	3	
3	7	2	2	3	3
4	3	2	2	3	3
5	9	4	4	2	2
6	1	4	2	3	3
7	4, 6	2, 2	1, 1	2, 1	2, 3
10	2	2	2	3	3
11	5	3	2	4	3
12	14	1	1	3	3
13	13	4	2	3	3
14	8, 10, 11, 12, 15	4, 1, 3, 4, 4	2, 1, 2, 2, 2	4, 4, 3, 3, 4	3, 2, 3, 3, 3

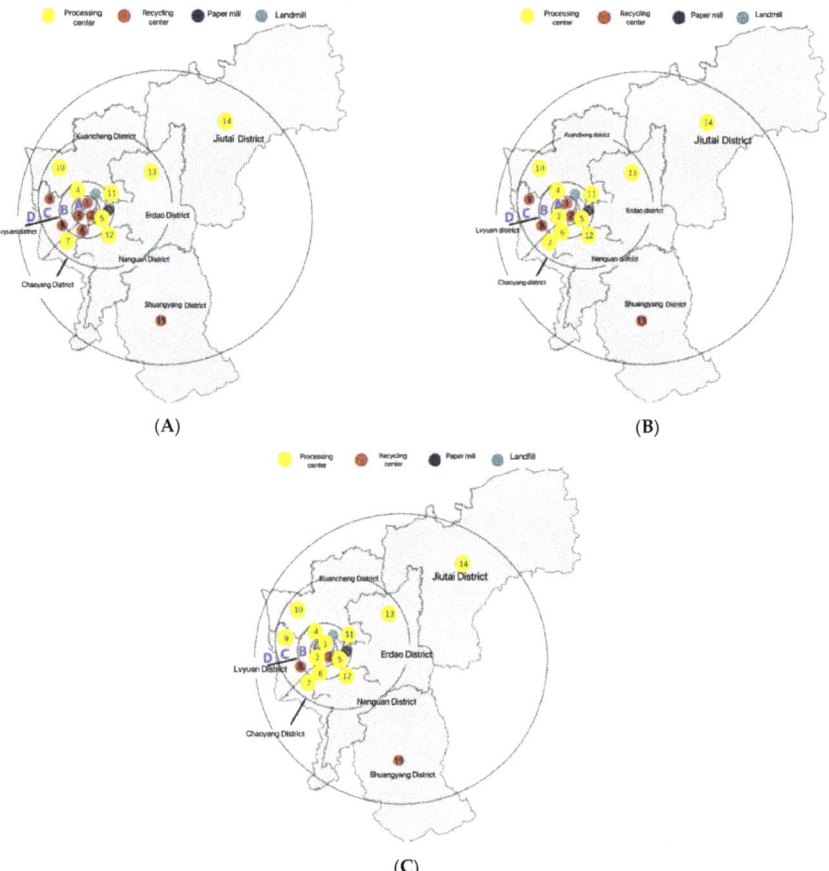

Figure 18. (A) Schematic diagram of the location of each node of the class I sample solution. (B) Schematic diagram of the location of each node of the class II sample solution. (C) Location diagram of nodes of Class III sample solutions.

The coordinates of the point selected for class II are $(3.340 \times 10^7, 2.023 \times 10^5)$, which is noted as the sample solution for class II, i.e., the total cost is 3.340×10^7 CNY and the carbon emission is 2.023×10^5 kg. The first, second, third, and forth parts of the chromosome corresponding to this point are coded as

$$\begin{bmatrix} 6 & 10 & 4 & 7 & 11 & 7 & 3 & 14 & 5 & 14 & 14 & 13 & 13 & 12 & 14 \end{bmatrix}$$
$$\begin{bmatrix} 4 & 2 & 1 & 2 & 3 & 2 & 2 & 4 & 4 & 1 & 3 & 4 & 4 & 1 & 4 \end{bmatrix}$$
$$\begin{bmatrix} 2 & 2 & 3 & 1 & 2 & 1 & 2 & 2 & 4 & 1 & 2 & 2 & 2 & 1 & 2 \end{bmatrix}$$
$$\begin{bmatrix} 3 & 3 & 1 & 2 & 4 & 1 & 3 & 4 & 2 & 4 & 3 & 3 & 3 & 3 & 4 \end{bmatrix}$$
$$\begin{bmatrix} 3 & 3 & 2 & 2 & 3 & 3 & 3 & 2 & 2 & 3 & 3 & 3 & 3 & 3 \end{bmatrix}$$

The above codes were decoded to obtain the recycling centers responsible for each processing center, the models used, and the technologies used, as shown in Table 11. The location of each node is shown in Figure 18B.

The coordinates of the point selected for class III are $(3.363 \times 10^7, 1.961 \times 10^5)$, which is noted as the sample solution for class III, i.e., total cost is 3.363×10^7 CNY and carbon emission is 1.961×10^5 kg. The first, second, third, and fourth parts of the chromosome corresponding to this point are coded as,

$$\begin{bmatrix} 6 & 10 & 4 & 7 & 11 & 12 & 3 & 14 & 5 & 9 & 14 & 1 & 13 & 12 & 7 \end{bmatrix}$$
$$\begin{bmatrix} 3 & 4 & 3 & 3 & 3 & 4 & 2 & 4 & 2 & 2 & 3 & 3 & 4 & 4 & 4 \end{bmatrix}$$
$$\begin{bmatrix} 1 & 2 & 3 & 1 & 3 & 3 & 2 & 2 & 4 & 1 & 4 & 2 & 2 & 1 & 2 \end{bmatrix}$$
$$\begin{bmatrix} 3 & 3 & 1 & 2 & 3 & 2 & 3 & 3 & 3 & 4 & 4 & 4 & 3 & 3 & 3 \end{bmatrix}$$
$$\begin{bmatrix} 2 & 3 & 2 & 2 & 3 & 2 & 3 & 3 & 2 & 1 & 3 & 3 & 3 & 3 & 2 \end{bmatrix}$$

After the above encoding and decoding, the recycling centers, models, and technologies adopted by each processing center are obtained, as shown in Table 12. The location of each node is shown in Figure 18(C).

Table 12. Class III sample solution analysis.

Processing Center	Recycling Center in Charge	Road Section			Technical Processing
		1	2	3	
1	12	3	2	4	3
3	7	2	2	3	3
4	3	3	3	1	2
5	9	2	4	3	2
6	1	3	1	3	2
7	4, 15	3, 4	1, 2	2, 3	2, 2
9	10	2	1	4	1
10	2	4	2	3	3
11	5	3	3	3	3
12	6, 14	4, 4	4, 1	2, 3	2, 3
13	13	4	2	3	3
14	8, 11	4, 3	2, 4	3, 4	3, 3

Compare and analyze the sample solutions of class I, II, and III selected above: From the perspective of site selection, it can be seen that among the nodes selected by class I sample solutions, 2 nodes are located in region B, 5 nodes are located in region C, and 1 node is located in region D. Among the nodes selected by region B sample solutions, 1 node is located in region A, 3 nodes are located in region B, 5 nodes are located in region C, and 1 node is located in region D. Among the nodes selected by class III sample solutions,

2 nodes are located in region A, 4 are located in region B, 5 are located in region C, and 1 is located in region D, and the node selected by the sample solution of class III contains class II, and class II contains class I. From the perspective of the selected vehicle types, excluding some invalid codes such as starting and ending points being the same node, it can be seen that the transportation modes between nodes are widely selected, and all four types of vehicles have been applied. From the perspective of the selected technology, it can be seen that the same processing center can choose 2 or more kinds of processing technology, and each processing technology has an application. To sum up, after selecting the regional category, the specific location, vehicle type, and technology should be taken into consideration to optimize the whole system.

7. Conclusions

Green and low-carbon products are becoming increasingly popular, and green carbon reduction has become the mainstream way of consumption upgrading. This paper analyzes and summarizes the existing courier packaging recycling model, and establishes a new courier packaging recycling model based on the concept of sharing from a low-carbon perspective. From the perspective of engineering research, this paper proposes a complete set of reverse logistics network design process for express packaging, especially from the existing express network, and establishes a network optimization model by combining qualitative and quantitative analysis, which provides a certain technical reference value for similar projects. From the application value point of view, this paper defines the scope of region M. According to the population of each administrative region in region M, the design value is used to weight according to the population number to estimate the courier volume of each administrative region in region M. The location information of 535 courier points in region M was obtained and filtered. The courier packaging recycling mode adopted in region M was determined. This paper also randomly selects one sample solution from each of the three types of solution sets, conducts the coding interpretation of site selection, vehicle selection, and processing technology selection and gives an example design scheme. The express packaging recycling network constructed in this paper can avoid the waste of express packaging, reduce environmental pollution, and promote the sustainable development of social environment and economy for the social development of region M. For the express enterprises in region M, it can improve the utilization rate of express packaging, reduce the cost, actively assume social responsibility, and establish a good corporate image. There are shortcomings in this paper. Affected by the epidemic, there are large errors in the estimation of express business volume in each administrative region of M. The performance of the program written by the relevant algorithm is unstable, and the time complexity and space complexity are not considered, and the algorithm design and program writing should be further optimized. In future research, this aspect should be considered more comprehensively and carefully.

Author Contributions: Conceptualization, J.M. and J.C.; methodology, J.C.; software, J.C.; validation, X.L. and H.Z.; formal analysis, J.C. and C.L.; investigation, J.M.; resources, X.L.; data curation, J.C.; writing—original draft preparation, J.C.; writing—review and editing, H.Z.; visualization, C.L. and X.L.; supervision, C.L. and H.Z.; project administration, H.Z. and C.L. All authors have read and agreed to the published version of the manuscript.

Funding: This research received no external funding.

Data Availability Statement: Not applicable.

Acknowledgments: The authors thank the editor and the anonymous referees for their helpful comments and critics, and Professor Guangdong Tian for helpful discussions and guidance.

Conflicts of Interest: The authors declare no conflict of interest.

Appendix A

Table A1. Total population of each district in Region M.

Name of Administrative Region	Year		
	2020	2019	2018
Nanguan District	764,163	744,357	717,550
Kuancheng District	663,020	651,892	645,688
Chaoyang District	758,991	747,508	729,875
Erdao District	580,277	579,356	577,012
Lvyuan District	651,033	654,046	659,108
Shuangyang District	364,782	366,780	371,912
Jiutai District	667,942	671,291	679,336
Total population of Changchun	7,537,969	7,512,896	7,511,748

Table A2. The proportion of the population of each district in the total population of Changchun in M region.

Name of Administrative Region	The Percentage of the Population in the Current Year			
	2020	2019	2018	2018–2020
Nanguan District	10.14%	9.91%	9.55%	9.95%
Kuancheng District	8.80%	8.68%	8.60%	8.72%
Chaoyang District	10.07%	9.95%	9.72%	9.96%
Erdao District	7.70%	7.71%	7.68%	7.70%
Lvyuan District	8.64%	8.71%	8.77%	8.69%
Shuangyang District	4.84%	4.88%	4.95%	4.87%
Jiutai District	8.86%	8.94%	9.04%	8.92%

Table A3. Location of express points in Nanguan District.

Serial Number	Latitude/°N	Longitude /°E	Serial Number	Latitude/°N	Longitude/°E
1	43.837454	125.327664	51	43.85571	125.400205
2	43.789996	125.437189	52	43.843923	125.425986
3	43.88474	125.350858	53	43.803751	125.315023
4	43.893736	125.35813	54	43.750018	125.409793
5	43.834801	125.333301	55	43.899874	125.332733
6	43.827144	125.329905	56	43.827882	125.414442
7	43.840422	125.373367	57	43.878994	125.336723
8	43.826949	125.375575	58	43.896309	125.351509
9	43.882053	125.349496	59	43.882392	125.347125
10	43.842641	125.374858	60	43.905428	125.342984
11	43.906604	125.343757	61	43.861626	125.359128
12	43.844766	125.380254	62	43.844444	125.38038
13	43.813458	125.457464	63	43.813495	125.465922
14	43.897753	125.338467	64	43.802057	125.283431
15	43.782392	125.406786	65	43.85151	125.450023
16	43.820709	125.314338	66	43.891005	125.339234
17	43.842253	125.40775	67	43.903562	125.344714
18	43.827599	125.32845	68	43.891354	125.337182
19	43.830943	125.309065	69	43.81103	125.400753
20	43.879202	125.334329	70	43.835494	125.433065
21	43.827144	125.329905	71	43.789372	125.375345
22	43.796082	125.309145	72	43.871081	125.353375
23	43.869381	125.339793	73	43.893203	125.350009
24	43.839403	125.356681	74	43.897777	125.345988
25	43.842627	125.348033	75	43.915569	125.360708
26	43.805436	125.29279	76	43.77458	125.269852

Table A3. Cont.

Serial Number	Latitude/°N	Longitude /°E	Serial Number	Latitude/°N	Longitude/°E
27	43.908228	125.353404	77	43.788377	125.267272
28	43.833878	125.377279	78	43.872522	125.360277
29	43.793152	125.398239	79	43.80733	125.454246
30	43.861092	125.388539	80	43.828481	125.318853
31	43.843238	125.425431	81	43.798887	125.30516
32	43.840715	125.360151	82	43.793443	125.315005
33	43.812281	125.402488	83	43.837223	125.406287
34	43.834626	125.39462	84	43.844025	125.339175
35	43.85298	125.450993	85	43.792858	125.42437
36	43.832712	125.391496	86	43.841206	125.410059
37	43.835115	125.442014	87	43.792006	125.395835
38	43.893361	125.352221	88	43.852766	125.356367
39	43.8931	125.34364	89	43.899677	125.344485
40	43.89796	125.352507	90	43.802605	125.336546
41	43.860657	125.369726	91	43.880092	125.345643
42	43.838179	125.460384	92	43.899882	125.332816
43	43.826313	125.378839	93	43.833841	125.367847
44	43.83805	125.412816	94	43.840575	125.408217
45	43.834954	125.392255	95	43.833253	125.388789
46	43.893672	125.346473	96	43.82796	125.379248
47	43.903571	125.353122	97	43.835528	125.380312
48	43.790302	125.440001	98	43.811003	125.397103
49	43.82728	125.375988	99	43.821876	125.453335
50	43.837934	125.300282			

References

1. Yan, H.; Wu, L.; Yi, X.; Wang, D.D.; Li, X. Discussion on green express packaging. In Proceedings of the International Conference of Green Buildings and Environmental Management (GBEM), Qingdao, China, 23–25 August 2018.
2. Liang, H.P.; Li, J.G. Research on the creative design of express package recycling system basis on internet. *IOP Conf. Ser. Earth Environ. Sci.* **2020**, *463*, 012089. [CrossRef]
3. Xiao, Y.M.; Zhou, B.Y. Does the development of the delivery industry increase the production of municipal solid waste?-An empirical study of China. *Resour. Conserv. Recycl.* **2020**, *155*, 104577. [CrossRef]
4. High, X.; Liu, C.S. Research on customers' willingness to participate in express package recycling. In Proceedings of the 5th International Conference on Energy Materials and Environment Engineering, Kuala Lumpur, Malaysia, 12–14 April 2019.
5. Ding, Z.H.; Sun, J.; Wang, Y.W.; Jiang, X.H.; Liu, R.; Sun, W.B.; Mou, Y.P.; Wang, D.W.; Liu, M.Z. Research on the influence of anthropomorphic design on the consumers' express packaging recycling willingness: The moderating effect of psychological ownership. *Resour. Conserv. Recycl.* **2021**, *168*, 105269. [CrossRef]
6. Carfí, D.; Donato, A. Plastic-pollution reduction and bio-resources preservation using green-packaging game coopetition. *Mathematics* **2022**, *10*, 4553. [CrossRef]
7. Cheng, L.; Cao, G.R. Present situation and ideas of express packaging organization. *Adv. Graph. Commun. Media Technol.* **2017**, *417*, 697–703. [CrossRef]
8. Yang, H.T.; Li, W.L. Construction of express packaging recovery logistics system from the perspective of ecological innovation—Take Xinyang Normal University as an example. In Proceedings of the 25th Annual International Conference on Management Science and Engineering, Frankfurt, Germany, 17–20 August 2018.
9. Cai, K.H.; Xie, Y.F.; Song, Q.B.; Sheng, N.; Wen, Z.G. Identifying the status and differences between urban and rural residents' behaviors and attitudes toward express packaging waste management in Guangdong Province, China. *Sci. Total Environ.* **2021**, *797*, 148996. [CrossRef]
10. Duan, H.B.; Song, G.H.; Qu, S.; Dong, X.B.; Xu, M. Post-consumer packaging waste from express delivery in China. *Resour. Conserv. Recycl.* **2019**, *14*, 137–143. [CrossRef]
11. Ren, X.; Wang, Y.H. Design of express recyclable packaging bag based on green environmental packaging material. In Proceedings of the 5th International Conference on Environmental Science and Material Application (ESMA), Xi'an, China, 15–16 December 2019.
12. Guo, Y.L.; Luo, G.L.; Hou, G.S. Research on the evolution of the express packaging recycling strategy, considering government subsidies and synergy benefits. *Int. J. Environ. Res. Public Health* **2021**, *18*, 1144. [CrossRef]
13. Hua, Y.F.; Dong, F.; Goodman, J. How to leverage the role of social capital in pro-environmental behavior: A case study of residents' express waste recycling behavior in China. *J. Clean. Prod.* **2021**, *28*, 124376. [CrossRef]

14. Wu, S.S.; Gong, X.; Wang, Y.F.; Cao, J. Consumer cognition and management perspective on express packaging pollution. *Int. J. Environ. Res. Public Health* **2022**, *19*, 4895. [CrossRef]
15. Chen, F.Y.; Chen, H.; Yang, J.H.; Long, R.Y.; Li, W.B. Impact of regulatory focus on express packaging waste recycling behavior: The moderating role of psychological empowerment perception. *Environ. Sci. Pollut. Res.* **2019**, *26*, 8862–8874. [CrossRef] [PubMed]
16. Zheng, C.L.; Zhou, Y.Y. Multi-criteria group decision-making approach for express packaging recycling under interval-valued fuzzy information: Combining objective and subjective compatibilities. *Int. J. Fuzzy Syst.* **2022**, *24*, 1112–1130. [CrossRef]
17. Lin, G.; Chang, H.M.; Li, X.; Li, R.; Zhao, Y. Integrated environmental impacts and c-footprint reduction potential in treatment and recycling of express delivery packaging waste. *Resour. Conserv. Recycl.* **2022**, *179*, 106078. [CrossRef]
18. Harsaj, F.; Aghaeipour, Y.; Sadeghpoor, M.; Rajaee, Y. A fuzzy multi-objective model for a sustainable end-of-life vehicle reverse logistic network design: Two meta-heuristic algorithms. *Int. J. Value Chain Manag.* **2022**, *13*, 47–87. [CrossRef]
19. Gao, X.H.; Cao, C.J. A novel multi-objective scenario-based optimization model for sustainable reverse logistics supply chain network redesign considering facility reconstruction. *J. Clean. Prod.* **2020**, *270*, 122405. [CrossRef]
20. Nie, D.X.; Li, H.T.; Qu, T.; Liu, Y.; Li, C.D. Optimizing supply chain configuration with low carbon emission. *J. Clean. Prod.* **2020**, *271*, 122539. [CrossRef]
21. Guo, J.Q.; Wang, X.Y.; Fan, S.Y.; Gen, M. Forward and reverse logistics network and route planning under the environment of low-carbon emissions: A case study of Shanghai fresh food e-commerce enterprises. *Comput. Ind. Eng.* **2017**, *106*, 351–360. [CrossRef]
22. Reddy, K.N.; Kumar, A.; Sarkis, J.; Tiwari, M.K. Effect of the carbon tax on reverse logistics network design. *Comput. Ind. Eng.* **2020**, *139*, 106184. [CrossRef]
23. Yang, J.H.; Long, R.Y.; Chen, H.; Sun, Q.Q. A comparative analysis of express packaging waste recycling models based on the differential game theory. *Resour. Conserv. Recycl.* **2021**, *168*, 105449. [CrossRef]
24. Wu, J.; Azarm, S. Metrics for quality assessment of a multiobjective design optimization solution set. *J. Mech. Des.* **2001**, *123*, 18–25. [CrossRef]
25. Liu, Q.G.; Liu, X.X.; Wu, J.; Li, Y.X. Multiattribute group decision-making method using a genetic K-Means clustering algorithm. *Math. Probl. Eng.* **2020**, *2020*, 8313892. [CrossRef]
26. Deb, K.; Pratap, A.; Agarwal, S.; Meyarivan, T. A fast and elitist multiobjective genetic algorithm: NSGA-II. *IEEE Trans. Evol. Comput.* **2002**, *6*, 182–197. [CrossRef]
27. Liang, X.; Chen, J.B.; Gu, X.L.; Huang, M. Improved adaptive non-dominated sorting genetic algorithm with elite strategy for solving multi-objective flexible job-shop scheduling problem. *IEEE Access* **2021**, *9*, 106352–106362. [CrossRef]
28. Pulansari, F. The analysis of cost drivers to successful implementation of reverse logistics system. In Proceedings of the 1st International Conference on Industrial and Manufacturing Engineering (ICI and ME), Medan, Indonesia, 16–17 October 2018.
29. Xu, J.G.; Qiao, Z.; Liu, J.H. Study on cost control of enterprise reverse logistics based on the analysis of cost drivers. In Proceedings of the 3rd International Conference on Wireless Communications, Networking and Mobile Computing (WiCOM 2007), Shanghai, China, 21–25 September 2007.
30. Fang, X.H.; Li, N.; Mu, H. Research progress on logistics network optimization under low carbon constraints. In Proceedings of the International Conference on Green Development and Environmental Science and Technology (ICGDE), Changsha, China, 18–20 September 2020.
31. Wang, B.; Li, H.H. Optimization of Electronic Waste Recycling Network Designing. In Proceedings of the 5th International Conference on Electromechanical Control Technology and Transportation (ICECTT), Network, Nanchang, China, 15–17 May 2020.
32. Chen, M.; Yin, C.J.; Xi, Y.P. A new clustering algorithm Partition K-means. In Proceedings of the International Conference on Advanced Materials and Computer Science, Chengdu, China, 1–2 May 2011.
33. Ge, F.H.; Luo, Y. An improved K-means algorithm based on weighted euclidean distance. In Proceedings of the 3rd International Confrence on Theoretical and Mathematical Foundations of Computer (ICTMF 2012), Bali, Indonesia, 1–2 December 2012.
34. Deb, K.; Agrawal, R.B. Simulated binary crossover for continuous search space. *Complex Syst.* **1995**, *9*, 115–148.
35. Deb, K.; Goyal, M.A. Combined genetic adaptive search (GeneAS) for engineering design. *Comput. Sci. Inform.* **1996**, *26*, 30–45.
36. Vachhani, V.L.; Dabhi, V.K.; Prajapati, H.B. Survey of multi objective evolutionary algorithms. In Proceedings of the International Conference on Circuit, Power and Computing Technologies (ICCPCT), Nagercoil, India, 19–20 March 2015.
37. Osyczka, A.; Krenich, S. Evolutionary algorithms for multicriteria optimization with selecting a representative subset of Pareto optimal solutions. In Proceedings of the 1st International Conference on Evolutionary Multi-Criterion Optimization (EMO 2001), Zurich, Switzerland, 7–9 March 2001.
38. Takagi, T.; Takadama, K.; Sato, H. Supervised Multi-objective optimization algorithm using estimation. In Proceedings of the IEEE Congress on Evolutionary Computation (CEC), Padua, Italy, 18–23 July 2022.

39. Abubaker, A.; Baharum, A.; Alrefaei, M. Good solution for multi-objective optimization problem. In Proceedings of the 21st National Symposium on Mathematical Sciences (SKSM), Penang, Malaysia, 6–8 November 2013.
40. Froese, R.; Klassen, J.W.; Leung, C.K.; Loewen, T.S. The border K-means clustering algorithm for one dimensional data. In Proceedings of the IEEE International Conference on Big Data and Smart Computing (BigComp), Daegu, Republic of Korea, 17–20 January 2022.

Disclaimer/Publisher's Note: The statements, opinions and data contained in all publications are solely those of the individual author(s) and contributor(s) and not of MDPI and/or the editor(s). MDPI and/or the editor(s) disclaim responsibility for any injury to people or property resulting from any ideas, methods, instructions or products referred to in the content.

Article

Multi-Objective Optimization for Mixed-Model Two-Sided Disassembly Line Balancing Problem Considering Partial Destructive Mode

Bao Chao [1], Peng Liang [1], Chaoyong Zhang [1,*] and Hongfei Guo [2,*]

[1] The State Key Laboratory of Digital Manufacturing Equipment and Technology, Huazhong University of Science and Technology, Wuhan 430074, China
[2] School of Intelligent Systems Science and Engineering, Jinan University, Zhuhai 519070, China
* Correspondence: zcyhust@hust.edu.cn (C.Z.); ghf_2005@jnu.edu.cn (H.G.)

Abstract: Large-volume waste products, such as refrigerators and automobiles, not only consume resources but also pollute the environment easily. A two-sided disassembly line is the most effective method to deal with large-volume waste products. How to reduce disassembly costs while increasing profit has emerged as an important and challenging research topic. Existing studies ignore the diversity of waste products as well as uncertain factors such as corrosion and deformation of parts, which is inconsistent with the actual disassembly scenario. In this paper, a partial destructive mode is introduced into the mixed-model two-sided disassembly line balancing problem, and the mathematical model of the problem is established. The model seeks to comprehensively optimize the number of workstations, the smoothness index, and the profit. In order to obtain a high-quality disassembly scheme, an improved non-dominated sorting genetic algorithm-II (NSGA-II) is proposed. The proposed model and algorithm are then applied to an automobile disassembly line as an engineering illustration. The disassembly scheme analysis demonstrates that the partial destructive mode can raise the profit of a mixed-model two-sided disassembly line. This research has significant application potential in the recycling of large-volume products.

Keywords: multi-objective; mixed-model; two-sided; disassembly line balancing; partial destructive mode

MSC: 90B30

Citation: Chao, B.; Liang, P.; Zhang, C.; Guo, H. Multi-Objective Optimization for Mixed-Model Two-Sided Disassembly Line Balancing Problem Considering Partial Destructive Mode. *Mathematics* **2023**, *11*, 1299. https://doi.org/10.3390/math11061299

Academic Editor: Andrea Scozzari

Received: 30 December 2022
Revised: 30 January 2023
Accepted: 6 February 2023
Published: 8 March 2023

Copyright: © 2023 by the authors. Licensee MDPI, Basel, Switzerland. This article is an open access article distributed under the terms and conditions of the Creative Commons Attribution (CC BY) license (https://creativecommons.org/licenses/by/4.0/).

1. Introduction

The lifecycle of products is continually getting shorter due to the quick development of new technology and advances in science. Many products are quickly phased out due to outdated functions, or scrapped, leading to the generation of more and more waste [1]. Remanufacturing is the manufacturing of waste products as raw materials, which can effectively conserve energy and resources and significantly lowers production costs. Disassembly is the first and mandatory step of remanufacturing; it plays a significant role in recycling of resources [2–4].

Paced assembly lines are increasingly being used by recycling companies instead of the fixed disassembly position layout. They have a great advantage in efficiency while dealing with a significant volume of waste products. In the process of disassembly, the priorities among parts must be taken into consideration and the toxic residues must be removed. How to rationally assign the tasks to the stations on the paced line to achieve the optimal goals under these constraints is called the disassembly line balancing problem (DLBP), which was first proposed by Gupta and Gungor [5] and has garnered considerable interest from experts and scholars from related fields.

According to the different objectives and conditions, DLBPs mainly fall into two major types. As addressed in our study, the type of DLBP that aims to minimize the number of workstations for a given cycle time is called DLBP-I. DLBP- II has the objective of minimizing the cycle time with a fixed number of workstations. The majority of DLBP research is focused on Type-I, and based on this, the optimization aims are expanded to include additional factors to make it more practical for disassembly businesses. The following are some of the most commonly considered objectives: energy consumption [6,7], workload smoothness index [8], number of workers [9], disassembly profit [7], and line efficiency [10].

Complete disassembly necessitates the removal of every part, whereas partial disassembly only necessitates the removal of required and hazardous parts, leaving the remaining parts intact [11]. It is obvious that for disassembling businesses, the partial disassembly mode is more suited to lowering costs and raising productivity and profits. In addition to this, unlike assembly lines, disassembly lines are facing uncertainty factors, such as corrosion and deformation of the connectors, which makes it difficult for each part to be removed conventionally [12,13]. At the same time, the conventional disassembly mode is not suitable for the disassembling of low-value and long task time parts. Pointing to this condition, a partial destructive disassembly mode is considered in this article [7]. In this mode, the major parts of the waste products are conventionally disassembled, and the rest of the parts are destructively disassembled or discarded under cost considerations.

Single-model disassembly lines are designed to produce high volumes of standardized homogeneous products, making them unsuitable for customer demand with a wide range of products. Firms tend to add a new disassembly line for new waste product during the recycling process. This strategy has drawbacks such as higher disassembly costs, wasted layout space, and decreased disassembly efficiency. A more cost-effective alternative for the disassembly of waste products with comparable assembly structures is to achieve mixed disassembly of these products on the same disassembly line [14]. When disassembling on two-sided lines, the disassembly tasks could be distinct because of variations in part designs, or the disassembly of the same part might result in different operating times and value because of variations in waste products' quality [15]. There are few studies on the mixed model two-sided disassembling line problem, and the existing studies lack the consideration of the uncertainty of the product state and how to maximize the disassembly revenue through partial destructive disassembly.

It was proved that DLBP is an NP-complete problem [16]. Since the problem was proposed, various methods have been developed to solve it. Exact methods primarily use integer programming and dynamic programming to solve the DLBP in solvers, such as CPLEX, LINGO, and GUROBI [17,18]. With increasing DLBP scale, exact methods are unable to provide feasible disassembly solutions in a reasonable time, so heuristic and metaheuristic methods are proposed [19]. For heuristics, the AHP with PROMETHEE [20] and a greedy/2-opt algorithms [21] are mainly applied. For meta-heuristics, this includes traditional algorithms like genetic, simulated annealing, ant colony, artificial bee colony, etc., [22–24] and recently, other algorithms have been proposed, such as gravitational search, gray wolf, migrating birds optimization, etc. [25,26]. According to the findings, meta-heuristics are more computationally efficient than the other two types of approaches, and they can lead to satisfactory answers [27].

Although the existing literature has made great progress in the research of DLBP, there are still gaps in the following aspects: Above all, the current research on the mixed-model two-sided disassembly of large-volume waste products did not take into account the partial destructive mode and the tool changes during the disassembly process. Secondly, existing studies only focus on single objectives such as profit maximization or workstation minimization as optimization goals, without comprehensive consideration of various needs of enterprises. In the end, there is a lack of a feasible case to provide research for this type of problem.

In view of the shortcomings of the current research, this paper takes minimizing the number of workstations, minimizing the smoothness index, and maximizing the profit as the objectives, and studies the mixed-model two-sided disassembly line balancing problem suitable for large-volume waste products disassembling in the partial destructive mode. The main contributions can be listed as follows. Firstly, a new multi-objective mathematical model is developed for solving PD-MTDLBP. Secondly, an improved NSGA-II algorithm is proposed for multi-objective optimisation of PD-MTDLBP. Finally, a multi-model case transformed from a real disassembly scenario is provided.

The remainder of this paper is structured as follows. In Section 2, the partial destructive mixed-model two-sided disassembly line balancing problem (PD-MTDLBP) is described, and the MIP formulation of PD-MTDLBP is presented. In Section 3, the proposed approach for solving PD-MTDLBP is given in detail. In Section 4, a computational example to validate the performance of the proposed model and algorithm are given. Conclusions are then drawn in the final section, along with suggestions for further research avenues.

2. Problem Statement

2.1. Problem Description

In the arrangement of a two-sided disassembly line, the workstations are symmetrically positioned along both sides of the conveyor. The stations on the left and right sides refer to one another as a companion station. Together, they form a mated station. Each workstation has a corresponding operator and disassembly tools [28]. The disassembly task is subject to the disassembly direction constraint on the two-sided disassembly line, which can be divided into three types: left type (L), right type (R), and either type (E). Each type of task is only allowed to be disassembled in its corresponding direction.

A two-sided disassembly line is referred to as a mixed-model two-sided disassembly line if it is used to disassemble multiple waste products with similar structural characteristics in a mixed flow [29]. Each waste product has a task disassembly precedence relationship that can be combined to create a joint disassembly precedence diagram.

Generally speaking, destructive disassembly can increase the efficiency of disassembly, thereby lowering energy consumption and disassembly costs, but it can also make parts less valuable. Hence, parts that are not in high demand or not hazardous can be disassembled either conventionally or destructively. High-demand and hazardous parts, on the other hand, must be disassembled conventionally.

2.2. Mathematical Model

The mathematical model for PD-MTDLBP is as follows, and the parameters and variables required by the model are as shown in Appendix A.

$$\min f_1 = \sum_{s \in S} \sum_{k=1,2} W_{sk} \tag{1}$$

$$\min f_2 = \sqrt{\sum_{s \in S} \sum_{k=1,2} (T_{sk} - \max\{T_{sk}\})^2 / \sum_{s \in S} \sum_{k=1,2} W_{sk}} \tag{2}$$

$$\max f_3 = \sum_{i \in I} \sum_{e=1,2} x_i v_{ie} - \sum_{m \in M} \sum_{i \in I} \sum_{s \in S} \sum_{k=1,2} \sum_{e=1,2} (x_{isk} c_{ie} + x_{isk} t_{ie}^m (c_s + h_i c_h)) \\ - \sum_{s \in S} \sum_{k=1,2} \sum_{q \in Q} \sum_{i \in I} \sum_{j \in I} x_{iskq} x_{jsk(q+1)} z_{ij} t_t c_s - |S| c_f \tag{3}$$

s.t.

$$x_i = 1, \forall i \in \{i | h_i^m + d_i^m \geq 1\} \tag{4}$$

$$x_i \leq 1, \forall i \in \{i | h_i^m + d_i^m = 0\} \tag{5}$$

$$x_j = 1, \forall P_{ij} = 1, x_i = 1 \tag{6}$$

$$x_i e_i = 1, \forall i \in \{i | h_i^m + d_i^m \geq 1\} \tag{7}$$

$$e_i \leq 1, \forall i \in \{i | (h_i^m + d_i^m = 0) \wedge (x_i = 1)\} \tag{8}$$

$$\sum_{s\in S}\sum_{k=1,2} x_{isk} = 1, \forall i \in \{i|x_i = 1\} \tag{9}$$

$$\sum_{m\in M}\sum_{i\in I}\sum_{e=1,2} x_{isk}t_{ie}^m + \sum_{k=1,2}\sum_{q\in Q}\sum_{i\in I}\sum_{j\in I} x_{iskq}x_{jsk(q+1)}z_{ij}^t t_t \leq CT, \forall s \in S, k \in \{1,2\} \tag{10}$$

$$\sum_{s'\in S}\sum_{k\in K(j)} s' x_{js'k} \leq \sum_{s\in S}\sum_{k\in K(i)} s x_{isk}, \forall P_{ij} = 1, x_i x_j = 1 \tag{11}$$

$$\sum_{i\in I} y_{ibs} t_{ie}^m \geq \sum_{j\in I} y_{jas} t_{je}^m + \sum_{k\in K(a)} x_{ask} t_{ae}^m, \forall P_{ba} = 1, m \in M, s \in S, x_b x_a = 1 \tag{12}$$

$$\sum_{k=1,2} x_{isk} + \sum_{k=1,2} x_{jsk} \leq 1 + (y_{ijs} + y_{jis}), \forall ij \in I, s \in S \tag{13}$$

$$\sum_{i\in I} x_{isk} \leq nW_{sk}, \forall s \in S, k = 1,2 \tag{14}$$

$$\sum_{k=1,2} W_{sk} - 2G_s - F_s = 0, \forall s \in S \tag{15}$$

$$G_s \leq G_{s-1}, \forall s \in \{2,\ldots,|S|\} \tag{16}$$

In the objective functions, the number of workstations is minimized by Equation (1). Workloads on of the disassembly line are smoothed by Equation (2). Disassembly profit is maximized by Equation (3) [30]. In the constraints, Equations (4) and (5) represents that the parts that are hazardous or demanded must be disassembled; the rest of the parts are disassembled randomly [7]. All of a task's immediate predecessors must be completed in order for it to be performed, as shown in Equation (6). Equations (7) and (8) indicate that the parts that are hazardous or demanded must be disassembled in conventional mode, whilst others can be disassembled in destructive or conventional mode. Equation (9) denotes that the parts selected for disassembly must be assigned to a workstation. Equation (10) represents the cycle time constraint. For the whole disassembly line, the mated-station index of the immediate predecessor must not be greater than that of the immediate successor, as shown in Equation (11). Equation (12) represents the precedence constraint of tasks within the same workstation. Equation (13) represents the position constraint within the station, which defines the relative position between two tasks successively assigned to the same workstation. Equation (14) is the disassembly station and disassembly task constraint, so that the workstation is opened after the disassembly task is assigned. Equation (15) indicates that the total number of workstations is equal to the sum of the mated stations and companion stations [31]. Formula (16) indicates that the mated stations are started one by one.

3. The Proposed Method

For the purpose of solving multi-objective optimisation problems (MOP), meta-heuristic algorithms have been repeatedly shown to be very efficient. In this study, the non-dominated sorting genetic algorithm-II (NSGA-II) is improved and applied to address the proposed PD-MTDLBP. The NSGA-II algorithm is a Pareto-based approach, and its optimal solution set is essentially the non-inferior solution to the MOP. The NSGA algorithm is improved from the following aspects. Based on the multi-chromosomes encoding method proposed by Wang [7] et al., a decoding method suitable for PD-DLBP was constructed. Two processes, two-point crossover and single-point mutation, suitable for multi-chromosomes operations, are applied to generate new populations. The NSGA-II flowchart is depicted in Figure 1, and the detailed processes are given below.

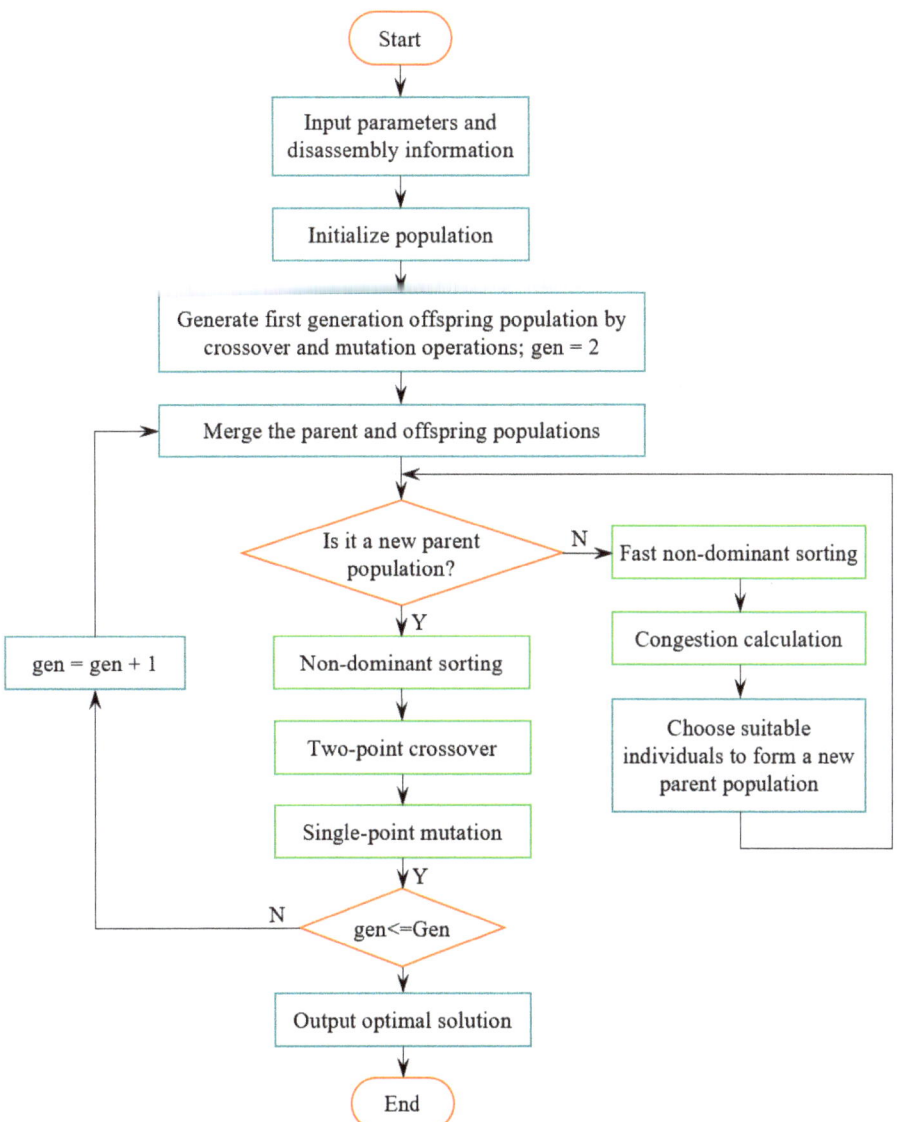

Figure 1. Flowchart of NSGA-II.

3.1. Encoding

Encoding, also known as the process of coming up with a workable disassembly task sequence, is the first and most important step in solving the PD-MTDLBP problem. Three integer vectors are employed for the encoding of the PD-MTDLBP based on the disassembly precedence matrix: the task sequence vector (TS), task decision vector (TD), and task mode vector (TM). Each vector is a one-dimensional array with N_t elements. The TS designates the order in which the tasks of the mix-model are carried out on the two-sided disassembly line.

The TD determines whether the tasks in the TS participate in the disassembly process, and its encoding process should meet Equations (4)–(6). The TM determines which mode the tasks involved in the disassembly should adopt. Its encoding process needs to satisfy Equations (7) and (8). Taking Figure 2, as an example, assuming that the hazard index of tasks 4 and 6 is 1, and is 0 for the others; and the demand index of task 2 and 11 is 1, and is 0 for the others. The TS, TD, and TM of a feasible initial solution can be constructed as shown in Table 1.

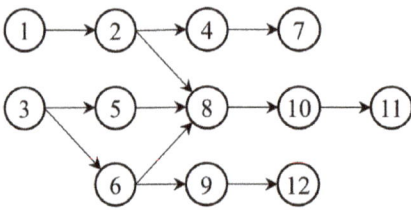

Figure 2. Disassembly precedence diagram.

Table 1. Encoding vector.

Task	1	2	3	4	5	6	7	8	9	10	11	12
TS	3	5	6	9	12	1	2	8	10	4	7	11
TD	1	1	1	0	1	0	1	1	1	1	0	1
TM	1	0	1	-	1	-	1	0	1	1	-	1

3.2. Decoding

During the decoding process, tasks are assigned to each workstation in the order specified in the task sequence vector, subject to cycle time and disassembly direction constraints. The decoding processes are as follows:

Step 1: Turn on the first mated station and begin decoding.

Step 2: Determine whether each model's mated station has received all of the tasks in the TS. Proceed to step 8 if so. If not, move on to step 3.

Step 3: Assign the first task i in the TS as the active task.

Step 4: If TD[i] = 1, proceed to step 5. Otherwise, remove current task from TS and return to step 2.

Step 5: Determine the disassembly time of the current task according to TM[i]. If there is a tool change, add the required time to the disassembly time.

Step 6: Assign the current task to the left or right side of the mated station if it has a definite disassembly direction (L or R). If E, place it on the side where there is more time for disassembly.

Step 7: If the cycle time constraint is met, assign the task to the current companion station, otherwise, assign the task to a new one. After the assignment, remove the current task from TS and go back to step 2.

Step 8: Output the decoding result.

3.3. Crossover

The crossover of the task sequence vector is usually carried out at random in numerous research. It is easy to produce infeasible individuals by this type of crossing. In this study, a two-point crossover operator is adopted to guarantee that the crossed individuals meet the precedence constraints.

The individuals TS_1 and TS_2 are used to designate two parents of the two-point crossover operation, as seen in Figure 3. Two crossover points P_1 and P_2 are randomly selected in the parent individuals to determine the section of crossover. Keep the sequences before P_1 and after P_2 in TS_1 unchanged. The sub-sequence {9, 12, 1, 2, 8, 10} between P_1 and P_2 in TS_1 becomes {1, 2, 9, 8, 12, 10} through mapping of the same sequence in TS_2, namely, the offspring individual N_1 = {3, 5, 6, 1, 2, 9, 8, 12, 10, 4, 7, 11}. Under these crossover operations, the offspring always satisfy the precedence constraint [32].

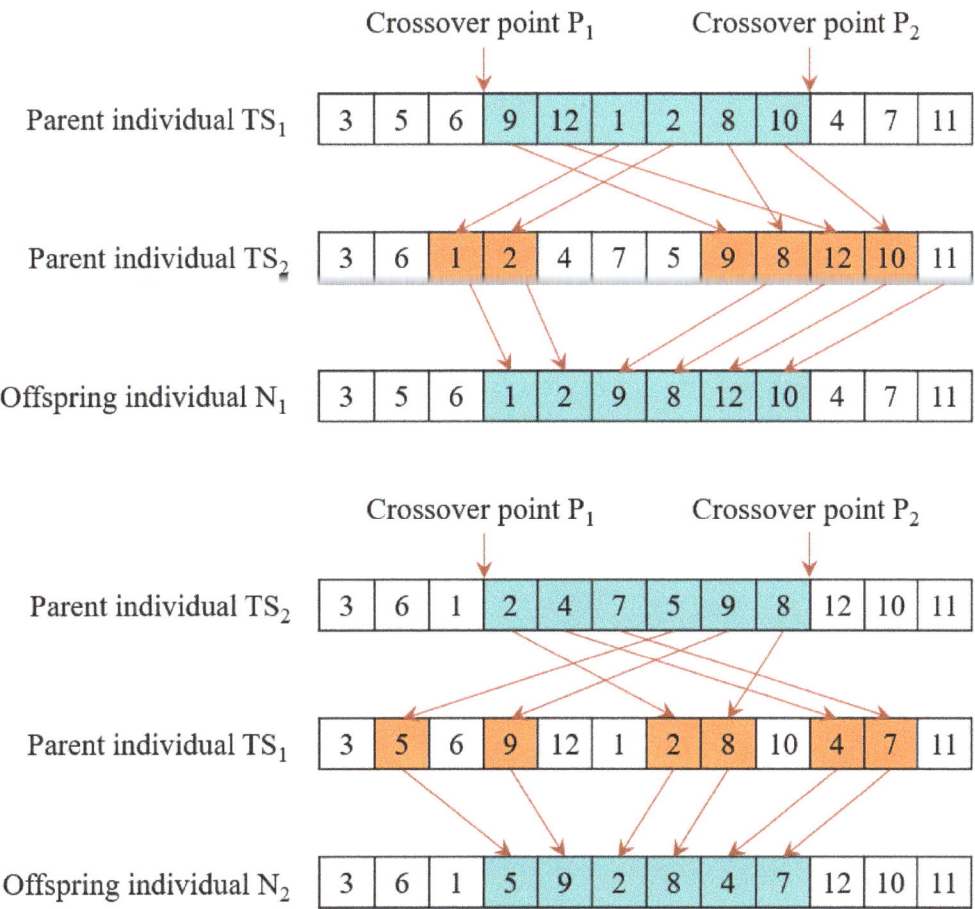

Figure 3. Individual crossover operation.

The crossover operation of the task decision vector and task mode vector is consistent with the crossover of the task sequence vectors. However, it should be noted that after the completion of the crossover of the task decision vector, the sequence should be checked and adjusted to ensure that the disassembly decision variable of all the predecessor tasks of the selected task is 1.

3.4. Mutation

A random mutation of the task sequence vector can also create infeasible individuals. A single-point mutation operator based on a precedence constraint is employed to find a feasible individual. The individual TS is regarded as the parent of the single-point mutation operation, as depicted in Figure 4. In TS, first a mutation point P is chosen at random, and the closest predecessor {3} and successor {8} tasks of the chosen task are identified. The chosen task {5} is then randomly inserted between the predecessor and successor to create the feasible individual set [33]. The offspring individual N {3, 5, 6, 1, 2, 4, 7, 9, 8, 12, 10, 11} is then chosen at random from the set.

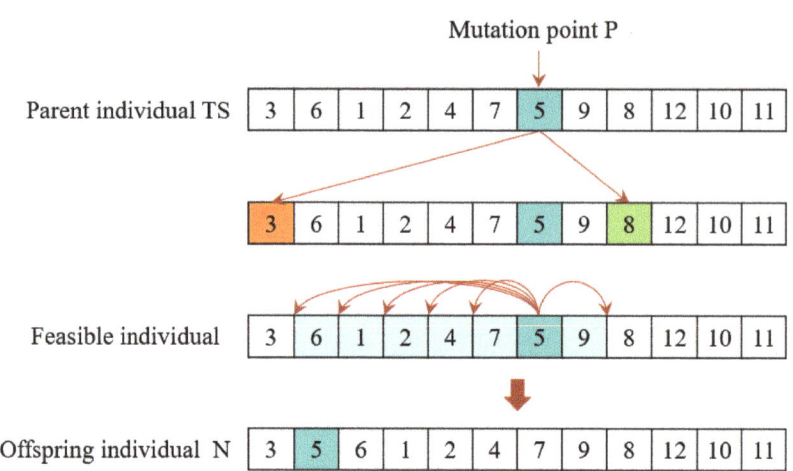

Figure 4. Individual mutation operation.

The task decision vector and task mode vector adopt the same mutation operation as the task sequence vector. Following the mutation of the task decision vector, the sequence should also be verified and corrected.

4. Case Study

A practical case of automobile is selected to verify the reliability and validity of the proposed model and method. Table 2 illustrates the 74 tasks that make up the entire process of disassembling an automobile. It includes information such as the hazardous property (h), the demanded property (d), the preferred operation direction (k), the disassembly mode $€$, the disassembly time (t) for three models (m), the revenue (v), and the type of tools (o) of each task. Figure 5 depicts the relationships between tasks in terms of priority. The precedence relationship, the preferred operation direction, and hazardous property for each task are taken from Liang [15] et al. The population and iteration times of the algorithm are set as 100 and 500. The crossover probability and mutation probability involved in the algorithm are set as 0.8 and 0.2, respectively. Minimum product set is $MPS = \{1, 1, 1\}$.

Table 2. Tasks information of the automobile disassembly.

No.	Parts	h	d	k	$e=1$					$e=0$				
					t			v	o	t			v	o
					m_1	m_2	m_3	-	-	m_1	m_2	m_3	-	-
1	Left engine hood hinge	0	0	L	20	18	17	19	6	2	2	2	14	9
2	Right engine hood hinge	0	0	R	17	21	13	19	1	2	2	2	14	9
3	Engine hood	0	1	E	10	15	12	833	6	1	2	1	625	9
4	Airbag	1	1	L	100	103	91	1296	6	9	9	8	972	7
5	Battery	1	0	R	33	39	39	110	5	3	4	4	83	8
6	Fuse Box	1	0	R	28	27	30	18	3	3	3	3	14	8
7	Waste fluid	1	0	E	13	8	16	20	6	2	1	2	15	7
8	Waste oil	1	0	E	195	202	143	2	3	17	17	12	2	7

Table 2. Cont.

No.	Parts	h	d	k	e = 1						e = 0					
					t			v	o	t			v	o
					m_1	m_2	m_3	-	-	m_1	m_2	m_3	-	-
9	Refrigerant	1	0	E	63	38	43	17	4	6	4	4	13	8
10	Left front wheel	0	0	L	41	31	31	130	1	4	3	3	98	7
11	Left rear wheel	0	0	L	27	41	29	130	5	3	4	3	98	7
12	Right front wheel	0	0	R	32	22	30	130	4	3	2	3	98	8
13	Right rear wheel	0	0	R	38	40	39	130	3	4	4	4	98	9
14	Left fender	0	0	L	22	20	21	31	6	2	2	2	20	0
15	Right fender	0	0	R	22	33	24	31	5	2	3	2	23	8
16	Left front bumper	0	0	L	43	23	43	182	5	4	2	4	137	8
17	Right front bumper	0	0	R	23	38	42	182	2	2	4	4	137	8
18	Front bumper	0	0	E	17	19	14	285	5	2	2	2	214	7
19	Air intake grille	0	0	E	29	18	22	107	2	3	2	2	80	8
20	Left lamps	0	0	L	31	24	26	944	2	3	2	3	708	9
21	Right lamps	0	0	R	25	42	30	944	1	3	4	3	708	7
22	Left front door	0	1	L	38	44	44	1149	1	4	4	4	862	9
23	Left rear door	0	1	L	29	45	48	1149	3	3	4	4	862	8
24	Right front door	0	1	R	51	38	48	746	4	5	4	4	560	9
25	Right rear door	0	1	R	50	34	42	746	2	5	3	4	560	8
26	Left trunk cover hinge	0	0	L	19	19	17	61	3	2	2	2	46	8
27	Right trunk cover hinge	0	0	R	20	15	17	61	2	2	2	2	46	9
28	Trunk cover	0	1	E	41	27	22	910	1	4	3	2	683	7
29	Spare wheel	0	0	E	23	20	32	83	5	2	2	3	62	7
30	Left rear bumper	0	0	L	35	24	28	159	4	3	2	3	119	9
31	Right rear bumper	0	0	R	28	33	38	159	5	3	3	4	119	9
32	Rear bumper	0	0	E	13	19	14	244	1	2	2	2	183	8
33	Radiator	0	0	E	56	56	48	742	1	5	5	4	557	9
34	Condenser	0	0	E	48	62	77	409	1	4	6	7	307	9
35	Coolant tank	1	0	E	70	71	53	452	5	6	6	5	339	8
36	Air cleaner	0	0	E	38	35	28	787	5	4	3	3	590	7
37	Wiper	0	0	E	33	32	32	123	5	3	3	3	92	8
38	Wiper motor	0	0	E	37	30	26	58	4	4	3	3	44	8
39	Left front windscreen	0	0	L	42	56	52	70	4	4	5	5	53	7
30	Right front windscreen	0	0	R	57	43	42	70	4	5	4	4	53	7
41	Front windscreen	1	0	E	30	32	18	248	3	3	3	2	186	8
42	Left rear windscreen	0	0	L	23	33	25	51	3	2	3	3	38	9
43	Right rear windscreen	0	0	R	33	33	26	51	3	3	3	3	38	8
44	Rear windscreen	1	0	E	24	23	20	156	5	2	2	2	117	9
45	Left seat	0	1	L	95	126	100	977	3	8	11	9	733	7
46	Right seat	0	1	R	137	134	149	1186	6	12	12	13	890	9
47	Armrest box	0	0	E	37	68	35	25	5	4	6	3	19	9
48	Fuel tank	1	0	R	43	76	77	637	6	4	7	7	478	7
49	Steering wheel	0	0	L	56	39	47	189	2	5	4	4	142	9
50	Left center console bolt	0	0	L	63	67	59	1	2	6	6	5	1	9
51	Right center console bolt	0	0	R	50	36	46	2	2	5	3	4	2	8
52	Center console panel	0	0	E	38	34	44	438	3	4	3	4	329	8

Table 2. Cont.

No.	Parts	h	d	k	$e=1$					$e=0$				
					t			v	o	t			v	o
					m_1	m_2	m_3	-	-	m_1	m_2	m_3	-	-
53	Dashboard	0	0	L	48	39	35	508	3	4	4	3	381	7
54	Shift handle	0	0	E	68	76	60	106	6	6	7	5	80	9
55	Brake rigging	0	0	L	89	103	77	226	2	8	9	7	170	9
56	Clutch pedal	0	0	L	27	25	35	81	2	3	3	3	61	9
57	Accelerator pedal	0	0	L	39	36	39	81	6	4	3	4	61	8
58	Air conditioner	0	1	E	47	64	70	660	5	4	6	6	495	8
59	Steering system	0	0	L	103	121	121	512	4	9	11	11	384	8
60	Carbon canister	1	0	E	14	13	13	23	1	2	2	2	17	8
61	Bottom guard board	0	0	E	26	30	27	70	2	3	3	3	53	9
62	Exhaust pipe	1	1	E	70	41	53	1440	1	6	4	5	1080	9
63	Drive shaft	0	1	E	99	164	109	577	1	9	14	10	433	7
64	Electric generator	0	0	E	103	100	96	392	1	9	9	8	294	9
65	Front suspension	0	0	E	122	102	109	64	1	11	9	10	48	7
66	Rear suspension	0	0	E	93	116	128	57	6	8	10	11	43	8
67	Engine	0	1	E	163	180	213	6188	4	14	15	18	4641	8
68	Transmission	0	1	E	117	156	93	6562	2	10	13	8	4922	8
69	Left decoration	1	0	L	47	47	80	91	1	4	4	7	68	9
70	Right decoration	1	0	R	45	76	56	62	4	4	7	5	47	7
71	Interior light	1	0	E	24	16	19	8	4	2	2	2	6	9
72	Audio system	0	0	E	44	30	35	244	4	4	3	3	183	9
73	Left wiring harness	0	0	L	35	35	39	385	3	3	3	4	289	7
74	Right wiring harness	0	0	R	21	33	31	331	1	2	3	3	248	7

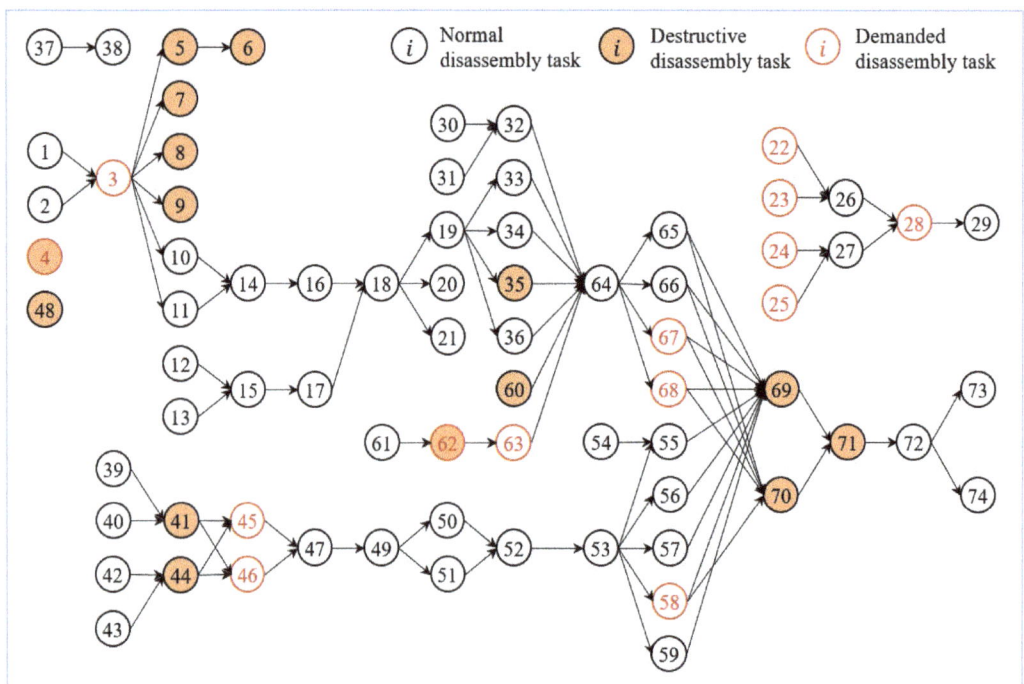

Figure 5. Precedence relationships among the parts of the waste automobile.

The cycle time of the disassembly line is 521 s. The conventional disassembly times of each model are randomly generated between 1/3~2/3 of the original task times. The destructive disassembly times are achieved by multiplying the conventional disassembly times by 1/12. The disassembly costs of different types of tools are shown in Table 3. The revenue generated from the conventional disassembly is randomly generated within the range of 20% to 50% of its market value. The revenue generated from the destructive disassembly is 3/4 of that from a conventional disassembly. The other auxiliary parameters are as follows: $c_s = 1$ RMB/s, $c_h = 0.2$ RMB/s, $c_f = 200$ RMB, $t_t = 2$ s.

Table 3. Disassembly costs of different types of tools.

o	1	2	3	4	5	6	7	8	9
c	6	10	8	4	7	9	2	5	3

NSGA-II algorithm has been run 10 times and 12 Pareto solutions have been obtained. The Pareto front of the algorithm is shown in Figure 6. The three objective function values of the Pareto front corresponding to Figure 6 are shown in Table 4. It can be seen from the results of f_1 and f_2 that there is a trade-off between the number of workstations and profit. This may be related to the longer disassembly time of high-value parts. However, from the results of f_3, there is no significant correlation between the smoothness index and the number of workstations or between the smoothness index and profit; this is because the station time varies between disassembly schemes. This is consistent with the conclusion of Wang [7] et al.

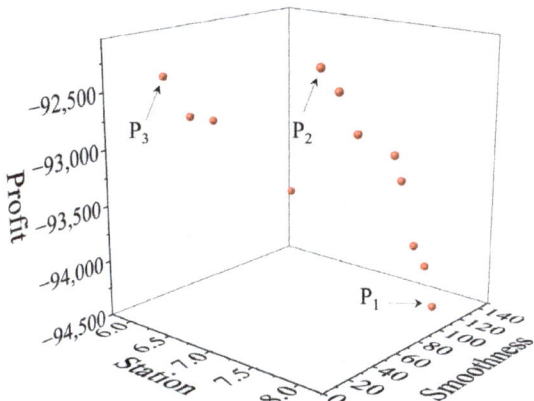

Figure 6. The Pareto front of NSGA-II.

In order to evaluate the benefits of the partial destructive mode, profits are calculated for each of the three modes (partial destructive mode, conventional mode, and destructive mode) as shown in Table 4. In the destructive mode, harmful parts and high-value parts are still disassembled in a conventional way, and the rest of the parts are disassembled destructively. The maximum values in the three results are highlighted in bold. It can be seen that in almost all results, the profit calculated under the partial destructive mode is the largest. The partial destructive mode clearly outperforms the conventional and destructive modes.

Table 4. The computational result of NSGA-II.

No.	f_1	f_2	$-f_3$		
			Partial Destructive Disassembly	Conventional Disassembly	Destructive Disassembly
1	6	67.4	**−92,893.6**	−91,939.6	−92,108.6
2	6	49.4	**−92,807.6**	−92,581.6	−92,126.6
3	6	29.6	−92,397.6	**−92,581.6**	−92,126.6
4	6	134.9	**−93,804.6**	−91,963.6	−92,084.6
5	8	15.9	−92,041.6	−91,939.6	**−92,084.6**
6	8	106.8	**−94,004.6**	−91,933.6	−92,072.6
7	8	44.9	**−92,638.6**	−91,945.6	−92,090.6
8	8	82.9	**−93,152.6**	−91,981.6	−92,090.6
9	8	95.7	**−93,770.6**	−92,557.6	−92,102.6
10	8	115.3	**−94,423.6**	−91,963.6	−92,126.6
11	8	29.8	**−92,260.6**	−91,969.6	−92,078.6
12	8	76.4	**−92,911.6**	−92,551.6	−92,102.6

The three points marked in Figure 6 correspond to schemes that obtain better value on each of the three objectives. These are point P_1 with the largest profit, point P_2 with the best smoothness, and point P_3 with the smallest workstation. The objective values (f_1, f_2, $-f_3$) of the three points are (8, 115.3, −94,423.6), (8, 15.9, −92,041.6), and (6, 29.6, −92,397.6), respectively. The Gantt charts corresponding to the three points are shown in Figures 7–9. It shows the task sequence, start, and end time of each task, and the tool changes between different tasks (filled with black in the figure). The disassembly scheme S_1 and S_2 are both performed on eight workstations. The optimal smoothness index can be obtained when scheme S_2 is adopted. A total of 19 tasks are destructively dismantled. Although it has minimal idle time, its profits are not the highest. When scheme S_1 is adopted, 22 tasks are destructively disassembled. The decrease in conventionally disassembled tasks, combined with the presence of the multi-constraint, resulted in a large amount of idle time, but it is still the most profitable scheme. In scheme S_3, 31 tasks are destructively disassembled so that more tasks can be performed in fewer workstations. In this case, the impact on profit mainly comes from revenue of the parts and disassembly time cost, while the impact on profit from starting a new workstation is not the main one. Thus, there is a situation where six workstations have no advantage over eight workstations.

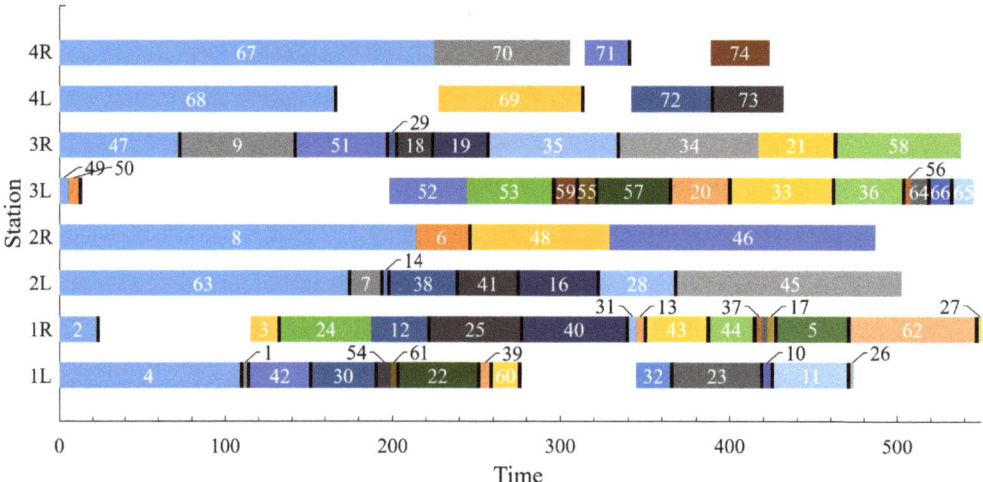

Figure 7. Gantt chart of disassembly scheme S_1.

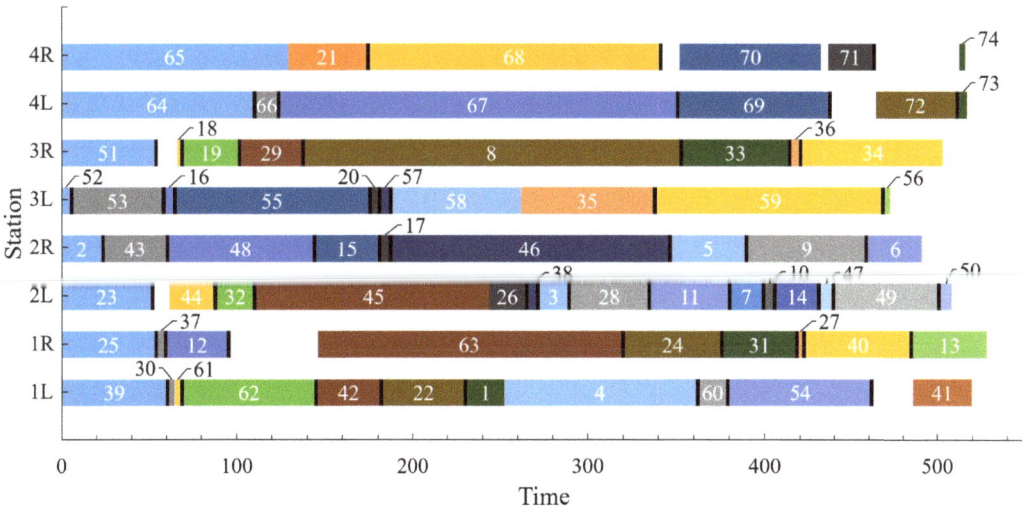

Figure 8. Gantt chart of disassembly scheme S_2.

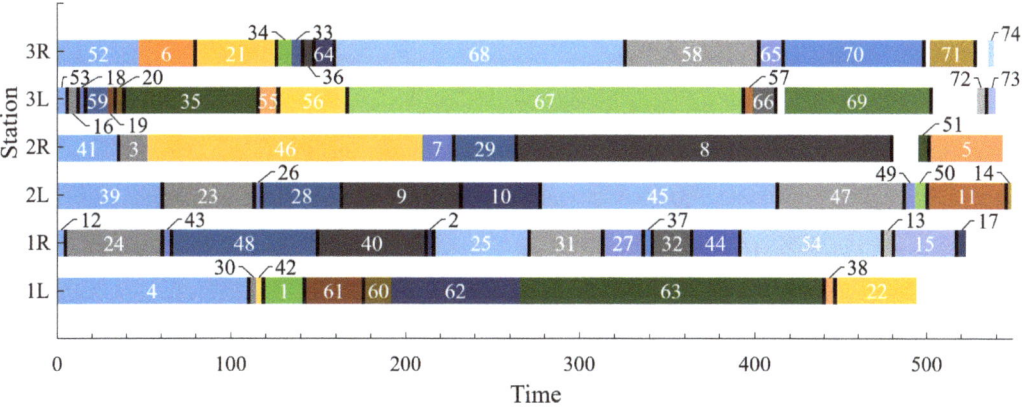

Figure 9. Gantt chart of disassembly scheme S_3.

The disassembly scheme S_1 with the maximum profit is selected to analyse the relationships among task profit, revenue, and cost, as shown in Figure 10. Here, the cost is expressed as a negative value. As the disassembly operation progresses, the cost increases gradually. Although four new mated stations are opened, the cost does not change dramatically. This indicates that the cost is mainly the time cost of disassembly. The profit of disassembly increases with the increase in revenue. Among them, when the high-value parts corresponding to Task 67 (Engine) and Task 68 (Transmission) are disassembled, the revenue and profit are dramatically improved. This is due to a fact that the revenue of these two parts is much higher than their disassembly cost.

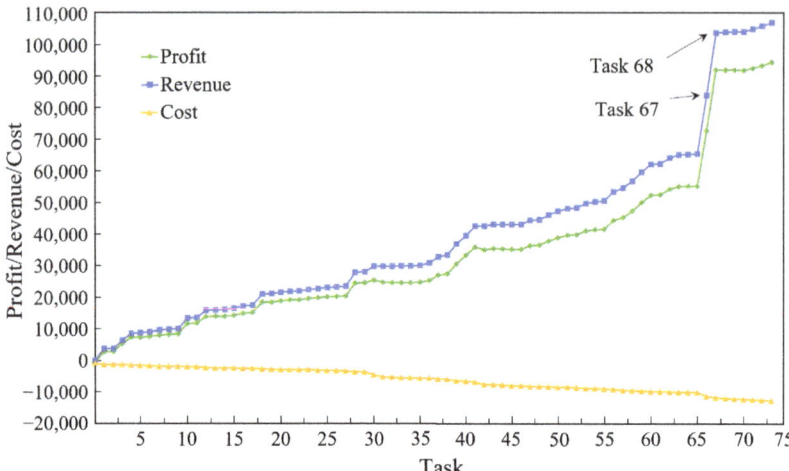

Figure 10. The relationships among task profit, revenue, and cost.

As can be seen from the above results, fewer workstations do not lead to higher profit. At the same time, better smoothness does not effectively increase profits. This is related to the characteristics of the partial destructive disassembly mode itself. When fewer workstations are pursued, more tasks may be destructively disassembled to assign more tasks in one workstation. When pursuing the best smoothness, high-value parts may be destructively disassembled in order to achieve the balance of tasks among workstations, thus they are unable to obtain higher benefits. For enterprises, profit is the first priority. When the factory site is sufficient, the disassembly scheme with a relatively large number of workstations but the highest profit should be selected.

5. Conclusions

This research innovatively designed a mixed-model two-sided disassembly line considering a partial destructive mode. Harmful parts and high-value parts are disassembled in a conventional mode, and other parts are disassembled randomly in a conventional or destructive mode. The impact of tool change on operation time is considered to more accurately describe the actual disassembly process. Then, the mathematical model of the disassembly process is established, and the three objectives of the number of workstations, the smoothness index, and the profit are optimized. In addition, in order to solve this combinatorial optimization problem efficiently, NSGA-II, which has been proved to be superior by many studies, is selected in this study, and the encoding, decoding, crossover, and mutation rules are redefined according to the characteristics of the problem. The results show that the partial destructive disassembly mode can maximize profits.

In this work, the mixed-model disassembly of large-volume products is studied from the perspective of a partial destructive mode, which provides a new research idea for the disassembly of waste products under uncertain conditions. The mathematical model and algorithm constructed in this paper can provide theoretical and technical guidance for the construction of large-volume products disassembly line.

Future research can be extended to many fields. This study did not take into account the correlation between parts. In the same disassembly sequence, whether the destructive disassembly of the predecessor will affect the disassembly mode of the successors is a problem worth further investigation. Further, disassembly lines for large-volume products can be combined with assembly lines for large-volume products, allowing economic and environmental indicators of the disassembly to assembly process to be considered at a more automated disassembly level.

Author Contributions: B.C.: Writing—Original draft, methodology. P.L.: software, data curation. C.Z.: validation, supervision. H.G.: validation. All authors have read and agreed to the published version of the manuscript.

Funding: This research was partially supported by the Project of International Cooperation and Exchanges NSFC [Grant No. 51861165202], the National Natural Science Foundation of China [Grant Nos. 51575211, 51705263, 51805330], the 111 Project of China [Grant No. B16019]. The authors thank the technical support from the Experiment Center for Advanced Manufacturing and Technology in the School of Mechanical Science & Engineering of HUST.

Data Availability Statement: The data that support the findings of this study are available from the corresponding author, upon reasonable request.

Conflicts of Interest: The authors declare no conflict of interest.

Appendix A

The parameters and variables required by the model are as follows:

- Indices:

i, j, a, b: Index of tasks, $i, j, a, b \in I$.
s, s' : Index of mated stations, $s, s' \in S$.
k : Side of the stations, left side, $k = 1$; right side, $k = 2$.
q : Position of the tasks within a workstation, $q \in Q$.
m : Product model, $m \in M$.

- Parameters:

I : Set of tasks, $I = \{1, 2, \ldots, i, \ldots, N_t\}$.
S : Set of mated stations, $S = \{1, 2, \ldots, s, \ldots, N_s\}$.
Q : Set of task positions, $Q = \{1, 2, \ldots, q, \ldots, N_q\}$.
M : Set of product model, $M = \{1, 2, \ldots, m, \ldots, N_m\}$.
t_{ie}^m : Disassembly time when the task i of model m adopts disassembly mode e.
t_t : Tool replacement time.
v_{ie} : Disassembly revenue when task i adopts disassembly mode e;
c_{ie} : Disassembly cost when task i adopts disassembly mode e;
c_s : Unit time cost of running the workstation.
c_h : The additional unit time cost to the workstation while handling hazardous tasks.
c_f : Fixed cost of starting workstation.
o_i : Type of tool for task i.
T_{sk} : Total disassembly time in workstation.
CT : Cycle time.
MPS : Minimum product set, $MPS = \{a_1, a_2, a_3, \ldots, a_M\}$.
a_m : Number of models m in MPS, $a_m = A_m/L$, $(m = 1, 2, \ldots, N_m)$.
A_m : Number of products m.
L : The greatest common divisor of all A_m.

- Decision variables:

x_i : 1, if task i is performed, 0, otherwise.
x_{isk} : 1, if task i is assigned to the k side of the mated station s, 0, otherwise.
x_{iskq} : 1, if task i is assigned to position q on k side of the mated station s, 0, otherwise.
e_i : 1, if the task i is disassembled conventionally, 0, if the task i is disassembled destructively.
W_{sk} : 1, if the k side of the mated station s is used, 0, otherwise.
G_s : 1, if the entire mated station s is used, 0, otherwise.
F_s : 1, if only one side of the mated station s is used, 0, otherwise.
y_{ijs} : For mated station s, 1, if task i is assigned to the s before task j, 0, otherwise.

- Indicator variables:

h_i : 1, if the task i is hazardous, 0, otherwise.
d_i : 1, if the task i is demanded, 0, otherwise.
z_{ij} : 1, if the disassembly tools for task i and task j are different, 0, otherwise.
P_{ij} : 1, if task j is an immediate predecessor of task i, 0, otherwise.

References

1. Rehman, S.U.; Kraus, S.; Shah, S.A.; Khanin, D.; Mahto, R.V. Analyzing the relationship between green innovation and environmental performance in large manufacturing firms. *Technol. Forecast. Soc. Chang.* **2021**, *163*, 120481. [CrossRef]
2. Guo, H.F.; Lian, X.; Zhang, Y.; Ren, Y.P.; He, Z.B.; Zhang, R.; Ding, N. Analysis of Environmental Policy's Impact on Remanufacturing Decision Under the Effect of Green Network Using Differential Game Model. *IEEE Access* **2020**, *8*, 115251–115262. [CrossRef]
3. Wu, J.Z.; Lian, K.L.; Deng, Y.L.; Jiang, P.; Zhang, C.Y. Multi-Objective Parameter Optimization of Fiber Laser Welding Considering Energy Consumption and Bead Geometry. *IEEE Trans. Autom. Sci. Eng.* **2022**, *19*, 3561–3574. [CrossRef]
4. Wu, J.Z.; Zhang, C.Y.; Lian, K.L.; Cao, H.J.; Li, C.B. Carbon emission modeling and mechanical properties of laser, arc and laser-arc hybrid welded aluminum alloy joints. *J. Clean. Prod.* **2022**, *378*, 134437. [CrossRef]
5. Gungor, A.; Gupta, S.M.; Pochampally, K.; Kamarthi, S.V. Complications in disassembly line balancing. In Proceedings of the 1st International Conference on Environmentally Conscious Manufacturing, Boston, MA, USA, 6–8 November 2000; pp. 289–298.
6. Wu, K.; Guo, X.W.; Liu, S.X.; Qi, L.; Zhao, J.; Zhao, Z.Y.; Wang, X. IEEE Multi-objective Discrete Brainstorming Optimizer for Multiple-product Partial U-shaped Disassembly Line Balancing Problem. In Proceedings of the 33rd Chinese Control and Decision Conference (CCDC), Kunming, China, 22–24 May 2021; pp. 305–310.
7. Wang, K.P.; Li, X.Y.; Gao, L.; Li, P.G. Energy consumption and profit -oriented disassembly line balancing for waste electrical and electronic equipment. *J. Clean. Prod.* **2020**, *265*, 121829. [CrossRef]
8. Paprocka, I.; Skolud, B. A Predictive Approach for Disassembly Line Balancing Problems. *Sensors* **2022**, *22*, 3920. [CrossRef]
9. Wu, T.F.; Zhang, Z.Q.; Yin, T.; Zhang, Y. Multi-objective optimisation for cell-level disassembly of waste power battery modules in human-machine hybrid mode. *Waste Manag.* **2022**, *144*, 513–526. [CrossRef]
10. Ren, Y.P.; Zhang, C.Y.; Zhao, F.; Triebe, M.J.; Meng, L.L. An MCDM-Based Multiobjective General Variable Neighborhood Search Approach for Disassembly Line Balancing Problem. *IEEE Trans. Syst. Man Cybern. Syst.* **2020**, *50*, 3770–3783. [CrossRef]
11. Liang, W.; Zhang, Z.Q.; Zhang, Y.; Xu, P.Y.; Yin, T. Improved social spider algorithm for partial disassembly line balancing problem considering the energy consumption involved in tool switching. *Int. J. Prod. Res.* **2022**, 1–17. [CrossRef]
12. Guo, H.F.; Zhang, L.S.; Ren, Y.P.; Li, Y.; Zhou, Z.W.; Wu, J.Z. Optimizing a stochastic disassembly line balancing problem with task failure via a hybrid variable neighborhood descent-artificial bee colony algorithm. *Int. J. Prod. Res.* **2022**, 1–15. [CrossRef]
13. Bentaha, M.L.; Marange, P.; Voisin, A.; Moalla, N. End-of-Life product quality management for efficient design of disassembly lines under uncertainty. *Int. J. Prod. Res.* **2022**, 1–22. [CrossRef]
14. Paksoy, T.; Gungor, A.; Ozceylan, E.; Hancilar, A. Mixed model disassembly line balancing problem with fuzzy goals. *Int. J. Prod. Res.* **2013**, *51*, 6082–6096. [CrossRef]
15. Liang, J.Y.; Guo, S.S.; Xu, W.X. Balancing Stochastic Mixed-Model Two-Sided Disassembly Line Using Multiobjective Genetic Flatworm Algorithm. *IEEE Access* **2021**, *9*, 138067–138081. [CrossRef]
16. McGovern, S.M.; Gupta, S.M. Combinatorial optimization analysis of the unary NP-complete disassembly line balancing problem. *Int. J. Prod. Res.* **2007**, *45*, 4485–4511. [CrossRef]
17. Lambert, A.J.D. Linear programming in disassembly/clustering sequence generation. *Comput. Ind. Eng.* **1999**, *36*, 723–738. [CrossRef]
18. Bentaha, M.L.; Battaia, O.; Dolgui, A. An exact solution approach for disassembly line balancing problem under uncertainty of the task processing times. *Int. J. Prod. Res.* **2015**, *53*, 1807–1818. [CrossRef]
19. Ren, Y.P.; Meng, L.L.; Zhao, F.; Zhang, C.Y.; Guo, H.F.; Tian, Y.; Tong, W.; Sutherland, J.W. An improved general variable neighborhood search for a static bike-sharing rebalancing problem considering the depot inventory. *Expert Syst. Appl.* **2020**, *160*, 113752. [CrossRef]
20. Avikal, S.; Mishra, P.K.; Jain, R. A Fuzzy AHP and PROMETHEE method-based heuristic for disassembly line balancing problems. *Int. J. Prod. Res.* **2014**, *52*, 1306–1317. [CrossRef]
21. McGovern, S.M.; Gupta, S.M. 2-opt heuristic for the disassembly line balancing problem. In Proceedings of the 3rd International Conference on Environmentally Conscious Manufacturing, Providence, RI, USA, 29–30 October 2003; pp. 71–84.
22. Cheng, C.Y.; Chen, Y.Y.; Pourhejazy, P.; Lee, C.Y. Disassembly Line Balancing of Electronic Waste Considering the Degree of Task Correlation. *Electronics* **2022**, *11*, 533. [CrossRef]
23. Kizilay, D. A novel constraint programming and simulated annealing for disassembly line balancing problem with AND/OR precedence and sequence dependent setup times. *Comput. Oper. Res.* **2022**, *146*, 105915. [CrossRef]
24. Cil, Z.A.; Mete, S.; Serin, F. Robotic disassembly line balancing problem: A mathematical model and ant colony optimization approach. *Appl. Math. Model.* **2020**, *86*, 335–348. [CrossRef]
25. Ren, Y.P.; Yu, D.Y.; Zhang, C.Y.; Tian, G.D.; Meng, L.L.; Zhou, X.Q. An improved gravitational search algorithm for profit-oriented partial disassembly line balancing problem. *Int. J. Prod. Res.* **2017**, *55*, 7302–7316. [CrossRef]
26. Guo, X.W.; Zhang, Z.W.; Qi, L.; Liu, S.X.; Tang, Y.; Zhao, Z.Y. Stochastic Hybrid Discrete Grey Wolf Optimizer for Multi-Objective Disassembly Sequencing and Line Balancing Planning in Disassembling Multiple Products. *IEEE Trans. Autom. Sci. Eng.* **2022**, *19*, 1744–1756. [CrossRef]
27. Lu, Q.; Ren, Y.P.; Jin, H.Y.; Meng, L.L.; Li, L.; Zhang, C.Y.; Sutherland, J.W. A hybrid metaheuristic algorithm for a profit-oriented and energy-efficient disassembly sequencing problem. *Robot. Comput. Integr. Manuf.* **2020**, *61*, 101828. [CrossRef]

28. Kucukkoc, I. Balancing of two-sided disassembly lines: Problem definition, MILP model and genetic algorithm approach. *Comput. Oper. Res.* **2020**, *124*, 105064. [CrossRef]
29. Macaskill, J. Production-line balances for mixed-model lines. *Manag. Sci.* **1972**, *19*, 423–434. [CrossRef]
30. Wang, K.; Li, X.; Gao, L.; Li, P.; Sutherland, J.W. A Discrete Artificial Bee Colony Algorithm for Multiobjective Disassembly Line Balancing of End-of-Life Products. *IEEE Trans. Cybern.* **2022**, *52*, 7415–7426. [CrossRef]
31. Delice, Y.; Aydogan, E.K.; Ozcan, U.; Ilkay, M.S. A modified particle swarm optimization algorithm to mixed-model two-sided assembly line balancing. *J. Intell. Manuf.* **2017**, *28*, 23–36. [CrossRef]
32. Tian, G.; Zhang, C.; Fathollahi-Fard, A.M.; Li, Z.; Zhang, C.; Jiang, Z. An Enhanced Social Engineering Optimizer for Solving an Energy-Efficient Disassembly Line Balancing Problem Based on Bucket Brigades and Cloud Theory. *IEEE Trans. Ind. Inform.* **2022**, 1–11. [CrossRef]
33. Tian, G.D.; Yuan, G.; Aleksandrov, A.; Zhang, T.Z.; Li, Z.W.; Fathollahi-Fard, A.M.; Ivanov, M. Recycling of spent Lithium-ion batteries: A comprehensive review for identification of main challenges and future research trends. *Sustain. Energy Technol. Assess.* **2022**, *53*, 102447. [CrossRef]

Disclaimer/Publisher's Note: The statements, opinions and data contained in all publications are solely those of the individual author(s) and contributor(s) and not of MDPI and/or the editor(s). MDPI and/or the editor(s) disclaim responsibility for any injury to people or property resulting from any ideas, methods, instructions or products referred to in the content.

www.ingramcontent.com/pod-product-compliance
Lightning Source LLC
LaVergne TN
LVHW070424100526
838202LV00014B/1521

MDPI
St. Alban-Anlage 66
4052 Basel
Switzerland
Tel. +41 61 683 77 34
Fax +41 61 302 89 18
www.mdpi.com

Mathematics Editorial Office
E-mail: mathematics@mdpi.com
www.mdpi.com/journal/mathematics